SHAKESPEARE AND THE SUPERNATURAL

Shakespeare and the supernatural

Edited by Victoria Bladen and Yan Brailowsky

Manchester University Press

Copyright © Manchester University Press 2020

While copyright in the volume as a whole is vested in Manchester University Press, copyright in individual chapters belongs to their respective authors, and no chapter may be reproduced wholly or in part without the express permission in writing of both author and publisher.

Published by Manchester University Press
Oxford Road, Manchester M13 9PL

www.manchesteruniversitypress.co.uk

British Library Cataloguing-in-Publication Data
A catalogue record for this book is available from the British Library

ISBN 978 1 5261 0906 4 hardback
ISBN 978 1 5261 0908 8 paperback

First published 2020

The publisher has no responsibility for the persistence or accuracy of URLs for any external or third-party internet websites referred to in this book, and does not guarantee that any content on such websites is, or will remain, accurate or appropriate.

Typeset
by Toppan Best-set Premedia Limited

We dedicate this volume to:
Emeritus Professor Chris Wortham, with love and gratitude

Victoria

my family, friends and colleagues, for their patience

Yan

Contents

List of figures	*page* ix
Notes on contributors	x
Acknowledgements	xiv
Introduction: Shakespeare and the supernatural – Victoria Bladen and Yan Brailowsky	1
I Embodying the supernatural	**29**
1 Shakespeare's political spectres – Victoria Bladen	31
2 'Rudely stamped': supernatural generation and the limits of power in Shakespeare's *Richard III* – Chelsea Phillips	50
3 Digital puppetry and the supernatural: double Ariel in the Royal Shakespeare Company's *The Tempest* (2017) – Anchuli Felicia King	70
II Haunted spaces	**85**
4 Demons and puns: revisiting the 'cellarage scene' in *Hamlet* – Pierre Kapitaniak	87
5 Performing the Shakespearean supernatural in Avignon: a challenge to the Festival – Florence March	114

III Supernatural utterance and haunted texts — 135

6 Prophecy and the supernatural: Shakespeare's challenges to performativity – Yan Brailowsky — 137

7 Puck, Philostrate and the *locus* of *A Midsummer Night's Dream*'s topical allegory – Laurie Johnson — 157

8 'Strange intelligence': transformations of witchcraft in *Macbeth* discourse – William C. Carroll — 173

IV Magic, music and gender — 191

9 Music and magic in *The Tempest*: Ariel's alchemical songs – Natalie Roulon — 193

10 From Prospero to Prospera: transforming gender and magic on stage and screen – Katharine Goodland — 218

V Contemporary transformations — 243

11 'I'll put a girdle round the earth in forty minutes': representing the supernatural in film adaptations of *A Midsummer Night's Dream* – Gayle Allan — 245

12 Ophelia and her magical daughters: the afterlives of Ophelia in Japanese pop culture – Yukari Yoshihara — 262

Index — 278

Figures

3.1	Digital Ariel in RSC's *The Tempest* 2017, in collaboration with Intel. Screen capture from DVD of live broadcast, Royal Shakespeare Company (RSC) and Opus Arte.	*page* 71
3.2	Double Ariel: live performer and digital avatar. Screen capture from DVD of live broadcast, RSC and Opus Arte.	72
3.3	Ariel reliving his confinement in the pine. Screen capture from DVD of live broadcast, RSC and Opus Arte.	79
8.1	Raphael Holinshed, *The firste volume of the Chronicles of England, Scotlande, and Irelande* (London, 1577). Detail: Macbeth, Banquo, and the Witches. STC 13568.5 Vol. 1 (folio), p. 243. (Used by permission of the Folger Shakespeare Library.)	176
10.1	Blair Brown as Prospera (2003). Photo credit: T. Charles Erickson.	220
10.2	Olympia Dukakis as Prospera (2012). Photo credit: Kevin Sprague.	223
10.3	Helen Mirren as Prospera, directed by Julie Taymor (2010, Miramax) (screen capture).	227
12.1	Ophelia of *Claymore* (2007, Nippon Television Network) at her death (screen capture).	268
12.2	Ophelia in *Romeo × Juliet*, directed by Fumitoshi Oizaki. By permission of GONZO. ©2007 GONZO · CBC · SPJSAT.	269
12.3	Ophelia from *Fatal Frame* (*Gekijô-ban: Zero*) (2014, Kadokawa, directed by Mari Asato) (screen capture).	271

Notes on contributors

Dr Gayle Allan is the Deputy Dean of Trinity College, University of Melbourne. Her research and teaching areas are Shakespearean film adaptations and stage history, and theories of jealousy in the early modern period. She is a member of the committee of the Australia and New Zealand Shakespeare Association (ANZSA).

Dr Victoria Bladen teaches literary studies and adaptation at The University of Queensland, Australia, and has published four Shakespearean text guides in the Insight Publications (Melbourne) series: *Measure for Measure* (2015), *Henry IV Part 1* (2012), *Julius Caesar* (2011) and *Romeo and Juliet* (2010). She co-edited *Supernatural and Secular Power in Early Modern England* (Farnham: Ashgate, 2015), *Shakespeare on Screen: Macbeth* (Rouen: Presses Universitaires de Rouen et du Havre, 2013) and a special issue of the *Australian Literary Studies* journal on *Afterlives of Pastoral* (2015). Victoria has published articles in several volumes of the *Shakespeare on Screen* series, including *Shakespeare on Screen: The Tempest and Late Romances* (Cambridge: Cambridge University Press, 2017), and co-edited *Shakespeare on Screen: King Lear* (Cambridge: Cambridge University Press, 2019).

Yan Brailowsky is Senior Lecturer in Early Modern British History and Literature at the University of Paris Nanterre. His publications include *The Spider and the Statue: Poisoned innocence in* A Winter's Tale (Paris: Presses universitaires de France, 2010), *William Shakespeare:* King Lear (Paris: SEDES, 2008), and co-edited collections on plays such as *The Winter's Tale* (2011) and *Love's Labour's Lost* (2015) and other topics: *Language and Otherness in Renaissance Culture* (2008), *Le Bannissement et l'exil en Europe au XVIe et XVIIe siècles* (2010), *Brevity is the soul of wit* (2015) and *Shakespeare and Africa* (2017). He is General Editor of *Angles* and Secretary of the French Shakespeare Society.

William C. Carroll is Professor of English at Boston University. His publications include *The Great Feast of Language in Love's Labour's Lost* (Princeton, NJ:

Princeton University Press, 1976); *The Metamorphoses of Shakespearean Comedy* (Princeton, NJ: Princeton University Press, 1985); and *Fat King, Lean Beggar: Representations of Poverty in the Age of Shakespeare* (Ithaca, NY: Cornell University Press, 1996). He has edited Thomas Middleton, *Women Beware Women* and *Thomas Middleton: Four Plays* (both New Mermaids), Shakespeare, *Macbeth: Texts and Contexts* (Bedford Shakespeare), *The Two Gentlemen of Verona* (Arden Third Series) and *Love's Labour's Lost* (New Cambridge Shakespeare). He is co-chair of the Shakespearean Studies Seminar at the Mahindra Center for the Humanities at Harvard University. In 2005–6 he served as president of the Shakespeare Association of America.

Katharine Goodland is Professor of English and director of the Master of Arts in English program at the City University of New York's College of Staten Island. She is the author of *Female Mourning and Tragedy in Medieval and Renaissance English Drama from the Raising of Lazarus to King Lear* (Farnham: Ashgate, 2006; Abingdon: Routledge, 2016) and co-editor of *A Directory of Shakespeare in Performance* (3 volumes, Houndmills: Palgrave Macmillan, 2006, 2011). Her articles on performance and early English drama have appeared in several journals and book collections; most recently, her essay 'Female Mourning, Revenge and Hieronimo's Doomsday Play' was published in *The Spanish Tragedy: A Critical Companion*, edited by Thomas Rist (London: Bloomsbury, 2016).

Laurie Johnson is Professor of English and Cultural Studies at the University of Southern Queensland, Australia. He is the author of *Shakespeare's Lost Playhouse: Eleven Days at Newington Butts* (Abingdon: Routledge, 2018), *The Tain of Hamlet* (Newcastle-upon-Tyne: Cambridge Scholars, 2013) and *The Wolf Man's Burden* (Ithaca, NY: Cornell University Press, 2001), and the editor (with John Sutton and Evelyn Tribble) of *Embodied Cognition and Shakespeare's Theatre: The Early Modern Body-Mind* (Abingdon: Routledge, 2014) and (with Darryl Chalk) of *Rapt in Secret Studies: Emerging Shakespeares* (Newcastle-upon-Tyne: Cambridge Scholars, 2010). He is the current president of the Australian and New Zealand Shakespeare Association and a member of the editorial board of *Shakespeare* journal.

Pierre Kapitaniak is Professor of Early Modern British Civilisation at the University Paul-Valéry Montpellier. He works on Elizabethan drama and early modern conceptions and representations of supernatural phenomena. He has published *Spectres, Ombres et fantômes: Discours et représentations dramatiques en Angleterre* (Paris: Honoré Champion, 2008) and co-edited *Fictions du diable: démonologie et literature* (Geneva: Droz, 2007). He has translated into French and edited Thomas Middleton's play *The Witch/La sorcière* (Paris: Classiques Garnier, 2012). His current work includes a long-term project with Jean Migrenne on translating early modern demonological treatises (publications to date: James VI's *Démonologie* (Grenoble: Jérôme Millon, 2010) and Reginald Scot's

La sorcellerie démystifiée (Grenoble: Millon, 2015)). He is also currently working with Jérôme Hankins on a new translation of *The Tempest*.

Anchuli Felicia King is a multidisciplinary artist who works primarily in live theatre. Her areas of interest include VFX and projection design, interactive technologies, music production, technodramaturgy and writing for performance. Currently based in New York, Felicia has worked with a wide range of companies and institutions, including Punchdrunk, PlayCo, 3LD Arts & Technology Center, Roundabout Theater, 59E59, Ars Nova, the Obie Awards, The Builders Association, Ensemble Studio Theater, NYTW and Red Bull Theater. She continues to work globally, with companies such as The Royal Court and Yellow Earth Theatre (London), Playwriting Australia, Sydney Theatre Company and Belvoir Theatre (Sydney), Melbourne Theatre Company (Melbourne), House of North (Berlin) and SHIFT Festival (Shanghai).

Florence March is Professor in Early Modern English Drama at University Paul-Valéry Montpellier (France) and a member of the Institute for Research on the Renaissance, the Neo-Classical Age and the Enlightenment, at the French National Centre for Scientific Research. She has published extensively on Shakespeare's function in South France festivals (Avignon, Montpellier and Nice), on Shakespearean stage configurations in twentieth- and twenty-first-century Europe and the relationship between stage and audience. She is co-editor in chief of *Cahiers élisabéthains*, a journal of English Renaissance studies, and associate editor of *Arrêt sur scène/Scene Focus*, a bilingual online journal in performance studies. She is a translator of drama in English at Maison Antoine Vitez (an international centre for drama translation).

Chelsea Phillips is an Assistant Professor of Theatre at Villanova University. She is also a professional dramaturge, an associate director for the International Perceptions of Pregnancy Researchers' Network and co-convenes the Pregnancy and Motherhood working group for the American Society for Theatre Research. Her current book project focuses on pregnancy and the eighteenth-century British stage. Her most recent article, 'Bodies in Play: Maternity, Repertory and the Rival Romeo and Juliets', was published in the May 2019 issue of *Theatre Survey*. She has also published in the international journals *Women's History* and *Testi e Linguaggi*, and the collection *Shakespeare Expressed: Page, Stage, and Classroom in Shakespeare and His Contemporaries* (Madison, NJ: Fairleigh Dickinson University Press, 2013).

Natalie Roulon teaches English at the University of Strasbourg, France. She is the author of *Les Femmes et la musique dans l'œuvre de Shakespeare* (Paris: Honoré Champion, 2011). She has also written a bilingual handbook on English for the performing arts, *L'Anglais des arts du spectacle* (Montpellier: L'Entretemps, 2012). Her main fields of research are women and music in English Renaissance literature. She has published on *All's Well That Ends Well*, *Henry IV Part I*,

Henry VIII, *Julius Caesar*, *Love's Labour's Lost*, *The Taming of the Shrew*, *The Tempest*, sonnet 130 and on the Swetnam Controversy. An article of hers on *Women Beware Women* is forthcoming.

Yukari Yoshihara is an associate professor at the University of Tsukuba, Japan. Her research is primarily in the field of Shakespeare and Japanese pop culture, and she has published on Shakespeare and manga in the journal *Multicultural Shakespeare*; on Japanese adaptations of *Othello*, in *Shakespeare and the Ethics of Appropriation* (Houndmills: Palgrave Macmillan, 2014), edited by Alexa Huang and Elizabeth Rivlin; on Shakespearean adaptation in Japanese culture in *Re-Playing Shakespeare in Asia* (Abingdon: Routledge, 2010), edited by Poonam Trivedi and Ryuta Minami; and in the journal *Shakespeare Survey*. She also co-edited *English Studies in Asia* (Kuala Lumpur: Silverfish Books, 2007).

Acknowledgements

We would like to thank everyone at Manchester University Press for their support of the project and assistance in bringing this volume to print. We would also like to thank all of the authors for their wonderful contributions and assistance during the editing process, and the anonymous peer reviewers of the essays and the volume for their valuable advice and feedback.

Introduction: Shakespeare and the supernatural

Victoria Bladen and Yan Brailowsky

Supernatural elements constitute a significant dimension of Shakespeare's plays: ghosts haunt political spaces and internal psyches; witches foresee the future and disturb the present; fairies meddle with love; natural portents and dreams foreshadow events; and a magus conjures a tempest from the elements. These aspects contribute to the dramatic power and intrigue of the plays, whether they are treated in performance with irony, comedic effect or unsettling gravity. Although Shakespeare's plays were written and performed for early modern audiences, for whom the supernatural, whether sacred, demonic or folkloric, was still part of the fabric of everyday life, these supernatural elements continue to enthral us, and maintain their power to raise a range of questions in more contemporary contexts. Supernatural elements implicitly question the border between the human and the non-human, and between the visible and the unseen. They also raise questions of control and agency that intersect with the exercise of power, a central focus across Shakespeare's *œuvre*.

Shakespeare drew on the supernatural in all of his dramatic genres and throughout his career, from the early histories (such as *Richard III* and *Henry VI, Part II*) to the late romances (such as *The Winter's Tale, Cymbeline* and *The Tempest*), in tragedies (*Julius Caesar, Hamlet* and *Macbeth*) and in comedy (*A Midsummer Night's Dream*), suggesting the importance of the supernatural in his approach to drama. Exploration of this dimension resonates with many of the central themes of the plays, raising theological, political and moral questions. His work invites critical analysis of how supernatural figures, elements and forces are constructed in the plays, raising various options for performance, and what assumptions and ambiguities arise from these representations. The chapters of this volume respond to this invitation in a range of ways, taking into account early modern and contemporary perspectives.

The first challenge in approaching the theme of the supernatural is that of definition.[1] The etymology of the term suggests something 'that transcends nature', according to the current definition in the *Oxford English Dictionary*

(OED). However, as Darren Oldridge observes in *The Supernatural in Tudor and Stuart England*, 'the boundaries between natural and supernatural phenomena have never been securely fixed' and this 'shifting border' in early modernity is particularly complex.[2] What constituted 'nature' and ordinary natural laws for Shakespeare and his contemporaries? The vast differences between our understandings of a mechanistic universe, with rational laws, causes and effects, and early modern conceptions of a divinely created nature generate the first issue in trying to determine what distinguishes the natural from the supernatural.

Magical nature

The realm of the 'natural' was imagined as alive with invisible spirits and forces that could be harnessed with the right knowledge, using what was understood as natural magic.[3] As Peter Marshall and Alexandra Walsham point out, there was a 'supernatural hyper-reality threaded through the natural order of creation'.[4] Nature was thought of as God's Second Book, a parallel green Bible and repository of divine truths.[5] As Christopher Wortham and David Ormerod suggest, whereas 'modern man looks at the world… medieval man looked through it. His attempt was not to describe the world, but to determine its meaning, and this meaning was to be fathomed in terms of the extent to which the world contained messages confirming and elaborating the revelation of divine scripture.' By comparison, the early modern viewpoint saw the world as 'an ordered and planned manifestation' with an underlying plan that could not 'be located immediately at a literal level'; it was the task of the scholar to see through the 'outward husk of reality' to 'its *nucleus*'.[6] The natural was thus a manifestation of the supernatural space of divine design; their version of nature was already infused with what, to us, is a supernatural conception.

Early modern authors made an additional distinction between the supernatural and the preternatural, which encompassed all that human knowledge could not explain but that did not contravene the laws of nature such as they were conceived. This could include the workings of dreams, certain meteorological phenomena or the flight of witches; these were thought of as belonging to the realm of the unexplained, not the inexplicable. To complicate things further, deeds attributed to otherworldly beings could be described as 'supernatural' even when they were understood by contemporaries as natural events, albeit sources of wonder, thus extending the term 'supernatural' to the preternatural.[7]

Phenomena that were unexplained could be investigated in a proto-scientific way; supernatural or preternatural subject matter did not preclude seemingly methodical investigations and ordered arguments. As Keith Thomas observes, 'God's sovereignty was thought to be exercised through regular channels, and the natural world was fully susceptible of study by scientists seeking causes and regularities'.[8] Similarly, Jane Davidson points out that, given the development of practices of observed realism in visual art, and the new scientific impulses, 'it was logical then that the mindset of careful observation and record was a part of the study of the supernatural as well'.[9]

In the Shakespearean canon, natural phenomena – such as storms, 'monstrous' births and screeching owls – often function as omens, their strangeness as generative of the uncanny as ghosts, spirits, witches and magic. These natural phenomena often serve as foreshadowing to the audience and as signs for characters to interpret, just as nature was read as a divinely created book of hidden truths. Monstrous births were ambiguous; they could be preternatural signs in nature's book that were potentially explainable; yet they could also be an act of God, suggesting sin or disorder in the natural world, as with Richard III, whose physical deformity was linked with his tyrannical rule and political disruption.

Miracles were understood as exceeding the laws of nature, evidence of God's particular intervention, beyond the ordinary workings of nature. The term *supra naturam*, as Oldridge points out, dated from the early Christian writers, and the term *supernaturalis* was first commonly used in the thirteenth century in the context of examining and classifying miracles.[10] However, by the sixteenth century the orthodox view was that the time of miracles had passed and that, while theoretically possible, miracles were now a highly rare occurrence.[11]

The supernatural in the early modern imagination

A lack of knowledge laid the groundwork for the construction of the supernatural, which countered a sense of powerlessness in the face of illness, death, birth deformities, acts of God and other inexplicable phenomena. Shakespeare's contemporaries were faced with short life expectancies, high rates of death in childbirth and the risk of many illnesses and diseases that were incurable, such as leprosy and the plague. Medical knowledge was poor and access to doctors limited; most people had little education or power to control their living conditions. In the face of a void of understanding, comforting and terrifying narratives entered the vacuum.

Supernatural agency could fill this existential or experiential void, positing a seemingly rational explanation for otherwise inexplicable occurrences. The ghost, in particular, exemplifies the porous border between the natural and the supernatural. For the Catholic Church, the ghost was a soul in Purgatory, caught in limbo between heaven and hell, thus able to cross the threshold between life and death to deal with unfinished business. However, this shifted after the Reformation with the rejection of Purgatory, described in the *Thirty-Nine Articles* (1571) as 'a fond thing vainly invented, and grounded upon no warranty of Scripture' (Article XXII). Now, ghosts and apparitions were thought more likely to be a demon or a demonic illusion designed to trick the observer.[12]

The fairies from folklore were also linked to the demonic and were often thought of as spirits of the deceased, or as possessive spirits in the case of bewitchment.[13] James VI, in his *Demonologie* (1597), had expressed the opinion that demons could disguise themselves as fairies, and John Aubrey, writing in the late seventeenth century, referred to 'those demons that we call fairies'.[14] Fairies were part of the animated natural world, alive with spirits, remaining a vibrant part of oral folklore, even in the face of emerging rationalism in the latter part of the seventeenth century.

Since nature was imagined as a network of invisible powers and spirits, it was assumed that these could be harnessed with the right knowledge, be it physics, astrology, alchemy or, simply, 'magic', a term encompassing a variety of beliefs and practices. Natural magic, working within the properties of nature, was the field of the local 'cunning' woman or man, providing medicinal advice and locating lost objects or people.[15] The practices of cunning men and women were not necessarily magic; it depended on whether charms were used to accompany the medicine, and often prayers accompanied charms, again blurring the lines.[16]

Magic imagines a form of control over objects, people and events. In classical antiquity, the term referred to the arts of the *magi*, Zoroastrian priests of Persia who were known to practise astrology, claim the power to cure people and pursue occult knowledge.[17] Given that the Zoroastrians were suspect foreigners from the perspective of the Greeks and Romans, from the outset magic was something potentially threatening and likely to arouse apprehension.[18] Natural magic was distinct, in theory, from demonic magic, which involved a pact with the Devil to access demonic power (rather than the power of natural properties). As Richard Kieckhefer outlines, in *Magic in the Middle Ages*:

> Broadly speaking, intellectuals in medieval Europe recognised two forms of magic: natural and demonic. Natural magic was not distinct from science, but rather a branch of science. It was the science that dealt with 'occult virtues' (or hidden powers) within nature. Demonic magic was not distinct from religion, but rather a perversion of religion. It was religion that turned away from God and toward demons for their help in human affairs.[19]

Perceptions of the status of magic in the medieval and early modern period differed widely. The Church had historically condemned the practice of magic; in *De Doctrina Christiana* (c. 426), Augustine unequivocally repudiated soothsayers and wizards who claimed they could invoke ghosts and spirits, associating them with demons:

> So all the specialists in this kind of futile and harmful superstition, and the contracts, as it were, of an untrustworthy and treacherous partnership established by this disastrous alliance of men and devils, must be totally rejected and avoided

by the Christian. 'It is not', to quote the apostle, 'because an idol is something, but because whatever they sacrifice they sacrifice it to devils and not to God that I do not want you to become the associates of demons'.[20]

Even 'white' magic was suspect, although in practice white witches often escaped heavy punishment.[21]

Anxiety over this issue was exacerbated by the historically indistinct lines between religion and magic in the medieval church, and between natural and demonic magic.[22] The Reformed Church argued that the rituals and ideology of the pre-Reformation Church were often close in character to the magic it condemned as demonic. Where precisely was the line to be drawn between prayers and charms? In theory, 'words and prayers… had no power in themselves, unless God chose to heed them; whereas the working of charms followed automatically upon their pronunciation', as if they had a performative power.[23] However, in practice, the concepts overlapped. As Thomas accurately describes, magic and religion were 'rival therapies' and, even after the Reformation, not mutually exclusive: 'there were magical elements surviving in religion, and there were religious facets to… the practice of magic'.[24]

Shakespeare's plays reveal various approaches to magic. In *Henry VI Part II*, Margery Jordan, described as a 'witch', and Roger Bolingbroke, a 'conjurer', partake in demonic 'exorcisms' (1.4.4), successfully proceeding to 'raise… ghosts' and 'spirits' (1.4.19, 21) using black magic, devil-like, in the '[d]eep night, dark night' (1.4.16).[25] Their arrest moments later makes it clear that such blasphemous spirit-raising is to be roundly condemned. In *The Tempest*, Prospero's magic is more ambiguous. Is he a practitioner of 'white magic' (also termed 'theurgy' and 'natural magic'), or is he also resorting to 'black magic' (also termed 'necromancy', 'nigromancy' or 'goety')?[26] How magic was classified often depended on who was practising it, giving greater weight to the supernatural agent.

The practice of magic was traditionally gendered and subject to class distinctions. Higher magic, ostensibly white magic, was based on learned, scholarly knowledge and seen as the preserve of male magicians, the respected magus figure revered (at least by some), often compared to celebrated contemporary examples. In this context, magic was considered as an extension of book-based knowledge, generally inaccessible to women through a lack of access to education and prejudice against female curiosity and power. Arguments against the involvement of women in affairs of Church and state were common, particularly in the wake of the Marian persecutions in England in the 1550s. In the eyes of John Calvin and other Protestant writers, women ought 'to keep themselves lowly and mild'.[27] Failure to do so was to risk public opprobrium, or worse.

The intellectual study of magic was predominantly a European phenomenon, emerging in Florence during the Italian Renaissance in the context of Platonism.

Works by writers such as Marsilio Ficino and Pico della Mirandola, given impetus by Ficino's Latin translation of the *Corpus Hermeticum*, spread through Europe via the writings of Paracelsus and Cornelius Agrippa. In England, these writings influenced figures such as Robert Fludd and John Dee, who dabbled in alchemy – the latter was adviser to Elizabeth I.[28]

The proto-science of alchemy came under the umbrella of natural magic and was part of the intellectual, scholarly pursuit of magic. The alchemical concept of *solve et coagula*, breaking up components using a liquid (*solve*) as a medium in order to transform and recreate, resonates with the themes and imagery of *The Tempest*.[29] On the premise of the early modern assumption that all sublunary matter was composed of the four elements – earth, fire, air and water – alchemy constituted a search for the fifth element, *quintessence*, of which all the superlunary, celestial bodies were believed to be composed.[30] It was the path to immortality, as well as the means of transforming base metals to gold. Within the sphere of intellectual, scholarly knowledge was also astrology, the study of the effects of the heavenly bodies on the sublunary world that assumed influence over the body and events.[31] Although it was generally considered the concern of the court, the nobility and the Church, given that it formed a cornerstone of medical knowledge, astrology impacted on many other branches of knowledge; traders of knowledge at all levels of society drew from astrological beliefs.[32]

In comparison with scholarly magic, lower magic was based on local, experiential and folkloric knowledge, not derived from bookish learning; this was the preserve of cunning women and men. Although this too was believed to be based on natural magic and an understanding of occult forces in nature, it was nonetheless often perceived as easily sliding into dubious, 'black' magic, requiring demonic assistance. Also, lower magic was often associated with the female witch, feared for her *maleficium*, the ability to cause harm to people and animals.[33] As Richard Kieckhefer states, '[i]t was men who were more likely to arouse anxiety by actually standing in magic circles and conjuring demons; it was women who were far more likely to be burned in the ensuing bonfires'.[34]

In *The Tempest*, the gendered polarity of magical practice is represented by the juxtaposition of Prospero, presented as an ennobled, scholarly sorcerer wronged by his enemies, and Sycorax, described as a 'foul witch' (1.2.259) (although since she never appears on stage, the audience only has Prospero's word for this). According to Prospero, she was exiled from Algiers for 'mischiefs manifold and sorceries terrible/To enter human hearing' (1.2.266–7). In the play's text, Shakespeare invites questions over Prospero's distinction between his magic and Sycorax's by using Medea's incantations in Ovid's *Metamorphoses* for Prospero's '[y]e elves of hills' speech (5.1.33). To further blur the lines, Prospero's power is generally performed through the agency of Ariel, who fulfils the traditional role of the witch's 'familiar'.

Notwithstanding Queen Elizabeth's reverence for an alchemist and astrologer such as John Dee, the political state generally took a dim view of magic, evidenced by the introduction of witchcraft legislation in England during the sixteenth century. In 1542 Henry VIII passed the first Witchcraft Act (subsequently repealed in 1547 by Edward VI); in 1563 Elizabeth I passed a new Witchcraft Act that punished those convicted of damage to property or persons by witchcraft with one year's imprisonment, and those convicted of murder by witchcraft with the death penalty. Originally, practitioners could only be prosecuted if their magic resulted in harm; however, the legislation became more draconian in 1604 under James I and the mere practice of magic, regardless of its consequences, could attract prosecution.[35] Underlying the fear of witchcraft that fuelled these prosecutions was the notion that the witch entered into a diabolical contract with the Devil.

The Devil was a paradoxical figure; although constituting humanity's adversary, he was an instrument of God's judgement, part of the divinely sanctioned executive.[36] As James I described, the Devil was 'God's hangman'.[37] As Philip C. Almond points out, 'the history of God in the West is also the history of the Devil, and the history of theology also the history of demonology'.[38] Satan was perceived as ever present in the world, along with his company of evil spirits, part of the network of invisible forces that charged the physical world. As Thomas relates, 'men thus became accustomed to Satan's immediacy'; and 'once the possibility of his personal appearance in this world had been accepted it was but a short cut to the notion that there were individuals who entered into semi-feudal contracts with him, mortgaging their souls in return for a temporary access of supernatural knowledge or power'.[39] This belief condemned thousands of unfortunates to persecution, torture and execution.

Enchantment, disenchantment and the theatre

Theatre proved a unique space for staging and processing shifting currents of belief and scepticism in relation to the supernatural.[40] In early modern England, the power of belief affected the theatrical experiences of many, particularly with the staging of devils, as evident in the report of an early performance of Christopher Marlowe's *Doctor Faustus* (c. 1592):

> at Exeter, an extra devil suddenly appeared among the actors on stage, causing a panic; in London the 'old Theater crackt and frighted the audience' during one performance, at others, the 'visible apparition' of the devil appeared on stage 'to the great amazement both of the Actors and Spectators'.[41]

For many, this was arguably theatre's *raison d'être*, as audiences flocked to the playhouses in anticipation of experiencing such 'great amazement'. As David Bevington reflects, '[t]he hope of such an event was possibly one fascination that drew audiences to the play [*Dr Faustus*], in somewhat the same fashion as spectators flock to the circus wondering if the high-wire artist will fall and be killed'.⁴²

Shakespeare's use of the supernatural in his plays attests to its cultural and theological prevalence in early modern society, not unlike the playwright's equally liberal use of pagan, mythological or folkloric traditions. It may have been as difficult for Shakespeare to resist the supernatural as it was for Renaissance humanists to produce art without turning to classical mythology. As Jean Seznec points out in *The Survival of the Pagan Gods*, mythological and supernatural tropes had an enduring appeal:

> One need but recall, in this connection, St Augustine or St Jerome and their inner conflicts. Their minds are haunted by the profane poetry which they ought to denounce; it has penetrated their very souls. In the twelfth century, a Guibert of Nogent, a Pierre of Blois, secretly cherish the ancients whom they deny in public. Hildebert of Lavardin reminds the faithful that they are children of Christ, not of Minerva or Venus, but celebrates in Latin verses the statues of the gods and their supernatural beauty.⁴³

As with mythological fables from Ovid and others which provided the basis for fabulous stories, the supernatural was too tempting to dismiss for a popular playwright seeking to elicit curiosity and wonder among playgoers – and to ensure his company's commercial success, as well as his own.⁴⁴ Shakespeare's engagement with the supernatural also linked his *œuvre* to the semi-mythical, semi-divine classical works produced by figures such as Homer and Ovid, a linking that arguably contributed to Shakespeare's appeal for nineteenth-century Romantics such as Victor Hugo, who was also interested in spiritism and extolled Shakespeare's sublime, almost supernatural 'genius'.⁴⁵

Shakespeare wrote in, and for, an enchanted world but one that was on the cusp of change, with the emergence of observational methods, proto-empiricism and sceptical discourses, as exemplified by works such as Reginald Scot's *The Discoverie of Witchcraft* (1584) and Francis Bacon's *Novum Organum* (1620), which reflected the impact of Protestant scepticism.⁴⁶ Scot argued that the time for miracles, oracles and prophecies had 'ceased', and that the preaching of a reformed faith had done away with Popish superstitions elsewhere: '[d]ivers writers report, that in *Germanie*, since *Luthers* time, spirits and divels have not personallie appeared, as in times past they were woont to doo'.⁴⁷ Bacon argued that 'prejudice' led men to continue to believe in the supernatural, as men are always tempted to use the 'same method... in every superstition, like astrology, dreams, omens, divine judgments and so on: people who take pleasure in such vanities notice the results when they are fulfilled, but ignore and overlook them when they fail'.⁴⁸

Shakespeare's work often gives voice to such scepticism through characters such as Edmund in *Lear*, who scoffs at beliefs that we are 'fools by heavenly compulsion, knaves, thieves, and treachers by spherical predominance' (1.2.107–8),[49] and Lafew in *All's Well That Ends Well*, who claims:

> [t]hey say miracles are past, and we have our philosophical persons to make modern and familiar things supernatural and causeless. Hence is it that we make trifles of terrors, ensconcing ourselves into seeming knowledge when we should submit ourselves to an unknown fear. (*All's Well*, 2.3.1–6)[50]

Such statements register that times were changing through the works of 'philosophical persons', such as Bacon, or demonologists like Scot who made 'trifles of terrors' and revealed, in his *Discoverie*, various tricks used by supposed sorcerers and witches to con the credulous. Despite these thinkers, who were still a minority, and the Church of England's attempts to stamp out superstitious and demonic practices, most people still gave credence to supernatural beliefs, and audiences brought these beliefs to the theatre. As Lafew acknowledges, belief in the supernatural still had currency for his audience, suggesting at least a shared willingness to submit 'to an unknown fear'.

The playwright himself may have been as sceptical *vis-à-vis* the supernatural as Edmund or Lafew, yet he also took 'pleasure in such vanities', using assorted beliefs in the supernatural to feed audiences' desire for theatrical wish-fulfilment. As Stephen Greenblatt has argued, Shakespeare and his contemporaries replaced the power of Catholic ritual with that of the dramatic experience, one in which audiences willingly partook, underscoring the theatrical nature of belief in the supernatural: '[t]he official church dismantles and cedes to the players the powerful mechanisms of an unwanted and dangerous charisma; in return the players confirm the charge that those mechanisms are theatrical and hence illusory'.[51]

From this viewpoint, theatre had a key role to play, shoring up man's need for enchantment in a disenchanted world. As Kevin Pask observes in *The Fairy Way of Writing*, the 'historical process of disenchantment represented an opportunity for the theatre, which could present "falsehoods" on the stage, at least in the form of fictions, with relative impunity. If popular magic no longer carried the ability to charm and to harm, it might still carry the potential to entertain. The fairy way of writing thus also belonged to the age of the new science'.[52] In other words, the gradual disenchantment of the world could be exploited by playwrights as they strove to re-enchant audiences by giving the supernatural a bodily incarnation, one as striking as the 'dreadful fancy' and 'ghastly sprite' that terrorises Lucrece:

> Imagine her as one in dead of night
> From forth dull sleep by dreadful fancy waking,
> That thinks she hath beheld some ghastly sprite,
> Whose grim aspect sets every joint a-shaking;
> What terror 'tis! (*The Rape of Lucrece*, ll. 449–53)

Early modern playgoers did not need to 'imagine' such sights; they could experience the supernatural, or at least a version of it, by going to the theatre. The theatre took on a cosmological meaning, re-establishing the world full of wonders that was in the process of being lost.

Shakespeare's work looks both forward and back, to brave new worlds opening up, and to modes of sceptical thought, as well as the rich veins of medieval thought, folkloric traditions, pre-Reformation theology and the inherited narratives on the supernatural. Emerging proto-scientific discourses co-existed with older ways of framing the world and early modern drama reflects this. As Kristen Poole has argued, the *locus* of the stage dramatised the tension between science and the supernatural; the theatre building, with its trap door and balcony, embodied a mental mapping: 'the geography of the supernatural and the afterlife, the geography of heaven and hell', at a time when maps were becoming increasingly important in framing early modern perceptions of their world, as key references to maps in *King Lear* and *Henry IV Part I* illustrate.[53] As Tiffany Stern recalls, the cosmic geographies that mapped the early modern mental world, of heaven, earth and hell, were inscribed in the very structures of the theatre itself.[54] In Shakespeare's Globe, the tangible reality of theatre performed and remediated these cross-currents of thought on the natural and the supernatural.

The concept of 'disenchantment' was first popularised by the sociologist Max Weber, who spoke of '*Entzauberung der Welt*' ('de-magi-fication of the world') to describe the process by which medieval society made the transition from a spiritual to a secular world view, from a God-infused cosmos to a proto-capitalist system.[55] Thomas's seminal study of *Religion and the Decline of Magic* (1971) traces, from a historical perspective, the gradual relinquishing of belief in magic and supernatural modes of thought that was tied to the development of Protestantism. In his concluding chapter, he quotes from the Epilogue of *The Tempest*: 'Now my charms are all o'erthrown,/And what strength I have's mine own – /Which is most faint' (*Tempest*, Epilogue 1–3), suggesting that Prospero's renunciation of magic reflects something of the broader processes of incipient disenchantment.[56] This disenchantment would develop further after the upheavals of the Civil War in the mid-seventeenth century, gaining ground with the establishment of the Royal Society (1660) and the beginnings of the Scientific Revolution.

Supernatural modes of thought proved resilient in the face of emerging discourses of scepticism and rationalism, and have survived in various ways into modernity.[57] Beliefs in witchcraft, sorcery, ghosts and astrology linger and retain their potency in many contemporary cultures, in some contexts with tragic consequences. In 2017, the United Nations held an Experts Workshop on Witchcraft and Human Rights in Geneva to address the torture and deaths arising from accusations of witchcraft around the world.[58]

Supernatural discourses arguably remain relevant to understanding humanity. As Philip C. Almond observes, the twenty-first century has seen a 'new Western engagement with the imaginary enchanted world of preternatural beings', adding that the 'modern enchanted world is one of multiple meanings where the spiritual occupies a space between reality and unreality. It is a domain where belief is a matter of choice and disbelief willingly and happily suspended.'[59] Ewan Fernie, in his insightful study of the demonic, has demonstrated its significance for understanding not only many of the most powerful texts of the Western canon but also core truths of the human psyche.[60] His work points to the importance of analysis of the supernatural for understanding early modernity as well as for holding up a mirror to our own complex selves.[61]

Outline of the volume

The contributions in this collection evidence a variety of critical approaches to the supernatural in Shakespeare. Several chapters focus on situating his work within historical contexts, displaying a shared focus on the role of the supernatural in an economy of knowledge and craft, artisanal and intellectual. Within this economy, power circulated and was negotiated; shared narratives fuelled the trading of knowledge and expertise. These historicist approaches illuminate the ways in which the supernatural created a productive discursive field for interrogating political, linguistic and theatrical questions, and how the supernatural challenges the use of language, providing alternative forms of communication (spectral, musical, alchemical, topical). Other chapters turn to questions of performance of the supernatural, and contemporary adaptations. They explore the ways in which the discursive field of the supernatural has been appropriated for a range of contemporary agendas and interpretations in various stage productions and screen adaptations. The contemporary era has brought new technical possibilities to staging the supernatural, yet contemporary discourses, for example on gender, require new interpretations and shifts to the playtext. Modern interpretations also face the challenge of reinvigorating the mystery of the supernatural and its dramatic power for a predominantly sceptical audience.

These different approaches inform each other, opening up various dialogues between the chapters; histories haunt texts and spaces, and have consequences for performance choices. The political and historical strands outlined in this introduction are taken up in different ways by all of the authors, particularly through the issue of embodiment, a key aspect of theatre which rests on a physical onstage presence, be it the actors', or the existence of a stage on which actors can perform the supernatural, as well as a theatre (or venue) in which audiences can view the actors and experience the paradox of supernatural embodiment.

Embodying the supernatural

Just as the concept of the supernatural challenges our ability to describe or circumscribe it through language, attempts to give the supernatural a material or bodily reality in a theatrical context are problematic. How is the supernatural embodied in Shakespeare's plays? Victoria Bladen's and Chelsea Phillips's chapters explore different types of supernatural bodies, invisible and legible. Bladen's chapter on 'Shakespeare's political spectres' examines the political dimensions of Shakespeare's ghosts in the context of the theory of the king's two bodies. The playwright was intensely interested in cases of rupture, where power had not passed legitimately to a new ruler, leaving unresolved the question of where the spirit of 'authentic' monarchy lay. By taking examples from *Hamlet*, *Julius Caesar*, *Richard III* and *Macbeth*, Bladen argues that this displaced spirit constitutes a type of 'second' ghost that haunts the monarch's throne. The ghosts in these plays function as signs of the additional spectre that remains unseen yet a traceable sign of disorder in the body politic.

The political disorder virtually embodied by ghosts could be more perceptibly incarnated in a human body marred by physical deformities. These deformities could, in turn, be taken as the evidence of 'supernatural generation'. Like Bladen's, Phillips's chapter is concerned with supernatural bodies; however, Phillips's focus is on the maternal body that functions as a potent site of intersection between natural and supernatural worlds, and the 'monstrous' birth that can function, like the 'second ghost', as a sign of disorder. In her chapter 'Rudely stamped', she outlines how the lack of adequate scientific, medical and biological knowledge created a vacuum filled by supernatural beliefs. The pregnant body was imagined to be susceptible to external forces, as evidenced by monstrous births such as that of Richard III. She divides 'supernatural generations' into four categories: some supernatural generations are marked by maternal impression and/or witchcraft that could have potent effects on a child (exemplified by Caliban, affected by his mother's witchcraft); generative events accompanied by portents, when births are followed by strange natural phenomena; births seen as prophecies or signs; and changeling children. Political disruption could lead to unnatural births, and these could facilitate conjuring, as in *Macbeth*. Explaining supernatural events, while not reducing their threat, could at least render the supernatural legible. Phillips situates Shakespeare's various references within the historical contexts of constructions of monstrosity, and then focuses on *Richard III*, arguing that the language of the supernatural in fact fails to adequately explain Richard's origins.

In Anchuli Felicia King's chapter on 'Digital puppetry and the supernatural', she examines the implications of presenting a 'double' Ariel using the digital puppetry of motion capture (mo-cap) technology in the 2017 Royal Shakespeare Company production of *The Tempest*. That year's season followed in the wake of the 400th anniversary of Shakespeare's death, inspiring director Gregory Doran to experiment with the supernatural dimensions of the play. The creative team were asked what technology Shakespeare would be using if he were alive today. The Jacobean masque form, which foregrounded technical innovation and stagecraft as a significant aspect of production, was a resonant precedent and inspiration. King provides valuable insights into the technical processes involved in mo-cap technology and examines how its abilities and limitations reflected and tapped into the play's themes of containment and liberty.

Her contribution further develops the question of the supernatural body. Whereas Bladen's and Phillips's chapters explore different types of supernatural body, invisible and legible, taking a symbolic approach to the challenge of embodiment, King explores how technology can reinterpret Ariel's magical body. In doubling it, through mo-cap technology, in what ways does it remind us of the uncanny and porous border between the physical and supernatural worlds? The limitations of the visual effects in this production, that resulted in the appearance of a 'trapped' Ariel double, resonate with the play's themes of control and power, central to early modern discourses on magic, as well as to the political issues raised by the supernatural. The 2017 RSC production divided critics, suggesting that attempts to stage the supernatural for contemporary audiences can prove challenging for directors.

Haunted spaces

In early modernity, the supernatural was utilised in various ways in religious, political and cultural discourses, from which the theatre drew and to which it contributed. The concept of a metaphysical space that surrounded the known world facilitated the construction of powerful abstract concepts and narratives. It assumed surveillance of the ordinary world by a cocooning divine presence who had made the world and continued to observe it. In Shakespeare's theatre, the physical space with its layers of earth, heaven and hell, within which the actor was located, echoed and was shaped by these metaphysical constructions; at the same time, in a reciprocal relationship, as Tiffany Stern observes, the physical theatre also 'dictated and circumscribed imaginative space for Shakespeare's audience' through 'its locational, visual and aural presence'.[62]

The sub-stage area was often associated with death and hell; bodies were lowered into it for burial scenes and devils might emerge from it, as in *Doctor Faustus*. In *Hamlet*, the ghost's voice emerges from 'the cellarage', seeming to originate from a subterranean space, suggesting an unquiet corpse or a demon.

Pierre Kapitaniak's contribution, 'Demons and puns', like Bladen's, re-examines the construction of the ghost, but in the context of a haunting of language and of a haunted theatrical space. He brings new angles on Hamlet's first encounter with the ghost, arguing that the scene may be better understood when placed in the context of medieval stage traditions and several sixteenth-century plays that provide precedents for Shakespeare's language and subterranean location of the ghost, rather than a demonological interpretation. Taking into account historical and performative considerations, Kapitaniak argues that the various nicknames that Hamlet gives the ghost do not necessarily invoke a demonic connotation, as is commonly assumed, but may well have their origins in previous theatrical precedents. These precedents, or traditions, suggest that embodying the supernatural requires a leap of faith, one in which audiences choose to believe, basing their choice on (often obscure) knowledge from the past.

While Kapitaniak's work of linguistic archaeology reinvestigates theatrical space of the ghost in terms of the haunting of past dramatic texts and their language formulations, Florence March's chapter 'Performing the Shakespearean supernatural in Avignon' examines a different type of haunted space: the *Cour d'Honneur* of the medieval papal palace in Avignon. Listed as a World Heritage site by UNESCO, the *Cour d'Honneur* is the central venue for the annual Festival d'Avignon, combining medieval history with contemporary theatrical practice. Its imposing structure, spectacular dimensions and history render it a daunting theatrical space and a challenge for productions. What are the implications for Shakespearean productions in this epic space with its layers of history and performance? As Marvin Carlson argues in *The Haunted Stage: the Theatre as Memory Machine*, theatre is a repository of memory and a particularly haunted space.[63] March analyses a series of productions from the mid-twentieth century to the present, considering how they approached staging the supernatural in this venue. She explores how history and the implications of the Shakespearean supernatural intersect in this evocative space, and how natural forces, such as the *mistral*, the fierce *provençal* wind, together with the monstrous dimensions of the walls of the court, stage a confrontation between the transient and the permanent.

Supernatural utterance and haunted texts

The supernatural also plays a semantic role in Shakespeare's work, as metaphor and utterance. Theatre can be a haunted space, but it can also haunt language. Yan Brailowsky discusses the manner in which the supernatural is expressed through language, especially in the guise of prophetic utterances, in his chapter 'Prophecy and the supernatural'. Using ordinary-language philosophy and plays taken from the tragedies and the histories (*Julius Caesar, Henry VI Part II,*

Richard II and *Macbeth*), this chapter shows that Shakespeare's prophecies are paradoxically non-performative on stage because they are never properly acknowledged as such. These prophecies can be efficacious off-stage, however, asserting the powers of the poet to contribute to the fashioning of history. Harking back to the freedom enjoyed by the *vates* (the poet-prophet) of Roman antiquity, Shakespeare uses prophetic utterances to question historical narratives and to provoke or interpret supernatural phenomena. In the process, the playwright makes language 'stutter', a concept borrowed from Gilles Deleuze's notion of *'bégaiement de la langue'*, using prophetic utterances which strengthen the power of language to make, or unmake, kings and kingdoms. By discussing prophecies and omens from a pragmatist perspective, Brailowsky questions early modern conceptions of the supernatural and contemporary notions of performativity, unsettling the idea that genealogies may be linear. If anything, supernatural genealogies are rhizomatic or reticular, an idea that Laurie Johnson takes up in exploring how a playtext's appropriation and development of supernatural dimensions can function as a response to local and contemporary concerns.

Johnson's chapter, 'Puck, Philostrate, and the *locus* of *A Midsummer Night's Dream*'s topical allegory', explores the relationship between mythical and folkloric, intertextual sources for Shakespeare's comedy and contemporary topical allusions. The intersection between these references contributes to the construction of the supernatural in the play. He firstly explores the potential sources for the name 'Puck', noting that the particular formulation appears to be Shakespeare's, although indebted to similar words for the sprite. Johnson then turns to the contemporary competition between George Buck and John Lyly for the position of Master of the Revels, then occupied by Edmund Tylney, to argue that Puck and Bottom may allude to Buck and Lyly, and that in 'Robin Goodfellow', there may be a further topical reference to Robert Devereux, Earl of Essex. Johnson sees the *locus amœnus* of the fairy realm as a space that Shakespeare uses to maintain control of the tension between the array of sources and topical references. He also highlights how the textual economy of the playwright in the Elizabethan theatre was bound up in the management of audience expectations. Fairies, while linked with ghosts and demons, also created an alternative courtly and political world, a mirror to the human world. They thus provided an ideal vehicle for constituting intertextual references to the Elizabethan court, as Johnson's theory of a topical allegory illustrates. Consequently, his work also resonates with the essays in the volume that focus on performance and adaptation, and how the supernatural in Shakespeare can be utilised and shaped to meet the contemporary concerns of a play's creatives and audience.

Johnson's and Kapitaniak's chapters point to the value of establishing a genealogy of constructions and accretions of the supernatural in dramatic texts and theatrical practices. William C. Carroll's work takes a similar approach, as well as illuminating, like Brailowsky and Johnson, how the supernatural functions as a productive discursive field for Shakespeare. In his chapter, 'Strange intelligence', Carroll traces the historiography of the Macbeth narrative, starting with brief early chronicle entries in the eleventh century that contain no supernatural elements, through later medieval accounts that introduce the Weird Sisters as a dream vision, and the suggestion that Macbeth's father was the Devil. Carroll shows that, with Hector Boece's 1527 account, there was a significant shift in which the Sisters change to actual figures encountered. The story was further developed in subsequent accounts, adding more depth to the supernatural dimension prior to Raphael Holinshed's *Chronicles*, Shakespeare's main source. Holinshed's 1577 edition included the famous illustration of the three Weird Sisters, depicting three well-dressed women of different ages. Carroll points to the variant constructions of the otherworldly characters, situating Shakespeare's play amidst discourses that range from the secular (such as George Buchanan's account, subsequent to Holinshed, in which the Weird Sisters only appear in a dream) to the supernatural. As Carroll argues, Shakespeare's play appears to be indebted to both narrative traditions. What emerges is a picture of a narrative that gradually accumulates a supernatural dimension through its various retellings, culminating in Shakespeare's playtext. Carroll's genealogical approach to *Macbeth* thus complements Johnson's reading of the *Dream*, showing how competing texts can reveal topical references and contemporary issues.

Magic, music and gender

Two chapters discuss cases in which a playtext such as *The Tempest* competes with itself as it strives to (re-)define magic and its practice through a multilayered reading of music, or by a performative troubling of gender. Natalie Roulon's chapter, 'Music and magic in *The Tempest*', examines the intellectual 'high' magic tradition; it explores the rich alchemical dimensions of *The Tempest*, focusing particularly on Ariel's songs. She brings a range of new insights to the play and its musical facets through the lens of early modern alchemical links and associations. Roulon argues that Ariel can be read as an 'Ariel-Mercurius' figure, an attendant spirit to Prospero as alchemist, without whom the Great Work cannot take place. Ariel's role as chemical spirit recalls Marsilio Ficino's *spiritus*, whose nature is similar to that of musical sound, and it is through his Orphic music that most of the characters on the island are led down the path to spiritual purification. Even though musical magic is presented with irony on several occasions, Ariel's songs all partake of the idealising current of the play, adumbrating the alchemical wedding of Ferdinand and Miranda, Alonso's regeneration and Ariel's well-deserved freedom. Roulon's rich historical research strengthens the case for reading *The Tempest* as an alchemical palimpsest.

Katharine Goodland's work shifts our attention to the intersection of gender and magic in her chapter 'From Prospero to Prospera'. Like Phillips, Goodland is concerned with the female body as a border; however, her focus is different interpretations of magical power. The gendering of magic becomes refocused with a female Prospera in various stage and screen adaptations. In *The Tempest*, Shakespeare sets up an opposition between male and female forms of magic in the figures of Prospero and Sycorax, so what happens when Propero's body becomes haunted by that of Sycorax, mother of the supposed 'monstrous' Caliban? Goodland focuses on one screen and two stage productions: Julie Taymor's screen adaptation of *The Tempest* (2010), starring Helen Mirren; the 2003 McCarter Theatre production, directed by Emily Mann with Blair Brown as Prospera; and the 2012 Shakespeare and Company production directed by Tony Simotes, with Olympia Dukakis as lead. Goodland analyses how reviewers and critics have responded to these female Prosperas, and the gendered lenses through which performances and production decisions are viewed. She argues that these three productions invite us to rethink the playtext's opposition between gendered forms of magic, and to be aware of the cultural and political discourses that frame our critical responses. In this way, her work links to Johnson's argument for the importance of taking into account contemporary intertexts that inform audience reception of the supernatural. Her chapter also returns us to the challenge of how to embody the supernatural, and resist the traditional gender divisions of magic between the lowly, dangerous witch and the respected, male, magus figure.

Contemporary transformations

In twentieth- and twenty-first-century performances and adaptations of Shakespeare, transcending nature has been explored through special effects in film, in popular fiction or on stage. How have contemporary productions and adaptations responded to the challenge of reinterpreting the supernatural? Gayle Allan, in her chapter 'I'll put a girdle round the earth in forty minutes', explores how various productions in the history of the *Dream* on screen have dealt with the fairy world, and the effects and implications of performance decisions, for example on whether the fairies will 'fly' and how light or sinister the mood will be. While our modern conception of fairies is inherited from the nineteenth century, early modern conceptions were much darker; as Diane Purkiss notes, fairies, above all, were considered '*dangerous*'.[64] In the *Dream*, even when fairies intend to be 'helpful' to humans, things can go wrong, and they can be cruel even to each other, as Oberon's trick is to Titania. Options in depicting the fairies on screen range from abstraction to literalism and, in making choices, a production needs first to decide what the fairies are. Allan notes that in the play's screen history there has been a strong impulse towards realism in attempting to immerse the audience in the otherworldly dimension. Fairy worlds in screen adaptations of the play invariably reflect the contemporary culture of the context in which the film was made, and Allan's analysis provides insights into the history of Shakespeare on screen and the depiction of the supernatural. Its consideration of the historical intertexts of each production recalls the historicist approach taken by several other chapters in this volume. Her work also points to the potential of the supernatural in Shakespeare to be adapted to vastly different cultures and genres.

As Maurizio Calbi has argued, Shakespeare is a constant spectral presence in contemporary culture.[65] Yukari Yoshihara explores the intriguing afterlives of Ophelia in Japanese pop-cultural appropriations and transformations in her chapter 'Ophelia and her magical daughters'. The paradoxical realism of the fairies in *Dream* contrasts with the otherworldly treatment reserved to a very human character from *Hamlet*, Ophelia, whose figure has haunted popular culture. While in Shakespeare's *Hamlet* there is no supernatural dimension to Ophelia, in her Japanese afterlives she has been transformed in a variety of ways. Ophelia has contributed to the 'dead wet girl' figure, common in Japanese horror genres. Far from remaining a passive victim, many iterations of Ophelia give her agency and supernatural powers. Yoshihara firstly considers the key, initiating role in the history of Shakespearean reception, and particularly the supernatural, of Natsume Soseki (1867–1916), the first Japanese Professor of English Literature at Tokyo Imperial University. She then provides a fascinating survey of Ophelia's various metamorphoses. Hayao Miyazaki rendered his Ophelia a sea goddess in *Ponyo* (2008); in the manga/anime series *Claymore*, created by Norihiro Yagi, Ophelia is a giant monster with a snake's tale; and in Gonzo's anime television series *Romeo × Juliet* (2007), Ophelia protects the Tree of Life of Neo Verona, a city in the air. The Shakespearean hypotext thus generates a space of exploration in contemporary Japanese pop culture, which opens up a new dimension of Ophelia as a supernatural character.

Taken together, the essays provide insights into an array of Shakespeare's plays, underlining the complexity of his use of the supernatural, as well as our own. The different chapters not only explore the manner in which Shakespeare negotiated with the supernatural, as if the supernatural were an external reality, but also the manner in which the playwright was an agent, a creator, rather than a mere witness, of the supernatural. They also evidence the ways that contemporary adaptations have added supernatural elements where these were absent from the original playtext. In so doing, *Shakespeare and the supernatural* collapses distinctions: histories haunt texts and spaces, informing performance choices, and contemporary culture provides echo chambers for the myriad forms taken by supernatural beliefs of the early modern era. Overall, the volume provides a cross-section of current work on Shakespeare, encompassing textual insights, historical contexts and interpretations of performance on stage and screen. It challenges us to rethink how we frame the world and construct the porous boundaries between the natural and supernatural. The volume also highlights the potential that performance offers us to explore this illuminating dimension of Shakespeare's work. In this ongoing project, Shakespeare's spectre and 'most potent art' will continue to haunt us.

Notes

1. On issues raised in defining the supernatural, see Victoria Bladen and Marcus Harmes, 'The Intersections of Supernatural and Secular Power', in Marcus Harmes and Victoria Bladen (eds), *Supernatural and Secular Power in Early Modern England* (Farnham and Burlington, VT: Ashgate, 2015), pp. 1–3.
2. Darren Oldridge, *The Supernatural in Tudor and Stuart England* (London and New York: Routledge, 2016), pp. 1–2.
3. On magic, see Owen Davies, *Magic: A Very Short Introduction* (Oxford: Oxford University Press, 2012) and Frank Klaassen, *The Transformations of Magic: Illicit Learned Magic in the Later Middle Ages and Renaissance* (Pennsylvania: Pennsylvania State University Press, 2013).
4. Peter Marshall and Alexandra Walsham (eds), *Angels in the Early Modern World* (Cambridge: Cambridge University Press, 2006), pp. 11–12. See also Peter Benes and Jane Montague (eds), *Wonders of the Invisible World: 1600–1900* (Boston, MA: Boston University Press, 1995); and Christine Göttler and Wolfgang Neuber (eds), *Spirits Unseen: The Representation of Subtle Bodies in Early Modern European Culture* (Leiden: Brill, 2008).
5. On the idea of nature as God's Second Book, see Klass van Berkel and Arjo Vanderjagt (eds), *The Book of Nature in Early Modern and Modern History* (Leuven: Peeters, 2006).
6. Christopher Marlowe, *Dr Faustus: The A-Text*, eds David Ormerod and Christopher Wortham (Perth: University of Western Australia, 1985).
7. Oldridge, *The Supernatural*, p. 3.
8. Keith Thomas, *Religion and the Decline of Magic* (New York: Charles Scribner's Sons, 1971), p. 80.
9. Davidson cites the compilation work, the *Malleus Omnibus* (1669), as a significant 'scientific work dealing with the supernatural' that counterbalanced other, more secular scientific works, such as those of Konrad Gesner, Edward Topsell and Nicolas Steno. Jane P. Davidson, *Early Modern Supernatural: The Dark Side of European Culture, 1400–1700* (Santa Barbara, CA: Praeger, 2012), pp. 5, 8–11.
10. Oldridge, *The Supernatural*, p. 1.
11. Thomas, *Religion and the Decline of Magic*, pp. 80, 107.
12. On ghosts generally, see John Newton and Jo Beth (eds), *Early Modern Ghosts* (Durham: University of Durham, 2002); Thomas, *Religion and the Decline of Magic*, chapter 19; and Kathryn Edwards, 'The History of Ghosts in early modern Europe: Recent Research and Future Trajectories', *History Compass*, 10:4 (2012), 353–66.

13 See generally Diane Purkiss, *Troublesome Things: A History of Fairies and Fairy Stories* (London: Penguin, 2000); and Thomas, *Religion and the Decline of Magic*, p. 185 and chapter 19.
14 Oldridge, *The Supernatural*, p. 9.
15 On cunning folk see Owen Davies, *Popular Magic: Cunning-folk in English History* (London and Oxford: Bloomsbury, 2007); Thomas, *Religion and the Decline of Magic*, chapter 8; and Judith Bonzol, '"In good reporte and honest estimacion amongst her neighbours": Cunning Women in the Star Chamber and on the Stage in Early Modern England', in Lisa Hopkins and Helen Ostovich (eds), *Magical Transformations on the Early Modern English Stage* (Farnham and Burlington, VT: Ashgate, 2014), pp. 169–84.
16 Thomas, *Religion and the Decline of Magic*, p. 192.
17 Richard Kieckhefer, *Magic in the Middle Ages* (Cambridge: Cambridge University Press, 2000), p. 10.
18 Ibid.
19 Ibid., p. 9.
20 Augustine, *De Doctrina Christiana*, ed. and trans. R. P. H. Green (Oxford: Clarendon Press, 1995), Book II, sec. 89, p. 99. For additional contextual documents delineating Augustine's influence on medieval and early modern conceptions of witchcraft, see Alan Charles Kors and Edward Peters (eds), *Witchcraft in Europe, 400–1700: A Documentary History* (Philadelphia: University of Pennsylvania Press, 2001).
21 Thomas, *Religion and the Decline of Magic*, p. 257.
22 See Thomas, *Religion and the Decline of Magic*, chapter 2.
23 Ibid., p. 61.
24 Ibid., p. 267.
25 *2 Henry VI*, in *The Riverside Shakespeare*, ed. G. Blakemore Evans (Boston, MA: Houghton Mifflin, 2nd edn, 1997).
26 Kieckhefer, *Magic in the Middle Ages*, p. 62; Barbara Howard Traister, *Heavenly Necromancers: The Magician in English Renaissance Drama* (Columbia, MO: University of Missouri Press, 1984).
27 John Calvin, *Sermons on the Epistle to the Ephesians* [1577], trans. A. Golding (Edinburgh: Banner of Truth Trust, 1973), p. 569. On the dangers of feminine curiosity, see Yan Brailowsky, 'From Genesitic Curiosity to Dangerous Gynocracy in Sixteenth-Century England', in Line Cottegnies, Sandrine Parageau and John J. Thompson (eds), *Women and Curiosity in Early Modern England and France* (Leiden: Brill, 2016), pp. 27–40.
28 Thomas, *Religion and the Decline of Magic*, pp. 224–5. On Dee's relationship with Elizabeth I, see Benjamin Woolley, *The Queen's Conjurer: The Science and Magic of Dr John Dee, Adviser to Queen Elizabeth I* (New York: Henry Holt and Company, 2001). See also Mickaël Popelard, *La figure du savant chez Shakespeare et Marlowe: rêves de puissance et ruine de l'âme* (Paris: Presses universitaires de France, 2010). An additional figure who may have had some influence on Shakespeare was Giordano Bruno, whose interest in hermeticism was analysed by Frances Yates in her landmark study *Giordano Bruno and the Hermetic Tradition* (Chicago: Chicago University Press, 1964).

29 For the process of *solve et coagula*, dissolution and coagulation, as essential to the alchemical process of refining the philosopher's stone, see Lyndy Abraham, *A Dictionary of Alchemical Imagery* (Cambridge: Cambridge University Press, 1998), p. 187.
30 Thomas, *Religion and the Decline of Magic*, p. 285.
31 *Ibid.*, p. 287.
32 *Ibid.*, pp. 285, 301, and generally chapters 10–12.
33 It is estimated by Brian Levack that there were approximately 90,000 prosecutions for witchcraft across Europe, of which around half resulted in executions. In Britain it is estimated there may have been up to 5,000 trials and 1,500–2,000 executions. The most common profile for those convicted and executed was elderly women. See generally Brian P. Levack, *The Witch-Hunt in Early Modern Europe* (Harlow: Pearson, 3rd edn, 2006). For alternative estimates from various authors see Allison P. Coudert, 'The Myth of the Improved Status of Protestant Women: The Case of the Witchcraze' in Jean R. Brink, Allison P. Coudert and Maryanne C. Horowitz (eds), *The Politics of Gender in Early Modern Europe* (Kirksville, MO: Sixteenth Century Journal Pubs, 1989), pp. 61–89.
34 Kieckhefer, *Magic in the Middle Ages*, p. xi. On the extensive field of witchcraft and the witch trials, as well as Levack's *The Witch-Hunt in Early Modern Europe*, see James Sharpe, *Witchcraft in Early Modern England* (Harlow: Longman, 2001); and Stuart Clark, *Thinking with Demons: The Idea of Witchcraft in Early Modern Europe* (Oxford: Oxford University Press, 1997).
35 Philip C. Almond, *England's First Demonologist: Reginald Scot & 'The Discoverie of Witchcraft'* (London: I. B. Tauris, 2011), pp. 14–16.
36 Thomas, *Religion and the Decline of Magic*, p. 469 and see generally pp. 469–92. On the Devil generally, see Philip C. Almond, *The Devil: A New Biography* (London: I. B. Tauris, 2014).
37 Thomas, *Religion and the Decline of Magic*, p. 472.
38 Almond, *The Devil*, p. 18.
39 Thomas, *Religion and the Decline of Magic*, pp. 471–3.
40 On the supernatural and the early modern stage, see Hopkins and Ostovich (eds), *Magical Transformations on the Early Modern English Stage*; Verena Theile and Andrew D. McCarthy (eds), *Staging the Superstitions of Early Modern Europe* (Farnham and Burlington, VT: Ashgate, 2013); and Ryan Curtis Friesen, *Supernatural Fiction in Early Modern Drama and Culture* (Brighton: Sussex Academic Press, 2010).
41 Leah S. Marcus, *Unediting the Renaissance: Shakespeare, Marlowe and Milton* (London and New York: Routledge, 1996), p. 42.
42 David Bevington, 'Introduction to *Doctor Faustus*', in David Bevington et al. (eds), *English Renaissance Drama: A Norton Anthology* (New York: W. W. Norton, 2002), p. 249; Andrew Sofer, 'How to Do Things with Demons: Conjuring Performatives in *Doctor Faustus*', *Theatre Journal*, 61:1 (2009), p. 2.
43 Jean Seznec, *The Survival of the Pagan Gods: The Mythological Tradition and Its Place in Renaissance Humanism and Art* (1940), trans. Barbara F. Sessions (Princeton, NJ: Princeton University Press, 1953), p. 266.

44 On the commercial needs of early modern theatre, see Paul Menzer, 'Crowd Control', in Jennifer A. Low and Nova Myhill (eds), *Imagining the Audience in Early Modern Drama, 1558–1642* (New York: Palgrave Macmillan, 2011), pp. 19–36.
45 Victor Hugo, *William Shakespeare* (Paris: A. Lacroix, Verboeckhoven et Cie, 1864). Despite Hugo's penchant for history and his living in the heyday of nineteenth-century positivism, the prolific writer was also fond of spiritism and participated in a number of table-turning *séances*.
46 Reginald Scot, *The Discoverie of Witchcraft*, ed. Montague Summers (New York: Dover Publications, 1972); Francis Bacon, *Francis Bacon: The New Organon*, eds Lisa Jardine and Michael Silverthorne, Cambridge Texts in the History of Philosophy (Cambridge: Cambridge University Press, 2000).
47 Scot, *The Discoverie*, p. 87. On the 'ceasing' of oracles, prophecies, and omens, see Book VIII. On Scot, see Almond, *England's First Demonologist*.
48 Bacon, *The New Organon*, Book I, sec. 46, p. 43.
49 William Shakespeare, *King Lear*, ed. Jay L. Halio (Cambridge: Cambridge University Press, 2005).
50 *The Norton Shakespeare*, eds Stephen Greenblatt, Walter Cohen, Suzanne Gossett, Jean E. Howard, Katherine Eisaman Maus and Gordon McMullan (New York: Norton, 3rd edn, 2016). See also Marco Mincoff, *Things Supernatural and Causeless: Shakespearean Romance* (Newark: University of Delaware Press, 1993) and Harry Berger Jr, *Making Trifles of Terrors: Redistributing Complicities in Shakespeare* (Stanford, CA: Stanford University Press, 1997).
51 Stephen Greenblatt, 'Shakespeare and the Exorcists', in *Shakespearean Negotiations: The Circulation of Social Energy in Renaissance England* (Berkeley: University of California Press, 1988), p. 120. Greenblatt compared *Lear* with Samuel Harsnett's *A Declaration of Egregious Popish Impostures*, published in 1603, which notably inspired the scenes in which Edgar plays Poor Tom.
52 Kevin Pask, *The Fairy Way of Writing: Shakespeare to Tolkien* (Baltimore, MD: Johns Hopkins University Press, 2013), p. 4.
53 Kristen Poole, *Supernatural Environments in Shakespeare's England: Spaces of Demonism, Divinity, and Drama* (Cambridge: Cambridge University Press, 2011), p. 3. On Shakespeare and maps, see Christopher Wortham, 'Meanings of the South: From the *Mappaemundi* to Shakespeare's *Othello*', in Anne M. Scott, Alfred Hiatt, Claire McIlroy and Christopher Wortham (eds), *European Perceptions of Terra Australis* (Farnham and Burlington, VT: Ashgate, 2011), pp. 61–81; and Peter Whitfield, *Mapping Shakespeare's World* (Oxford: Bodleian Library, 2015).
54 Tiffany Stern, '"This Wide and Universal Theatre": the Theatre as Prop in Shakespeare's Metadrama', in Farah Karim-Cooper and Tiffany Stern (eds), *Shakespeare's Theatres and the Effects of Performance* (London and Oxford: Bloomsbury, Arden Shakespeare, 2013).
55 Weber's thesis has been amply challenged since it was first used a century ago. See Nandini Das and Nick Davis (eds), *Enchantment and Dis-Enchantment in Shakespeare and Early Modern Drama: Wonder, the Sacred, and the Supernatural* (New York: Routledge, 2016), pp. 3–7; Sara Lyons, 'The Disenchantment/Re-Enchantment of the World: Aesthetics, Secularization, and the Gods of Greece

from Friedrich Schiller to Walter Pater', *The Modern Language Review*, 109:4 (2014), 873–95; and, more recently, Jason A. Josephson-Storm, *The Myth of Disenchantment: Magic, Modernity, and the Birth of the Human Sciences* (Chicago: Chicago University Press, 2017).
56 *The Tempest*, ed. David Lindley (Cambridge: Cambridge University Press, 2nd edn, 2013); Thomas, *Religion and the Decline of Magic*, p. 641.
57 Thomas, *Religion and the Decline of Magic*, pp. 248, 605; and Birgit Meyer and Peter Pels (eds), *Magic and Modernity: Interfaces of Revelation and Concealment* (Stanford, CA: Stanford University Press, 2003).
58 www.ohchr.org/en/issues/albinism/pages/witchcraft.aspx, accessed 14 April 2019. Also see the exhibition notes for the University of Queensland Art Museum's exhibition *Second Sight: Witchcraft, Ritual, Power* 2019, https://art-museum.uq.edu.au/second-sight-witchcraft-ritual-power, accessed 14 April 2019.
59 Almond, *The Devil*, p. 17.
60 Ewan Fernie, *The Demonic: Literature and Experience* (London and New York: Routledge, 2013).
61 Also see generally Josephson-Storm, *The Myth of Disenchantment*; and Stanley Jeyaraja Tambiah, *Magic, Science, Religion, and the Scope of Rationality* (Cambridge: Cambridge University Press, 1990).
62 Stern, "This Wide and Universal Theatre", p. 32.
63 Marvin Carlson, *The Haunted Stage: The Theatre as Memory Machine* (Ann Arbor: University of Michigan Press, 2001).
64 Purkiss, *Troublesome Things*, p. 8.
65 Maurizio Calbi, *Spectral Shakespeares: Media Adaptations in the Twenty-First Century* (Houndmills and New York: Palgrave Macmillan, 2013).

Bibliography

Abraham, Lyndy, *A Dictionary of Alchemical Imagery* (Cambridge: Cambridge University Press, 1998).

Almond, Philip, *The Devil: A New Biography* (London: I. B. Tauris, 2014).

—— *England's First Demonologist: Reginald Scot & 'The Discoverie of Witchcraft'* (London: I. B. Tauris, 2011).

Augustine, *De Doctrina Christiana*, ed. and trans. R. P. H. Green (Oxford: Clarendon Press, 1995).

Bacon, Francis, *Francis Bacon: The New Organon*, eds Lisa Jardine and Michael Silverthorne, Cambridge Texts in the History of Philosophy (Cambridge: Cambridge University Press, 2000).

Benes, Peter, and Jane Montague (eds), *Wonders of the Invisible World: 1600-1900* (Boston, MA: Boston University Press, 1995).

Berger, Harry Jr, *Making Trifles of Terrors: Redistributing Complicities in Shakespeare* (Stanford, CA: Stanford University Press, 1997).

Bladen, Victoria and Marcus Harmes, 'The Intersections of Supernatural and Secular Power', in Marcus Harmes and Victoria Bladen (eds), *Supernatural and Secular Power in Early Modern England* (Farnham and Burlington, VT: Ashgate, 2015), pp. 1–14.

Bevington, David, et al. (eds), *English Renaissance Drama: A Norton Anthology* (New York: W. W. Norton, 2002).

Bonzol, Judith, '"In good reporte and honest estimacion amongst her neighbours": Cunning Women in the Star Chamber and on the Stage in Early Modern England' in Lisa Hopkins and Helen Ostovich (eds), *Magical Transformations on the Early Modern English Stage* (Farnham and Burlington: Ashgate, 2014), pp. 169–84.

Brailowsky, Yan, 'From Genesitic Curiosity to Dangerous Gynocracy in Sixteenth-Century England', in Line Cottegnies, Sandrine Parageau and John J. Thompson (eds), *Women and Curiosity in Early Modern England and France* (Leiden: Brill, 2016), pp. 27–40.

Butterworth, Philip, *Magic on the Early English Stage* (Cambridge: Cambridge University Press, 2005).

Calbi, Maurizio, *Spectral Shakespeares: Media Adaptations in the Twenty-First Century* (Houndmills and New York: Palgrave Macmillan, 2013).

Calvin, John, *Sermons on the Epistle to the Ephesians* [1577], trans. A. Golding (Edinburgh: Banner of Truth Trust, 1973).

Carlson, Marvin, *The Haunted Stage: The Theatre as Memory Machine* (Ann Arbor: University of Michigan Press, 2001).

Clark, Stuart, *Thinking with Demons: The Idea of Witchcraft in Early Modern Europe* (Oxford: Oxford University Press, 1997).

Coudert, Allison P., 'The Myth of the Improved Status of Protestant Women: The Case of the Witchcraze' in Jean R. Brink, Allison P. Coudert and Maryanne C. Horowitz (eds), *The Politics of Gender in Early Modern Europe* (Kirksville, MO: Sixteenth Century Journal Pubs, 1989), pp. 61–89.

Das, Nandini, and Nick Davis (eds), *Enchantment and Dis-Enchantment in Shakespeare and Early Modern Drama: Wonder, the Sacred, and the Supernatural* (New York: Routledge, 2016).

Davidson, Jane P., *Early Modern Supernatural: The Dark Side of European Culture, 1400–1700* (Santa Barbara, CA: Praeger, 2012).
Davies, Owen, *Magic: A Very Short Introduction* (Oxford: Oxford University Press, 2012).
—— *Popular Magic: Cunning-folk in English History* (London and Oxford: Bloomsbury, 2007).
Edwards, Kathryn, 'The History of Ghosts in early modern Europe: Recent Research and Future Trajectories', *History Compass*, 10:4 (2012), 353–66.
Fernie, Ewan, *The Demonic: Literature and Experience* (London and New York: Routledge, 2013).
Friesen, Ryan Curtis, *Supernatural Fiction in Early Modern Drama and Culture* (Brighton: Sussex Academic Press, 2010).
Göttler, Christine, and Wolfgang Neuber (eds), *Spirits Unseen: The Representation of Subtle Bodies in Early Modern European Culture* (Leiden: Brill, 2008).
Greenblatt, Stephen, *Shakespearean Negotiations: The Circulation of Social Energy in Renaissance England* (Berkeley: University of California Press, 1988).
Hopkins, Lisa, and Helen Ostovich (eds), *Magical Transformations on the Early Modern English Stage* (New York: Routledge, 2014).
Hugo, Victor, *William Shakespeare* (Paris: A. Lacroix, Verboeckhoven et Cie, 1864).
Josephson-Storm, Jason A., *The Myth of Disenchantment: Magic, Modernity, and the Birth of the Human Sciences* (Chicago: Chicago University Press, 2017).
Kieckhefer, Richard, *Magic in the Middle Ages* (Cambridge: Cambridge University Press, 2000).
Klaassen, Frank, *The Transformations of Magic: Illicit Learned Magic in the Later Middle Ages and Renaissance* (Pennsylvania: Pennsylvania State University Press, 2013).
Kors, Alan Charles, and Edward Peters (eds), *Witchcraft in Europe, 400–1700: A Documentary History* (Philadelphia: University of Pennsylvania Press, 2001).
Levack, Brian P., *The Witch-Hunt in Early Modern Europe* (Harlow: Pearson, 3rd edn, 2006).
Low, Jennifer A., and Nova Myhill (eds), *Imagining the Audience in Early Modern Drama, 1558–1642* (New York: Palgrave Macmillan, 2011).
Lyons, Sara, 'The Disenchantment/Re-Enchantment of the World: Aesthetics, Secularization, and the Gods of Greece from Friedrich Schiller to Walter Pater', *The Modern Language Review*, 109:4 (2014), 873–95.
Marcus, Leah S., *Unediting the Renaissance: Shakespeare, Marlowe and Milton* (London and New York: Routledge, 1996).
Marlowe, Christopher, *Dr Faustus: The A-Text*, eds David Ormerod and Christopher Wortham (Perth: University of Western Australia, 1985).
Marshall, Peter, and Alexandra Walsham (eds), *Angels in the Early Modern World* (Cambridge: Cambridge University Press, 2006).
Menzer, Paul, 'Crowd Control', in Jennifer A. Low and Nova Myhill (eds), *Imagining the Audience in Early Modern Drama, 1558–1642* (New York: Palgrave Macmillan, 2011), pp. 19–36.
Meyer, Birgit, and Peter Pels (eds), *Magic and Modernity: Interfaces of Revelation and Concealment* (Stanford, CA: Stanford University Press, 2003).

Mincoff, Marco, *Things Supernatural and Causeless: Shakespearean Romance* (Newark: University of Delaware Press, 1993).

Newton, John, and Jo Beth (eds), *Early Modern Ghosts* (Durham: University of Durham, 2002).

Oldridge, Darren, *The Supernatural in Tudor and Stuart England* (London and New York: Routledge, 2016).

Pask, Kevin, *The Fairy Way of Writing: Shakespeare to Tolkien* (Baltimore, MD: Johns Hopkins University Press, 2013).

Poole, Kristen, *Supernatural Environments in Shakespeare's England: Spaces of Demonism, Divinity, and Drama* (Cambridge: Cambridge University Press, 2011).

Popelard, Mickaël, *La figure du savant chez Shakespeare et Marlowe: rêves de puissance et ruine de l'âme* (Paris: Presses universitaires de France, 2010).

Purkiss, Diane, *Troublesome Things: A History of Fairies and Fairy Stories* (London: Penguin, 2000).

Scot, Reginald, *The Discoverie of Witchcraft*, ed. Montague Summers (New York: Dover Publications, 1972).

Seznec, Jean, *The Survival of the Pagan Gods: The Mythological Tradition and Its Place in Renaissance Humanism and Art* (1940), trans. Barbara F. Sessions (Princeton, NJ: Princeton University Press, 1953).

Shakespeare, William, *King Lear*, ed. Jay L. Halio (Cambridge: Cambridge University Press, 2005).

—— *The Tempest*, ed. David Lindley (Cambridge: Cambridge University Press, 2nd edn, 2013).

—— *The Norton Shakespeare*, eds Stephen Greenblatt, Walter Cohen, Suzanne Gossett, Jean E. Howard, Katherine Eisaman Maus and Gordon McMullan (New York: Norton, 3rd edn, 2016).

—— *The Riverside Shakespeare*, ed. G. Blakemore Evans (Boston, MA: Houghton Mifflin, 2nd edn, 1997).

Sharpe, James, *Witchcraft in Early Modern England* (Harlow: Longman, 2001).

Sofer, Andrew, 'How to Do Things with Demons: Conjuring Performatives in *Doctor Faustus*', *Theatre Journal*, 61:1 (2009), 1–21.

Stern, Tiffany, '"This Wide and Universal Theatre": the Theatre as Prop in Shakespeare's Metadrama', in Farah Karim-Cooper and Tiffany Stern (eds), *Shakespeare's Theatres and the Effects of Performance* (London and Oxford: Bloomsbury, Arden Shakespeare, 2013).

Tambiah, Stanley Jeyaraja, *Magic, Science, Religion, and the Scope of Rationality* (Cambridge: Cambridge University Press, 1990).

Theile, Verena, and Andrew D. McCarthy (eds), *Staging the Superstitions of Early Modern Europe* (Farnham and Burlington, VT: Ashgate, 2013).

Thomas, Keith, *Religion and the Decline of Magic* (New York: Charles Scribner's Sons, 1971).

Traister, Barbara Howard, *Heavenly Necromancers: The Magician in English Renaissance Drama* (Columbia, MO: University of Missouri Press, 1984).

van Berkel, Klaas, and Arjo Vanderjagt (eds), *The Book of Nature in Early Modern and Modern History* (Leuven: Peeters, 2006).

Whitfield, Peter, *Mapping Shakespeare's World* (Oxford: Bodleian Library, 2015).
Woolley, Benjamin, *The Queen's Conjurer: The Science and Magic of Dr John Dee, Adviser to Queen Elizabeth I* (New York: Henry Holt and Company, 2001).
Wortham, Christopher, 'Meanings of the South: From the *Mappaemundi* to Shakespeare's *Othello*', in Anne M. Scott, Alfred Hiatt, Claire McIlroy and Christopher Wortham (eds), *European Perceptions of Terra Australis* (Farnham and Burlington, VT: Ashgate, 2011), pp. 61–81.
Yates, Frances, *Giordano Bruno and the Hermetic Tradition* (Chicago: Chicago University Press, 1964).

Part I
Embodying the supernatural

1

Shakespeare's political spectres

Victoria Bladen

This bodes some strange eruption to our state

(*Hamlet*, 1.1.68)

In Elizabethan and Jacobean England, ghosts were problematic, a concept associated with Catholic constructions of the afterlife and with folkloric traditions that Protestantism sought to displace. However, ghosts proved to be popular figures on the stage, and Shakespeare and his contemporaries were highly attuned to the theatrical power of the spectral. In Shakespeare's plays, the monarch's throne is a particularly haunted space. In *Richard III* (1597), *Julius Caesar* (1599), *Hamlet* (1600) and *Macbeth* (1606), political leaders, or those close to the centres of power, are subject to visitations from ghosts who had held power themselves or been murdered as part of the brutal process of obtaining or maintaining power. Thus, the ghosts not only unsettle, rendering the boundary between the living and the dead porous, but also implicitly challenge monarchs' positions, undermining assumptions of legitimacy and supervising political change.

Shakespeare's ghosts draw attention to early modern assumptions about the transfer of monarchical power. Pursuant to the theory of the king's two bodies, a monarch was conceptually divided into mortal (the body natural) and immortal parts (the body politic).[1] The spirit, the essence of divine and legitimate kingship with a mandate from God, passed seamlessly, in theory, to the next legitimate ruler. However, what happened in cases where power did not legitimately pass into a successor's mortal body? The spirit of 'authentic' monarchy could be left disembodied, not re-vested in a new body. Shakespeare's work evidences a deep interest in such scenarios of political rupture where power had not transferred legitimately or was contested, leaving unresolved the question of where 'legitimate' right was vested. In the plays that present such scenarios, we can think of the displaced spirit of legitimate rule as an additional spectral presence, haunting the sphere of the crown, and disturbing those wielding power illegitimately. The ghosts we encounter in the plays register this additional spectral presence that we do not see but feel the effect of; they implicitly highlight a flawed system, undermining the concept of stable, sanctioned rule passing undisturbed to the next legitimate ruler. This chapter explores the political dimensions of Shakespeare's ghosts, examining how and to what end they haunt political spaces, and the ways in which they resonate with the additional spectre, the second ghost, of the disembodied legitimate ruler, and thus disturb the parameters of monarchy itself.

The nature of the ghost

A ghost, by its very nature, evades rational categories, with the appearance of a body that no longer exists, that may speak with a mouth that can no longer utter sound. The spectre embodies death yet defies it, challenging and transgressing the border between life and death. As Jacques Derrida described, the ghost is 'some thing that remains difficult to name: neither soul nor body, and both one and the other'.[2] The ghost is a figure of rupture, disturbing and intriguing.

Catholic doctrine allowed for ghosts to be understood as souls from Purgatory, seeking intercession; the only challenge was to be sure of an apparition's orthodoxy.[3] The idea of Purgatory had been central to late medieval theology, an appealing concept of an intermediate zone in which it was possible to work towards entry to heaven and benefit from the efforts of the living to also work towards one's release.[4] However, Protestantism abolished the concept and condemned belief in spirits, arguing that what had previously been explained as ghosts were in fact devils, and that purgatory had no scriptural foundation.[5] As Kathryn A. Edwards notes, 'the most direct response of early modern intellectuals was to equate ghosts and demons'.[6] Ludwig Lavater articulated the new, orthodox Protestant position on ghosts in his *Of Ghosts and Spirites Walking by Night* (1569). Yet, as Catherine Stevens has explored, even in this account that attempts to contain belief in ghosts, the powerful draw of the concept threatens to elude containment.[7] Jo Beth points out, in *Early Modern Ghosts*, that with the post-Reformation redefinition of ghosts, 'categories started to merge in popular thought, creating beings which combined elements of both ghost and demon. Even where they were still thought of as spirits of the dead, ghosts began to be tainted with the elements ascribed to their demonic counterparts by the clergy.'[8] Hamlet expresses this doubt when he observes '[t]he spirit that I have seen/May be a dev'l' (2.2.517–18).[9]

Whether perceived as a spirit of the dead or as a demon, ghosts retained their potency. Edwards aptly describes ghosts as 'a universal experience in early modern Europe', and among the themes common to early modern accounts of ghosts she notes is the presumption that the apparition had a purpose, frequently justice or revenge.[10] This was reflected on the stage and, in Shakespeare's work, that purpose is invariably political, directed at matters central to the state. There are fourteen ghosts that appear in the plays in focus here:[11] the long list of victims of *Richard III* (Prince Edward, Henry VI, Clarence, Rivers, Grey, Vaughan, the young princes killed in the Tower, Hastings, Lady Anne and Buckingham), the ghost of Julius Caesar, Old Hamlet and Banquo. All of these ghosts are victims of murder; they 'embody', in their intangible, spectral way, the violence of the throne, a reminder of the cost of power.

The ghosts function as complex *memento mori*. They are specific reminders of death for the characters experiencing the ghost in the play, recalling the murders that led to the ghost's condition, while also functioning as general reminders of inevitable death for the play's audience. In *Hamlet*, the ghost of Old Hamlet is a natural counterpart of Yorick's skull that Hamlet holds in the graveyard scene; they are complementary remnants of human death.[12] Yet paradoxically, ghosts also evidence life after death, as well as ongoing surveillance of the space of the living by the dead. All of the ghosts in Shakespeare's plays evidence knowledge of what is going on in the living world and purport to intervene in direct or indirect ways; they are able to effect tangible results despite their ephemeral nature, often through affecting the mind of the witness.

A key question that critics have asked of Shakespeare's ghosts is whether they have an independent existence or are the product of the witness's mind, a projection of the intense mental crisis a character is undergoing.[13] Contemporary directors of stage and screen generally have considerable flexibility in how they resolve this issue whereas, in the early modern theatre, the embodied presence of the actor playing the ghost would have suggested an actual supernatural presence, rather than a figment of the imagination.[14] Most of the ghosts only appear to one person, with the exception of *Hamlet* where the ghost of Old Hamlet is seen by several other witnesses, not just Hamlet, in Act 1, Scene 1. In *Richard III*, Richard and Richmond are asleep when they encounter the ghosts, rendering the spectres more dreamlike. In *Julius Caesar*, although Brutus is awake, it is late and he is no doubt sleepy.[15] Macbeth is awake, although gripped by guilt, making Banquo plausible as a hallucination. Yet whatever crisis the witness's mind is undergoing, there is a clear link in all these plays with events at the state level.

Shakespeare's ghosts appear in the wake of political crisis. In *Hamlet*, Horatio makes this link explicit: '[t]his bodes some strange eruption to our state' (1.1.68). Such a state results where a legitimate ruler has been murdered, such as Old Hamlet or Duncan, or, in the case of *Richard III*, where a series of legitimate potential rulers and heirs have been killed. In *Julius Caesar*, the rupture results from the pseudo-regicide that registers the death of the republic leading to the beginning of empire. Who a ghost appears to also has political relevance; ghosts appear to figures who either were involved in the murder (Macbeth, Richard III, Brutus) or to the figure who potentially has the power to redress the wrong (Hamlet, Richmond).

It is political trauma that opens up the boundaries between the living and the dead, and this state is often described as registered and manifest in the natural world. For example, in *Julius Caesar* it is reported by Calphurnia that 'horrid sights' have been seen by the watch: '[a] lioness hath whelped in the streets;/And graves have yawn'd, and yielded up their dead'. Images of warriors 'fought upon the clouds' and 'ghosts did shriek and squeal about the streets' (2.2.16–24).[16] In *Macbeth*, after the death of Duncan, the Old Man reports that a falcon was killed by a mousing owl (2.4.12–13) and Ross recalls that Duncan's horses 'turned wild in nature', 'a thing most strange and certain' (2.4.14–16), to which the Old Man adds ''[t]is said they ate each other' (2.4.18). Although some characters express scepticism about cosmic signs (such as Cicero in *Julius Caesar*, 1.3.34), generally the plays suggest that supernatural and unnatural occurrences register political disturbance that reverberates through nature. The ghosts form part of these signs.[17]

The second ghost

As markers of political disturbance, Shakespeare's ghosts recall the invisible yet present second ghost. They are advocates and vehicles for the voice of the additional spectre of political legitimacy. A monarch was conceived of as a haunted body in itself, infused with the spirit of divinely ordained rule. As Ernst Kantorowitz outlined in his seminal study, while the physical body was mortal, the *dignitas* or office of the king was conceived as immortal. Every monarch was considered self-begotten and eternal, arising naturally from the death of the previous monarch like a phoenix.[18]

Although we do not see this additional spectre, yet we see its traces. The ghosts we experience register the breach that has occurred, the vacuum of legitimate rule and the intangible spirit of legitimacy that remains suspended, not vested, within the dysfunctional political worlds of the plays. Thrones are inhabited by figures who not only occupy them illegitimately, but are essentially unfit to constitute monarchs and unable to be divinely sanctioned. Thus, not only does the legitimate ruler not occupy the throne but the throne is positively occupied by regicides, the antithesis of legitimacy. The situation is more complex in *Julius Caesar* in that the legitimate rule at stake, from the conspirators' perspective, is the threatened republic. Paradoxically, since the assassination ultimately fails to prevent the shift to empire, Caesar's corpse becomes a sign of the dead republic. At the same time, ironically, the supernatural signs of disturbance in the play, together with the prophecy of the Ides of March, suggest that Julius Caesar was already a monarch, a concept more familiar to Shakespeare's original audiences than a republic. As Calphurnia observes, nature's signs are reserved for monarchs: '[w]hen beggars die there are no comets seen;/The heavens themselves blaze forth the death of princes' (2.2.30–31).

Rulers who hold power illegitimately, such as Macbeth, Claudius and Richard III, express anxieties, directly or indirectly, in relation to their illegal possession of the throne. It is expressed, for example, through lack of sleep (Macbeth), inability to pray (Claudius) or the manic attempts to remove all potential obstacles (Richard, Macbeth). In these illegitimate rulers, there is the suggestion that their rule is tainted with the demonic. Such suggestions include: in *Macbeth*, the idea of Seyton/Satan as his companion (5.5), in *Richard III* the many references to the Devil (e.g. 1.2.48; 1.2.223) and in *Hamlet*, in addition to Claudius's inability to pray (3.3.97), various references by Hamlet (3.4.76; 3.4.170). Just as, in the wake of Reformation theory, there was blurring between 'legitimate' spirits and the demonic in the conception of ghosts, here there is the idea that not only is the spirit of legitimacy disembodied, but that the throne has been hijacked by the demonic. These suggestions clearly indicate that there has been no transmission of authentic monarchical power between rulers. I will now turn to consider the ghosts that respond to this state of affairs, looking firstly at returning ghostly rulers in *Hamlet* and *Julius Caesar*, and then at the ghosts of victims of political violence in *Richard III* and *Macbeth*.

Ghostly former rulers

The first question raised in *Hamlet* is what *is* the apparition – a legitimate spirit of Hamlet's father, or a demon: the opening line '[w]ho's there?' (1.1.1) resonates with this central question. Horatio's fear, that the spectre may lead Hamlet to his death (1.4.69–74), raises the possibility that the ghost is demonic. Likewise, Hamlet questions whether the ghost is 'a spirit of health or goblin damned' (1.4.40). The dubious nature of the ghost is emphasised by its location, on the battlements of the castle, the *locus* where borders are defended from enemies without, and the time it appears, after midnight and before dawn. If the ghost is legitimate, what does it want? The ghost appears to crave remembrance – 'remember me' (1.5.91) – and revenge – 'Revenge his foul and most unnatural murder' (1.5.25), although it is not specified how he expects Hamlet to carry this out – 'howsomever thou pursuest this act' (1.5.84).

As Derrida observes of ghosts, 'there is something disappeared, departed in the apparition itself'.[19] In *Hamlet*, the ghost is a remnant of the previous political state of Denmark, the body politic of which is figuratively suggested to be a corpse – 'something is rotten in the state of Denmark' (1.4.90). When Horatio describes 'buried Denmark' (1.1.47) in reference to Old Hamlet, the image emphasises the idea of the political state as a corpse. Furthermore, when, after the death of Polonius, Hamlet puns that 'the body is with the King, but the King is not with/The body' (3.5.26–7), the line resonates with the split that has occurred in the state. True kingship lies not with Claudius, while the true king is no longer embodied.

The current political state of Elsinore paradoxically renders impossible what the ghost asks of Hamlet. Claudius, the regicide, physically occupying the throne yet devoid of the spirit of right rule, blocks the avenue of redress.[20] There is no rightful king to whom Hamlet can appeal for justice, since the legitimate spirit is disembodied and thus disabled from action. Hamlet, in his inertia and inability to act, mirrors this state of stasis. Denmark is an elective monarchy, so there was no automatic right for Hamlet to take the throne upon the death of his father, yet the voting body has elected Claudius in ignorance of his crime, so Hamlet has likely been deprived of the throne.[21] This underlines the parallels between Hamlet and the spectre of legitimate rule; both occupy states of limbo disengaged from the space of the throne. What the ghost demands of Hamlet, revenge, is also theologically dubious, since revenge was considered the right of God, and murder was a sin.[22] It was also, of course, dangerous, since to kill a king, however dubious his ascension to the throne, was treason.[23] In acting against Claudius, Hamlet would have no legal protection or religious justification. Hamlet is trapped by duties of obedience to various levels of patriarchal control – his father, the state and God.

Hamlet's description of Claudius as 'a king of shreds and patches' (3.4.102) is insightful and goes beyond suggesting that the king is a joke. The reference to motley aligns the king with Yorick, the court jester, now dead and rotting in the graveyard. In terms of his kingship, Claudius is a mere corpse, like the jester, lacking the live spirit of monarchy. Several theorists and critics have interpreted Hamlet's failure to kill Claudius, when he is ostensibly praying, through the lens of the theory of the king's two bodies. Jacques Lacan comments: '[w]hat stays Hamlet's arm? It's not fear – he has nothing but contempt for the guy – it's because he knows that he must strike something other than what's there.'[24] Similarly, Slavoj Žižek writes that '[Hamlet] knows that in so far as this sublime body is a pure semblance, it would forever slip out of his reach – his blow would always strike empty.'[25] Both insights accurately discern the hollow state of Claudius, of semblance, not substance. Yet does Hamlet desire to *strike* the spectre of monarchy? This assumption is problematic; Hamlet's stated reason for hesitation in this scene, the concern that Claudius may go to heaven since he appears to be praying (3.3.75–87), seems the more convincing reason.

The spectre of kingship has affinities with both the ghost of Old Hamlet and Hamlet himself; all three are in suspended states. As a disembodied spirit, Old Hamlet is physically unable to enact revenge, so he attempts to act through his son; however, Hamlet is similarly stymied. Haunted by his father, he is like a pseudo-monarch, a royal figure also dispossessed of the throne and haunted by the knowledge that legitimate rule is misplaced in Denmark. His suspended state of inaction and indecision is directly linked to his political state of limbo. The dramatic power of the play is created through the unendurable suffering of linked father and son, held in tension and unable to be released. The political significance of Old Hamlet's ghost is that it creates an impossible overlap of regimes. That the ghost is a former ruler generates an implicit conflict of authority, undermining the living ruler, himself illegitimate. The old regime lingers, challenging and politically engaged, rendering both regimes impotent and suspended. Ultimately, the stalemate can only be released through the tragic bloodbath at the end, which clears the throne of its half-monarch, opening the way for a new era of rule, thus ending the separation of the king's two bodies and vesting the spirit of right rule in Fortinbras.[26]

At the opening of *Julius Caesar*, the senators are confronted with a threatened republic. With the growing power of the living Caesar, there is an immanent loss of power vested in the Senate, yet Caesar has not yet taken the crown so, at the time of the assassination, the state of limbo has already been initiated, power passing, through the people, from republic towards monarchy. Again, Shakespeare's interest in in-between political states is evident, scenarios in which it is not precisely clear where legitimate power resides. Right rule has become spectral, as the republic slides towards a monarchy but a monarch is not yet vested; Caesar's ghost resonates with and recalls this political spectre. There is also a pervasive sense of metaphysical surveillance well before the appearance of the ghost. Turmoil in nature is reported and observed, interpreted by several characters as registering and anticipating the political crisis.

Caesar's death fractures the political body, while the world of the play suggests a breach of the natural order. Calphurnia interprets the unnatural signs as a mark of Caesar's greatness (2.2.30–31), his quasi-monarchical status inciting the supernatural registering of the imminent events. Caesar is killed lest he become a monarch, yet paradoxically, once dead, the transformation seems to have already occurred. Nature and the metaphysical realm appear to behave as if he were a king, proving the fears of the republicans and rendering the assassination a regicide. Alternatively, it is not the death of Caesar himself that Nature expresses as trauma, but rather the death of the republic and the political void into which vacuum Octavius will ultimately step, ushering in the new political regime of empire. On this reading, Caesar's death paradoxically signals and stands in for the death of the republic, his corpse a sign of the political body.[27] On either reading, despite the ostensible triumvirate claiming power, legitimate rule becomes a spectral presence. In terms of its political function, Caesar's ghost marks the boundary between republican and monarchical government. If his corpse recalls the dead republic, his ghost reminds us of the floating spirit of government that is unvested.

The ghost of Caesar, like Banquo's ghost for Macbeth, could be staged or filmed as an internal phenomenon, reflecting Brutus's conscience, since the ghost is only seen by Brutus and not by any of his attendants.[28] At the same time, the playtext suggests it as an external phenomenon; the dimming of Brutus's candle heralds the ghost's coming (4.3.279), a common early modern belief.[29] At first, Brutus thinks he is imagining the vision: 'I think it is the weakness of mine eyes/That shapes this monstrous apparition' (4.3.280–81). He then expresses the same doubts that Hamlet does, as to whether the ghost's origins are divine or demonic: '[a]rt thou some god, some angel, or some devil' (4.3.83). In response to Brutus's demand as to what the ghost is, the ghost claims '[t]hy evil spirit, Brutus' (4.3.286). This suggests a connection between Brutus and the ghost; it belongs to Brutus, the essence of Brutus's deed that weighs on his conscience despite his rational justifications for the act. Given that the ghost also functions as a referent of the second ghost, the spectre of suspended legitimate governance, this statement also suggests a connection between Brutus and the political spectre. In the play it is Brutus who is most connected with the idea of guarding the republic, which deepens the horror of the act he feels compelled to orchestrate to save that ideal. Although Brutus seems to calmly accept the ghost's pronouncement that he will see him again at Philippi (4.3.287–90), that the ghost weighs on him is evidenced later on in the play, particularly when Brutus sees his death as fulfilling the revenge impulse of the ghost.

Caesar himself, throughout the play, is a unique space for exploring the idea of the king's two bodies. He is seemingly divided into material and metaphysical facets, 'immortal Caesar' (1.2.60), an idea of greatness. Even Caesar conceives of himself as a dual identity, as both a man and a public concept. He speaks of this metaphysical aura as a separate identity when he describes himself in the third person. The gap between these two facets, fragile mortal and immense metaphysical presence, articulates the idea of the king's two bodies. The statues of Caesar, referred to in the first scene (1.1.63–4), suggest an abstract ideal of what Caesar is; they underscore the spectral political dimension to his identity. The idea of him as great is more potent than the mortal man. Cassius struggles to reconcile the abstract idea of Caesar's greatness with the reality of the fragile, physical dimension of the man, the 'sick girl' (1.2.128), as he recounts an episode where Caesar nearly drowned (1.2.100–31). Not only is Caesar subject to fainting spells, but also, like Macbeth, he lacks children; in the worlds of Shakespeare's plays this is commonly a sign of lacking political legitimacy. After the assassination, it is the abstract idea of Caesar that grows in power. In Caesar's words, he is not only monarchical but god-like. Ironically, he claims his constancy just before he is murdered (3.1.61–2). Yet in fact, Caesar's claim of constancy proves prophetic; the abstract idea of his greatness is unaffected by the death and in fact seems to grow once his spirit is no longer fettered by his fragile body.

The spectral power of Caesar pervades the battlefield. Cassius, at his death, cries 'Caesar, thou art revenged,/Even with the sword that killed thee' (5.3.45–6). Brutus cries, after the deaths of Cassius and Titinius, 'O Julius Caesar, thou art mighty yet;/Thy spirit walks abroad and turns our swords/In our own proper entrails' (5.3.94–6). In the final scene he reports again to Volumnius that '[t]he ghost of Caesar hath appeared to me/Two several times by night

– at Sardis once,/And this last night here in Philippi fields./I know my hour is come' (5.5.17–19). He interprets this second encounter as the sign that he will die that day. With his final speech, he sees his death as the fulfilment of the ghost's purpose: 'Caesar, now be still./I killed not thee with half so good a will' (5.5.51). However, Caesar's ghost has a political significance that extends beyond a simple appearance as revenge for murder. It is a fulcrum that registers not only a shift of power but also a change in the form of government, and the rupture of the life/death boundary is appropriate for such an upheaval to the mode of rule. Throughout the battle scenes there is a melancholic sense of the larger death that subsumes the fates of the individuals, the death of the republic that, with the shift to empire, becomes itself a spectral presence.

Ghostly political victims

The uncanny return of Richard III's corpse in the twenty-first century provided an apt coda to Shakespeare's construction of a king haunted by the returning dead.[30] The ghosts in *Richard III*, appearing to him the night before the battle of Bosworth, register and recall the collateral damage of Richard's journey to political power. They also, in their excessive number and in their close relation to Richard, are signs of his unnatural occupation of the throne, that his rule is against the natural order of things as presented in the world of the play. Whereas Macbeth's illegitimacy is signalled in his lack of progeny, Richard III's is marked in his body; he bears the physical warning signs of what he will wreak. Shakespeare's language articulates this unfitness; even Richard describes himself as 'rudely stamped', 'deformed' and 'unfinished' (1.1.16, 20), while those around him commonly refer to him using demonic ('foul devil', 1.2.48) or animal imagery ('hedgehog', 1.2.100; 'dog', 1.3.212; 'elvish-marked, abortive, rooting hog', 1.3.224).

The ghosts condemn Richard and assert their power to affect the mind: '[l]et me sit heavy on thy soul tomorrow' (5.3.116). They remind Richard of his actions – 'Think how thou stabb'st me in my prime of youth' (5.3.117); paradoxically, in their ephemeral forms they embody his deeds. They are his political record, the returning abject objects that he sought to cast away.[31] The ghosts claim an active role in the upcoming battle, assuring Richmond that: 'the wrongèd souls/Of butchered princes fight in thy behalf' (5.3.119–20). In their addresses to both Richard and Richmond, they supervise the political changeover, like a supernatural court that bears witness. The ghosts preside, satisfied, over Richard's imminent loss of power. Just as their lives were the stepping stones on the way to power for Gloucester, it is fitting that he re-encounters them on the return journey away from power. At the same time, in appearing to Richmond, there is the sense that the ghosts are ushering in a new reconciliation and embodiment of the second ghost in a legitimate monarch's body.

The ghosts each repeat the words '[d]espair and die' (5.3.124), the epistrophe and alliteration adding force, with the repetition and iambic rhythm giving the effect of a magic chant. The ability of the ghosts to curse credits them with the power to affect the mortal world, and implies the efficacy of words even from beyond the grave. It also continues the vein of cursing throughout the play, and links the ghosts with the figure of Margaret, who is like a quasi-ghost haunting Richard's court, a remnant of the previous monarch's reign. She is a voice prophesying the impending horror of his reign, and the subsequent ghosts echo and repeat her verbal assault. The fact that Richard is affected by the ghosts – 'how dost thou afflict me' (5.3.177) – conveys their power and reiterates the potency of words. This continues a theme evident throughout the play: characters' words come back to haunt them.

In the context of this larger order, as Stephen Greenblatt outlines, the ghosts 'are not merely psychological projections but metaphysical emissaries. The dead do not simply rot and disappear, nor do they survive only in the memories and dreams of the living: they are an ineradicable presence, a part of the structure of reality, an uncanny age group capable of blessing and cursing.'[32] The ghosts in *Richard III* imply divine surveillance and a metaphysical structure that the events are part of. Although the returning dead are always disruptive, there is nevertheless the sense that the ghosts of *Richard III* are rightfully present. There is solemn order to their coming. They appear in logical sequence, and repeat each other's mantras. They continue the heavy sense of ritual in the play overall, and function as witnesses in a divine court case, their presence providing accumulating evidence until the weight of it against Richard is overwhelming. In their dual role, they not only condemn Richard but also stand as harbingers of Henry, heralding the arrival of the next monarch. As a court of spirits, they confer legitimacy, and Henry is constructed as embodying the legitimate spirit of rule.

As Greenblatt observes, the play stages Richard's destruction and 'the ritual that lingers over the play is an exorcism'.[33] The ghosts supervise this expulsion and purging from the body politic of a figure who is not only presented as illegitimately occupying the throne, but as positively unnatural, anti-human and demonic. Richard is an agent of chaos before order is restored, embodied in the figure of Henry. The play draws on the fascination of the audience with seeing unnatural rule, the spectre of the crown usurped, the throne as a site of murderous riot and a bloody Carnival before Lent is restored with the first Tudor king. The ghosts of *Richard III* reiterate the rupture of the political state and dislodged spirit of legitimacy. Their political significance also lies in their challenge to the 'pastness' of the past. Richard's miscalculation, like Macbeth's, is to assume that murder could erase his victims' existence. Instead, they layer the present with their lingering presence, and at the dream scene, Richard confronts the horror of the palimpsest, the past layering and tainting the present.

At the conclusion of the play, Richmond imagines England as a wounded body and claims that, with his victory, 'civil wounds are stopped' (5.5.39-40). The implication is that he will reunite the king's two bodies into a healthy whole under Tudor rule, of particular relevance to an Elizabethan audience as subjects of Henry's granddaughter.

Shakespeare's interest in returning victims of political violence continued with his later tragedy *Macbeth*, where again the supernatural is concentrated on the political centre. The Weird Sisters appear to be particularly concerned with who has and will have power, and it is their potent conveyance to Macbeth of the supposedly pre-ordained future that inspires and precipitates his actions. The vision of the dagger in Act 2, Scene 1 is an extension of this invitation to Macbeth to actively create his political future. He questions whether the spectral weapon arises from within or outside himself, yet it appears 'as palpable' (2.1.40) as the dagger he draws in response.

In Act 2, Scene 2, after the killing of Duncan, although no ghost of the king appears, there is, nevertheless, an uncanny presence that seems to join the Macbeths and come between them. This begins a process of division that corrodes the marriage and ensures their line will remain unfruitful, a sign of their political illegitimacy; from this point on, the couple will move steadily apart. The traces of this invisible presence are evident from a close analysis of their dialogue. Firstly, Lady Macbeth is startled by an owl shrieking, responding with '[h]ark! Peace!' (2.2.2). When Macbeth enters with the bloody daggers and asks '[w]ho's there? What ho!' (2.2.8), he reacts in fear to a sound that is not Lady Macbeth's voice (alternatively, he fails to recognise her voice). Lady Macbeth does not answer him, and seems to assume that what Macbeth hears (or Macbeth's voice) is the guards waking (2.2.9-10). Her urging of 'Hark!' (2.2.11) suggests that she has heard something more, yet Macbeth says nothing further after entering. When she asks '[m]y husband?' (2.2.13), he does not answer her and instead states 'I have done the deed' (2.2.14). Then he proceeds to ask his own question: '[d]idst thou not hear a noise?' (2.2.14).

Macbeth appears to have heard a noise that he cannot account for. When Lady Macbeth asks her own question: '[d]id not you speak?' (2.2.16), this suggests that either Macbeth did not recognise his own voice, if his was the voice he heard, or what Lady Macbeth heard previously was not Macbeth's voice. Macbeth does not answer her question and instead asks yet another: '[w]hen?' (2.2.17). Although Lady Macbeth clarifies that what she heard was when he descended, Macbeth leaves her question hanging, unanswered. Macbeth also refers to hearing a voice: '[m]ethought I heard a voice cry, "Sleep no more! Macbeth does murder sleep"' (2.2.38-9) and, when Lady Macbeth questions him, he claims that the voice cried 'to all the house' that 'Macbeth shall sleep no more!' (2.2.44-6).

Throughout this passage there is a disconnect between the pair. A *non-voice* is heard. The disturbing presence relates both to the dislocated spirit of legitimacy, wrenched from Duncan's corporeal body, and to the presence of weird space, that is the trace and effect of the Sisters in excess of the scenes where they are actually present.[34] This uncanny 'unscene' ghost creates a wedge between the married pair and they appear no longer to be able to answer each other's questions, to communicate. The sense of an unsettling presence is continued as the series of knocks begins, and although it has a rational explanation, in the eventual entry of Macduff and Lennox (at 2.3.18), this does not remove the uncanny effect of the sound that seems to respond to the Macbeths' deed. The divide between them will increase as the play progresses, as their suppressed guilt corrodes Lady Macbeth's sanity and solidifies Macbeth's murderous drive.

Macbeth's mental composure is further strained upon the appearance of Banquo's ghost. The first thing that strikes us is that Banquo is keeping a promise. He had promised to attend the banquet and, to Macbeth's horror, he does; the strength of his word survives the boundary of the grave. The adherence to this promise, across the divide of life and death, recalls Lady Macbeth's earlier, violent assertion of the binding nature of promises (1.7.54–9). Banquo's appearance from one perspective is, paradoxically, an act of loyalty (in stark contrast to Macbeth's murderous disloyalty to his king). Yet it is also, at the same time, a profound threat.

By filling the space at the dinner table, Banquo closes the circle of attendees, thus excluding Macbeth, according to Macbeth's vision: '[t]he table's full' (3.4.47). The iambic pentameter's three-feet pause before Macbeth utters these lines resonates with the uncanny space that Banquo creates. This is not just an act in relation to a place at dinner; it is an act with political implications. The power that Macbeth wields over the kingdom is encapsulated and embodied in the circle of his thanes. The dinner circle represents the solidarity and strength of Macbeth's rule, and eating together is a ritual that affirms loyalty; it is a promise of arms, fidelity and recognition of the right to rule. In this scene, the thanes gather yet Macbeth is excluded. Instead, it is Banquo's spirit, the father of future kings, that fills the circle. The action of the ghost is a type of ghostly political usurpation; to Macbeth's eyes at least, the ghost takes the place, literally, of the king. It supplants him, despite its intangible presence. Banquo's ghost thus plays the role of the second ghost, the displaced spirit of legitimacy. His ghostly presence reminds us of the disconnect between the body of the unlawful monarch, Macbeth, and the legitimate ghostly body that floats, unvested. The appearance of Banquo's ghost, which implicitly makes a statement about political legitimacy, also points to the future, and links this episode with the subsequent scene where Macbeth encounters the Weird Sisters again and is shown the vision of Banquo's long line of future kings (4.1.111–23). The vision constitutes another form of spectral presence haunting the sphere of the throne, the ghosts of future monarchs.

Despite being ephemeral and silent, Banquo's ghost is able to make a physical and political impact. It becomes the silent voice of the political spectre by forcing Macbeth to make what almost amounts to a public confession of guilt, or at least knowledge of Banquo's murder: '[t]he times has been/That, when the brains were out, the man would die./And there an end. But now they rise again...' (3.4.80–82). It also has the effect of revealing Macbeth as infirm, another sign of his unfitness to rule and his lack of legitimate occupation of the throne.

Macbeth strives in vain for a secure throne. As the play progresses, he becomes increasingly fearful because his hold on the crown is so fragile; paradoxically, the more people he kills to cement his hold on the throne, the further it slips from his grasp. This striving is in vain because the spirit of legitimacy is absent. Although we don't 'see' this spectre, we experience its trace in the uncanny presence evident after Duncan's murder, and in the apparition of Banquo. A non-king and yet the father of kings, Banquo is a spectral sign of legitimate rule. This is particularly evident in his virility; even dead he is potent, not only a father, but a founder of a rich line. The prophecy and the vision of political fecundity horrify Macbeth who, by comparison, is a political dead-end. These two aspects, the uncanny post-regicide presence and the spectral, fertile Banquo, are reminders of the political ghost of legitimacy that fails to be embodied in Macbeth. The political significance of Banquo lies in his reminding Macbeth, and Shakespeare's first audiences, of the 'legitimate' mode of patrilinear succession that existed prior to Macbeth's murder of Duncan, and that will resume after Macbeth's death, initially through Malcolm, and subsequently through Banquo's line, through to his supposed heir James I.

Conclusions

Shakespeare was cognisant of the theatrical power of the revenant, the horror of the transgressed boundary such as Macbeth articulates in response to Banquo's ghost. Ghosts constitute unfinished business; they register state rupture and appear with political purpose. They challenge the status quo and voice their opposition, through silence, dreams or calls to arms. They witness, supervise and protest. They also physically intervene, despite their ephemeral intangibility, and affect the mental states of the living. As borderline creatures, they flourish on the borders between regimes, protesting at change or usurpation, or ushering in a new ruler.

The ghosts raise a series of questions about what it is to be human, composed of material and metaphysical components. They manifest the split, appearing as a trace of the bodily form that no longer exists. The concept of the king's two bodies, of a spirit of legitimacy and a physical receptacle, constitutes a natural parallel for the idea of the ghost. Thus, the ghostly and the political seem a natural fit in these plays. The political is spectral, involving the powerful phantom of a 'true heir', a mirage of 'legitimate' rule. Political right is a fugitive spectre that figures jostle and kill for. That it is elusive and contested points to the ephemeral nature of the spirit of legitimate kingship that Shakespeare explores and challenges.

Both ghosts and the space of the crown in these plays are sites of severance and share the experience of violence. The ghosts are a sign of the violent wrenching of spirit from body, while the dual bodies of the monarch that constitute the crown are split in all of these plays. There has been no smooth transition of legitimate spirit from one ruler to the next. Instead, violent ruptures have left the crown as an empty shell, vulnerable through its lack of legitimate spirit. Shakespeare was deeply interested in such states of crisis and political limbo, and in these four plays the presence of ghosts resonates with flawed political systems in the wake of rupture. The ghosts are aligned with the ephemeral concept of legitimate rule, yet point to the fraught nature of power transitions. Thus, the throne is haunted by ghosts whose function is not only to enact various types of remonstrance, warning or revenge but also to reiterate the violence and flawed nature of the system. The ghosts Shakespeare presents, and their counterpart in the spectre of legitimate rule, thus constitute a critique of early modern assumptions about the transfer of legitimate rule. The ghosts' power to unsettle goes beyond their transgression of the life/death border to challenge the foundations of monarchy itself.

Ghosts performed significant cultural work on the early modern stage. The court was haunted by actors playing monarchs, the theatre creating spaces in which questions of power and its exercise could be explored and played with. Monarchs themselves were highly cognisant of the power and potential threat of the stage, as when Elizabeth I recognised the analogue in the performance of *Richard II* commissioned by the Earl of Essex prior to his ill-fated rebellion. Furthermore, to present ghosts on the stage suggested that the actions of monarchs were subject to supernatural surveillance. Ghosts imply a divine supervision of the exercise of political power, rendering the space of the throne spectral, a conduit for supernatural communion. The sphere of the crown becomes a porous boundary to the invisible world, and for a character to see a ghost was to confront the visibility and vulnerability of the material world to the invisible. As supposedly divinely ordained agents of God, monarchs were already in theory under supernatural watch, and the ghosts can seem extensions of this. In an era when monarchs held extensive and often unchecked powers, to present ghosts on the stage was to remind audiences that monarchs' actions were subject to judgement from the invisible world. While God could not be represented, ghosts gestured towards the spaces beyond the living, implying the potential for monarchs to be held accountable. The process of watching a play thus enacted and reflected that concept of supernatural spectatorship, rendering the audience in one sense spectral, and creating the unsaid invitation to critique the political sphere.

Notes

1 See generally Ernst Kantorowitz, *The King's Two Bodies: A Study in Mediæval Political Theology* (Princeton, NJ: Princeton University Press, 1957). Also see Slavoj Žižek, *For They Know Not What They Do: Enjoyment as a Political Factor* (New York: Verso, 2nd edn, 2002), p. 255.
2 Jacques Derrida, *Specters of Marx: The State of the Debt, the Work of Mourning, and the New International*, trans. Peggy Kamuf (New York and London: Routledge, 1994), p. 6.
3 Kathryn A. Edwards, 'The History of Ghosts in early modern Europe: Recent Research and Future Trajectories', *History Compass*, 10:4 (2012), p. 355.
4 On Purgatory generally see Peter Marshall, *Beliefs and the Dead in Reformation England* (Oxford: Oxford University Press, 2002); Jacques Le Goff, *The Birth of Purgatory*, trans. Arthur Goldhammer (Chicago: University of Chicago Press, 1984); Craig M. Koslofsky, *The Reformation of the Dead* (London: Macmillan, 2000); and Stephen Greenblatt, *Hamlet in Purgatory* (Princeton, NJ, and Oxford: Princeton University Press, 2001).
5 Edwards, 'The History of Ghosts', p. 355.
6 *Ibid.*, p. 358.
7 Catherine Stevens, '"You Shal Reade Marvellous Straunge Things": Ludwig Lavater and the Hauntings of the Reformation', in Marcus Harmes and Victoria Bladen (eds), *Supernatural and Secular Power in Early Modern England* (Farnham and Burlington, VT: Ashgate, 2015). Edwards also notes that the extensive pamphlet literature about apparitions produced in and for Protestant territories, especially England and Germany, continued to express traditional attitudes to ghosts that would have been categorised as Catholic superstition pursuant to orthodox Protestant ideology: Edwards, 'The History of Ghosts', p. 359.
8 Jo Beth, '"In the Divell's Likenesse": Interpretation and Confusion in Popular Ghost Belief', in John Newton and Jo Beth (eds), *Early Modern Ghosts* (Durham: University of Durham, 2002), p. 72.
9 All Shakespearean quotations are taken from the Norton edition: Stephen Greenblatt, Walter Cohen, Suzanne Gossett, Jean E. Howard, Katherine Eisaman Maus and Gordon McMullan (eds), *The Norton Shakespeare* (New York: Norton, 3rd edn, 2016).
10 Edwards, 'The History of Ghosts', pp. 353, 356, 361.
11 In addition to those listed, there are also the ghosts of Posthumus's parents in *Cymbeline*, whose roles are less overtly political, although again *Cymbeline* involves rupture at the state level, given the separation between the king and the lost princes, and the threat of the queen and her son Cloten.

12 See Victoria Bladen, 'The Ghost and the Skull: Rupturing Borders between the Living and the Dead in Filmed *Hamlets*', in Sarah Hatchuel and Nathalie Vienne-Guerrin (eds), *Shakespeare on Screen: Hamlet* (Le Havre: Publications des Universités de Rouen et du Havre, 2011).

13 See for example John Jump, who outlines the key questions Shakespeare's ghosts raise: John Jump, 'Shakespeare's Ghosts', *Critical Quarterly*, 12 (1970), p. 339.

14 See generally Bladen, 'The Ghost and the Skull', and Pierre Kapitaniak, 'Hamlet's Ghost on Screen: The Paradox of the Seventh Art', in Hatchuel and Vienne-Guerrin (eds), *Shakespeare on Screen: Hamlet*.

15 Jump, 'Shakespeare's Ghosts', p. 339.

16 Also see the events described by Casca (*Julius Caesar*, 1.3.3–32). Again, in *Hamlet* Horatio recounts how '[a] little ere the mightiest Julius fell,/The graves stood tenantless and the sheeted dead/Did squeak and gibber in the Roman streets', and celestial events such as comets and eclipses also functioned as harbingers of doom (1.1.112–24).

17 Cicero's scepticism anticipates that of Edmund in *Lear* (1.2.108–17). In *Richard III*, it is the monarch's 'unshapen' (1.2.236) body itself that functions as a sign of cosmic disturbance and breach of the natural order: '[b]ehold, mine arm/Is like a blasted sapling withered up' (3.4.73–4).

18 Kantorowitz, *The King's Two Bodies*, pp. 386–401.

19 Derrida, *Specters*, p. 6.

20 On the political *impasse* see Andrew Hadfield, 'The Power and Rights of the Crown in *Hamlet* and *King Lear*: "The king – the king's to blame"', *The Review of English Studies*, 54 (2003).

21 Hamlet states that Claudius '[p]opped in between th'election and my hopes/Thrown out his angle for my proper life' (5.2.65–6).

22 The Biblical prohibition against revenge, '[t]he Lord shall fight for you, therefore hold you your peace' (Exodus 14.14) was on the cover of the Geneva Bible. Also see Romans 12:19 and Deuteronomy 32:35.

23 As Hadfield writes, 'political assassination, successful or not, invariably ended in the death of the perpetrator'; Hadfield, 'Power and Rights', p. 576.

24 Jacques Lacan, 'Death and the Interpretation of Desire in *Hamlet*', in Shoshan Felman (ed.), *Literature and Psychoanalysis* (Baltimore, MD: Johns Hopkins University Press, 1982), p. 51.

25 Žižek, *For They Know Not*, p. 256.

26 'But I do prophesy th'election lights/On Fortinbras – he has my dying voice' (5.2.334).

27 On Shakespeare's interest in republican ideas, see Andrew Hadfield, *Shakespeare and Republicanism* (Cambridge: Cambridge University Press, 2005) and 'Tarquin's Everlasting Banishment: Republicanism and Constitutionalism in *The Rape of Lucrece* and *Titus Andronicus*', *Parergon*, 19:1 (2002).

28 For explorations of Julius Caesar on screen generally see Sarah Hatchuel and Nathalie Vienne-Guerrin (eds), *Shakespeare on Screen: The Roman Plays* (Rouen and Le Havre: Publications des Universités de Rouen et du Havre, 2009).

29 Greenblatt et al. (eds), *Norton Shakespeare*, p. 1740.

30 www.richardiii.net/leicester_dig.php. Accessed 2 December 2018.

31 On the returning abject, see Julia Kristeva, *Powers of Horror: An Essay on Abjection*, trans. Leon S. Roudiez (New York: Columbia University Press, 1982).
32 Greenblatt et al. (eds), *Norton Shakespeare*, p. 559.
33 *Ibid.* p. 560.
34 For an exploration of the idea of the Sisters as generating weird space, see Victoria Bladen, 'Weird Space in *Macbeth on Screen*', in Sarah Hatchuel, Nathalie Vienne-Guerrin and Victoria Bladen (eds), *Shakespeare on Screen: Macbeth* (Rouen and Le Havre: Presses Universitaires de Rouen et du Havre, 2013).

Bibliography

Beth, Jo, '"In the Divell's Likenesse": Interpretation and Confusion in Popular Ghost Belief', in John Newton and Jo Beth (eds), *Early Modern Ghosts* (Durham: University of Durham, 2002), pp. 70–8.

Bladen, Victoria, 'Weird Space in *Macbeth* on Screen', in Sarah Hatchuel, Nathalie Vienne-Guerrin and Victoria Bladen (eds), *Shakespeare on Screen: Macbeth* (Rouen and Le Havre: Presses Universitaires de Rouen et du Havre, 2013), pp. 81–106.

—— 'The Ghost and the Skull: Rupturing Borders between the Living and the Dead in Filmed *Hamlets*', in Sarah Hatchuel and Nathalie Vienne-Guerrin (eds), *Shakespeare on Screen: Hamlet* (Le Havre: Publications des Universités de Rouen et du Havre, 2011), pp. 143–74.

Derrida, Jacques, *Specters of Marx: The State of the Debt, the Work of Mourning, and the New International*, trans. Peggy Kamuf (New York and London: Routledge, 1994).

Edwards, Kathryn, 'The History of Ghosts in early modern Europe: Recent Research and Future Trajectories', *History Compass*, 10:4 (2012), 353–66.

Greenblatt, Stephen, *Hamlet in Purgatory* (Princeton, NJ, and Oxford: Princeton University Press, 2001).

—— 'Richard III', in Stephen Greenblatt, Walter Cohen, Suzanne Gossett, Jean E. Howard, Katherine Eisaman Maus and Gordon McMullan (eds), *The Norton Shakespeare*, (New York: Norton, 3rd edn, 2016), pp. 555–62.

Hadfield, Andrew, *Shakespeare and Republicanism* (Cambridge: Cambridge University Press, 2005).

—— 'Tarquin's Everlasting Banishment: Republicanism and Constitutionalism in *The Rape of Lucrece* and *Titus Andronicus*', *Parergon*, 19:1 (2002), 77–104.

—— 'The Power and Rights of the Crown in *Hamlet* and *King Lear*: "The King – the King's to Blame"', *The Review of English Studies*, 54 (2003), 566–86.

Hatchuel, Sarah, and Nathalie Vienne-Guerrin (eds), *Shakespeare on Screen: The Roman Plays* (Rouen and Le Havre: Publications des Universités de Rouen et du Havre, 2009).

Jump, John, 'Shakespeare's Ghosts', *Critical Quarterly*, 12 (1970), 339–51.

Kantorowicz, Ernst Hartwig, *The King's Two Bodies: A Study in Mediæval Political Theology* (Princeton, NJ: Princeton University Press, 1957).

Kapitaniak, Pierre, 'Hamlet's Ghost on Screen: The Paradox of the Seventh Art', in Sarah Hatchuel and Nathalie Vienne-Guerrin (eds), *Shakespeare on Screen: Hamlet* (Rouen and Le Havre: Publications des Universités de Rouen et du Havre, 2011), pp. 175–90.

Koslofsky, Craig M., *The Reformation of the Dead* (London: Macmillan, 2000).

Kristeva, Julia, *Powers of Horror: An Essay on Abjection*, trans. Leon S. Roudiez (New York: Columbia University Press, 1982).

Lacan, Jacques, 'Death and the Interpretation of Desire in *Hamlet*', in Shoshan Felman (ed.), *Literature and Psychoanalysis* (Baltimore, MD: Johns Hopkins University Press, 1982), pp. 11–52.

Lavater, Ludwig, *Of Ghostes and Spirites Walking by Nyght and of Strange Noyses, Crackes, and Sundry Forewarnynges, Whiche Commonly Happen Before the Death of Menne, Great Slaughters, [and] Alterations of Kyngdomes* [1569], trans. Robert Harrison (London, 1572).

Le Goff, Jacques, *The Birth of Purgatory*, trans. Arthur Goldhammer (Chicago: University of Chicago Press, 1984).
Marshall, Peter, *Beliefs and the Dead in Reformation England* (Oxford: Oxford University Press, 2002).
Shakespeare, William, *The Norton Shakespeare*, eds Stephen Greenblatt, Walter Cohen, Suzanne Gossett, Jean E. Howard, Katherine Eisaman Maus and Gordon McMullan (New York: Norton, 3rd edn, 2016).
Stevens, Catherine, '"You Shal Reade Marvellous Straunge Things": Ludwig Lavater and the Hauntings of the Reformation', in Marcus Harmes and Victoria Bladen (eds), *Supernatural and Secular Power in Early Modern England* (Farmham and Burlington, VT: Ashgate, 2015), pp. 141–62.
Žižek, Slavoj, *For They Know Not What They Do: Enjoyment as a Political Factor* (New York: Verso, 2nd edn, 2002).

2

'Rudely stamped': supernatural generation and the limits of power in Shakespeare's *Richard III*

Chelsea Phillips

The maternal body was a site for the intersection of the natural and supernatural worlds in early modern England.[1] In part this was because 'maternal and midwiving bodies delivered both ordinary, earthly matter and a miracle deserving of reverence.'[2] It was also attributable in part to the mysteries surrounding the maternal body's biology. Ruled by nature, divine in pattern, the generative body was 'a site of imagination and contest', perpetually constructed as susceptible to outside influence.[3] This could come from anywhere: the mother, the father, the child, a neighbour, the sovereign. The womb was unruly by its very nature: it could wander, create false conceptions and shape the child to resemble a monster as easily as its parents. Largely beyond human control, the womb was opaque, obscuring its contents from prying eyes or medical intervention.[4] When strange conceptions or 'monstrous' births – from the Latin *monstrum*, meaning marvelous and suggesting a divine portent or sign – took place, pamphlets and medical texts both capitalised on the fascination the events caused and attempted to allay cultural anxiety about presumed supernatural influence on the generative process.[5] The strategy for allaying these anxieties usually involved revealing the secret cause of the defect, making legible the forces (divine, malignant, social or physiological) presumed to interfere with successful reproduction. In doing so, these publications often attempted to set clear boundaries for what could, and could not, reasonably be considered under human control. Shakespeare's plays similarly capitalise upon and allay anxiety regarding supernatural influence on the processes of human generation, entering into a wider social discourse surrounding the limits of both human and supernatural power.

In *Shakespearean Maternities*, Chris Laoutaris refers to the opacity of the early modern generative process as 'an epistemological process in which disruption, uncertainty, contention and exchange were the constitutive and sometimes even deconstructive principles'.[6] Generative success was only truly measurable when the child was born: alive, whole, legitimate and ideally male, with a clear resemblance to its father. Visual markers of success are often described in metaphors of mechanical means of reproduction, such as coining, printing or stamping, as when in *The Winter's Tale* Leontes praises Florizel's mother with '[y]our mother was most true to wedlock, Prince,/For she did print your royal father off,/Conceiving you' (5.1.123–5).[7] Walter Benjamin claimed '[t]he presence of the original is the prerequisite to the concept of authenticity', and this is precisely the case in moments when characters validate paternity and maternity through visual resemblance.[8] The ideal generative process created perfect, legitimate copies. Just as these mechanical means of production could develop defects, however, so could human reproduction print off or 'rudely stamp' legitimate issue, of which Richard III is the prime example.

In this chapter, I aim to survey the intersections of supernatural powers and human generation (conception, pregnancy, birth, parenting) in Shakespeare's plays, examining how Shakespeare constructs these intersections and explores the limits of supernatural power. These supernatural generations fall into three categories: (1) Those marked by *maternal impression* and/or *witchcraft*; (2) *Calamitous births* resulting from sin (usually of one or both parents or a close relative) or instability within the social or political world; and (3) *Changeling* children and other supernatural offspring.

For each category, I offer examples from Shakespeare's plays, followed by a reading of one example that teases out the way Shakespeare constructs the supernatural and its constraints. I conclude by applying these initial observations to an analysis of Richard III's origins as recounted in *Henry VI, Part 3* and *Richard III*. As contextual information, I will first offer brief examples of the way religious, medical and other texts construed monstrosity and the supernatural.[9]

Monstrosity and the supernatural

In the early modern imagination, monstrous births could arise from a variety of causes, from the natural if extra-ordinary to the decidedly supernatural. Maternal impression, whereby the power of the individual pregnant woman's imagination marked the child, was perhaps the least supernatural cause and yet widely discussed. In the usual course of events, the womb's impressive power moulded the child into a copy of its parents, with the seed from both parents providing the pattern and raw material.[10] It was, however, an indiscriminate force; a woman frightened by a dog might give birth to a dog or to a hirsute infant. In this case, the mother's fright could override the natural pattern of the parents, replacing it with the thing that made a stronger impression on her mind.[11]

Witchcraft and the power of maternal impression were similar in action and result, with the largest difference being intent and blame. A woman unexpectedly frightened by a dog was not to blame if the fright affected her child, as she clearly harboured no evil intent and had little or no control over the event.[12] A witch, however, might deliberately punish a woman in a kind of parody of maternal impression, perhaps in an attempt to disguise her actions. In the pamphlet *A certain relation of the hog-faced gentlewoman called Mistris Tannakin Skinker...* (1640), a pregnant woman refuses alms to an old woman suspected of witchcraft. The woman mutters a curse that the 'hoggish' nature of the woman imprint on the child, and the child is born with a hog's snout.

Divine judgement could also misshape the child. Such births were often construed as a form of punishment of one or both parents, or even the larger community, the nation or humankind.[13] In some cases, then, those who appear to be punished may be no more to blame than the woman frightened by a dog whose child is born covered in hair. This is especially true in times of national crisis. Monstrous birth could occur as part of a larger trend of unnatural events in times of political turmoil or upheaval and therefore be construed as reflective of disruption and disorder, abstracting the cause from the specific individuals involved. Such births, however, made concrete the danger of such volatile times: the state depended on the (re)production of healthy citizens.

Medical texts supported the idea of monstrosity as divine judgement, while also offering physiological causes. John Sadler's *The Sicke Woman's Private Looking-Glasse* (1636) attempts to give women the ability to recognise the causes of their sickness so they might seek the correct remedy, and explores both natural and unnatural causes of monstrosity: 'the cause of [monstrous] generation,... is either Divine or Naturall. The Divine cause proceeds from the permissive will of God, suffering parents to bring forth such abominations, for their filthie and corrupt affections which are let loose unto wickednesse.'[14] Like the pamphlets, Sadler qualifies this general truth with 'there are many borne depraved which ought not to bee ascribed unto the infirmity of the parents'.[15] In these cases, natural causes must be explored: these include an imbalance in the womb or the seed of either partner, which might cause insufficiency (born less than fully formed) or excess (extra limbs) in the child, as well as maternal impression. Maternal impression had great power during conception, but was particularly fearful because it remained a danger throughout pregnancy. Sadler, in his chapter on monsters, essentially ascribes to the power of maternal impression (an internal process) what other texts ascribe to witchcraft (an external influence). He thus reveals simultaneously a scepticism towards witchcraft and a bias in favour of an ever more powerful understanding of the womb's potential for 'natural' malignancy, for 'there is no disease so ill but may procede from the evill quality of it'.[16]

Considering the progression of pamphlets surrounding monstrous birth (from the admittedly small sample cited here), there seems to be a perceptible change over time in attitudes toward monstrous births. The earliest 'monstrous birth' announcements, dating from the 1560s, are broadsheets containing an image of the 'monster' (human or animal), a somewhat standardised verse injunction to pray and repent, as well as the details of where and when the birth took place, and perhaps the names of corroborating witnesses. Only a few decades later, these single sheets have transformed into multipage pamphlets offering detailed background information on the circumstances of the birth, including the characters of those involved (the parents, the midwife and so forth). Though generally asserting the author's inability to discern the cause of the monstrosity, the pamphlets offer specific clues readers might use to come to their own conclusions.[17] From single broadsheets claiming monstrous births as a kind of collective social punishment from God, 'monstrous birth' pamphlets begin to craft narratives in which there is a localised cause of the birth; it is the result of direct sin, or an act of witchcraft perpetuated by a single individual on a single individual.

Folk belief also shaped the understanding of and response to the supernatural's perceived influence on human generation. Susan Schoon Eberly's 'Fairies and the Folklore of Disability: Changelings, Hybrids, and the Solitary Fairy' traces folk beliefs in fairy changelings to recognisable congenital defects, building on previous work linking birth defects with the development of lore about 'fairy-takings'. Commonalities among different disorders, such as inhibited growth rates or a diminished ability to speak, may explain conceptions of different races of fairy folk. Supernatural explanations for a child's disability, or an inexplicable failure to thrive, helped to ease the grieving process for parents, as well as assigning blame to an external, wild force beyond the control of the parents or the midwife.

In early modern England, then, births that did not follow recognised patterns of nature had many possible explanations. They might indicate an internal flaw in the mother's body or mind; they might point to the presence of witchcraft in the community; signal divine judgement on the parents, the community or the state; or be the result of fairy-takings. Understanding each possibility, and how to guard against it, was of vital importance, for successful generation was in many ways early modern society's most important form of labour. The production of legitimate, healthy citizens and rulers maintained order and hierarchy and prevented the cataclysms prevalent when questions of succession arose. Such cataclysms could in turn disrupt reproductive processes, signalling a symbiotic relationship between the body politic and the bodies of individual citizens.

Shakespeare's supernatural generations

Caliban most clearly illustrates the power of maternal impression and witchcraft to shape a child. Sycorax escaped execution by 'pleading the belly', drawing on the legal precedent that spared pregnant women from execution, but she is unable to protect her child from the natural magic of maternal impression.[18] Her son bears clear, readable physical marks of her evil influence, which an audience may recognise and, presumably, avoid. Caliban's lack of human shape is mirrored in Prospero's description of his mother, who 'with age and envy/ Was grown into a hoop' (1.2.259–60). Sycorax's body transformed over time, but she passed this disfigurement in its entirety to her son. His freckles suggest an overflux of menstrual blood at his conception, meaning his mother broke sexual taboos as well as being a practising witch.[19] Not knowing Caliban's history, Stephano and Trinculo designate him a 'moon-calf' to account for his odd shape. The moon-calf label implies that Caliban's birth violated natural order. In addition to its associations with imbecility, instability and deformity, 'moon-calf' was a term for false conception in both humans and animals.[20]

In Caliban's case, his mother is clearly to blame for his temperament and his appearance, and her marking of him is indelible. We do not know who his father was – Prospero suggests the devil, though the term 'hag-seed' implies that he was spontaneously generated in his mother's womb – but his identity matters little, for we need look no further than the mother to discover the cause of this monster, '[w]hich any print of goodness wilt not take' (1.2.355). In giving Caliban's evil nature and physical deformity a local habitation and a name, Shakespeare acknowledges that monstrous nature/nurture exists, but also reassures his audience that that they may avoid it and, perhaps more importantly, recognise it through physical signs.

Throughout the canon, calamities in nature frequently portend personal or political unrest. A storm rages the night of Duncan's murder in *Macbeth*, while the assassins plot in *Julius Caesar*, and while Lear rages and the country teeters on the brink of civil war. Prospero conjures a storm to right personal and political wrongs; a bolt of lightning punishes the incest of Antiochus and his daughter in *Pericles*. When associated with the moment of birth, meteorological signs can foreshadow a person's fate, or their capacity for greatness or evil. Marina's stormy birth foreshadows the trials and travels she will undergo before reuniting with her family. In contrast, at Glendower's birth 'the frame and huge foundation of the earth/Shaked like a coward', (*1 Henry IV*, 3.1.15–6) which he proceeds to claim foretells he will shake England, and gives him power to conjure the devil. As a cure to any fear this might create, Hotspur plays the role of sceptic, protesting Glendower's insistence that his birth was prophetic:

> Diseased nature oftentimes breaks forth
> In strange eruptions; oft the teeming earth
> Is with a kind of colic pinch'd and vex'd
> By the imprisoning of unruly wind
> Within her womb; which, for enlargement striving,
> Shakes the old beldam earth and topples down
> Steeples and moss-grown towers. At your birth
> Our grandam earth, having this distemperature,
> In passion shook. (*1 Henry IV*, 3.1.25–33)

Hotspur's scepticism functions as the limiting, rationalising force surrounding these strange portents; what Glendower believes was a sign of his greatness was in fact the earth breaking wind. Hotspur's cynicism is confirmed when they fail to overcome Henry's army, proving the emptiness of Glendower's claims. While in retrospect it might be possible to discover the meaning of strange meteorological events, prophesying from them is foolish.[21]

Just as unnatural events reveal or portend political, social or personal upheaval, unnatural births become a sign of such disturbances. The nation's body politic, when diseased by war, famine or political unrest, is unable to correctly form its progeny: '[m]onstrous births made for powerful polemic in times of monarchical insecurity in particular, mobilizing the discursive connection between the bloody activities of the birthroom and the state'.[22] In these moments of crisis, the infected political body enters the bodily wombs of pregnant women, reshaping children in its image; we see this, for example, in the 'unfathered heirs and loathly births of nature' (4.4.122) in *Henry IV, Part 2*. Unrest could create other kinds of unnatural births: for example, the lioness that 'hath whelped in the streets' in *Julius Caesar* (2.2.17). The lioness, a wild, untamed thing, either mistakes the streets of the capital as a place over which she has dominion and in which she may give birth in safety, or is unexpectedly overcome by her labour.

When Macbeth approaches the witches in Act 4, Scene 1, demanding further information about his fate, his request to speak with their masters requires the supernatural use of talismans of unnatural birth. These unnatural births fuel their supernatural conjuring, which in turn brings about Macbeth's downfall. Before Macbeth enters, the witches' charm includes some eighteen distinct body parts from a variety of species. One of the few human ingredients, the 'finger of birth-strangled babe/Ditch-delivered by a drab' (4.1.31-2), is explicitly tied to a generation outside the normal bounds of order, an unnatural birth.[23] To allow their masters to speak to Macbeth directly, the witches add the grease from a murderer's gibbet to the fire and the blood of a sow 'that hath eaten/ Her nine farrow' (4.1.80-1) to the cauldron. This inhuman, cannibalistic maternity brings forth the apparitions and potentially helps to shape them, as though they are being impressed with the cauldron's contents like a child within a womb. The witches' masters appear to Macbeth as a 'bloody child' and 'a child crowned with a tree in his hand', underlining the play's preoccupation with dynasty, mocking Macbeth's lack of children and highlighting the strong associations between birth and the supernatural that exist in the play. Much earlier, in Act 1, Scene 5, Lady Macbeth offers her body to 'spirits' (familiars), who will feed on it in the parody of maternal nurture that made witchcraft so wholly disturbing in early modern England. Given that the encounter with the witches happens in Act 4, Scene 1, in the context of burgeoning national instability, we might ask if even the existence of the baby's finger and the sow's blood is attributable to the political upheaval of Macbeth's unnatural rule. In the final balance, of course, Macduff, himself the result of an unnatural, though *medical*, birth, overcomes the supernatural generations associated with Macbeth and replaces them with legitimate, fairly formed sovereignty. Macbeth's reliance on the supernatural brings about his downfall, just as a village witch might do harm but will ultimately succumb to divine order and judgment.

The final category of supernatural generation is that of the changeling child or other supernatural offspring. Only *A Midsummer Night's Dream* contains an actual changeling, but many plays contain references to them. In *Hamlet*, Marcellus assures us that fairies cannot 'take' children during the 'season… wherein our saviour's birth is celebrated', (1.1.139–40) both introducing the fear of fairy-taking, and providing the audience with one of its limiting factors. Henry IV wishes that fairies had changed his Hal for a Hotspur in the cradle (*I Henry IV*, 1.2.86–8). Perdita is mistaken for a changeling when the shepherd finds her on the coast of Bohemia. Pericles briefly fears Marina is a fairy when they meet in Mytilene.

In Act 2, Scene 2 of *A Midsummer Night's Dream* Titania and Oberon meet in the forest. The fairy king and queen are fighting, bickering over a little changeling boy Titania keeps from Oberon. When Oberon challenges her, Titania explains that the boy is the son of a 'vot'ress of mine order' (2.1.123) who died in childbirth. Titania recounts the affection she had for this mortal woman, as she 'gossiped by [Titania's] side' (125). This gossiping references one or both of two things: either that the votaress and Titania used to attend the gossip's feasts during the births and lying-ins of women in labour, or that the votaress was herself a gossip at the births of Titania's children. In either case, Titania directly engages in human rituals of birth, despite her supernatural nature. Furthermore, her reasons for taking the child, potentially a source of considerable anxiety for parents, mitigate her actions. She does not take the child out of spite or to be mischievous or covetous; she takes it because of the love and duty she owed her mortal companion. Even Oberon's desire for the child is recognisable as a form of human ritual. He wants the child as a page, a legible position within the fairy hierarchy, for it mimics the human practice of sending children out of the home for fostering and apprenticing.

Oberon's desire for the child, and her refusal to give in, has spread discord, floods and famine throughout the country. Titania refers to herself and Oberon as the 'parents and originals' of these disasters. Instead of the normal year's cycle of birth, growth, harvest and death, fuelled by harmony between the fairies, they have created monstrous births, redoubled copies of their strife, with their dissension. When all is forgiven and order restored, the fairies provide a blessing to the new married couples that specifically protects their future children from 'the blots of Nature's hand…/Never mole, hare-lip, nor scar,/ Nor mark prodigious, such as are/Despiséd in nativity' (5.1.39–43). The fairies, whose quarrels over a stolen human child caused famine, and whose kind steal human babies, are ultimately both more merciful and more human than they appear, using their powers to bless and protect instead of steal and corrupt.

In Shakespeare's plays, characters offer explanations for supernatural events, trace their origins or find commonality with supernatural creatures. Across time and genre, the supernatural, though threatening, is rendered legible through these processes. When the supernatural is divinely punished or confined by human laws and customs, boundaries of power become visible.

Richard III's ambiguously supernatural origins

From these more general observations, I turn to a consideration of Richard III's birth as described in *Henry VI, Part 3* and *Richard III*, and drawn from Polydore Vergil, Sir Thomas More and Raphael Holinshed. Richard's origins defy easy explanation, and he is variously cast as the result of each of three intersecting points of supernatural and human generation. Beginning with his association with changelings and other supernatural offspring, I will work backwards through the characterisation of his birth as calamitous, ending with maternal impression and witchcraft.

In Act 3, Scene 2 of *Henry VI, Part 3*, Richard explains to the audience why he will pursue the crown instead of the peaceful pleasures of 'a lady's lap' (3.2.148). Love is further from Richard than the crown:

> Why, love forswore me in my mother's womb,
> And, for I should not deal in her soft laws
> She did corrupt frail nature with some bribe
> To shrink mine arm up like a withered shrub,
> To make an envious mountain on my back –
> Where sits deformity to mock my body –
> To shape my legs of an unequal size,
> To disproportion me in every part,
> Like to a chaos, or an unlicked bear whelp
> That carries no impression like the dam. (3.2.153–62)

Though 'love' is feminine, Richard does not explicitly tie this love to his mother, instead implying that nature and love compacted together to shape him without his mother's knowledge or complicity. From this point onward in this play and in *Richard III*, many characters offer theories for why Richard is the way he is, frequently focusing on his outward deformity as a metaphor for inner corruption. In this section, I am interested in the way the language of the supernatural attempts, but fails, to adequately explain Richard's origins.

Michael Torrey's 'The Plain Devil and Dissembling Looks' explores the physiognomy of Richard III – the belief that the external body reflected the status of the mind and soul. Torrey claims that, 'despite obvious signs of his wickedness, he repeatedly ensnares his victims, using lies and histrionics to mask his seemingly obvious villainy... Richard's construction as a *deformed deceiver*, in other words, reproduces the surprising ambivalence of physiognomical discourse.'[24] While Torrey's assertion that Richard's appearance is belied by his deceptive speaking is true – and his citation of qualified physiognomic texts compelling – the play can also be read as containing a warning not to allow sweet words to cloud the divine judgment physiognomy reveals, rather than an ambiguity about physiognomy's veracity.

Margaret, Richard's most implacable enemy, makes a forceful statement about his physiognomy, but also ties his appearance to an explicitly supernatural origin:

> Thou elvish-marked, abortive, rooting hog,
> Thou that wast sealed in thy nativity
> The slave of nature and the son of hell,
> Thou slander of thy mother's heavy womb,
> Thou loathéd issue of thy father's loins (1.3.225–30).

Instead of receiving the 'stamp' of legitimacy and fair form in the womb, Richard was marked by elves, 'sealed' (confirmed) as the lowest creature in nature, or even explicitly supernatural ('the son of hell'). As such, he betrays his parents and 'slanders' his mother's womb. The descriptions of Richard's deformities and his difficult childhood are similar to early modern beliefs about changeling children, and in the above passage, Margaret explicitly suggests that fairies are partially responsible for Richard's condition.

Richard's childhood also reflects common beliefs about changeling children. In her discussion with the young Duke of York, Richard's mother remembers: '[h]e was the wretched'st thing when he was young,/So long a-growing and so leisurely,/That, if this rule were true, he should be gracious' (2.4.18–20).[25] A failure to thrive or grow was a hallmark of changelings, who either did not grow at all, or grew at a slower pace than human children. As Linda Charnes points out, there are several discrepancies surrounding Richard's birth and childhood.[26] He was born with teeth, but Richard claims to have been 'sent before my time/Into this breathing world scarce half made up' (1.1.20–1). Richard's paradoxical under- and over-gestated state – born with teeth, but small and slow to grow – underscore his decidedly abnormal status while complicating the ability of those around him to pinpoint a specific cause.

Susan Schoon Eberly highlights 'misshapen limbs... irritability, constant crying, and ravenous appetite' as further indicators of a changeling child.[27] Richard certainly possesses misshapen limbs and, according to his mother, his infancy was 'tetchy and wayward' (4.4.169), implying that he was a particularly difficult and oversensitive infant. 'Wayward' deserves further consideration, however, in light of the way Richard's deformities echo descriptions of supernatural changelings. In the Folio of *Macbeth*, the so-called 'Weird' Sisters are the 'weyard/weyward' sisters, conjuring associations not simply with vagrancy but also the Anglo-Saxon root *wyrd*, fate or destiny. As Magreta de Grazia and Peter Stallybrass charge, in Shakespeare's England:

> the boundaries that separate *weyward/weyard/weird/wayward* into four discrete and mutually exclusive lexical units had not yet been drawn and systematically reproduced. Until dictionaries fixed these boundaries, cognates blurred, phonetically and orthographically, without regard to the post-lexical determinations that subsequently divided them. Whether Holinshed or Shakespeare or a given scribe or compositor of either author's work determined a given form is less significant than the capacity of a word in the language preregulative or generative phase to take multiple forms.[28]

Wayward, then, resonates orthographically with both physical and metaphysical meanings, just as do most other features of Richard's birth. Though clearly no one considers Richard a changeling once he is an adult, the features of his early life align with superstitions surrounding these fairy oddities: malformed, slow to grow, inexplicably difficult and monstrous. The problem, of course, is that Richard's deformities were visible from birth; he is not a fair human child replaced with an inferior fairy babe, and therefore he cannot be a changeling, unless he was somehow exchanged while still within his mother's womb, as Margaret suggests.

Failing the changeling explanation, ideas that Richard is in actuality some kind of other supernatural beast emerge: 'O ill-dispersing wind of misery!/O my accursed womb, the bed of death!/A cockatrice hast thou hatch'd to the world,/Whose unavoided eye is murderous' (4.1.52–5). The cockatrice could not only turn people to stone, but was supposedly born when a toad or snake incubated a chicken's egg, simultaneously making Richard an alien being in his mother's womb and her womb a reptilian creature. This impossibly unnatural generation coming from the Duchess' womb emphasises the way the supernatural becomes the only means of understanding the depths of Richard's depravity. Again, as in Richard's soliloquy in Act 3, Scene 2 of *Henry VI, Part 3*, the Duchess here emphasises the autonomy of her womb, which has done something over which she had no control or knowledge.

Margaret has a complex relationship with the Duchess, alternately suggesting sympathy and blame for her as Richard's mother. He 'slander[ed]' his mother's womb, his deformity belying her continence and virtuous nature, which suggests Margaret's sympathy for the mother. In other passages, however, Margaret blames the Duchess for Richard. In their final encounter, Margaret casts her womb as the kennel from which Richard, a hell-hound – harbinger of death and hunter of souls – escaped: '[f]rom forth the kennel of thy womb hath crept/A hell-hound that doth hunt us all to death' (4.4.47–8). Like the reference to a cockatrice, the imagery of a woman whose womb kennels hounds makes both mother and son supernatural. Margaret's description recalls Scylla in

Greek mythology, a beautiful nymph cursed or poisoned and turned into a monster. Scylla retained her human upper half, but her lower half transformed into a snake or fish, with six dogs' heads circling her waist. She lived on one side of the strait between the rocks of Scylla and Charybdis. When sailors (like Odysseus) came too close, she appeared and consumed her victims with the dogs' heads. In visual renderings, the dogs' heads appear to emerge from her womb or genitals. Ovid's *Tristia* refers to Scylla's '*esse canes utero sub virginis*' ('dog-clustered groin'), and in his *Epistulae ex Ponto*, he refers to her 'misshapen womb [from which] monsters bark'.[29] The spectres of Scylla and the cockatrice create monsters of Richard and his mother, compromising the clear separation between their bodies asserted in source texts, which take care to render his mother blameless in her son's monstrosity.

When Henry VI confronts Richard in the Tower just before his death, he offers us the first outsider view of Richard's birth and similarly expunges the Duchess of any culpability:

> Thy mother felt more than a mother's pain,
> And, yet brought forth less than a mother's hope,
> To wit, an indigested and deforméd lump,
> Not like the fruit of such a goodly tree.
> Teeth hadst thou in thy head when thou wast born,
> To signify thou camest to bite the world. (*3 Henry 6*, 5.6.49–54)

Henry clearly absolves both parents of any wrongdoing that might explain Richard's appearance. The source material renders the Duchess even more sympathetic with descriptions of his birth: More writes that she could not be delivered 'uncut', meaning the midwife or surgeon had to cut her perineum to get the child out. Henry suggests that the reasons for Richard's unnatural shape are clear now, in retrospect, if they were not clear at the time of his birth. This retroactive application of prophecy to the strangeness of Richard's appearance perhaps diffuses anxieties surrounding the lack of clear reasons for it at the time. If Richard's actions *now* can justify the seemingly meaningless horror of *then*, then no violation of human understanding of the supernatural has occurred. In a compelling parallel, Polydore Vergil uses Richard III, among others, as evidence that 'the title of Glocester... hath been fetall, and foreshewed the destruction of them who should enjoy it'.[30] Though inadvertent, Vergil's spelling of 'fatal' hints at the ties between death and origin in the character of Richard.

Before he dies, Henry tells Richard that

> The owl shriek'd at thy birth, – an evil sign;
> The night-crow cried, aboding luckless time;
> Dogs howl'd, and hideous tempest shook down trees;
> The raven rook'd her on the chimney's top,
> And chattering pies in dismal discords sung (*3 Henry 6*, 5.6.44–8).

Not only did a storm accompany Richard's birth, he had a flock of ill-omened birds for an augury. The owl's shriek usually portended death; instead of dying at birth or killing his mother, however, the owl apparently warns of Richard as an omen of death himself. The despairing cries of these birds are echoed in Richard's account of the birthing chamber, when '[t]he midwife wonder'd and the women cried/"O, Jesus bless us, he is born with teeth!"' (*3 Henry 6*, 5.6.74–5).

Evil signs accompany Richard's birth, but the birth itself is also prophetic. The discordant cacophony with which Richard entered the world is also echoed in his self-identification with 'a chaos': '[t]o shape my legs of an unequal size;/ To disproportion me in every part,/Like to a chaos, or an unlick'd bear-whelp/ That carries no impression like the dam' (*3 Henry 6*, 3.2.159–62). In Greek origin myths, chaos was both the formless void containing the materials from which life (both divine and demonic) sprang, and, if not the first, then certainly one of the earliest primordial deities. Chaos was a disorderly generative force. Ovid's *Metamorphoses* opens with a description:

> Before the Sea & Lande were made, and heaven that all doth byde,
> In all the worlde one onely Face of Nature dyd abide.
> Whiche Chaös hight, a huge rude heape, and nothing else but even
> A heavie lump and clottered clod of sedes together driven,
> Of things at strife amonge them selves for want of order due…
> No kinde of thing had proper shape, but eache confounded other.
> For in one selfe same body strove, the whot [sic] and colde together. (Ovid, *The Fyrst Fower Bookes* [1565], p. A1)

Chaos serves as the womb of the world, and its disordered nature echoes the permeable and ungovernable early modern womb that could so corrupt human generation. Specifically, Richard refers to the fact that chaos contains all the necessary parts, but none of the divine shape, just as he contains all the parts of a man, but lacks form, coming out as an 'indigested… lump'.[31] Richard will also function as 'a chaos' during *Richard III*, thrusting the nation back into a void in which he thrives, crafting himself as the saving deity who can restore order. Margaret's kennel analogy for the Duchess of York's womb aligns her womb with the primordial void from which Richard emerged. These multiple associations serve to collapse the distinct boundaries between Richard and his mother, life and death. Richard both is chaos, and emerges from it; his mother's womb, therefore, is also chaos. Richard and her womb, being chaos, are both generative and destructive. The Duchess calls her womb 'accursed womb of death' because it gave Richard life. Ill-omened, supernaturally unnatural, Richard's life brings hell-hound-like death to those around him. He has become death, and by association so has she.

It is no wonder, then, that the Duchess laments the power she had but did not use when pregnant: 'O, she that might have intercepted thee,/By strangling thee in her accursed womb/From all the slaughters, wretch, that thou hast done!' (4.4.137–9). Ignorant of what she carried, she (and her womb) failed to take action upon Richard's body until it was too late. The personification of her womb, like her claims that 'from my dugs he drew not this deceit' (2.2.30), is an attempt to assert blamelessness in the form of a separation between their bodies, a separation threatened by social understandings of the supernatural monstrosity, and perpetual references to Richard's origins and abortive appearance.

I now come, finally, to the questions of maternal impression in relation to the stories of Richard's generation. After nearly two plays of hearing how Richard is 'rudely stamp'd' and 'neither like [his] sire nor dam', it is perhaps surprising to hear him tasking Buckingham with convincing the public that Edward IV was illegitimate and Richard his father's true son in 'form and nobleness of mind' (*Richard III*, 1.1.16 and *3 Henry 6*, 2.2.135).[32] In Polydore Vergil's *English History* (*Anglia Historia*), Vergil writes that Richard induced a preacher named Ralph Sha to allege the bastardy of his brother Edward through an accusation of adultery against his mother, hence barring Edward IV from the succession. Sha offered as proof that 'king Edward was nether in physnomy nor shape of body lyke unto Richard the father; for he was highe of stature, tother very little; he of large face; tother short and rownd. Howbeyt, yf suche matters were well consyderyd, no man could dowt but Richard, now in place, was the dukes trew soone, who by right owght to inherit.'[33]

Richard claims to resemble his father in name and in shape, making his father little, short and round. Despite Buckingham's best attempts, however, the shocked silence of the crowd implies they are unable to reconcile Richard's claims to resemble his father with the figure they know. When Richard confronts the Commons with his performance of piety, however, it is in part his claiming of faults that alters their minds:

> First if all obstacles were cut away,
> And that my path were even to the crown,
> As my ripe revenue and due by birth
> Yet so much is my poverty of spirit,
> So mighty and so many my defects,
> As I had rather hide me from my greatness. (*Richard III*, 3.7.156–61)

He is no longer denying his shape in comparing himself to his father, but enacting the recognition and purgation of a sinful body. Buckingham's narrative transfers Richard's physical deformities onto England – 'blemished', wanting 'proper limbs', 'defaced', 'shoulder'd' and 'oblivion' – and suggests that, like the prayers Richard uses to purge himself of sin, he is the antidote for the country's ills:

> it is your fault that you resign
> The supreme seat, the throne majestical…
> To the corruption of a blemished stock…
> This noble isle doth want her proper limbs;

> Her face defaced with scars of infamy,
> Her royal stock graft with ignoble plants,
> And almost shoulder'd in the swallowing gulf
> Of blind forgetfulness and dark oblivion. (*Richard III*, 3.7.117–29)

The 'swallowing gulf' of Richard's chaos is now the gulf that threatens them all. In rewriting his brother and nephew's nativities, Richard creates a void in the state that he can then shape in his own image. While this can be understood, Janet Adelman suggests, as Richard's fantasy of male subjecthood, it also aligns Richard with the maternal body that can shape her offspring.

Despite all that can be said about Richard and supernatural generation, drawing a singular, clear conclusion is difficult. Richard is a portent of divine judgment decades before he enacts his villainy, complicating the belief in relatively immediate causes of monstrosity. His mother did not see a cockatrice, copulate with a hell-hound or a fairy, or practise witchcraft. Before Richard, she produced 'two mirrors of [Richard Plantagenet's] semblance' (2.2.51), affirming the continence of her generative body. No political upheaval at the day or time of Richard's birth is cited; his monstrous birth, much like an unnatural storm, only gains specific meaning after the fact. Like a storm, however, there are simply too many possible explanations and attributions, and the application of his monstrosity to the present civil war is in some ways as arbitrary as Glendower's appropriation of the comet and earthquake the day he was born. How, then, should we read Richard? Murray Krieger reads Richard as having a clear supernatural purpose, suggesting that he is a purging force who clears the remnants of the old, factious, guard away so that Henry Tudor might bring peace and unity to England.[34] In such an explanation, Richard does not need to be a changeling or the product of witchcraft; he has, despite his demonic nature, a divine purpose. When he has served that purpose, divine judgment takes him, in part through the restoration of his mother's agency.

At the end of *Richard III*, the mother who has been powerless to control her son, within or without the womb, finally manages to exploit her imaginative impressive powers on him in the form of a curse:

> Therefore take with thee my most heavy curse;...
> My prayers on the adverse party fight;
> And there the little souls of Edward's children
> Whisper the spirits of thine enemies
> And promise them success and victory.
> Bloody thou art, bloody will be thy end;
> Shame serves thy life and doth thy death attend. (*Richard III*, 4.4.188–96)

What would have been an inexcusable sin during pregnancy – the manipulation of maternal impression to curse her son – becomes a necessary sacrifice to save England; an infanticidal action is justified by the maternal care she shows her country and Edward's children. The Duchess' curse manifests in the ghosts' visitation the night before battle, breaching Richard's mental defences, undermining his sense of self. Though he has talked of love forsaking him before, the lack of love in this scene suddenly hits home. It is as if, in his tent, we see a re-enactment of love abandoning Richard in the womb, leaving him to wither and die. Once the Duchess claims her maternal power to purge her womb, and England, of Richard's false conception, Richmond, the rightful semblance of its majesty, may thrive. After Bosworth, Richmond foretells a period of peace prominently marked with the language of successful generation (italicised):

> O now let Richmond and Elizabeth,
> The true succeeders of each royal house,
> By God's *fair* ordinance *conjoin* together,
> And let their *heirs* – God, if thy will be so –
> Enrich the time to come with *smooth-faced* peace,
> With *smiling plenty* and *fair prosperous* days!
> Abate the edge of traitors, gracious Lord,...
> Let them not live to taste this land's *increase*
> That would with treason wound this fair land's peace!
> Now civil wounds are stopp'd, peace lives again:
> That she may long live here, God say amen! (*Richard III*, 5.5.29–41)

Now that the false conception and false monarchy of Richard III is purged, Richmond and Elizabeth can begin the process of producing 'fair[ly]' formed, 'smooth-faced' issue, restoring the order of nature.

Shakespeare's later plays continue to play out themes introduced in *Richard III*, of both physical deformity and human malignancy. Richard III's visible villainy transforms into an internal, invisible villainy. Iago, like Richard, speaks masterfully and constructs the appearance of truth where none exists. When Iago's plot unravels, Othello looks 'down toward his feet but that's a fable' (5.2.292), hoping in vain to see the cloven feet that would mark him a devil. What Othello knows, however, is that there will be no supernatural explanation for Iago's evil, no physical marker he could or should have recognised. The lack of supernatural explanation for Iago's villainy both reassures (he is a man and subject to human law) and disturbs (for now men can engender evil rivalling that of devilish fiends). From motiveless Iago, Shakespeare's portrait of Macbeth and Lady Macbeth is reassuring in both its humanity, and the portrait of evil driven by supernatural soliciting. Though, like Iago, the Macbeths bear no physical signs of their sins, they do bear crippling psychological wounds. Evil may not always be easy to recognise, but those going outside the bounds of nature will pay eventually and order will be restored. Shakespeare's last look at physical deformity tells a very different and less ambiguous tale than does Richard III. Caliban's disfigurement rewrites the mystery of Richard III's. Much like a 'monstrous birth' pamphlet, Shakespeare gives his audience a clear backstory, an (unfavourable) assessment of Sycorax's character and clear reasons for Caliban's distemper and malformation. As Caliban, like Richard, is a fully grown adult in the play, however, we are presented with a character about whom questions of nature *and* nurture may be asked, and it is in the tension between the two that richness and ambiguity can reside.

Early modern explorations of the causes, symptoms and results of the supernatural world's influence on reproduction reveals a desire to understand the limits and modes of human control over reproduction while offering a landscape of potential explanations for that beyond such control. From the extra-ordinary but still 'natural' process of maternal impression to the specific malignancy of witchcraft or fairy-taking, to the calamitous monstrosity of personal sin or political upheaval, early modern generation was construed as a natural process intimately entwined with and susceptible to outside influence. While no singular explanation of monstrous birth existed, both pamphlets and the sample of plays surveyed here ultimately aimed to allay anxiety about seemingly supernatural intrusions on human generation by asserting the role and will of the divine (whether Christian or pagan/mythic) to bless good citizens and stable, rightful rulers with favourable generation.

Notes

1 Many thanks to Victoria Bladen, Yan Brailowsky, Colleen Kennedy, and those who offered insight and feedback on this chapter.
2 Caroline Bicks, *Midwiving Subjects in Shakespeare's England* (Burlington, VT: Ashgate, 2003), p. 171.
3 Kathryn M. Moncrief and Kathryn R. McPherson (eds), *Performing Maternity in Early Modern England* (Farnham and Burlington, VT: Ashgate, 2007), p. 1.
4 The exceptions are instances when the mother died, for example, and surgeons opened the body in an attempt to save the child, or other cases calling for surgical intervention. Since the law protected pregnant women from execution until after they had given birth, the bodies of criminals given to medical organisations for autopsy never included pregnant women. Laoutaris rightly observes that 'the maternal body *known* was the maternal body in crisis': Chris Laoutaris, *Shakespearean Maternities: Crises of Conception in Early Modern England* (Edinburgh: Edinburgh University Press, 2008), p. 11.
5 Susan Schoon Eberly, 'Fairies and the Folklore of Disability: Changelings, Hybrids, and the Solitary Fairy', *Folklore*, 99:1 (1988), p. 59.
6 Laoutaris, *Shakespearean Maternities*, p. 12.
7 All Shakespeare quotations are taken from *The Norton Shakespeare*, based on the Oxford Edition, eds Stephen Greenblatt, Walter Cohen, Jean E. Howard, and Katherine Eisaman Maus (New York: W.W. Norton and Company, 1st edn, 1997).
8 Walter Benjamin, 'The Work of Art in the Age of Mechanical Reproduction', in Hannah Arendt (ed.), *Illumination: Essays and Reflections*, trans. Harry Zohn (New York: Schocken Books, 1969), p. 220.

9 For much more exhaustive analyses of these and many other sources, see Deborah Willis *Malevolent Nurture: Witch Hunting and Maternal Power* (Ithaca: Cornell University Press, 1995); Janet Adelman, *Suffocating Mothers: Fantasies of Maternal Origin in Shakespeare's Plays, Hamlet to The Tempest* (New York: Routledge, 1992); and Gail Kern Paster, *The Body Embarrassed: Drama and the Disciplines of Shame in Early Modern England* (Ithaca, NY: Cornell University Press, 1993).

10 Aristotle wrote that the man provided the pattern, the woman the matter to be printed upon, and most early modern treatises followed this general division; see Thomas Laqueur, *Making Sex: Body and Gender from the Greeks to Freud* (Cambridge, MA: Harvard University Press, 1999), pp. 28–32.

11 Powerful cravings could also mark a child, though usually less drastically. A woman who longed for strawberries and could find none might have a child with a strawberry-shaped birthmark somewhere on its body; husbands were therefore encouraged to provide their wife with the food she craved to prevent such markings.

12 Maternal impression is complex, and not always without blame for the woman involved. For example, she might attempt to wield her body's impressive power to conceal adultery by imagining her husband while having sex with a lover. In such a world, paternity is always uncertain, a possibility that may be in Leontes' mind when he rejects the infant Perdita despite her supposed resemblance to him.

13 *A true relation of the birth of three monsters in the city of Namen in Flanders* (1609), for example, tells of a 'woman of good birth, and reputed alwayes vertuous in her living' (A4) whose prideful, wealthy sister refused her aid during her pregnancy. The woman fell into labour and produced three monsters, each of which prophesied divine punishment for mankind and then died. Here, as in many other tales, it is the unnatural withholding of charity and aid to others that provokes divine wrath, which is partially enacted through the pregnant body of the blameless sister. The monsters, importantly, do not specifically attack the sister (though she does die), but turn their warning toward a wider social ill. *A true relation…* both teaches the exercise of charity, and calls for general repentance.

14 John Sadler, *The Sicke Woman's Private Looking-Glasse* (London: Printed by Anne Griffin, 1636), p. 135.

15 *Ibid.*, p. 136.

16 *Ibid.*, p. A6.

17 *The true reporte of the forme and shape of a monstrous childe* (1562) tells of a woman and her husband whose first child together was monstrous. Both partners had previously been married and had completely normal offspring. They conceived the monstrous child out of wedlock.

18 Ernest B. Gilman frames Sycorax's transportation as part of a new, alternative way for the state to dispose of its unwanted citizens. Though they could still be condemned to execution, in the late sixteenth and throughout the seventeenth century pregnant women were increasingly transported, not executed, after they gave birth. Ernest B. Gilman, 'Sycorax's "Thing"', in Dennis Kezar (ed.), *Solon and Thespis: Law and Theater in the English Renaissance* (Notre Dame, IN: Notre Dame University Press, 2007).

19 Sycorax's depiction as a supernatural-unnatural mother continues with Prospero's account of Ariel's treatment. Unable to bend Ariel to her will, she imprisons him in a cloven pine for twelve years in punishment. The unruly child, refusing to take its mother's stamp, is forced back into the womb, the site of ultimate maternal control. Sycorax's death, like that of a woman dying in childbirth, leaves Ariel imprisoned within her matrix until Prospero, magus-*cum*-man-midwife, appears and forces the womb to open and yield its contents.
20 This usage, the earliest recorded meaning, dates from 1565, and continues into the mid-seventeenth century ('Mooncalf, n.' *Oxford English Dictionary Online*).
21 Edmund in *King Lear* displays a similar scepticism.
22 Bicks, *Midwiving Subjects*, p. 102.
23 In his Witchcraft Act of 1604, James specifically named the use of human body parts in conjuring as an abominable act associated with witchcraft.
24 Michael Torrey, '"The Plain Devil and Dissembling Looks:" Ambivalent Physiognomy and Shakespeare's *Richard III*', *English Literary Renaissance*, 30:2 (2000), p. 126.
25 The rule to which she refers is 'sweet flowers are slow and weeds make haste' (2.4.15).
26 Linda Charnes, 'The Monstrous Body in *King Richard III*', in Hugh Macrae (ed.), *Critical Essays on Shakespeare's Richard III* (Richmond, VA, and New York: G.K. Hall, 1999).
27 Eberly, 'Fairies', pp. 63, 64.
28 Magreta De Grazia and Peter Stallybrass, 'The Materiality of the Shakespearean Text', *Shakespeare Quarterly*, 44:3 (1993), p. 266.
29 Marianne Govers Hopman, *Scylla: Myth, Metaphor, Paradox* (Cambridge: Cambridge University Press, 2012), p. 225.
30 Polydore Vergil, *Three Books of Polydore Vergil's English History*, ed. Sir Henry Ellis (London: The Camden Society, 1844), p. 75.
31 In George Sandys' 1621 translation, '[o]ne face had Nature, which they *Chaos* nam'd:/An vndigested lump' in Ovid, *The First Five Bookes of Ovids Metamorphosis*, trans. George Sandys (London: 1621), p. 1. This echoes Henry VI's description of Richard as 'indigested and deformed lump' (*3 Henry 6*, 5.6.51). According to the 1691 Latin edition, Ovid reads *rudis indigestaque moles*, clearly suggesting 'indigested' but also resonating with the English 'mole', a term for a false conception. See Ovid, *Metamorphose[o]n libri XV ad fidem editionis Heinsianae accurate emendati cum notis Minellianis* (London: F. Collins, 1691), Book 1, l. 6, p. 28.
32 The Norton editors follow the Oxford edition in substituting 'face' for 'form' because of Richard's obvious deformity (*Richard III*, 3.7.14). 'Form', however, appears in both the Folio and Quarto.
33 Vergil, *Three Books*, pp. 183–5.
34 Murray Krieger, 'The Dark Generations of Richard III', in Hugh Macrae (ed.), *Critical Essays on Shakespeare's Richard III* (Richmond, VA, and New York: G. K. Hall, 1999), pp. 146–60.

Bibliography

A certain relation of the hog-faced gentlewoman called Mistris Tannakin Skinker... (London: John Okes, 1640). Early English Books Online.

A true relation of the birth of three monsters in the city of Namen in Flanders (London: Simon Stafford, 1609). Early English Books Online.

The true reporte of the forme and shape of a monstrous childe (London: Thomas Marshe, 1562). Early English Books Online.

Adelman, Janet, *Suffocating Mothers: Fantasies of Maternal Origin in Shakespeare's Plays, Hamlet to The Tempest* (New York: Routledge, 1992).

Benjamin, Walter, 'The Work of Art in the Age of Mechanical Reproduction', in Hannah Arendt (ed.), *Illumination: Essays and Reflections*, trans. Harry Zohn (New York: Schocken Books, 1969).

Bicks, Caroline, *Midwiving Subjects in Shakespeare's England* (Burlington, VT: Ashgate, 2003).

Charnes, Linda, 'The Monstrous Body in *King Richard III*', in Hugh Macrae (ed.), *Critical Essays on Shakespeare's Richard III* (Richmond, VA, and New York: G. K. Hall, 1999), pp. 273–8.

De Grazia, Magreta, and Peter Stallybrass, 'The Materiality of the Shakespearean Text', *Shakespeare Quarterly*, 44:3 (1993), 255–83.

Eberly, Susan Schoon, 'Fairies and the Folklore of Disability: Changelings, Hybrids, and the Solitary Fairy', *Folklore*, 99:1 (1988), 58–77.

Gilman, Ernest B., 'Sycorax's "Thing,"' in Dennis Kezar (ed.), *Solon and Thespis: Law and Theater in the English Renaissance* (Notre Dame, IN: Notre Dame University Press, 2007), 99–123.

Hopman, Marianne Govers, *Scylla: Myth, Metaphor, Paradox* (Cambridge: Cambridge University Press, 2012).

Kern Paster, Gail, *The Body Embarrassed: Drama and the Disciplines of Shame in Early Modern England* (Ithaca, NY: Cornell University Press, 1993).

Krieger, Murray, 'The Dark Generations of Richard III', in Hugh Macrae (ed.), *Critical Essays on Shakespeare's Richard III* (Richmond, VA, and New York: G. K. Hall, 1999), pp. 146–60.

Laoutaris, Chris, *Shakespearean Maternities: Crises of Conception in Early Modern England* (Edinburgh: Edinburgh University Press, 2008).

Laqueur, Thomas, *Making Sex: Body and Gender from the Greeks to Freud* (Cambridge, MA: Harvard University Press, 1999).

Moncrief, Kathryn M., and Kathryn R. McPherson (eds), *Performing Maternity in Early Modern England* (Farnham and Burlington, VT: Ashgate, 2007).

More, Sir Thomas, *The History of King Richard the Third*, eds Gerard B. Wegemer and Travis Curtright (Dallas, TX: The University of Dallas, Center for Thomas More Studies, 2013).

Ovid, *Metamorphose[o]n libri XV ad fidem editionis Heinsianae accurate emendati cum notis Minellianis* (London: F. Collins, 1691).

—— *The First Five Bookes of Ovids Metamorphosis*, trans. George Sandys (London: 1621). Early English Books Online.

—— *The Fyrst Fower Bookes of P. Ouidius Nasos worke, intitled Metamorphosis*, trans. Arthur Golding (London: Willyam Seres, 1565). Early English Books Online.

Sadler, John, *The Sicke Woman's Private Looking-Glasse* (London: Printed by Anne Griffin, 1636). Early English Books Online.

Shakespeare, William, *The Norton Shakespeare, based on the Oxford Edition*, eds Stephen Greenblatt, Walter Cohen, Jean E. Howard and Katherine Eisaman Maus (New York: W. W. Norton and Company, 1st edn, 1997).

Torrey, Michael, '"The Plain Devil and Dissembling Looks:" Ambivalent Physiognomy and Shakespeare's *Richard III*', *English Literary Renaissance*, 30:2 (2000), 123–53.

Vergil, Polydore, *Three Books of Polydore Vergil's English History*, ed. Sir Henry Ellis (London: The Camden Society, 1844).

Willis, Deborah, *Malevolent Nurture: Witch Hunting and Maternal Power* (Ithaca, NY: Cornell University Press, 1995).

3

Digital puppetry and the supernatural: double Ariel in the Royal Shakespeare Company's *The Tempest* (2017)

Anchuli Felicia King

While critical discourse around the art of puppetry dates back to the period of German Romanticism, if not earlier,[1] attempts at establishing a theoretical body around puppetry have emerged only recently in the English-speaking world.[2] Writing about puppets, masks and object theatre has often been submerged into other disciplines, including 'folklore, anthropology, semiotics, art history, theatre history, drama, and performance studies'.[3] The relatively recent accretion of this varied body of writing into the unified field of 'puppet theory' has a new challenge in considering how this ancient form, which for centuries has been harnessed for spectacles of the mythic, magic and supernatural, might exist in dialogue with contemporary digital technologies.

In his chapter for the 2001 anthology *Puppets, Masks and Performing Objects*, Steve Tillis argues that the question of what constitutes 'live' puppetry has been largely overshadowed by technological advancements. For Tillis, 'computer graphics figures', particularly those controlled by motion capture, are 'conceptually new' and therefore 'owe their conception to the newness of the medium in which they exist'.[4] In the same anthology, theorist Stephen Kaplin offers these musings on the then-burgeoning field of live motion-capture ('mo-cap'): '[a]t this level of technology, the complexity of the systems themselves creates impediments… [however] it is only a matter of time before some enterprising puppeteer converts one for use in a theatrical performance'.[5]

That future, it seems, has arrived. While mo-cap remains costly and counterintuitive, major breakthroughs have been made in the use of motion-capture puppets on stage, allowing digital creatures to 'transcend their intangibility'[6] and evolve into a genre-defying hybrid form. In late 2016, the latest in real-time motion capture was placed on spectacular display in Gregory Doran's production of *The Tempest* at the Royal Shakespeare Company (RSC), in which the character of Ariel (played with spritely charm by Mark Quarterly) was accompanied in real time by his computer-generated (CG) double (see figure 3.1).

Digital puppetry and the supernatural

3.1 Digital Ariel in RSC's *The Tempest* 2017, in collaboration with Intel.

The critical response to the use of this burgeoning technology was telling. While Doran's production was widely lauded by theatre critics, they remained generally ambivalent about the use of digital puppetry in rendering Shakespeare's sprite. Critics noted that the use of mo-cap felt more like 'a one-off experiment… than a signpost to the future'[7] and that Ariel's CG avatar, while undeniably breathtaking, was 'ultimately gimmicky'[8] and had a tendency to 'upstage the actors'.[9] Tellingly, in his review for *The Guardian*, Michael Billington noted that while the simultaneous presentation of Quarterly with his digital avatar was impressive, it produced the 'odd sense that we are watching a Double Ariel' (see figure 3.2).

Billington's critique draws into sharp focus the theatrical challenge of using mo-cap in live performance. Mo-cap hinges on the synchronic performance of digital puppet and puppeteer yet, unlike traditional forms of puppetry, the digital avatar traditionally obscures the puppeteer entirely. The 'odd sense' of watching a digitally doubled Ariel that Billington describes in his review has certain resonances with the contemporary discourse around the 'uncanny valley', a term coined by Japanese roboticist Masashiro Mori that has long since entered the cultural *Zeitgeist*. According to Mori, as a virtual character approaches the asymptote of perfect human mimesis, it begins to inversely dip into a valley of repugnance, thereby alienating the viewer.[10]

Puppet theorists can shed some light on this phenomenon. Colette Searls proposes that digital puppets, like uncanny digital avatars, provoke visual discomfort because they actually violate 'the necessity of distance between performer and performed object/image'.[11] While Searls's assessment is compelling,

3.2 Double Ariel: live performer and digital avatar.

she misses a dramaturgical question: are there situations in which it is useful – aesthetically, thematically or indeed ethically – for digital puppets to be uncanny doubles? Indeed, can these doubled digital puppets create a space of theatrical liminality, thereby invoking the audience's bewilderment or wonderment, as the traditional puppet theatre has done for centuries?

As such, I intend to centre my examination on this production's 'Double Ariel' and the various ways it made use of the uncanny medium of mo-cap to engage with *The Tempest*'s themes of liminality, and specifically Ariel's liminal textual status as a supernatural entity. I will begin by discussing Doran's production as it relates to the broader body of staging practices associated with *The Tempest*, and the play's aesthetic debt to the Jacobean masque tradition. I will then turn my attention to Ariel's digital puppet specifically, and the technodramaturgy of this 'Double Ariel'.

I use the term 'technodramaturgy' to refer to the interplay between traditional dramaturgies and the innate, often concealed dramaturgies of technical systems themselves (software, hardware or mechanical). Rather than viewing these as two separate dramaturgies, 'technodramaturgy' views these two disciplines as an interlocked body of dramaturgies, feeding each other in an iterative loop. By deconstructing the technical systems used to render Ariel's avatar, I hope to demonstrate how processes of iterative technodramaturgy can lead to theatrical discoveries, and in so doing, I defend the use of this burgeoning technology in classical works. In the case of the RSC *Tempest*, this technology heightened the wonderment and spectacle of the supernatural, thus enabling contemporary audiences to parallel the experience of playgoers in the early modern era when superstitious beliefs were common currency.

A quaint device

Coming on the heels of the 400th anniversary of Shakespeare's death, the RSC's 2017 season bore a certain historical weight, one which no doubt drove RSC Artistic Director Gregory Doran to break new technical ground. Doran claims that the idea to employ mo-cap in his production arose from his reflections on *The Tempest* itself, and its debt to the Jacobean masque tradition, which had historically served as a platform for showcasing innovative stagecraft.[12]

Doran asked his staff to consider 'what effects Shakespeare might have employed if he were alive today', and he was sent a video by the RSC's Digital Director Sarah Ellis, of a 'floating' leviathan, rendered through a mix of mo-cap and augmented reality. Struck by this technology as a modern analogue for the awe-inducing spectacle of the Jacobean masque, Doran encouraged Ellis to reach out to Intel's research director, resulting in a two-year partnership between the RSC, Intel and innovators in mo-cap technology, Imaginarium Studios.[13]

In examining the critical ambivalence towards the use of mo-cap in Doran's production, we might begin by investigating his assertion that this technological conceit arose from *The Tempest* and its debt to the masque tradition. As a genre that thrived on spectacle, the masque heralded major innovations in stage machinery, including developments in the use of back shutters, perspective scenery and a variety of manual apparatuses.[14] In fact, as Jerzy Limon argues, the Jacobean masque is a form so driven by stagecraft that it is often preferable to read the masque not as a hermetically sealed text but as a body of staging practices, a 'theatrical, three-dimensional emblem in which the stage-picture… functions as the emblem's icon'.[15] With spectacle and innovation being at the core of the masque tradition, it is compelling to think of mo-cap as a kind of contemporary, digital manifestation of Jacobean spectacle. Yet to what extent can we say that mo-cap relates to the body of staging practices around *The Tempest* specifically?

First published in the 1623 Folio, *The Tempest* is accompanied by remarkably coherent and detailed stage directions. Despite ongoing debate over whether the stage directions were written in by the playwright himself,[16] they remain useful for framing issues of staging in the play. Deconstructing these stage directions in a series of essays from 1938, John C. Adams made a particularly compelling claim about a stage direction from Act 3, Scene 3, in which Ariel appears as the Harpy, conjuring a richly laid banquet before 'with a quaint device the Banquet vanishes'.[17] While this effect would normally suggest the use of a conventional Elizabethan trapdoor, Adams argues that the phrase 'quaint device' here suggests 'a new and ingenious property… unlike anything normally used in the playhouse'. Taking the inference a step further, he remarks: 'Have our discoveries any bearing on Shakespeare's choice of harpy costume for Ariel?... When Ariel "clasps his wings upon the Table" their outstretched expanse would wholly conceal the banquet.'[18]

Adams infers that innovations in Elizabethan stage machinery were key to *The Tempest*. Yet his assertion is particularly audacious because it implies that Ariel's presentation of the Harpy, far from being a carefully considered allusion, arose from the 'quaint device' itself. Adams suggests that aspects of Ariel's characterisation resulted from a kind of technodramaturgy: that the relationship between character and stage machinery was not a one-way street, but fed each other in a kind of iterative loop – or as Finn Ross, the video designer for Doran's production, described it when I spoke to him in late 2017, the result of an 'opinion matrix' – triangulating the creative offerings of Imaginarium's technologists with the production team's dramaturgical choices.[19]

Ross described how the production team aspired to a 'nuanced' rather than a 'slavish' use of their own quaint device. The design team settled on a guiding principle for the use of the digital puppet, driven by their desire to create a transformative Ariel that would still remain grounded by a single human performance. 'When Ariel was there as himself as a character... speaking directly with Prospero, then he would just be himself, as Mark,' Ross said, 'and then whenever Ariel was conjuring something... when he was a magical manifestation... then he would appear as a sort of avatar.'[20]

Of course, this rule necessitates some dramaturgical wheedling. Ariel is something of an enigma in the canon, a Protean figure with no clear textual precursors. An 'incomparably comprehensive demon,'[21] Ariel's textual origins have been variously attributed to esoteric magic, Jacobean witchcraft beliefs, Jewish and Christian demonology, and elemental symbology.[22] His slippery textual status is clearly reflected in the play's performance history, with his casting and characterisation fluctuating widely given a period's aesthetic and ideological preoccupations. In several instances, directors have even cast multiple actors in the role, from a bifurcated 'boy' and 'girl' Ariel in the Restoration[23] to an eleven-actor Ariel at the New York Shakespeare Festival in 1981.[24]

Like so many of Shakespeare's sprites, Ariel echoes the dramaturgical function of godly messengers in the classical tradition. Charting *The Tempest*'s literary debt to the *Aeneid*, Jan Kott notes that Ariel's role in *The Tempest* is not unlike that of Virgil's Mercury and various Homeric messengers, who 'are only seen by the mortals to whom they choose to speak... at the same time visible and invisible.'[25] Like Virgil's Mercury, Ariel's power is seemingly limitless yet it is invoked only when essential to his master's will, and thereby the unfolding human drama.

Indeed, I would argue that Shakespeare plays on this very tension, pitting Ariel's broad supernatural powers against their comparatively restrained theatrical use. This duality is precisely what makes the various instances and descriptions of Ariel's magic so vivid and surprising as *The Tempest* unfolds; we believe he can do anything, but he can only perform what Prospero (and the dramatist) bids him.

To render this tension at the core of Ariel's supernatural nature, Doran's production decided to establish the spirit as two mirrored bodies, discrete yet inextricably linked. This 'Double Ariel' was not so much a divided spirit as a refracted one, recalling Ariel's description of dividing and burning in many places aboard the King's vessel (1.2.231–35). Indeed, as Quarterly spoke this very line, his airy counterpart split in three, 'flaming distinctly' on the topmast, yards and bowsprit (*Tempest*, 1.2.235–6). In this way, Ariel's acts of magic, both enacted and described, were literalised by his digital complement.

Part of Ariel's supernatural capabilities, of course, is his capacity for presenting other roles – a water nymph, the Harpy and the goddess Ceres. Shapeshifter that he is, Ariel thus functions as an agent of spectacle, participant in the grand performance over which Prospero resides, one tellingly facilitated by sprites he refers to as his 'demi-puppets' (5.1.45). I would argue that we can view Ariel as a bifurcated performer, at once puppet and puppeteer, controlling other performative bodies as he is controlled himself. Quarterly's 'Double Ariel' arguably appears to be symptomatic of Ariel's textual status as a liminal, supernatural entity rather than a gimmicky technological imposition.

This is particularly true when we consider the question of Ariel's agency, and his status as a vassal to Prospero. The conditions of Ariel's servility, as well as his continued petitions for freedom, are rich with theatrical possibility precisely because they are left undefined in the playtext. An endlessly changeable spirit, Ariel can be read as both servile and potent, blithe and burdened, devoted and adversarial.[26] This is reflected in the play's performance history, with the master–servant relationship between Ariel and Prospero proving to be highly interpretable, existing everywhere on the spectrum from loving to violently antagonistic – as indeed was the case when Simon Russell Beale, the Prospero of Doran's production, played him in 1993.[27]

Quarterly's 'Double Ariel', rather than producing a stable interpretation of Ariel's captivity, actually theatricalised the fluid discourse of Ariel as captive, flitting not only between simulation and corporeality, but also between confinement and autonomy. The idiosyncrasies of the live mo-cap technical pipeline fundamentally informed this characterisation. However, in order to understand how this technodramaturgy arose, it is important to understand firstly the technical pipeline at play.

A touch of a button

Ariel's digital puppet is the result of the following five-stage pipeline:

1 the actor's Xsens mo-cap suit and/or facial rig sends data to the Xsens mo-cap software;

2 a game engine (UE or Unreal Engine) acts as a container and imposes the Xsens mo-cap data onto a 3D model, which has been pre-rigged in 3D modelling software (i.e. Blender or Maya);
3 the game engine (UE) sends out live virtual camera feed to D3 media servers;
4 D3 media servers send video feed over Cat5 (very fast Ethernet connections) to projection mapping software (i.e. MadMapper, Isadora, Touch Designer);
5 mapping software sends mapped video feed to projectors.

Every stage in this pipeline requires an enormous amount of graphic processing power and therefore has the potential to produce latency (delay, or blurring) between the data captured by the actor's mo-cap suit and the digital avatar. Doran's production represents a significant innovation in this field, with Intel and Imaginarium reducing this latency to only 2–3 frames, with an interesting exception I will return to. As a result, the major technical coup of this *Tempest* was the fact that, to the human eye, there was no visible disjuncture between Quarterly's actions and that of his digital counterpart – a Double Ariel. Yet the idiosyncrasies of this pipeline manifested themselves in other ways, with meaningful implications for Ariel's characterisation.

At the first stage of the pipeline, much of Quarterly's performance had to accommodate the technical needs of the mo-cap hardware, a custom Xsens MVN wireless mo-cap suit. Quarterly's suit was fitted with 136 individual nodes, each essentially a high-functioning accelerometer that captured the movement of Quarterly's individual joints. The suit had to fit snugly over Quarterly's entire body, limiting potential costuming choices. However, production designer Stephen Brimson Lewis ingeniously harnessed this constraint, highlighting the doubled nature of this airy spirit by painting Quarterly's suit to match the silvery texture of his digital avatar.

The suit's demands had another notable effect on Ariel's dramaturgy. Doran had initially blocked Quarterly centre-stage as the clear 'puppeteer' of his digital counterpart, so that the actor or 'embodied' Ariel would always be interacting with Prospero directly. However, it quickly became apparent in technical rehearsals that Quarterly's movement needed 'a significant amount of… re-conception' in order to clear the visual field for the projected avatar.[28] The result was an uncanny oscillation between puppet and puppeteer, with Quarterly and his avatar alternating in their physical dominance over the space. When the avatar was the primary speaker, Quarterly was confined to the balcony and a thin corridor upstage, prowling the space in semi-darkness. By contrast, when Quarterly dominated, the avatar would dissolve into obscurity. As such, the two Ariels oscillated back and forth in an endlessly compellingly visual dance, with the free movement of one Ariel resulting in the confinement of his double.

Just as the technical constraints of the suit manifested themselves in Ariel's doubled characterisation, so too did the technical constraints of the head-mounted display. In order to capture the movement of his face, Quarterly had to wear a HMD, a helmet fitted with a high-resolution camera. Unlike the data produced by Quarterly's suit, where each node merely captured the pitch/yaw/roll of each joint, the HMD had to transmit significantly more data, as the points of articulation in a human face are often only a few millimetres apart, requiring extremely high resolution and fidelity. As such, even though it was fed through the same technical pipeline, the HMD produced significantly more latency. The production team's solution was to restrict the use of the HMD to a single scene (Ariel's appearance as the Harpy), and to process Quarterly's vocal performance, using 'heavily amplified and affected' microphone effects to create an artificial delay, thereby synchronising Quarterly's voice with the facial capture. For the rest of the production, the avatar merely 'recalled' pre-captured facial expressions – happy, sad, angry. These were intricately choreographed to match Quarterly's performance, to produce the effect of total simultaneity.

All this evidences Intel and Imaginarium's extraordinary efforts to reduce, and even conceal, any latency between Quarterly and his avatar. After all, part of the spectacle of using mo-cap in live performance is the ability to display to an audience that the data is being captured and rendered simultaneously.

Yet the 'doubling' of Ariel is equally a result of the system itself. As Moeslund and Granum note in their comprehensive survey of motion-capture systems, an important benefit of 'direct model' capture (i.e. the use of an *a priori* humanoid, 3D model) is that the system can be calibrated using a 'similarity measure', which is typically accomplished by comparing the performer's poses to those performed by the model in the system, and calibrating accordingly.[29] From an engineering perspective, direct model mo-cap relies on simultaneity as its baseline metric. Simultaneity was not only a desirable theatrical outcome, it was the optimal manifestation of the technical system. The use of a 'similarity measure' is particularly important in direct model mo-cap, owing to the fact that an animated 3D model is actually made up of three separate components: a skeletal rig (the model's locomotive joints), a skeletal mesh (the model's sculpting or 'body'), and the skin (the model's texturing and occlusion masks). For this reason, the three models built for Ariel (the 'base' avatar, the water nymph and the Harpy) all bear a remarkable resemblance to each other. While skinned differently, the models rely on the same skeletal rig and roughly the same mesh. As such, these changing skins operated as digital breakaways, altering the puppet's visual form while remaining consistent to the base puppet. Ariel's digital puppet had continuous breakaways, reconfiguring his form while remaining fundamentally bound to the same morphology. This produced a compelling tension in Ariel's characterisation: for all his shapeshifting malleability, his avatar remained essentially trapped in the same physical container.

Imaginarium and Intel's next stage in the pipeline was to transfer these 3D models into an interactive gaming engine, a software container in which the 3D model can be fed the live mo-cap data. For this purpose, they chose to use

Unreal Engine, a popular suite of game development tools. A key component of the Unreal Engine, one central to Doran's production, is the use of a 'virtual camera' actor. In gaming platforms, what we typically think of as a player's 'perspective' or viewpoint is actually determined by the placement of a virtual camera in 3D space.

Translating this 3D virtual world to a proscenium theatre presented a curious conundrum. In Doran's production, the final image that the audience saw of Ariel's sprite was from the perspective of a virtual camera actor. Placed in front of Ariel's digital avatar in 3D space, the virtual camera sent out a high-definition live camera feed, a rectangular frame 1,920 pixels wide and 1,080 pixels long, to the projectors – a 2D live video stream of a 3D world. To fit within the rectangular frame of the virtual camera, Ariel's avatar had to be restricted by tight X, Y and Z parameters. Any illusion that the sprite was freely moving through 3D space had to be imposed retroactively, with video designer Finn Ross using conventional projection mapping techniques to manually shift this 2D video feed, at what he described as 'a touch of a button', onto the various surfaces of Lewis' set.

This pipeline produced an uncanny quality to the avatar's movement in the theatre space. Even though the avatar appeared to be moving freely, it was essentially confined in 3D space. Regardless of whether the audience could consciously perceive the cause of this disjunction, it produced a clear divergence between the movement of the avatar and that of the performer. The organic 'free' movement of Quarterly's body through space was sharply juxtaposed against the avatar's strangely restricted motion, creating the eerie sense that the avatar was trapped by the very surfaces it occupied.

This effect was amplified by the use of two key scenic elements, referred to as the 'cloud' and the 'vortex', two translucent cylinders of gauze used as projection mapping surfaces to create the illusion that the avatar was hovering. The 'vortex' was a fixed column centre-stage, and the 'cloud' was rigged to a mechanised fly system in the grid, allowing it to float across the stage. Yet the tight physical parameters of these cylinders resulted in numerous instances of clipping, with the avatar's limbs disappearing outside the edge of the frame. This clipping only served to amplify the effect that the avatar was caged by the cylinders he occupied.

Just as the tight 3D parameters of the avatar produced an uncanny quality to the pair's mirrored movement, so too did the tight confines of these containers produce the image of a thoroughly paradoxical sprite, at once airborne and earth-bound, floating through space while being confined by it. This was perhaps rendered most vividly in a stage image from Act 1, with Ariel reliving his confinement by Sycorax in a cloven pine (see figure 3.3). With Quarterly standing inside the vortex cylinder onto which his digital double was being projected, the two Ariels stood in physical opposition while mutually entrapped, highlighting both Quarterly's corporeality and his double's illusoriness. At every stage

3.3 Ariel reliving his confinement in the pine.

of the pipeline, Doran and his team harnessed the constraints of digital puppetry to render an ethereal and multifarious Ariel, endlessly oscillating between freedom and entrapment.

This kind of iterative technodramaturgy allows for a productive interchange between technological innovation and dramatic considerations. I would argue that Quarterly's digital sprite greatly enhances not only our engagement with the multifarious sprite, but also our broader engagement with the supernatural world of Shakespeare's playtext and its inherent performative debt to the masque tradition. Indeed, the awe-inducing ethereality of Ariel's digital puppet actually seems to have contributed to some of the critical hostility towards the use of mo-cap, with reviewers noting that Ariel's awe-inducing puppet felt like 'disappointing literalism' of *The Tempest*'s magic.[30]

I will therefore conclude by musing that the critical ambivalence towards this digital puppet seems largely inseparable from a kind of literary preservationist impulse around this particular play – the persistent Shavian bias (as Mark Shenton noted in his review) that 'the customary magic of the play resides… in the simpler glories of Shakespeare's script'.[31] While it is impossible to know to what extent this bias reflects the experience of the RSC's viewing public, I did observe that the general tenor of audience reviews on sites like seatplan.com seemed rather conversely inclined. One audience member marvelled at finally seeing Ariel as 'superhuman, growing in size and floating', while another noted that 'far from dreading the magical sequences… as I've always done before, I was eagerly anticipating them tonight'.[32] For certain spectators, the magic of this Double Ariel offered a compelling case for the use of mo-cap for this production. As the technology is still novel, it has the capacity to elicit wonder and awe among today's audiences, analogous in some ways to the responses that new stage machinery may have produced among playgoers in early seventeenth-century England. In this sense, mo-cap is a highly innovative digital technique that can translate the effects of the supernatural for contemporary audiences – if not a window into the past, at least 'a signpost to the future'.

Notes

1 Some of the material in this article was previously published in Felicia Anchuli King, '"These are not natural events": Ariel's Technodramaturgy in the Royal Shakespeare Company's *The Tempest*', *HowlRound: Theatre Commons* (11 January 2018), https://howlround.com/these-are-not-natural-events, accessed 15 December 2018.
2 Dassia N. Posner, Claudia Orenstein and John Bell, 'Introduction', in Dassia N. Posner, Claudia Orenstein and John Bell (eds), *The Routledge Companion to Puppetry and Material Performance* (Abingdon: Routledge, 2014), p. 7.
3 John Bell, 'Puppets, Masks, and Performing Objects at the End of the Century', in John Bell (ed.), *Puppets, Masks, and Performing Objects* (Cambridge, MA: MIT Press, 2001), p. 5.
4 Steve Tillis, 'The Art of Puppetry in the Age of Media Production', in Bell (ed.) *Puppets, Masks, and Performing Objects*, p. 179.
5 Stephen Kaplin, 'A Puppet Tree: A Model for the Field of Puppet Theatre', in Bell (ed.), *Puppets, Masks, and Performing Objects*, p. 25.
6 Colette Searls, 'Unholy Alliances and Harmonious Hybrids', in Posner, Orenstein and Bell (eds), *The Routledge Companion to Puppetry and Material Performance*, p. 296.
7 Michael Billington, '*The Tempest* Review: Beale's superb Prospero haunts Hi-tech Spectacle', in *The Guardian* (18 November 2016), www.theguardian.com/stage/2016/nov/18/the-tempest-review-simon-russell-beale-rsc, accessed 4 November 2018.
8 Fiona Mountford, '*The Tempest*, theatre review: Set Sail for a Choppy Journey', in *The London Evening Standard* (7 July 2017), www.standard.co.uk/go/london/theatre/the-tempest-theatre-review-set-sail-for-a-choppy-journey-a3681726.html, accessed 4 November 2018.
9 Dominic Cavendish, 'The RSC's *Tempest*: *Lord of the Rings*-style Magic and the Welcome Return of Simon Russell Beale', *The Telegraph* (18 November 2016), www.telegraph.co.uk/theatre/what-to-see/the-rscs-incredible-tempest-brings-lord-of-the-rings-style-magic/, accessed 4 November 2018.
10 Masashiro Mori, 'The Uncanny Valley', *IEEE Robotics and Automation*, 19:2 (2012), p. 98.
11 Searls, 'Unholy Alliances and Harmonious Hybrids', p. 301.
12 Daniel Pollack-Pezner, 'Two Ways to Bring Shakespeare into the Twenty-First Century', *The New Yorker* (2 December 2016), www.newyorker.com/books/

page-turner/two-ways-to-bring-shakespeare-into-the-twenty-first-century, accessed 15 December 2018. See also Orgel's critical introduction, *The Tempest*, ed. Stephen Orgel (Oxford: Oxford World's Classics, 2008), pp. 43–50. All references are to this edition.
13 Pollack-Pezner, 'Two Ways to Bring Shakespeare into the Twenty-First Century'.
14 Richard Southern, *Changeable Scenery: Its Origins and Development in the British Theatre* (London: Faber & Faber, 1999), p. 34.
15 Jerzy Limon, *The Masque of Stuart Culture* (Newark: University of Delaware Press, 1990), p. 78.
16 MacDonald P. Jackson, 'Stage Directions and Speech Headings in Act 1 of *Titus Andronicus* Q (1594): Shakespeare or Peele?', *Studies in Bibliography*, 49 (1996), p. 134.
17 William Shakespeare, *The Tempest*, ed. Orgel.
18 John C. Adams, 'The Staging of *The Tempest*, III.iii', *The Review of English Studies*, 14:56 (1938), p. 409.
19 Personal interview with Finn Ross, 25 October 2017.
20 *Ibid.*
21 Robert R. Reed, 'The Probable Origin of Ariel', *Shakespeare Quarterly*, 11:1 (1960), p. 61.
22 W. Stacy Johnson, 'The Genesis of Ariel', *Shakespeare Quarterly*, 2:3 (1951), p. 210.
23 Amanda Eubanks Winkler, 'Sexless Spirits?: Gender Ideology and Dryden's Musical Magic', *The Musical Quarterly*, 93:2 (2010), p. 301.
24 John Beaufort, 'Shakespeare Shipwrecked by a "Tempest" in New York's Central Park', *The Christian Science Monitor* (20 July 1981), www.csmonitor.com/1981/0720/072000.html/, accessed 4 November 2018.
25 Jan Kott, 'The *Aeneid* and *The Tempest*', *Arion: A Journal of Humanities and the Classics*, new series, 3:4 (1976), p. 427.
26 Reed, 'The Probable Origin of Ariel', p. 64.
27 Billington, '*The Tempest* Review'.
28 Ross interview, 2017.
29 Thomas B. Moeslund and Erik Granum, 'A Survey of Computer Vision-Based Human Motion Capture', *Computer Vision and Image Understanding*, 81:3 (2001), p. 245.
30 Pollack-Pezner, 'Two Ways to Bring Shakespeare into the Twenty-First Century'.
31 Mark Shenton, '*The Tempest* review at the Royal Shakespeare Theatre, Stratford-upon-Avon – "Gimmicky, but Simon Russell Beale Soars"', *The Stage* (17 November 2016), www.thestage.co.uk/reviews/2016/the-tempest-review-at-the-royal-shakespeare-theatre-stratford-upon-avon/, accessed 4 November 2018.
32 SeatPlan.com, audience reviews of *The Tempest*, https://seatplan.com/london/the-tempest/, accessed 2 April 2018.

Bibliography

Adams, John C., 'The Staging of *The Tempest*, III.iii', *The Review of English Studies*, 14:56 (1938), 404–19.

Beaufort, John, 'Shakespeare Shipwrecked by a "Tempest" in New York's Central Park', *The Christian Science Monitor* (20 July 1981), www.csmonitor.com/1981/0720/072000.html/, accessed 4 November 2018.

Bell, John, 'Puppets, Masks, and Performing Objects at the End of the Century', in John Bell (ed.), *Puppets, Masks, and Performing Objects* (Cambridge, MA: MIT Press, 2001), pp. 5–17.

Billington, Michael, '*The Tempest* Review: Beale's superb Prospero haunts Hi-tech Spectacle', *The Guardian*, 18 November 2016, www.theguardian.com/stage/2016/nov/18/the-tempest-review-simon-russell-beale-rsc, accessed 4 November 2018.

Cavendish, Dominic, 'The RSC's *Tempest*: *Lord of the Rings*-style Magic and the Welcome Return of Simon Russell Beale', *The Telegraph*, 18 November 2016, www.telegraph.co.uk/theatre/what-to-see/the-rscs-incredible-tempest-brings-lord-of-the-rings-style-magic/, accessed 4 November 2018.

Jackson, MacDonald P., 'Stage Directions and Speech Headings in Act 1 of *Titus Andronicus* Q (1594): Shakespeare or Peele?', *Studies in Bibliography*, 49 (1996), 134–48.

Johnson, W. Stacy, 'The Genesis of Ariel', *Shakespeare Quarterly*, 2:3 (1951), 205–10.

Kaplin, Stephen, 'A Puppet Tree: A Model for the Field of Puppet Theatre', in John Bell (ed.) *Puppets, Masks, and Performing Objects* (Cambridge, MA: MIT Press, 2001), pp. 18–25.

King, Felicia Anchuli, '"These are not natural events": Ariel's Technodramaturgy in the Royal Shakespeare Company's *The Tempest*', *HowlRound: Theatre Commons* (11 January 2018), https://howlround.com/these-are-not-natural-events, accessed 15 December 2018.

Kott, Jan, 'The *Aeneid* and *The Tempest*', *Arion: A Journal of Humanities and the Classics*, new series, 3:4 (1976), 424–51.

Limon, Jerzy, *The Masque of Stuart Culture* (Newark: University of Delaware Press, 1990).

Moeslund, Thomas B., and Erik Granum, 'A Survey of Computer Vision-Based Human Motion Capture', *Computer Vision and Image Understanding*, 81:3 (2001), 231–68.

Mori, Masashiro, 'The Uncanny Valley', *IEEE Robotics and Automation*, 19:2 (2012), 98–100.

Mountford, Fiona, '*The Tempest*, theatre review: Set Sail for a Choppy Journey', *The London Evening Standard* (7 July 2017), www.standard.co.uk/go/london/theatre/the-tempest-theatre-review-set-sail-for-a-choppy-journey-a3681726.html, accessed 4 November 2018.

Pollack-Pezner, Daniel, 'Two Ways to Bring Shakespeare Into the Twenty-First Century', *The New Yorker* (2 December 2016), www.newyorker.com/books/page-turner/two-ways-to-bring-shakespeare-into-the-twenty-first-century, accessed 15 December 2018.

Posner, Dassia N., Claudia Orenstein and John Bell, 'Introduction', in Dassia N. Posner, Claudia Orenstein and John Bell (eds), *The Routledge Companion to Puppetry and Material Performance* (Abingdon: Routledge, 2014), pp 1–12.

Reed, Robert R., 'The Probable Origin of Ariel', *Shakespeare Quarterly*, 11:1 (1960), 61–5.
Ross, Finn, Personal interview with the author, 25 October 2017.
Searls, Colette, 'Unholy Alliances and Harmonious Hybrids', in Dassia N. Posner, Claudia Orenstein and John Bell (eds), *The Routledge Companion to Puppetry and Material Performance* (Abingdon: Routledge, 2014), pp. 294–307.
Seatplan.com, 'Audience Reviews of *The Tempest*', https://seatplan.com/london/the-tempest/, accessed 2 April 2018.
Southern, Richard, *Changeable Scenery: Its Origins and Development in the British Theatre* (London: Faber & Faber, 1999).
Shakespeare, William, *The Tempest*, ed. Stephen Orgel (Oxford: Oxford World's Classics, 2008).
Shenton, Mark, '*The Tempest* review at the Royal Shakespeare Theatre, Stratford-upon-Avon – "Gimmicky, but Simon Russell Beale Soars,"' *The Stage* (17 November 2016), www.thestage.co.uk/reviews/2016/the-tempest-review-at-the-royal-shakespeare-theatre-stratford-upon-avon/, accessed 4 November 2018.
Tillis, Steve, 'The Art of Puppetry in the Age of Media Production', in John Bell (ed.), *Puppets, Masks, and Performing Objects* (Cambridge, MA: MIT Press, 2001), pp. 172–85.
Winkler, Amanda Eubanks, 'Sexless Spirits?: Gender Ideology and Dryden's Musical Magic', *The Musical Quarterly*, 93:2 (2010), 297–328.

Part II

Haunted spaces

4

Demons and puns: revisiting the 'cellarage scene' in *Hamlet*

Pierre Kapitaniak

A spectre is haunting the first Act of *Hamlet* – the spectre of the Old King.[1] The 'cellarage scene', on which this chapter intends to focus, is the final sequence of the last scene from Act 1; it follows Hamlet's interview with the Ghost (1.5.113–88)[2] and stages the latter in an ambiguous and disconcerting way. This sequence used to be a stumbling block of many theories about the apparition's nature throughout the twentieth century,[3] and by 2002 E. Pearlman still felt it necessary to warn against 'the excesses of pneumatological, psychological, and latterly cultural criticism that the scene has provoked'.[4] Almost two decades later, this short sequence still resists clarification, beyond the mere recognition of its value as comic relief. Although critical debate about the Ghost's nature seems to have tipped the balance in favour of a Purgatorial soul in the wake of Greenblatt's influential book *Hamlet in Purgatory*,[5] for some critics the possibility of a devilish ghost remains a potent argument in understanding the play.[6] Forsaking the doctrinal subtleties, other critics have turned to more popular medieval antecedents of *Hamlet*'s ghostly figure.[7] This chapter follows a similar trail, arguing that the 'cellarage scene' looks back towards medieval stage traditions that survived into the late sixteenth century. The couple formed by the subterranean Ghost and Hamlet is reminiscent of that of the Devil and the Vice in the morality plays. Indeed, several aspects of the sequence deserving closer examination may be directly related to the medieval stage traditions: the plurality of the oath, Hamlet's disrespectful tone, and the nicknames given by Hamlet to the Ghost. The latter, especially, suggest other meanings than that of a Protestant demonic spirit, while the whole sequence may be seen both as a living tableau on the stage and as comic relief,[8] part of Hamlet's wider propensity for puns.

A Chester mystery and multiple oaths

A century ago, Joseph Quincy Adams explained the repeated oaths and the ensuing movements in Act 1, Scene 5 through a parallel with an episode from the Book of Numbers.[9] In chapters 23 and 24, Balak, king of the Moabites, tries to have the refugees from the Exodus cursed by the prophet Balaam. Displeased with what he hears, Balak changes places several times, passing from the hills of Baal to Mount Pisgah, and to Mount Peor. Each time, he hopes that the new perspective will bring a change in the prophet's words. After three attempts at cursing, which God turns into a blessing, Balaam prophesies once more before leaving Balak. In the fourteenth century, this episode was integrated into a mystery play belonging to the Chester cycle – *Balaack and Balaam*[10] – in which Balaam looks around the stage seeking the right place for his prophecies. The play survives in two later manuscripts that present significant variants. Adams collated them to obtain Balaam's four successive positions, which he identified with the four cardinal points and the four corners of the stage. It seems to me that, on the contrary, the two versions must be examined separately. In the 1591 manuscript, there is an inconsistency between the stage directions and the text, because one of the prophecies is missing.[11] The 1607 text offers a much more coherent organisation. The three blessings are followed by the final prophecy, the staging of which departs from the three cardinal points, pointing at the sky.[12] Thus there are three curses that become blessings. R. M. Lumiansky and David Mills even suggest that this ternary structure 'may also be indicative of the nature of staging, where the actor could only face in three directions'.[13] In *Hamlet*, four oaths are punctuated by the Ghost's interventions:

Ham.   Never make knowne what you have seene to night…

Ghost.   Sweare. *Ghost cries under the Stage*…

[*Ham.*] Never to speake of this that you have seene…

Ghost.   Sweare…

[*Ham.*] Never to speake of this that you have heard…

Ghost.   Sweare by his sword…

[*Ham.*] Heere as before,… never shall… note
        That you knowe ought of me, this doe sweare…

Ghost.   Sweare. (Second Quarto (Q2), 1.5.143–79)[14]

However, as in the 1591 text of *Balaack and Balaam*, the number of cues does not correspond to the number of movements, since the three versions of the tragedy only mention two displacements: 'then weele shift our ground… once more remooue good friends' (Q2, 1.5.156–62). The three men do not seem to move between the first two oaths demanded by Hamlet, which are identical.

The presence of 'here' in a line of the First Quarto edition (Q1) confirms this hypothesis: 'Here consent to sweare' (Q1, 594). Despite the four oaths, there are only two indisputable shifts in *Hamlet* and consequently three places where the characters gather.

So many similarities can hardly be coincidental; all the more so as, when writing *Hamlet*, Shakespeare might only have had access to the lacunary 1591 manuscript of the mystery play or may have seen it staged. Of course, the Biblical episode is more likely to have influenced Shakespeare than the Chester cycle, especially as there seems to be no widespread dramatic convention of the kind. Yet what is striking is that the two scenes present similar incongruities.

Among critics, the idea of fitting the four oaths into a more regular ternary structure of the three places dates back to A. C. Bradley, who was the first to remark on the progression of the 'threefold oath'.[15] His argument is founded on meaning and reduces the first two synonymous oaths to one. Hamlet thus swears his friends to silence about what they saw, what they heard and what they know of his own projects. John Dover Wilson and many modern editors of the play apply this reading by incorporating stage directions ('*They swear*') after the second, third and fourth orders of the Ghost.[16]

It is therefore difficult to affirm with certainty whether Horatio and Marcellus swear one, two, three or four times, or whether they do not, since no original stage direction mentions any action and no witness actually swears aloud. This lack of evidence may indicate that swearing is not the main purpose of the sequence, but that its aim is purely spectacular. Above all, the audience remembers the subterranean cries and sees a group of three men move about the stage. One of the reasons for such staging is simply pragmatic: by placing themselves on the three sides of the stage in contact with the audience, the actors make sure that everybody enjoys a very symbolic tableau and that everybody hears the Ghost's cry.[17] Indeed, as the latter utters only one word, it is certainly better perceived the second or third time, and it may be for that very reason that the first displacement occurs only after the second cry.

The treatment of this sequence presents another similarity between the two plays. Disappointed by Balaam's words, Balak gets angry after the blessings and the tone he adopts when speaking to the prophet suddenly changes and becomes very disrespectful:

> What the dyvell ayles thee, thow populart?
> Thy speach is not worth a farte!...
> Thow preachest, populard, as a pye;
> the dyvell of hell thee destroye!
> (*Balaack and Balaam*, ll. 296–7; 312–13)

Balak uses insults like 'papelard' (that is hypocrite, with a possible pun on 'pope', given the spelling) and '[mag]pie', whose familiar meaning was that of a chatterbox. One cannot help relating those to the numerous nicknames with which Hamlet addresses the Ghost, but their situation and significance are quite different. In the mystery play, the disrespectful tone is triggered by the king's wrath,[18] while in *Hamlet*, there is no anger – at most some malice. Likewise, the relationship between Balak and Balaam has nothing in common with that between Hamlet and the Ghost. The king of the Moabites is a figure of authority and his wrath, as well as his language, are not surprising. Hamlet, on the other hand, is supposed to bow to the Ghost's paternal authority yet his tone betrays disrespect. If Shakespeare had seen the Chester play, or read one of the manuscripts, it is then possible that Balak's anger might have suggested Hamlet's tone.

Morality devils and Hamlet's tone

For Adams, the gravity of the Biblical intertext was hardly compatible with the grotesqueness of the 'cellarage scene', but such an interpretation ill accounts for Hamlet's levity in the presence of the subterranean Ghost. The Ghost's tale and Hamlet's soliloquy that ensues have built up a tension that does not endure in the following sequence. There is an ambiguity here that comes from the Prince's contradictory attitude towards his father's ghost when the latter returns to swear the witnesses to silence. The sequence is framed by two cues from Hamlet that remain in keeping with what precedes:

> Yes by *Saint Patrick* but there is *Horatio*,
> And much offence to, touching this vision heere,
> It is an honest Ghost that let me tell you…
> …
> Rest, rest, perturbed spirit (Q2, 1.5.135–7, 190)

Indeed, 'honest Ghost' and 'perturbed spirit' suggest a tormented soul and the mention of Saint Patrick echoes the 'sulphrus and tormenting flames' earlier depicted by the Ghost. However, these expressions hardly fit in with the sudden surge of familiar and rather disrespectful nicknames used by Hamlet for the Ghost:

> Ha, ha, boy, say'st thou so, art thou there trupenny?
> Come on, you heare this fellowe in the Sellerige,
> …
> Well sayd olde Mole, can'st work i'th earth so fast,
> A worthy Pioner, once more remooue good friends (Q2, 1.5.150–62)

These two cues, as well as '*Hic et ubique*' (l. 156), directly answer the Ghost's voice, the fourth injunction being followed by 'rest, perturbed spirit' (l. 180). The singular levity of Hamlet's first three interventions has inspired numerous questions and interpretations trying to infer from them the nature of the Ghost speaking from below.[19]

It has been assumed since Samuel Johnson that the couple formed by Hamlet and the Ghost is reminiscent of the Vice and the Devil that haunted the medieval stages,[20] yet this is usually stated quite vaguely, merely evoking a convention that is still present in the minds of the Elizabethan audience. Yet both Lysander William Cushman and Bernard Spivack showed that this 'famous' couple was far from being an old medieval tradition.[21] Indeed, out of approximately sixty moral interludes that have survived, nine stage the Devil (Lucifer, Satan or Belial) and only three develop a comic scene between the Vice and the Devil. Moreover, these three plays are late moralities that date back to the second half of the sixteenth century: Ulpian Fulwell's *Like Will to Like, Quoth the Devil to the Collier* (1568), Thomas Garter's *The Most Virtuous and Godly Susanna* (1569) and Thomas Lupton's *All for Money* (1577).[22] At the time of *Hamlet*, then, the couple formed by the Vice and the Devil appears to have been a rather recent tradition and, all in all, a limited one. All the same, the motif seems to have been quite popular with the audience and when in 1603 Samuel Harsnett writes of these 'old Church-playes' that staged a 'devil so vice-haunted', he goes back a few decades rather than centuries.[23]

Of the three plays, it is the first that provides the most fertile model for Hamlet's behaviour. *Like Will to Like, Quoth the Devil to the Collier* opens with a monologue by Nichol Newfangle ('the Vice'), soon joined by Lucifer, and Newfangle's first reaction sets the general tone of the scene:

Sancte benedicite, who have we heere?
Tom tumbler or els some dauncing beare,
Body of me it were best goe no neere,
For ought that I see it is my Godfather Lucifer. (*Like Will to Like*, ll. 35–8)

On seeing Tom ('the Collier of Croydon'), Newfangle decides to recruit him for his master and Tom agrees to dance with the Devil before leaving the stage. When Lucifer asks Newfangle to pay homage, the latter complies but still voices his disrespect by addressing the Devil as 'bottel nosed godfather' (ll. 167–9). Then follows a scene during which Newfangle plays at distorting each line of praise ordered by Lucifer:

Lucifer. All haile Oh noble Prince of hel,

Newfangle. All my dames cow tailes fel down into the wel.

Luc. I wil exalt thee above the clowdes,

New. I wil sault thee and hang thee in the shrowds.

Luc. Thou art the inhauncer of my renowne,

New. Thou art haunce the hangman of Callis town,

> *Luc.* To thee be honour alone,
>
> *New.* To thee shall come our hobling Jone.
>
> *Luc.* Amen.
>
> *New.* Amen. (ll. 170–79)

After his master has left, Newfangle confesses he has been scared and the absence of Lucifer makes his insults more audacious: he twice calls him 'the whorson Devil' (ll. 187, 189).

Bernard Spivack remarks that, according to Henslowe, the Earl of Pembroke's company staged a play at the Rose whose title was 'the devell licke unto licke'.[24] If it was indeed Fulwell's interlude, the Rose was the likeliest place for William Haughton to see it, as his *Grim the Collier of Croydon, or the Devil and his Dame* was most likely staged there shortly before *Hamlet*.[25] Beyond the obvious source for the character of Grim the collier, the play offers several textual parallels with the interlude, even though the situations differ, thus attesting to the popularity of the scene, if not of the entire play. In Haughton's play, Robin the devil decides to help Grim in his quest for Joan's love, but without Robin's knowledge. The playwright thus illustrates the proverbial title of the morality, to which Robin explicitly refers at the end of his monologue: 'I am on *Grim*'s side, for long time ago/The Devill call'd the Collier like to like' (*Grim the Collier of Croydon*, 4.1.30–31). Remaining invisible, Robin fights beside Grim against his rival Clack and insults Clack as well, mainly for the audience's delight: 'Now Miller, Miller, dustipoule,/I'le clapper-claw your Jobbernoule' (4.1.91–92).[26] In the following act, Robin stops being invisible and joins a banquet to eat 'a mess of Cream' with Grim, Joan and parson Shorthose who is to marry them:[27]

> *Robin.* Ho, ho, ho my Masters, no good Fellowship!
> Is *Robin Goodfellow* a Bug-bear grown… *Robin falleth to eat*.
> That he is not worthy to be bid sit down.
>
> *Grim.* O Lord save us! sure he is some Country-devil, he hath got a Russet-coat upon his face.
>
> *Short.* Now *benedicite*! who is this?
> I take him for some fiend I wiss. (5.1.65–72)

This passage recalls the opening of *Like Will to Like* with Robin's exclamation ('Ho, ho, ho') and above all Shorthose's reaction, which reproduces almost word for word Newfangle's '*Sancte benedicite*, who have we heere'.

If Haughton was able to see the interlude at the Rose, then Shakespeare would have had no difficulty in doing so too, as he might also have seen Haughton's own play. And a closer reading reveals similarities between those two texts and the end of the first act of *Hamlet*. There are four features common to Fulwell and Shakespeare. First, both present a couple formed by father and son figures: Newfangle keeps calling Lucifer his 'godfather'. Second, Newfangle and Hamlet use very familiar and disrespectful language, which subverts the authority imposed by filiation. The third point concerns the presence of a Latin formula: Newfangle, like Shorthose, greets Lucifer with '*Sancte benedicite*' and Hamlet greets the Ghost with '*Hic et ubique*'.[28] Lastly, *Like Will to Like* opens with Newfangle's exclamation – 'Ha, ha, ha, ha, now like un to like it wil be none other' – which is echoed by Hamlet when he hears the Ghost's voice: 'Ha, ha, come you here' (Q1, 593); 'Ha, ha, boy, say'st thou so' (Q2, 1.5.865); 'Ah ha boy, sayest thou so' (First Folio (F1), 1.5.846). Juxtaposing the three versions shows that only the latest (generally preferred by modern editors) differs from Fulwell's spelling,[29] while keeping the same sounds.

In contrast, the insults uttered in the two scenes present no similarities, either lexical or thematic. Fulwell focuses on lust and the body register ('bottel nosed godfather'),[30] while Shakespeare favours mining images: 'fellowe in the Sellerige', 'old mole' and 'worthy pioner'. Nevertheless, the chronological proximity of *Grim the Collier of Croydon* (1600) may well have merged the motif of the Vice and the Devil with that of the collier and the devil that Haughton inherited from Fulwell.

Nicknames and the ghost's nature

The comparison with the infernal couple led many twentieth-century commentators to use this sequence to confirm the diabolical nature of the Ghost, either as a devil in disguise imitating Hamlet's father,[31] or as a diabolic soul of the poisoned king.[32] What motivated such readings, above all, was the medieval tradition of naming the space beneath the stage *hell*. The nicknames used by Hamlet are thus interpreted as potentially diabolic, all the more so as in the European tradition it is customary to use diminutives for Satan.[33] Even those who reject the diabolic thesis acknowledge that the 'cellarage scene' welcomes suspicion about the Ghost's honesty: for some it only underlines the apparition's general ambiguity, for others it even proves its good faith.[34] But does Hamlet's vocabulary stigmatise the Ghost as devil? Hamlet addresses it successively as 'boy', 'truepenny', 'this fellowe in the Sellerige', 'old mole' and 'worthy pioner',[35] but although these five nicknames may share a demonic connotation, they may share other common connotations as well.

'Boy'

A survey of the moralities reveals that 'boy' is never uttered by the Vice about the Devil, but that it is usually quite the contrary. In *Enough is as Good as a Feast* (1560), Satan speaks of the Vice, who has just left, in the following terms: 'Oh my boy Covetouse' (l. 1355); in *Susanna*, the Devil treats Ill Report in the same fashion (ll. 44, 77). In his last apparition in *Like Will to Like* Lucifer pronounces a similar formula, associating 'boy' with the characteristic exclamation 'Ho, ho, ho, mine own boy make no more delay,/ But leap upon my back straight way' (*Like Will to Like*, ll. 1165–6). The same is true of other moralities, which implies that in *Hamlet*, 'boy' can hardly be a diabolic nickname. It refers to the Vice and underlines above all the paternal relationship, as shown by the other terms in *Susanna* – 'Chylde' and 'Sonne'. Therefore, if the connotation of 'boy' is diabolic, then it is Hamlet that takes on the devil's role, not the Ghost. I have shown elsewhere that the exclamations that accompany the appearances of the Devil differ from those accompanying the Vice: the former is associated with the 'o' sound, resembling a howling or roaring, while the 'a' sound connoting laughter is customary of the latter.[36]

Moreover, in *Hamlet*, the prince's exclamation when he discovers the Ghost under the stage ('Ha, ha, boy') also appears as an immediate echo of his own response to Horatio's apostrophe – 'Hillo, ho, ho, boy come, and come!' (Q2, 1.5.821) – and it is hard to envisage an infernal connotation in Horatio's case. These exclamations rather function as markers, since they indicate the beginning of the whole sequence and the beginning of the oath. The successive presence of two different formulae is not Shakespeare's innovation, since there is a similar scene in a comedy by Thomas Dekker which may well have influenced *Hamlet*. Performed by the rival company the Lord Admiral's Men in 1599, *Old Fortunatus* opens with Fortunatus playing with his echo in the woods:

Fortunatus. So, ho, ho, ho, ho.

Eccho within, Ho, ho, ho, ho.

Fort. There boy.

Eccho. There boy.

Fort. And thou bee'st a goodfellow, tell me how thou cal'st this wood.

Eccho. This wood.

Fort. I this wood, and which is my best way out.

Eccho. Best way out.

Fort. Ha, ha, ha, thats true, my best way out, is my best way out, but how that out will come in, by this Maggot I know not, I see by this we are all wormes meate: well, I am very poore and verie patient, Patience is a vertue: would I were not vertuous, thats to say, not poore, but full of vice (thats to say, ful of chinckes) Ha, ha, so I am, for I am so full of chinckes… (*Old Fortunatus*, ll. 1–16)

Beside the allusion to worms, the same shift from 'ho, ho, ho' to 'ha, ha, ha' confirms that the latter is connected with the Vice and not with the Devil. Indeed, Fortunatus himself associates his laughter with the morality character by punning on 'vertue' and 'vice'. Similarly, the use of 'boy' is by no means related to the devil, as Fortunatus knows perfectly well that he is conversing with his echo. In contrast, an additional common feature between the two scenes is that Fortunatus and Hamlet both address an invisible voice: the echo's comes from 'within', the Ghost's from below.

'Truepenny'

When Marston alludes to *Hamlet* in *The Malcontent* (1604), he merges several of Hamlet's lines:

> Mal. Illo, ho, ho, ho, arte there olde true penny? *Exit Celso.*
> Where hast thou spent thy selfe this morning? I see flattery in thine eies, and damnation in thy soule. Ha thou huge rascall!
>
> Men. Thou art very merry.
>
> Mal. As a scholler *futuens gratis*: How dooth the divell goe with thee now? (*The Malcontent*, 3.1.127–32)

Here is a real digest of Shakespeare's scene, including the Latin formula and the direct mention of a devil, which strongly suggests that it might be another nickname for Satan. Harold Jenkins reached such a conclusion, resting his case on a scene from *Friar Bacon and Friar Bungay* (1589), in which Miles (the wizard's servant) talks with a demon being ironical about his honesty: 'heers a plaine honest man, without welt or garde… Now surely hers a courteous devil, that for to pleasure his friende wil not stick to make a jade of himselfe, but I pray you goodman friend let me move a question to you' (*Friar Bacon and Friar Bungay*, ll. 1955–76). At the end of the dialogue, Miles goes to hell riding on the devil's back, which is reminiscent of Newfangle's exit on Lucifer's back in Fulwell's interlude, or of Worldly Man's exit in *Enough is as Good as a Feast*. Yet neither Fulwell, nor Wager, or Greene use the term 'truepenny'. Leslie Hotson offers another precedent for this expression in Martin Marprelate's controversy. In *An Almond for a Parrot* (1589), Thomas Nashe mocks Martin as 'the good olde true-pennie *Marprelate*'.[37] Hotson connects this quotation with John Lyly's *Whip for an Ape, or Martin Displaied* (1589), which gives Martin the part of the Vice left vacant by Tarlton's death.[38] Moreover, Hotson specifies that '[l]ike "true Roger" or "trusty Roger", *truepenny* is used in irony. Littleton's Latin dictionary defines it as *veterator vafer*, "old crafty knave". The bad penny is always turning up.'[39] The possibility of an anti-clerical allusion finds another echo in a play staged shortly after *Hamlet* – *The Second Part of*

The Return from Parnassus, or The Scourge of Simony (1603). Here is what Academico says when he mocks old Stercutio, who has come to settle his son Immerito's debts:

> *Acad.* What have we heere, old trupenny come to towne, to fetch away the living in his old greasy slops, then Ile none:
>
> *Im.* Well father, I will not, upon this condition, that when thou have gotten me the *gratuito* of the living, thou will likewise disburse a little mony to the bishops poser, for there are certaine questions I make scruple to be posed in.
>
> *Acad.* He meanes any question in Lattin, which he counts a scruple, oh this honest man could never abide this popish tounge of Latine, oh he is as true an English man as lives. (*The Second Part of The Return from Parnassus*, 2.4.4–25)

However, the association with Martin Marprelate or with the ignorant old man does not necessarily lead to a diabolic connotation.

A third possible reading of 'truepenny' is provided by the character of Tom Trupeny in Nicholas Udall's *Ralph Roister Doister* (1552), published in 1567. When Lady Christian Custance asks Trupeny to fetch Sir Tristram Trusty, he immediately obeys her, promising to be as fast as possible. When he returns, not as swiftly as he had promised, he tries to justify his delay by Trusty's slowness:

> *C. Custance.* Trupenie dyd promise me to runne a great pace,
> My friend Tristram Trusty to fet into this place…
>
> *Trupeny.* Ye are a slow goer sir, I make God avow.
> My mistresse Custance will in me put all the blame,
> Your leggs be longer than myne: come apace for shame.
>
> *C. Custance.* I can thee thanke Trupenie, thou hast done right wele.
>
> *Trupeny.* Maistresse since I went no grasse hath growne on my hele,
> But maister Tristram Trustie here maketh no speede. (*Ralph Roister Doister*, 4.5.1–11)

The nickname that Hamlet gives the Ghost may thus take another meaning: it underlines the Ghost's celerity and announces its extraordinary movements under the stage.

'This fellowe in the Sellerige'

If this last reading is correct, it provides a non-diabolic link with 'this fellowe in the Sellerige' in the following line, as well as with the formula '*hic et ubique*' in the second cue. In general, the infernal connotation of this expression is justified by the association of the space under the stage with hell,[40] but such a simplification does not take into account the lexical peculiarity of 'cellarage'. According to the *Oxford English Dictionary*, Shakespeare is the first to use 'cellarage' in the sense of 'cellar'.[41] Such a word could therefore be surprising and thus insist on the place from where the Ghost is speaking, making the usual connotation less immediate. Of course, later 'cellarage' became widespread and the two meanings were associated for Shakespeare's successors. Around 1617 Anthony Brewer used this very word in *The Lovesick King*, merging the scene from *Hamlet* and Haughton's comedy. In his play, two characters are particularly interesting: Randal, 'a Coal-Merchant' and his servant Grim 'the Collier'. Not only does the latter evoke a memorable place for colliers ('they say there are a new sort of Colliers crept up neer *London*, at a place call'd *Croydon*', 3.19–20), but in a quarrel, among the titles he confers on himself one reminds us of our preoccupation: 'Shall *Grim* the Collyer that has been thus long Controler of the Cole-pits, chief Sergeant of the Selleridge, nay the very Demigorgan of the Dungeon, be call'd a Fresh-water Fellow?'[42] The juxtaposition of all these titles amalgamates the collier, the miner and the 'fellowe in the Sellerige' with the Devil, suggested here through the distortion of Demogorgon, a mysterious infernal divinity.

Like 'cellarage', Hamlet's Latin formula may be interpreted in two ways. The most widespread interpretation goes back to John Dover Wilson in *What Happens in Hamlet*.[43] Wilson mainly trusted his intuition to claim that *Hic et ubique* must be understood as a formula for conjuring demons.[44] He first developed this argument about Horatio's presence with the guards: as a 'scholar', Horatio is the only one to master Latin, and thus able to address the spirit. From there he deduced the role of Hamlet's Latin remark. It is interesting to note that both propositions raise serious problems of coherence, for Horatio never utters a word of Latin and Hamlet never evokes the least protection he could get from the Latin he uses. The advocates of the Ghost's diabolic nature also insist on the ubiquity of the apparition implied by the formula, despite the fact that both God and the Devil could be ubiquitous.[45] For Stephen Greenblatt the same formula was reminiscent of Catholic liturgy for the dead and thus pointed to Purgatory.[46] Arthur McGee proposed another allusion to ubiquity,[47] which he found in the parody of morality that Jonson staged at the beginning of *The Devil is an Ass* (1616): '[w]hat is he, calls upon me, and would seem to lack a *Vice*?/Ere his words be halfe spoken, I am with him in a trice;/ Here, there, and every where, as the Cat is with the mice' (1.1.44–6). Though at first sight the association seems to be present, Iniquity attributes this gift to his own abilities – not to Satan's. Moreover, the Vice compares this power to that of a cat playing with its prey, suggesting that this ubiquity does not correspond to a strict theological concept, but that it rather serves as a hyperbole for speed, as I demonstrated above for 'truepenny'.[48]

One last problem remains. When Hamlet pronounces the Latin formula, it cannot be justified by the Ghost's movement under the stage, because it is not certain that the characters move between the Ghost's first two cries. It is also hard to imagine that Hamlet comments on how quick the Ghost is to join the group of three men after it left at line 91, for the two moments are separated by a long monologue. Confronting the quoted examples of *Hamlet* and *The Devil is an Ass*, together with a similar allusion in *Twelfth Night* where Sebastian speaks of ubiquity on seeing Viola dressed as Cesario (5.1.220–22), reveals that in all three cases ubiquity rhetorically emphasises the surprise created by the apparition of Viola, of the Ghost and of Iniquity. This value of *Hic et ubique* even finds an internal confirmation in *Hamlet*. During its second visitation of Horatio and the guards, the Ghost being about to leave displays exactly the same talent which puzzles the terrified witnesses: '*Bar*. Tis heere./*Hor*. Tis heere./*Mar*. Tis gone' (Q2, 1.1.140–41). It is strange that no critic has ever thought of relating the two descriptions of the same supernatural power, and it is even stranger that no one thinks of accusing the Ghost of devilish ubiquity in this first scene. At that moment in the play, the only element the critics acknowledge as diabolic is the crowing of the cock that makes the Ghost fade. In his edition of *Hamlet*, Jenkins notes, with other commentators in his wake, that in the nineteenth century the Ghost's exit was sometimes performed by several actors, without linking it to the end of the act.[49] Hibbard suggests that these cues divert the audience's attention from the Ghost, covering its exit.[50] But if the first display of this power does not demonise the Ghost, why should the second?

'Mole'

Of the two remaining nicknames – 'mole' and 'pioner' – neither was used in moralities staging the Vice and the Devil, but Nevill Coghill found an occurrence of 'mole' in a comedy adapted from Plautus's *Amphitryon* – *Jack Juggler* (1555). Jack boasts of his conjuring powers as follows: 'I wil conjure the mole and God before.'[51] From the apparent opposition between 'God' and 'mole', Coghill inferred that the latter was a nickname of Satan and that 'Shakespeare has carefully planted the suggestion that the Ghost's voice, at this point in the play, seems to Hamlet of diabolic origin'.[52] Although Robert William Dent rejected this reading, arguing that it was unique in sixteenth-century drama, Battenhouse provided another parallel in Pierre le Picard who devotes a chapter to 'la talpe', in which the following mention is found: 'ceste beste a une example de deable'.[53] Nevertheless, the example is quite far from English drama and insufficient to establish a popular convention.

Another meaning equally appropriate for the scene in *Hamlet* may be found in yet another late morality, the only one to evoke the mole. The eponymous hero of *The Pedlar's Prophecy* (1561) rhymes 'moles' with 'coles' in one of the numerous prophecies: 'Therfore the most of them [i.e. Justices] saith he, shalbe turned into moles,/Because they are covetous, and in heart blinde:/Yet som of them shalbe turned into black birds, called coles,/Them he meane, that be ever gentle and kinde' (*The Pedlar's Prophecy*, ll. 1294–7). This passage belongs to a long scene in which Pedlar lists the metamorphoses that will punish the different layers of the population and above all 'men in their offices'. After the priests and the ministers, after the gentlemen, the fate that awaits the judges has two versions: the bad will become 'moles', the good 'black birds, called coles', though all will end up in hell. It is most likely that 'cole' here means more than just a black bird, and that the author puns here on the other meaning of 'cole', referring to a conjuring trick or jugglery, or even to 'cole-prophet', a soothsayer or magician.[54] In this context, the mole becomes a symbol of the soul, recalling the subterranean character of its infernal or Purgatorial abode. From the chronological point of view, this anonymous morality and Holinshed's chronicles are the most probable sources for the 'mole'. Thomas Creede published a quarto edition of *The Pedlar's Prophecy* in 1595 and,[55] as early as 1597, Shakespeare became interested in the mole in *The First Part of Henry IV*, when he took up Holinshed's prophecy: '[t]his was doone (as some have said) through a foolish credit given to a vaine prophesie, as though king Henrie was the moldwarpe, curssed of Gods owne mouth'.[56] In both prophecies the mole symbolises the damned soul in hell, which is quite close to the condition of the Ghost.

One last play shortly preceding *Hamlet* develops the image of the 'mole', using terms even more reminiscent of the 'cellarage scene'. At the end of the first part of the Parnassus trilogy – *The Pilgrimage to Parnassus* (1598) – Ingenioso denounces that it is easier to get rich though trade than through learning and adds the example of his host: '[s]eest thou not my hoste Johns of the Crowne, who latelie lived like a moule .6. yeare under the grounde in a cellar, and cried anon, anon Sir, now is mounted upon a horse of twentie marke, and thinkes the earth too base to beare the waighte of his refined bodie?' (5.116–21). Four very precise lexical parallels make the resemblance between the two texts more than a coincidence: like the Ghost, John is compared to a mole; like the Ghost, he is underground, and more precisely in a cellar; and like the Ghost, he cries.

More recently Margreta de Grazia observed that 'mole' links the Ghost to the earthly body in keeping with a more physical representation of ghosts in early modern ballads,[57] while for Ricard McCoy or Sarah Outterson-Murphy, the underground imagery mainly insists on the presence of an actor in flesh under the stage.[58]

'Pioner'

Similarly, 'worthy pioner' plays essentially on the area where the Ghost evolves during the sequence. It is just such meaning that William D'Avenant seems to retain when he combines the two in *Albovine* (1628): 'The Mole's the subtle Pioner:/For when she undermines the earth, her slow/Motion makes no noise' (3.1.291–3). In fact, no play before or after *Hamlet* associates 'pioner' with a diabolic context. On this point, the critics willing to systematise the demonisation of the Ghost in this scene have based their arguments on lexical convergence with demonological treatises, favouring two English sources: the English translation of Ludwig Lavater's *Of ghostes and spirites walking by nyght*, reprinted in 1596, and Reginald Scot's *The Discoverie of Witchcraft* (1584), which in fact borrows the whole section from Lavater. Both authors report on the existence of mine-haunting demons and both mention the term 'pioners':

> Pioners and diggers for mettal, do affirme, that in many mines, there appeare straunge shapes and spirites, who are apparelled like unto other labourers in the pit. These wander up and down in caves and underminings. (Lavater)[59]
>
> They also assault them that are miners or pioners, which use to worke in deepe and darke holes under the earth. (Scot)[60]

Neither passage is enough to make 'pioner' a devil's nickname, since the words unequivocally denote human beings – witnesses or victims – and not underground demons. Of course, Lavater writes that the latter like to put on a miner's shape, but he never uses 'pioner' to speak of them. Moreover, what Lavater writes afterwards totally contradicts Hamlet's attitude: '[t]hey very seldome hurte the laborers (as they say) except they provoke them by laughing and rayling at them: for then they threw gravel stones at them, or hurt them by some other means.'[61] Hamlet adopts the only attitude that Lavater advises against in his treatise: he laughs at and mocks the Ghost. And yet nothing happens; the Ghost does not throw gravel at him, nor hurt him by any other means. If Shakespeare had had Lavater in mind, would it make sense to go against the logic of his source?[62] In fact, most arguments about this nickname rest on the shift in meaning that the critics operate between 'pioner' and 'collier', and which is essentially intuitive.[63] On the other hand, it is worth observing that Shakespeare avoids the word 'collier', even though he exploits its infernal connotation in *Twelfth Night*, which might in fact imply that Shakespeare did *not* wish to suggest too sulphurous a ghost.

Thus, none of the nicknames chosen by Hamlet is overtly associated with the devil, and consequently none allows any clear insight into the Ghost's nature. Rather, their common feature is a reference to the area under the stage as the space commonly associated with the Devil, and the deflating of the dramatic illusion during this sequence, repeatedly reminding the audience of the actor moving under the stage.

Hamlet's antics and comic relief

The nature of this underground orator is not the sole question raised by Hamlet's familiar tone. It also leads us to interrogate what drives the young prince to act in this manner. Eleanor Prosser wittily evoked the different theories explaining this scene: '[w]e find that Shakespeare is tricking his audience by stopping for a playful parody; the printer is tricking the reader by including a scene from the old "Ur-Hamlet"; the Ghost is tricking Hamlet; Hamlet is tricking the Ghost; Hamlet and the Ghost together are tricking the two amazed observers'.[64] Two more tricks could be added to the list, even more fanciful. H. D. F. Kitto suggested that Hamlet alone hears the Ghost, as he later does in the closet scene, and that Horatio's amazement is attributable to Hamlet's strange behaviour.[65] Linda Kay Hoff carried the argument even further: there is no ghost in this scene and Hamlet plays a ventriloquist's trick to impress his friends and swear them to silence.[66] Prosser's own conclusions seem as questionable: 'Shakespeare made the Ghost act like a devil because he wanted his audience to notice that it acts like a devil'.[67] The only one to act here is Hamlet, not the Ghost, unless one considers the place it speaks from as a profession of faith. But this would mean forgetting what happened just before: for the sake of coherence, the Ghost can only come back beneath the stage since the morning light which it has fled prevents it from appearing again. For his own part, Martin Dodsworth rejected Prosser's interpretation on the ground that it is Hamlet – and not the Ghost – on which the audience's attention focuses in the scene, and offered his own theory: 'Hamlet suggests that the Ghost is of no account, but he may be doing so because he is afraid or because he wants to conceal his complicity with it from his companions'.[68] But assuming that the familiar tone diminishes the Ghost's importance, its repeated cries and Hamlet's use of them seem the very last way to hide this complicity. André Lorant explained Hamlet's agitation by melancholy, which was known at the time to provoke a hysterical state close to madness.[69] The melancholy hypothesis is appealing. On the one hand, Hamlet's character illustrates the different clichéd representations of this disease throughout the play; on the other, the oath sequence becomes more coherent when related to what Horatio says about the prince before the latter follows the Ghost: '[h]e waxes desperate with imagination' (Q2, 1.4.87). A little earlier Horatio had already warned his friend against the danger of facing an evil spirit who would 'tempt' him and 'draw [him] into madness' (Q2, 1.4.69–74).

Yet it is just as easy to assume that, when he meets his friends again at the end of Act 1, Hamlet does his best to allay Marcellus and Horatio's suspicions using his friend's suggestion of madness. This is how Peter Mercer saw it:

> To his companions of this night he must therefore minimise the importance of this extraordinary event and at the same time maximise the need for secrecy. If these are contradictory necessities they may be easiest embraced by a manic performance, a pretence of utter distraction, the 'wild and whirling words' that so astonish Horatio and Marcellus. What is essential is that they are sworn to secrecy. The portentousness, the pity and the fear, of the meeting with his father's spirit is smothered by a frenetic hilarity which presents Hamlet as a conjurer

and the Ghost as a familiar devil. It is also, no doubt, a necessary release of tension.[70]

Although Hamlet's 'performance' is still interpreted as conjuring a devil rather than a spirit, Mercer had the merit of recognising the importance of the comic dimension of the scene, which has since become widely accepted, though its precise mechanism has been little explored. As a rule, the comic elements that are mentioned are limited to the nicknames given by Hamlet to the Ghost, whereas they could be but the tip of the iceberg. Analysing the formula '*Hic et ubique*', Christopher Devlin suggested an explanation which is neither theological, nor theatrical, but liturgical:

> Encouraged by one fairly obvious reference to the Roman Breviary, one may find another in Hamlet's first reaction to the Ghost, 'Angels and ministers of grace defend us'... For the prayer in the Office of St Michael, 'May we be defended on earth by thy ministers in heaven' is accompanied by an antiphon which invokes the Angelic protection HIC ET UBIQUE... An ironic echoing of the Liturgy may be sufficient explanation of Hamlet's odd irruption into Latinity, 'Hic et ubique!', when the Ghost moans beneath him.[71]

If Hamlet is indeed being ironical about liturgy, this remark may be part of a wider network of anti-clerical satire present throughout the scene, notably in the meaning of 'truepenny' as associated with Martin Marprelate's controversy, in Hamlet's allusion to Purgatory ('by St Patrick') and, as suggested by Linda Kay Hoff, in the oath itself, considered by the Protestants as a superstition.[72] More generally, Rainer Pineas has shown the evolution of the medieval Vice figure towards a Catholic vice in the strongly anti-papist Protestant polemic drama.[73] Read in this light, Hamlet's remark on 'an honest ghost' may in turn become an anti-Catholic gibe. A similar interpretation is also possible when Hamlet replies to Horatio's doubts:

> *Hora.* O day and night, but this is wondrous strange.
>
> *Ham.* And therefore as a stranger give it welcome,
> There are more things in heaven and earth Horatio
> Then are dream't of in your philosophie, but come. (Q2, 1.5.163–6)

Indeed, Hamlet's answer first plays on a proverb ('give the stranger welcome') and on the meaning of 'strange'. It is only logical that the joke should carry on and in the two following lines Hamlet should kindly mock Horatio and, beyond, the theological theories on ghosts. Moreover, the end of line 166 – 'but come' – marks a change in tone, and given that afterwards Hamlet seems to have regained his respect for the Ghost, his remark on philosophy still belongs to the jovial register.

Following up on Devlin's liturgical contextualisation, Stephen Greenblatt privileged a serious reading of such allusions as evidence of the resilience of

Purgatorial beliefs. He added many other references to the Catholic ritual in England and showed that one of the prayers for the dead (*pro quiescentibus in cimiterio*) associated the Latin formula with the souls' rest and with Purgatory: '*Avete, omnes animæ fideles, quarum corpora hic et unique requiescunt in pulvere*'. Greenblatt concluded that 'the words *hic et ubique*, addressed to the spirit who seems to be moving beneath the earth, seem to be an acknowledgement of the place where his father's spirit is imprisoned'.[74] Yet it seems to me as likely that such words would be an acknowledgement of the place from where the actor playing the spirit is speaking. Maurice Charney suggested a similarly ironic reading for the last of Hamlet's comments on the Ghost: 'rest, rest, perturbed spirit'. For Charney, Hamlet reminds the audience that the Ghost had moved a lot under the stage and needs rest.[75] The prince puns on the two meanings of 'perturbed' – a restless actor out of breath and one of the wandering souls that '*requiescunt in pulvere*'. For after all, that is the real reason for the multiple oath taken by the characters onstage: there are no theological or legal obligations to repeat the oath let alone to shift grounds to do so. What calls for such a staging is the Globe's open stage itself, which is surrounded by the audience on three sides. Repeating the oath three times offers the public the view of an emblematic tableau, while making the most of the comic effect generated by fast movements to which 'rest, rest' puts an end. Thus 'perturbed spirit' comes last in a long list of names, the common point of which is to recall the Ghost's position in the theatrical space and consequently to shatter for a moment the dramatic illusion.

A third element adding up to the comic dimension of the scene seems never to have been envisaged. From his very first apparition, Hamlet shows a developed taste for puns and for the subversion of meaning in his dialogues with Claudius and with his mother. At the critical moment when Hamlet decides to follow the silent Ghost, it is with a pun that he gets rid of his friends trying to thwart him: '[i]le make a ghost of him that lets me' (Q2, 1.4.85), and later he shows the same propensity for puns when he kills Polonius. One might wonder whether all the nicknames used by Hamlet whenever he hears the Ghost might not be yet another implicit pun on the ambiguity of the Ghost's injunction to 'swear', that is to take an oath or to use profanity. The illustration offered by Shakespeare himself for this action in *The Second Part of Henry VI* might perfectly describe Hamlet's behaviour: '[o]ft have I seene the haughty Cardinall.../ Sweare like a Ruffian, and demeane himselfe/ Unlike the Ruler of a Common-weale' (1.1.183–7). The pun on 'swear' becomes even more likely if Shakespeare was indeed influenced by the Chester mystery play on Balaam for, in addition to providing the structure of the oath, the curses wished for by Balak may have suggested the shift in meaning from 'curse' to 'oath'. As for the reason for such a double meaning and the comic dimension of the play, they may well be an illustration of that 'antic disposition' that Hamlet asks his companions to keep secret. And, as each time he chooses to demonstrate it, '[t]hough this be madnesse, yet there is method in't' (2.2.202–3).

The ironic treatment of the ghostly figure shares a more general attitude of playwrights towards ghosts. The doubt about the Ghost's nature is a constitutive element not of this supernatural figure but of Hamlet; this is what makes tragedy radically different from theology. The gap between the demonised ghosts of the theologians and the visiting souls of the playwrights may be noticed in similar form between the divine canon against revenge and the avenging impulse of the individual. In both cases drama indisputably favours emotion over reason. This difference appears clearly at the end of the first act of *Hamlet*. The scene definitely establishes the Ghost as a figure of authority for, despite Hamlet's familiarity, it is thanks to its repeated injunctions that Marcellus and Horatio take the oath, when they were quite unwilling to comply with Hamlet's request. And when it returns later in the queen's closet, it still embodies authority, even though its very reality is being questioned.

Notes

1 This chapter is based on an earlier and broader investigation published in Pierre Kapitaniak, *Spectres, ombres et fantômes: Discours et représentations dramatiques en Angleterre, 1576–1642* (Paris: Honoré Champion, 2008).
2 Unless otherwise stated, all references to William Shakespeare, *Hamlet*, eds Ann Thompson and Neil Taylor (London: Arden Shakespeare, 2006).
3 John Dover Wilson, *What Happens in Hamlet* (Cambridge: Cambridge University Press, 1935), p. 78; Eleanor Prosser, *Hamlet and Revenge* (Stanford, CA: Stanford University Press, 1967), p. 139; Jean-Marie Maguin, 'Hamlet: Angel and Devil', in Pierre Iselin (ed.), *William Shakespeare: Hamlet* (Paris: Didier-Erudition, 1997), p. 73.
4 E. Pearlman, 'Shakespeare at Work: The Invention of the Ghost', in Arthur F. Kinney (ed.), *Hamlet: New Critical Essays* (London: Routledge, 2002), p. 83.
5 On the Purgatorial Ghost: Steven Greenblatt, *Hamlet in Purgatory* (Princeton, NJ: Princeton University Press, 2001); Pearlman, 'Shakespeare at Work', pp. 81–2; John Freeman, 'This Side of Purgatory: Ghostly Fathers and the Recusant Legacy in *Hamlet*', in Dennis Taylor and David Beauregard (eds), *Shakespeare and the Culture of Christianity in Early Modern England* (New York: Fordham University Press, 2003), pp. 222–59; Richard Wilson, *Secret Shakespeare: Studies in Theatre, Religion and Resistance* (Manchester: Manchester University Press, 2004), p. 118; David Beauregard, '"Great Command O'ersways the Order": Purgatory, Revenge, and Maimed Rites in *Hamlet*', *Religion and the Arts*, 11 (2007): 45–73; and Allison Shell, *Shakespeare and Religion* (London: Methuen Drama, 2010), p. 114. Preceding Greenblatt, Anthony Low also defended a Ghost from purgatory in '*Hamlet* and the Ghost of Purgatory: Intimations of Killing the Father', *English Literary Renaissance*, 29 (1999): 443–67.

6 See for instance Verena Theile, 'Early Modern Literary Engagements with Fear, Witchcraft, the Devil, and that Damned Dr Faustus', in Verena Theile and Andrew D. McCarthy (eds), *Staging the Superstitions of Early Modern Europe* (Farnham: Ashgate, 2013), p. 82; Brett E. Murphy, 'Sulphurous and Tormenting Flames: Understanding the Ghost in *Hamlet*', *Shakespeare in Southern Africa*, 26 (2014), 117–22.

7 Andrzej Wicher, '"The dread of something after death" – The relationship between Shakespeare's *Hamlet* and some medieval dream visions and ghost stories', *Studia Anglica Posnaniensia*, 45:1 (2009), 137–52; Catherine Belsey, 'Shakespeare's Sad Tale for Winter: *Hamlet* and the Tradition of Fireside Ghost Stories', *Shakespeare Quarterly*, 61:1 (2010), 1–27.

8 For the living tableau, see Alan C. Dessen, *Recovering Shakespeare's Theatrical Vocabulary* (Cambridge: Cambridge University Press, 1995), p. 14 and Marion O'Connor, 'Snakeskins, Mirrors & Torches: Theatrical Iconography & Middleton's *The Witch*', *Research Opportunities in Renaissance Drama*, 41 (2002), 15–28.

9 J. Q. Adams, 'Some Notes on *Hamlet*', *Modern Language Notes*, 28 (1913), p. 40.

10 Adams refers to the play as *Processus Prophetarum* which, in fact, corresponds to a play from the Towneley cycle. *Balaack and Balaam* is the subtitle of the fifth play in the Chester cycle in one of the manuscripts. The entire play has another title – *The Cappers* – and is composed of two episodes: *Moses and the Law* and *Balaack and Balaam*. A. B. Harbage dated this cycle between 1377 and 1382, and it was performed until 1575. My quotations come from the manuscripts on which R. M. Lumiansky and D. Mills based their edition of *The Chester Mystery Cycle* (1974–86) and which respectively date back to 1591 (MS. Huntington 2) and to 1607 (MS. Harley 2124).

11 After the first two prophecies indicated by stage directions at ll. 279 and 303, Balak mentions three blessings (316), before uttering a fourth (319).

12 Three cardinal points are mentioned at ll. 216, 240 and 264, and the final prophecy is at l. 312.

13 R. M. Lumiansky and D. Mills (eds), *The Chester Mystery Cycle* (Oxford: Oxford University Press, 1986), p. 71.

14 Although the references are from the Arden Edition, 2006, the text and spelling are original as indicated within brackets: here the Second Quarto edition.

15 A. C. Bradley, *Shakespearean Tragedy* (London: Macmillan, 1905), pp. 412–13.

16 William Shakespeare, *Hamlet*, ed. Harold Jenkins (London: Methuen, 1982), pp. 225–7 and note p. 459; William Shakespeare, *Hamlet*, ed. G. R. Hibbard (Oxford: Oxford University Press, 1987), pp. 194–5; William Shakespeare, *The Norton Shakespeare*, eds Stephen Greenblatt, Walter Cohen, Jean E. Howard and Katherine Eisaman Maus (New York: W. W. Norton, 1997), p. 1687–8; *Norton Shakespeare* (3rd edn, 2015), p. 1784; William Shakespeare, *Complete Works*, ed. Stanley Wells and Gary Taylor (Oxford: Clarendon, 2005), pp. 690–1; William Shakespeare, *Complete Works*, ed. Jonathan Bate and Eric Rasmussen (Basingstoke: Macmillan, 2007), p. 1941–2. Less consistently, Frank Kermode provides the stage direction only after the last oath (*The Riverside Shakespeare*, Boston: Houghton Mifflin, 1997), p. 1199. In contrast, there are no stage directions in Ann Thompson and

Neil Taylor's edition (pp. 224–6), nor in the latest New Cambridge Shakespeare, where Philip Edwards lucidly comments '[p]erhaps at this point Horatio and Marcellus silently swear on the hilt of Hamlet's sword… There is no indication in the text of when, if ever, the formal oath is taken' (Cambridge University Press, 2019), p. 119.

17 In a note to 1.5.149, Thompson and Taylor relate a modern Globe anecdote that gives strength to my argument here: '[i]t turned out however not to be practicable to have the Ghost speak from under the stage at the London Globe in 2000: the actor could not be heard by the audience; nor could he hear his cues' (p. 223).

18 *Cf.* Numbers 24:10; *Balaam and Balaack*, 163*ff.*

19 It may be worth pointing out that the presence of the Ghost under the stage is an exceptional motif in Elizabethan drama, found only in two inseparable tragedies – *Hamlet* and *Antonio's Revenge* – as well as in a later play inspired by *Hamlet*: *The Seven Champions of Christendom* (1635). See Kapitaniak, *Spectres*, p. 340.

20 *The Plays of William Shakespeare, with the corrections and illustrations of various commentators. To which are added notes by S. Johnson* (London: Woodfall et al., 1768), vol. 5, p. 367.

21 L. W. Cushman, *The Devil and the Vice in the English Dramatic Literature before Shakespeare* (Halle: M. Niemeyer, 1900), pp. 16–44 and 145; Bernard Spivack, *Shakespeare and the Allegory of Evil* (New York: Columbia University Press 1958), pp. 130–1.

22 Ulpian Fulwell's *Like Will to Like, Quoth the Devil to the Collier* (London: Iohn Allde, 1568; repr. Edward Allde, 1587); Thomas Garter's *The Most Virtuous and Godly Susanna* (London: Hugh Jackson, 1578); Thomas Lupton's *All for Money* (London: Roger Warde and Richard Mundee, 1578).

23 Samuel Harsnett, *A Declaration of egregious Popish Impostures* (London: Iames Robert, 1603), pp. 291–92.

24 Spivack, *Shakespeare and the Allegory of Evil*, p. 253.

25 The play was printed only in 1662 (in *Gratiae Theatrales, or A choice of Ternary of English Plays*, London: R. D., 1662), but thanks to Henslowe's diary we know that it was performed by the Lord Admiral's Men on 6 May 1600 at the Rose. See Alfred Harbage, *Annals of English Drama* (London: Methuen, 1964), p. 76.

26 According to the *Oxford English Dictionary*, 'dusty-poll' was a nickname for a miller and 'jobbernowl' designated a blockhead or just a blockish or stupid head. As for 'clapper-claw', Robin puns both on the character's name (Clack) and on his profession, as 'clapper' may refer to a contrivance in a mill (also 'clack' or 'clap'), while 'clapperclaw' means to thrash or drub.

27 Shorthose was the name of a thief, accomplice to the notorious highwayman Galamiell Ratsey, whose *Second Part of his madde prankes and adventures* published in 1605 after his execution alludes to *Hamlet* (sig. Br).

28 In *Susanna*, Ill Report also has recourse to a Latin formula, but when the devil is not there: 'Oh oh, *Est nomen Mulieris*' (l. 532).

29 For the other spelling, several entries of the Vice in *The World and the Child* (1522) are introduced with 'Aha'. *Cf.* also Ambidexter in *Cambyses*: 'A, A, now I have it, I have it in deed./My name is Ambidexter' (ll. 148–9).

30 Lupton's morality play directly reflects this aspect of Fulwell's text. The many insults with which Sin addresses Satan strongly recall Newfangle's: 'evill faste knave', 'bottell nosed knave', 'Sir good face' and 'snottie nose' (ll. 348–460). *Cf.* also Ill Report speaking to the Devil: 'you shitten slave, you crookte nose knave' (*Susanna*, l. 33).
31 S.A. Blackmore, *The Riddles of Hamlet* (Boston, MA: Stratford, 1917), p. 156; Nevill Coghill, *Shakespeare's Professional Skills* (Cambridge: Cambridge University Press, 1964), pp. 12–14.
32 R. W. Battenhouse 'The Ghost in *Hamlet*: A Catholic Linchpin?' *Studies in Philology*, 48:2 (1951), p. 179; Prosser, *Hamlet and Revenge*, pp. 140–1; Arthur McGee, *The Elizabethan Hamlet* (New Haven, CT: Yale University Press, 1987), pp. 68–74.
33 See Robert Muchembled, *A History of the Devil: From the Middle Ages to the present*, trans. Jean Birrell (Cambridge: Polity Press, 2003), pp. 15–16.
34 The former interpretation is defended by Nigel Alexander, *Poison, Play and Duel: A Study in Hamlet* (London: Routledge, 1971), p. 50; Kenneth Muir, *Shakespeare's Tragic Sequence* (Liverpool: Liverpool University Press, 1972), p. 59; and M. C. Andrews, 'Professor Prosser and the Ghost', *Renaissance Papers* (1974), pp. 27–8. Among the advocates of the latter see Jenkins (ed.), *Hamlet*, p. 459, and Martin Dodsworth, *Hamlet Closely Observed* (London: Athlone Press, 1985), p. 62.
35 The first two do not figure in Q1.
36 Kapitaniak, *Spectres*, pp. 653–6.
37 Thomas Nashe, *Works*, ed. R. B. McKerrow (Oxford: Blackwell, 1958), vol. III, p. 348. It is noteworthy that the reference to Nashe is more than likely, for in the scene from Dekker's *Old Fortunatus*, Fortunatus makes a direct allusion to Nashe's pamphlet: 'my tongue speakes no language but an Almond for Parrat' (ll. 57–8).
38 John Lyly, *Works*, ed. R. W. Bond (Oxford: Clarendon Press, 1902), vol. III, p. 417.
39 Leslie Hotson, *Shakespeare's Motley* (London: R. Hart-Davis, 1952), p. 116.
40 *Cf.* 'the dongyon where the deuyll dwelleth': Spivack, *Shakespeare and the Allegory of Evil*, p. 255.
41 See *OED*, 'cellarage', n. 1; the sixteenth-century meaning of this word was that of a tax on wine kept in a cellar.
42 Anthony Brewer, *The love-sick king, an English tragical history with the life and death of Cartesmunda* (London: Rob. Pollard and John Sweeting, 1655), 3.47–50.
43 It was notably taken up by J. E. Hankins, *The Character of Hamlet* (Chapel Hill: University of North Carolina Press, 1941), p. 157; Coghill, *Shakespeare's Professional Skills*, pp. 10–11; Prosser, *Hamlet and Revenge*, p. 140; Jenkins (ed.), *Hamlet*, p. 458; and McGee, *The Elizabethan Hamlet*, p. 68.
44 When Prosser takes up this idea, she backs it with a quotation from Fletcher's *The Night Walker*: '[l]ets call the butler up, for he speaks Latine,/And that will daunt the devil' (2.105–6). One might also remember the conjuration scenes in *Doctor Faustus* and in *Friar Bacon and Friar Bungay*.
45 See Coghill, *Shakespeare's Professional Skills*, p. 110; Prosser, *Hamlet and Revenge*, p. 140; Jenkins (ed.), *Hamlet*, p. 458; McGee, *The Elizabethan Hamlet*, p. 68.

46 Greenblatt, *Hamlet in Purgatory*, p. 235.
47 McGee, *The Elizabethan Hamlet*, p. 68.
48 It is similar to the allusions we can find in Reginald Scot's *Discoverie of Witchcraft* (London: Henry Denham for William Brome, 1584), where Scot makes fun of such impossible feats, underlining their speed rather than the actual being in two places at the same time. See 'The Epistle to Coldwell and Readman', sig. A8^v.
49 Jenkins (ed.), *Hamlet*, p. 175; Thompson and Taylor (eds), *Hamlet*, p. 161.
50 Hibbard (ed.), *Hamlet*, p. 152.
51 *An enterlude for children to play named Iack Iugler* (London: John Allde, *c*.1570), sig.[Aiii]^r.
52 Coghill, *Shakespeare's Professional Skills*, p. 12; Prosser, *Hamlet and Revenge*, p. 140; and Roy Wesley Battenhouse, *Shakespearean Tragedy* (Bloomington: Indiana University Press, 1969), p. 247, take this hypothesis for granted.
53 'This beast is an example of the devil', quoted by Roy Wesley Battenhouse, 'The "Old Mole" of *Hamlet*: I.v.162', *Notes and Queries*, 216 (1971), 145–6. Battenhouse takes up Pierre le Picard's quotation from the Polish edition of *Hamlet*: William Shakespeare, *Hamlet*, ed. Witold Chwalewik (Warsaw: Wydawnictwo Polskiej Akademii Nauk, 1963), p. 150.
54 *Cf. OED* articles 'cole' n. 2 and 'cole-prophet'.
55 The identity of the publisher is of utmost importance here. Indeed, the English reprint of Lavater's treatise in 1596 was the work of Thomas Creede, who was also responsible for several quarto editions of Shakespeare's plays from 1594 to 1602. Ludwig Lavater, *Of ghostes and spirites walking by nyght* (London: Thomas Creede, 1596).
56 William Shakespeare, *King Henry IV, Part 1*, ed. A. R. Humphreys (London: Methuen, 1960), Appendix III, p. 171. Shakespeare's equivalent line is '[w]ith telling me of the Moldwarpe and the Ant' (3.1.143).
57 Margreta de Grazia, *Hamlet without Hamlet* (Cambridge: Cambridge University Press, 2007), p. 29.
58 Richard McCoy, *Faith in Shakespeare* (Oxford: Oxford University Press, 2013), p. xii; Sarah Outterson-Murphy, '"Remember me:" The Ghost and its spectators in *Hamlet*', *Shakespeare Bulletin*, 34:2 (2016), pp. 264–5.
59 Lavater, *Of ghostes*, I.xvi, p. 73.
60 Scot, *Discoverie*, chap. III, p. 494.
61 Lavater, *Of ghostes*, pp. 73–4.
62 It is certainly not coincidental that both Dover Wilson and Jenkins stop quoting Lavater just before the passage I have just quoted: Dover Wilson, *What Happens*, p. 81; Jenkins (ed.), *Hamlet*, p 458.
63 Dover Wilson, *What Happens*, p. 81; McGee, *The Elizabethan Hamlet*, p. 70.
64 Prosser, *Hamlet and Revenge*, pp. 140–1; Dover Wilson, *What Happens*, p. 81.
65 H. D. F. Kitto, *Form and Meaning in Drama* (London: Methuen, 1956), p. 256.
66 Linda Kay Hoff, *Hamlet's Choice: Hamlet, a Reformation Allegory* (Lewiston, ME: Edwin Mellen Press, 1988), p. 262.
67 Prosser, *Hamlet and Revenge*, p. 141.
68 Dodsworth, *Hamlet Closely Observed*, p. 62.

69 André Lorant, *Hamlet* (Paris: Aubier, 1988), p. 56. *Cf.* also Northrop Frye, *Northrop Frye on Shakespeare*, ed. Robert Sandler (New Haven, CT: Yale University Press, 1986), pp. 82–100.
70 Peter Mercer, *Hamlet and the Acting of Revenge* (London: Macmillan, 1987), pp. 170–1. Similarly, Jean-Marie Maguin suggested that this 'frenetic hilarity' is a means for Hamlet to set the Ghost at a distance and regain his critical judgement, temporarily lost (Maguin, 'Hamlet: Angel and Devil', p. 74).
71 Christopher Devlin, *Hamlet's Divinity* (Carbondale: Southern Illinois University Press, 1963), pp. 31–2. This argument is taken up by R. F. Fleissner in 'Subjectivity as an Occupational Hazard of "Hamlet Ghost" Critics', *Hamlet Studies*, 1:1 (1979), p. 29.
72 Hoff, *Hamlet's Choice*, p. 262.
73 Rainer Pineas, *Tudor and Early Stuart Anti-Catholic Drama*, coll. 'Bibliotheca humanistica et reformatorica', vol. 5 (Nieuwkoop: B. de Graaf, 1972), p. 47.
74 Greenblatt, *Hamlet in Purgatory*, p. 235.
75 Maurice Charney, *Style in Hamlet* (Princeton, NJ: Princeton University Press, 1969), p. 172.

Bibliography

Adams, Joseph Quincy, 'Some Notes on *Hamlet*', *Modern Language Notes*, 28 (1913), 39–43.
Alexander, Nigel, *Poison, Play and Duel: A Study in Hamlet* (London: Routledge, 1971).
Andrews, Michael Cameron, 'Professor Prosser and the Ghost', *Renaissance Papers* (1974), 19–29.
Anon., *An enterlude for children to play named Iack Iugler* (London: John Allde, c.1570).
Battenhouse, Roy Wesley, *Shakespearean Tragedy: Its Art and its Christian Premises* (Bloomington: Indiana University Press, 1969).
—— 'The 'Old Mole' of *Hamlet*: I.v.162' *Notes and Queries*, 216 (1971), 145–6.
—— 'The Ghost in *Hamlet*: A Catholic Linchpin?' *Studies in Philology*, 48:2 (1951), 161–92.
Beauregard, David, '"Great Command O'ersways the Order": Purgatory, Revenge, and Maimed Rites in *Hamlet*', *Religion and the Arts*, 11 (2007): 45–73.
Belsey, Catherine, 'Shakespeare's Sad Tale for Winter: *Hamlet* and the Tradition of Fireside Ghost Stories', *Shakespeare Quarterly*, 61:1 (2010), 1–27.
Blackmore, S. A., *The Riddles of Hamlet* (Boston, MA: Stratford, 1917).
Bradley, Andrew Cecil, *Shakespearean Tragedy* (London: Macmillan, 1905).
Brewer, Anthony, *The love-sick king, an English tragical history with the life and death of Cartesmunda* (London: Rob. Pollard and John Sweeting, 1655).
Charney, Maurice, *Style in Hamlet* (Princeton, NJ: Princeton University Press, 1969).
Coghill, Nevill, *Shakespeare's Professional Skills* (Cambridge: Cambridge University Press, 1964).
Corbin, Peter, and Douglas Sedge, *Three Jacobean Witchcraft Plays* (Manchester: Manchester University Press, 1986).
Cushman, Lysander William, *The Devil and the Vice in the English Dramatic Literature before Shakespeare* (Halle: M. Niemeyer, 1900).
de Grazia, Margreta, *Hamlet without Hamlet* (Cambridge: Cambridge University Press, 2007).
Dessen, Alan C., *Recovering Shakespeare's Theatrical Vocabulary* (Cambridge: Cambridge University Press, 1995).
Devlin, Christopher, *Hamlet's Divinity* (Carbondale: Southern Illinois University Press, 1963).
Dodsworth, Martin, *Hamlet Closely Observed* (London: Athlone Press, 1985).
Fleissner, R. F., 'Subjectivity as an Occupational Hazard of "Hamlet Ghost" Critics', *Hamlet Studies*, 1:1 (1979), 23–33.
Fletcher, John, *The Woman's Prize or The Tamer Tamed* [1611], in *Comedies and Tragedies Written by Francis Beaumont and Iohn Fletcher* (London: Printed for Humphrey Robinson and for Humphrey Moseley, 1647).
Freeman, John, 'This Side of Purgatory: Ghostly Fathers and the Recusant Legacy in *Hamlet*', in Dennis Taylor and David Beauregard (eds), *Shakespeare and the Culture of Christianity in Early Modern England* (New York: Fordham University Press, 2003), pp. 222–59.

Frye, Northrop, *Northrop Frye on Shakespeare*, ed. Robert Sandler (New Haven, CT: Yale University Press, 1986).
Fulwell, Ulpian, *Like Will to Like, Quoth the Devil to the Collier* (London: Iohn Allde, 1568; repr. Edward Allde, 1587).
—— *Grim the Collier of Croydon, or the Devil and his Dame*, in *Gratiae Theatrales, or A choice of Ternary of English Plays* (London: R. D., 1662)
Garter, Thomas, *The Most Virtuous and Godly Susanna* (London: Hugh Jackson, 1578).
Greenblatt, Stephen, *Hamlet in Purgatory* (Princeton, NJ: Princeton University Press, 2001).
Hankins, John Erskine, *The Character of Hamlet* (Chapel Hill: University of North Carolina Press, 1941).
Harbage, Alfred, *Annals of English Drama* (London: Methuen, 1964).
Harsnett, Samuel, *A Declaration of egregious Popish Impostures* (London: Iames Robert, 1603).
Hoff, Linda Kay, *Hamlet's Choice: Hamlet, a Reformation Allegory* (Lewiston, ME: Edwin Mellen Press, 1988).
Hotson, Leslie, *Shakespeare's Motley* (London: R. Hart-Davis, 1952).
Jonson, Ben, *The Devil is an Ass and Other Plays*, ed. M. J. Kidnie (Oxford: Oxford University Press, 2000).
Kapitaniak, Pierre, *Spectres, ombres et fantômes: Discours et représentations dramatiques en Angleterre, 1576–1642* (Paris: Honoré Champion, 2008).
Kitto, H. D. F., *Form and Meaning in Drama: A Study of Six Greek Plays and of Hamlet* (London: Methuen, 1956).
Lavater, Ludwig, *Of ghostes and spirites walking by nyght* [1572] (London: Thomas Creede, 1569).
Lorant, André, *Hamlet* (Paris: Aubier, 1988).
Low, Anthony, 'Hamlet and the Ghost of Purgatory: Intimations of Killing the Father', *English Literary Renaissance*, 29 (1999): 443–67.
Lumiansky, R. M. and David Mills (eds), *The Chester Mystery Cycle* (Oxford: Oxford University Press, 1986).
Lupton, Thomas, *All for Money* (London: Roger Warde and Richard Mundee, 1578).
Lyly, John, *The Complete Works of John Lyly*, ed. R. W. Bond (Oxford: Clarendon Press, 1902).
Maguin, Jean-Marie, 'Hamlet: Angel and Devil', in Pierre Iselin (ed.), *William Shakespeare: Hamlet* (Paris: Didier-Erudition, 1997), pp. 67–80.
McCoy, Richard, *Faith in Shakespeare* (Oxford: Oxford University Press, 2013).
McGee, Arthur, *The Elizabethan Hamlet* (New Haven, CT: Yale University Press, 1987).
Mercer, Peter, *Hamlet and the Acting of Revenge* (London: Macmillan, 1987).
Muchembled, Robert, *A History of the Devil: From the Middle Ages to the present*, trans. Jean Birrell (Cambridge: Polity Press, 2003).
Muir, Kenneth, *Shakespeare's Tragic Sequence* (Liverpool: Liverpool University Press, 1972).
Murphy, Brett E., 'Sulphurous and Tormenting Flames: Understanding the Ghost in Hamlet', *Shakespeare in Southern Africa*, 26 (2014), 117–22.

Nashe, Thomas, *The Works of Thomas Nashe*, ed. R. B. McKerrow (Oxford: Blackwell, 1958).
O'Connor, Marion, 'Snakeskins, Mirrors & Torches: Theatrical Iconography & Middleton's *The Witch*', *Research Opportunities in Renaissance Drama*, 41 (2002), 15–28.
Outterson-Murphy, Sarah, '"Remember me": The Ghost and its spectators in *Hamlet*', *Shakespeare Bulletin*, 34:2 (2016), 253–275.
Pearlman, E., 'Shakespeare at Work: The Invention of the Ghost', in Arthur F. Kinney (ed.), *Hamlet: New Critical Essays* (London: Routledge, 2002), pp. 71–84.
Pineas, Rainer, *Tudor and Early Stuart Anti-Catholic Drama*, coll. 'Bibliotheca humanistica et reformatorica', vol. 5 (Nieuwkoop: B. de Graaf, 1972).
Prosser, Eleanor, *Hamlet and Revenge* (Stanford, CA: Stanford University Press, 1967).
Ratsey, Galamiell, *Second Part of his madde prankes and adventures* (1605).
Scot, Reginald, *The Discoverie of Witchcraft* (London: Henry Denham for William Brome, 1584).
Shakespeare, William, *Hamlet*, ed. Philip Edwards (Cambridge: Cambridge University Press, 2019).
—— *Hamlet*, eds Ann Thompson and Neil Taylor (London: Arden Shakespeare, 2006).
—— *Hamlet*, ed. G. R. Hibbard (Oxford: Oxford University Press, 1987).
—— *Hamlet*, ed. Harold Jenkins (London: Methuen, 1982).
—— *Hamlet*, ed. Witold Chwalewik (Warsaw: Wydawnictwo Polskiej Akademii Nauk, 1963).
—— *King Henry IV, Part 1*, ed. A. R. Humphreys (London: Methuen, 1960).
—— *The Norton Shakespeare*, eds Stephen Greenblatt, Walter Cohen, Jean E. Howard and Katherine Eisaman Maus (New York: W. W. Norton, 1997), p. 1687–8; 3rd edn, eds Stephen Greenblatt, Walter Cohen, Jean E. Howard, Katherine Eisaman Maus and Gordon McMullan (New York: W. W. Norton, 2016).
—— *Complete Works*, ed. Jonathan Bate and Eric Rasmussen (Basingstoke: Macmillan, 2007).
—— *Complete Works*, ed. Stanley Wells and Gary Taylor (Oxford: Clarendon, 2005).
—— *The Riverside Shakespeare*, ed. Frank Kermode (Boston, MA: Houghton Mifflin, 1997).
—— *The Plays of William Shakespeare, with the corrections and illustrations of various commentators. To which are added notes by S. Johnson* (London: Woodfall et al., 1768).
Shell, Allison, *Shakespeare and Religion* (London: Methuen Drama, 2010).
Spivack, Bernard, *Shakespeare and the Allegory of Evil* (New York: Columbia University Press, 1958).
Theile, Verena, 'Early Modern Literary Engagements with Fear, Witchcraft, the Devil, and that Damned Dr Faustus', in Verena Theile and Andrew D. McCarthy (eds), *Staging the Superstitions of Early Modern Europe* (Farnam: Ashgate, 2013), pp. 59–82.
Wager, William, *A comedy or enterlude intituled, Inough is as good as a feast very fruteful, godly and ful of pleasant mirth* (London: Iohn Allde, 1570).
Wicher, Andrzej, '"The dread of something after death" – The relationship between Shakespeare's *Hamlet* and some medieval dream visions and ghost stories', *Studia Anglica Posnaniensia*, 45:1 (2009), 137–52.

Wilson, John Dover, *What Happens in Hamlet* (Cambridge: Cambridge University Press, 1935).
Wilson, Richard, *Secret Shakespeare: Studies in Theatre, Religion and Resistance* (Manchester: Manchester University Press, 2004).

5

Performing the Shakespearean supernatural in Avignon: a challenge to the Festival

Florence March

Shakespeare ranks among the favourite playwrights whose works have been staged in the international Avignon Festival, founded in 1947 with a performance of *Richard II*. The Elizabethan dramatist still stands as a reference point in this festival of popular theatre addressing large audiences in all sorts of venues – most of which were not originally designed for the theatre. According to Jean Vilar, the Festival's founder, Shakespeare proved the playwright most fitted to measure up to the Honour Court of the medieval Popes' Palace, a monument designated a UNESCO World Heritage Centre as well as the cradle and centre of the festival, whose spectacular dimension challenges all the productions it hosts. Pregnant with history, the epic venue is haunted by ghosts from the past, its *genii loci*, with whom the apparitions dramatised in many Shakespearean plays must negotiate. Such negotiation is all the more complicated as the spatial configuration of the court not infrequently generates another type of ghostly manifestation when the *mistral*, a fierce provençal wind, swirls in the open-air quadrangle surrounded by monumental stone walls, like an invisible force which either magnifies or endangers the performance.

Drawing on the complete *corpus* of Shakespearean productions in the Honour Court that staged supernatural manifestations between 1947 and 2016, this chapter proposes to explore the interactions between text, performance and venue. A *locus* of conflicts, whether they actualise the hero's inner turmoil or oppositions between characters, apparitions also embody the challenging confrontation between performance and venue, theatrical event and spectacular monument, the transient and the permanent. As a metatheatrical motif, supernatural creatures question not only the theatrical medium but also the theatricality of the venue and their compatibility. The Shakespearean supernatural thus challenges the Avignon Festival while paradoxically confirming its mission as a platform for experimentation, a laboratory for the performing arts and a showcase of contemporary theatre.

Twenty-seven Shakespearean productions were programmed in the Honour Court of the Popes' Palace over the seventy times the festival took place between 1947 and 2016, fifteen of them involving supernatural elements. There were two stagings of *Macbeth*, by Jean Vilar (1954 and 1956) and by Jean-Pierre Vincent (1985), who was then the head administrator of the Comédie-Française; four productions of *Hamlet*, respectively by Georges Wilson, who was director of the Théâtre National Populaire (TNP) later known as the Théâtre national de Chaillot (1965), Benno Besson, the director of the Volksbühne in Berlin at the time (1977), Patrice Chéreau, then director of Théâtre Les Amandiers at Nanterre (1988), and Thomas Ostermeier, the director of the Schaubühne in Berlin (2008); four productions of *Richard III*, by Roger Planchon, who directed the Théâtre de la Cité of Villeurbanne, later to become the TNP (1966), Terry Hands, then involved with the Royal Shakespeare Company (1972), Robert Sturua, the director of the Rustaveli Theatre in Tbilisi (1981), and Georges Lavaudant (1984); two stagings of *The Winter's Tale*, successively by Jorge Lavelli (1980) and Luc Bondy (1988); one production each of *A Midsummer Night's Dream* by Jean Vilar (1959), of *As You Like It* by Benno Besson (1976) and of *The Tempest* by Alfredo Arias, then director of the Commune Theatre at Aubervilliers in the northern suburbs of Paris (1986). This *corpus* also includes a marginal case, Planchon's *Richard III*, which he refused to stage in the Honour Court, preferring an alternative venue in the same architectural ensemble: the square overlooked by the Petit Palais, only a few dozen metres away from the Popes' Palace – which has only ever been used in that 1966 festival.

This diachronic approach to the Shakespearean supernatural in performance faces the issue of memory, a crucial one where the ephemeral art of the theatre is concerned, as the productions under study are unequally documented. This is further complicated by the fact that, for each production, I was looking for traces of specific, sometimes fleeting passages: the ghost scenes in *Hamlet* and *Richard III*, the apparitions in *Macbeth*, the allegory of Time and the magical transformation of the statue in *The Winter's Tale*, the fairies in *A Midsummer Night's Dream*, the spirits in *The Tempest*, and the *deus ex machina* in *As You Like It*. I constituted my research object by confronting sources as varied as video and tape recordings (whenever possible), photos, programmes, press packs and reviews, working notes, correspondence and interviews. Although Vilar's productions are the oldest performances in the *corpus*, they rank among the best documented projects for Vilar was already well aware of the importance of data archiving to build up a budding history of the Avignon Festival.[1]

The archival material shows that performing the supernatural requires an in-depth exploration of theatrical codes and devices. Its spectacular dimension, which relies on particularly rich soundscapes and imagery, stimulates both the artists' and the spectators' imagination. Valérie Nativel appropriately points out that the word 'shape' that designates the ghost of Hamlet's father at the beginning of the tragedy gives free rein to the director's creativity.² The supernatural questions the very notion of performance, sitting on the dividing line between the visible and the invisible, the audible and the inaudible – characters in the plays are divided in two categories: those who can see and hear the apparitions and those who cannot. Faced with the need to materialise the immaterial onstage, theatre pushes back its boundaries. As Jean Vilar's and his collaborators' working notes indicate, representing the apparitions proved an ongoing problem throughout the long run of *Macbeth*, from its creation in the Honour Court in 1954 to its reprise in the 1956 Festival and in four consecutive seasons of the TNP between 1954–5 and 1957–8. Uncertainties persist regarding the costume of Banquo's ghost, performed by Jean Deschamps. A note on the first dress rehearsal on 18 July 1954, only two nights before the premiere, specifies: 'Banquo's ghost – a hood?' Further down, on a different page, another mention of Banquo's ghost reads like a reminder that the manner in which he was to be represented was still a problem to be resolved.³ For the play's revival at the TNP in 1955, a wig provided an unsatisfactory answer. A note on costumes and props reads 'Deschamps's wig'. In their rehearsal notes on the banquet scene, technical director René Besson and costume designer Mario Prassinos wrote respectively, 'Deschamps's wig: needs to be changed' and 'Deschamps's ghost: wig is no good'.⁴ Another note on the technical preparation asks: 'Will the witches be alive?'⁵ Embodied by three actresses, the witches spoke in disembodied voices, although this hybrid combination evolved between 1954 and 1956 to take into account the spectators' reactions. As audiences complained that the stereophonic effects made the witches inaudible, Vilar eventually gave them up, asking his actresses to speak in reedy voices instead. Patrice Chéreau was also aware of the issues raised by the performance of the ghost in *Hamlet*. The significant differences between Elizabethan and contemporary audiences in the reception of the supernatural create a challenge for productions wishing to generate surprise, fear and amazement in rational spectators who no longer believe in ghosts, all the while avoiding at all costs ridiculous situations that could turn tragedy into farce. To create a supernatural illusion, Chéreau carefully documented his project, going as far as commissioning a French translation of John Dover Wilson's *What Happens in Hamlet*, in which the Shakespearean critic analysed the three different theological points of view on ghosts defended by Marcellus, Horatio and Hamlet.⁶ The supernatural and the theatre intersect in so far as supernatural elements fuel the spectacular on stage while questioning the codes and limits of theatre as a medium, as well as the mechanisms of illusion. The supernatural is thus a powerful vector for theatricality and metatheatricality.

The special interaction between the supernatural and the theatre may also be accounted for by their shared structural characteristics. Equally concerned with the issue of illusion, whether metaphysical or theatrical, they are grounded on structural duplication. According to philosopher Clément Rosset, illusion is a phenomenon rooted in the dialectic of the real and its double. It takes place when the deceptive double is momentarily mistaken for its real counterpart, which is displaced, put aside.[7] Etymologically, *super-natural* means that another world is situated 'above' or 'upon' the natural one in reference to which it is defined. The supernatural is defined as the co-existence of two worlds and their interplay, as can be seen in the plays in this *corpus*, where dramatic power derives from the interaction of human characters with ghosts, witches, fairies, spirits and other creatures from the underworld, the netherworld or some other parallel world. The theatre juxtaposes two realities: the real world embodied by the audience and the fictional world represented on stage that alternately substitutes itself for the former or co-exists with it, depending on the spectator's moments of illusion or lack thereof. Revealingly, in the plays under study, the word 'shadow', defined by the *Oxford English Dictionary* as a copy, a counterpart, and thus involving a duplicatory schema, is used interchangeably to designate an apparition or an actor, tightly interweaving the supernatural and theatre. In *Macbeth*, the witches call themselves 'shadows' and the eponymous character designates Banquo's ghost as a 'horrible shadow' before comparing life with 'a walking shadow, a poor player'.[8] In *Richard III*, both Ratcliff and Richard refer to the ghosts that haunt the latter in his sleep as 'shadows' – a term the protagonist also uses twice to speak about his theatrical disposition.[9] In *A Midsummer Night's Dream*, Puck calls Oberon, king of the fairies, 'king of the shadows', before using the term as a synonym for actors in the epilogue: 'If we shadows…'.[10] In the *corpus* of Shakespearean productions for the Honour Court in Avignon, the structural motif of the double at a dramatic level is transposed onstage using several strategies, notably visual duplication, soundscapes and scenography.

Visual duplication materialises the dual perception that metaphysical and theatrical illusion jointly induce in the characters that are haunted by these apparitions, as well as in the audience. Costume design may thus give the impression that the characters, who are under the illusion that they see these apparitions and who serve to mediate the audience's gaze, see double. In Vilar's *Macbeth*, Jean Deschamps wore the same costume in two different colours, dark green and black when he played the living Banquo, and white with inlays of red felt symbolising blood when he embodied Banquo's ghost. In Besson's and Ostermeier's productions of *Hamlet*, the same actor (respectively Dominique Serreau and Urs Jucker) performed the ghost of the late king and his murderer, King Hamlet's brother Claudius. Besides emphasising their kinship by signalling them as twins, the device blurred the difference between supernatural and natural worlds, suggesting continuity and reinforcing doubts about the material existence of the apparition. The costumes designed by Ezio Toffolutti, black for the ghost and white for the king, showed them as inverted doubles. In this ambivalent colour code, the white costume was not only emblematic of kingship; it merged with the colour of the medieval stone wall in the Honour Court, already relating Claudius to the past, turning him into a shadow of himself, as if he were another ghost. In his production of *The Winter's Tale*, Bondy implemented a different strategy to achieve a similar effect: Hermione and Perdita wore exactly the same white dress, making the young woman the living double of her mother's statue.

Another strategy of duplication in the productions at issue consisted in having two soundscapes interfere onstage, suggesting that the characters under the illusion, as well as the audience, were hearing double. Recorded voices, voice-overs and radio microphones were meant to produce distance and eeriness. The Honour Court echoed with ominous laughter in the storm scene at the beginning of Vilar's *Macbeth*, while voice-overs dubbed the soundtrack of the tempest in the opening scene of Arias' production. Vilar's witches used microphones to provide a contrast with human voices, emphasising at sound level the co-existence of the supernatural and natural worlds. In Ostermeier's *Hamlet*, Jucker also spoke into a microphone when playing the Ghost, differentiating his performance as the Ghost from his role as Claudius without breaking their continuity. In the role of Macbeth, Vilar listened to the recording of his own voice in the dagger scene, but this device that artificially externalised his conscience was much criticised in Avignon and removed from the reprise two years later. Similarly, Lavaudant replaced the apparitions with voice-overs to evoke Richard's split self in the ghost scene, a strategy that according to some critics proved counterproductive as it paradoxically amplified and distanced the inner voices haunting the protagonist as he progressively turned himself into a ghost-like figure.[11]

Scenography also participated in visual duplication. Wilson seems to have combined or alternated strategies to stage the Ghost in *Hamlet*: actor Jean Martinelli, dressed in armour, was doubled by a light projection on the wall of the Honour Court.[12] Ostermeier similarly opted for a dual representation, both material and immaterial. The king's apparition was systematically filmed by Hamlet (Lars Eidinger), whose differing views on the world after his father's death was conveyed by the eye of a video camera, and screened on a curtain of metal beads. In Act 3, Scene 4, the Ghost stood by the curtain, which simultaneously mediated its image, emphasising its theatricality. This duplication process emphasised the double function of the curtain as a porous border between the natural and supernatural worlds, and as the *locus* of metatheatricality, since it hosted both the shadow and the shadow's shadow. The curtain metonymically embodied the power of theatre to self-reflexively summon and dispel illusions. The dual structure of the performance was mirrored by the twofold audience, in the auditorium and onstage, the latter being further split between Hamlet, who could hear and see the Ghost, and Gertrude, who could not.

Scenography sometimes reproduced the monumental wall of Elsinore Castle, in a synecdochic *mise-en-abyme* of the venue. For *The Tempest* directed by

Arias, Roberto Plate designed a stone wall with three arcades, partly in ruins, opening onto an unknown world inhabited by spirits. Plate's wall thus doubled the wall of the Honour Court and its capacity to create and sustain an illusion. In the space between the two walls, theatre and the supernatural met and merged. For Chéreau's production of *Hamlet*, Richard Peduzzi designed the stage platform as a wooden replica of the wall, as if 'the Avignon wall had fallen down in one piece and the print of its ruin had been drawn on the floor'.[13] Several trapdoors in the platform opened onto the underworld. The wall and stage thus hinged the representations of the natural and supernatural worlds as inverted doubles. For Bondy's *The Winter's Tale* in the same year's festival, Peduzzi also designed a huge wooden wall, itself replicated on a smaller scale by wooden panels that encased Hermione's statue in an endless *mise-en-abyme*. The scenography emphasised the dual structure that underlies metaphysical and theatrical illusions, and highlighted the ability of the Honour Court to reveal the theatricality of the supernatural. In one particular case, Planchon's staging of *Richard III*, the entire venue was doubled, as the show took place in the square in front of the stone façade of the Petit Palais, an alternative to the Popes' Palace at the foot of which it is located.

In Avignon, the Shakespearean supernatural results from a negotiation with the Honour Court and its *genii loci*. With its huge proportions, and walls steeped in history, the Court qualifies as extra-ordinary and provides an ideal setting for staging the supernatural. Monstrous in all senses of the term, it makes a show of its gigantic dimensions (from the Latin *monstrare*: 'show'). A magic box, a catalyst of creativity, it inspires spectacular scenographies. Created for the Royal Shakespeare Company in 1970 and programmed at the Comédie-Française in March 1972 before coming to the Avignon Festival later in July, Terry Hands's *Richard III* was hailed for its imaginative boldness, particularly in the final act staging the battle of Bosworth, 'presented as a weird dance, conducted by an allegorised figure of Death who led the ghosts towards Richard and delivered the final dagger thrust'.[14] The monumental, medieval court magnified the already spectacular *danse macabre*, as 'the ghosts come to torment the king grew in huge numbers on the stone wall'.[15] The shadows onstage and the shadows' shadows reflected on the façade combined to suggest an impressive crowd scene. The Honour Court enlarged Hands's inventive stage reading of the supernatural in Shakespeare's text to create successful site-specific theatre. The show won the award for the best production of the year from the French Syndicat de la Critique. The *locus* of apparitions and disappearances, the Court alternately reveals and conceals, playing with the dialectic of the visible and the invisible. For Chéreau's *Hamlet*, Peduzzi designed a stage platform that looked like 'a cabinet of wonders': trapdoors, drawers and elevators created positive and negative spaces as columns and their capitals popped out and sank down into the Palladian façade that lay flat on the ground.[16]

In Besson's successive productions of *As You Like It* and *Hamlet* in 1976 and 1977, pipelines all around the acting area spat out and sucked in the characters. Bright orange-coloured in *As You Like It*, they looked like hellmouths in *Hamlet*. The binary dramatic structure of *The Winter's Tale* predisposes it to illusionary effects on stage. Lavelli took advantage of this potential to implement a theatre of machines: the trapdoors in the black-lacquered mirror floor released characters, ferocious bears, a wooden horse, swings and a bed covered in soft, silky cushions. At each scene change, a huge white veil came down to cover the stage and actors. When it was raised, the actors had vanished into thin air. Powerful images progressively built up towards the supernatural dénouement, the magic of which infused the entire show, as evidenced by the semantic field of fantasy and wonder running through press reviews.[17] Similarly, the huge grey-and-white chessboard of Lavaudant's *Richard III* concealed traps, and in Vincent's *Macbeth* the witches and Banquo's ghost came up through a haze of smoke that paradoxically revealed the magic potential of the Avignon Honour Court.

The visual creativity that the Honour Court inspires finds its counterpart in spectacular soundscapes. Maurice Jarre, the inventor of musical stereophony, was the first to experiment with the Popes' Palace. For Vilar's creation of *Macbeth*, he mixed studio recordings (of bagpipes, to add a splash of Scottish atmosphere, for instance) and live sound performed by musicians hidden beneath the stage, playing with the huge space's volume to express all the shades, sonorities and colours of his composition.[18] He used an *ondes Martenot*, the eerie wavering notes of which reverberated in the court and enhanced the mysterious, poignant atmosphere of Shakespeare's tragedy. Jarre also composed the 'dramatic music'[19] of *A Midsummer Night's Dream* directed by Vilar, who claimed that the comedy could not be reduced to a mere fairy-tale, nor treated in a playful manner:[20] 'we had to work in a state of stunned confusion, in a hypnotic condition, in a daze naturally induced by the in-depth study of the play'.[21] Vilar stated '[t]he music won't be melodic (apart from the elves' songs), but rather spasmodic'.[22] Jarre accordingly worked on tempo and silences to suggest the 'palpitations of the night'.[23]

As a critic put it in a review of Wilson's *Hamlet*, '[t]he Papal Palace... provides the shadows, faces and words with a magic setting'.[24] According to Yves Bonnefoy, who translated *Hamlet* for Chéreau's production, the horizontal façade designed by Peduzzi confers on bodies an enigmatic character.[25] The *mise-en-abyme* of the monumental wall thus enhances the poetic function of the venue, its capacity to make the familiar unfamiliar and to turn the real into a riddle. The illusionistic power of the court exerts itself not only on the artists but also on the spectators, whose imagination it stimulates. For Vilar, the self-sufficient presence of the wall made the use of theatrical artifice unnecessary and even counterproductive.[26] Hands similarly asserted the necessity to 'excite the audience's imagination'.[27] In Lavelli's staging of *The Winter's Tale*, the eerie veils that shroud the stage are first and foremost suggestive. They invite the spectators to give free rein to their imagination and dream.[28]

Thus, the Honour Court superimposes its own mystery onto the performances it hosts. The sense of 'ghostliness' that, according to Herbert Blau, characterises theatrical performance in general, seems to be magnified in the papal city.[29] For Vincent, 'there are several layers of ghosts in Avignon'.[30] Through the centuries, the Popes' Palace was used for several purposes: erected in the Middle Ages to host the popes in Avignon, it became a prison after the French Revolution and served as military troop headquarters during the twentieth century, before becoming a World Heritage Site and a theatre venue from 1947 onwards.[31] Historical ghosts blend in with historic ones, such as Vilar's, or those of famous actors like Gérard Philipe and Maria Casarès, and those of the thousands of spectators who have participated in building up the mythic history of the Honour Court. The spectators' role in the hauntological process at work in the Court was the subject of Frédéric Nauczyciel's 2008 exhibition 'Public/Faces',[32] re-titled 'Those who are watching us' in 2009. Avignon audiences were photographed from the stage as they were watching a play, the exposure time being equal to the performance time. As a result, the blurred figures captured through the lens of the camera are depersonalized and acquire a historical dimension, evoking the ghostly cohorts of those who have haunted the court over seventy years. For French theatre director Ariane Mnouchkine, 'this place [the Honour Court] is full of ghosts, but they are benevolent ones'.[33] Yet the *genii loci* that have come to haunt it over the centuries have not always looked upon the theatre favourably. Vincent regrets that his production of the Scottish play encountered so many obstacles in Avignon, whereas its reprise at the Comédie-Française was quite successful: '[i]t may be that in the case of *Macbeth*, the ghosts have something to do with it, they are definitely unfavourable to it, the play's ghosts versus those of the [Avignon Honour] court'.[34] Vilar had already experienced mishaps with the Scottish play, the premiere of which was disastrous. Ill and overworked, he had fainted twice on that day and had memory issues with his role as Macbeth. Despite the presence of a doctor in the wings and of prompters placed at strategic points, he had to sit down with his back to the audience and read the text of a monologue, which a mistimed spotlight revealed to the whole audience. These circumstances were all the more regrettable as the audience already doubted the capacity of the frail poet to embody a butcher. On top of this, Jarre had been accidentally hit on the head by an iron bar that very same day and, as the conductor, had to be replaced by actor Gérard Philipe.[35] Thirty years later, Vincent had to face the *mistral*, which invited itself to the premiere with gusts up to 100 km/h, worsened by the quadrangular space. Playing tricks on the actors, the wind turned the tragedy into a comedy, as Macbeth had to hold on to his crown and Lady Macbeth's maid had to cling to her wide dress to prevent the queen from being carried away by the fierce wind. The *mistral* stole the show that night.

According to Vilar, the Honour Court is 'a theatrical place, but in the worst sense of the term', 'a bad theatrical place, because too pregnant with History'.[36] The spectacular element (the wall) resists the spectacular event (the performance), opposing monument to movement and permanence to transience. The staging of the supernatural seems particularly appropriate to reconcile these opposites. It is not then surprising that '[i]n Avignon, the bare stone was immediately matched by Shakespeare…',[37] an author who frequently dramatised the supernatural in his plays. In the Shakespearean productions under study, the supernatural alternately sets the monument into movement and petrifies the performance, animates the Court and disembodies the actors, personifies the venue and confers a monstrous dimension to the shows it hosts.

Performing the supernatural sets the monument into motion in various ways. In the now legendary ghost scene of Chéreau's *Hamlet*, the late king made a grand entrance riding a galloping horse. The striking image, reminiscent of the Horsemen of the Apocalypse and *The Triumph of Death* by Pieter Brueghel,[38] combined with a powerful sound effect as the steed's swift hooves drummed on the wooden platform. Right from the opening, through the mediation of the duplicated wall, Chéreau announced his intention to re-encode the spectacular façade of the Honour Court so as to foster a dialogic relationship with the performance. In Ostermeier's *Hamlet*, the see-through curtain of metal beads not only revealed and concealed the Ghost, but the wall on which it was superimposed and its porous theatricality contaminated the monument, the function of which it redefined. In Arias's production of *The Tempest*, the Honour Court was again put into movement obliquely and metonymically through the performance of Ariel on the reproduction of the wall. Three actresses alternately appeared and disappeared through the arcades and breaches so as to suggest the spirit's ubiquity. In the ghost scene in *Richard III* directed by Hands, the dancing shadows and their magnified reflection on the wall combined stage and monument in the same movement. Vilar's working notes for his creation of *Macbeth* show his deep concern to ensure the fluid and rapid succession of the twenty-six tableaux in two and a half hours, especially given that 'a translation slows down the pace' of the performance.[39] Omnipresent in the tragedy, the supernatural was a constant vector of dynamism in the Honour Court.

Sometimes, on the contrary, the supernatural temporarily freezes all movement. In Bondy's production of *The Winter's Tale*, the posture of the petrified Hermione suggested she had been surprised while in motion and was ready to resume her gesture. The magic statue thus embodied the dialectic of monument and movement, a phenomenon enhanced by the two wooden panels that framed her and looked like a reduced copy of the huge wooden wall onstage, itself evoking both a vertical stage and a double of the Court's façade. Two theatrical modes met and merged with the supernatural statue. Eight years earlier, the motif of petrification already ran through Lavelli's *The Winter's Tale*. In the opening scene, a huge white veil uncovered motionless characters who seemed asleep. When Leontes suddenly broke into a fit of madness, his cry 'Too hot, too hot!'[40] had a chilling effect: the maids of honour stopped dancing, striking a pose, and the music and whispering ceased. Such sequences paved the way for Hermione's transformation into a statue.

The figure of the ghost, in particular, plays a specific role in the encounter of the Honour Court with theatre performance, as it mediates between past and present, life and death, motion and immobility. In both Besson's and Chéreau's productions of *Hamlet*, the king's spectre was dressed in armour, like a medieval knight reviving the memory of the Popes' Palace and the legend underlying the play. The Ghost epitomised the historical dimension of the venue while making a show of itself, thus being doubly spectacular. Relying on the semantic field of theatricality that develops in Shakespeare's text with each apparition of Hamlet's late father, director Daniel Mesguich coined a portmanteau word, 'spectracle', to define the spectre-as-spectacle.[41] In a similar vein, the first version of Jean-Louis Curtis's French translation of *Macbeth* for Vilar insisted on Banquo's ghost as illusion rather than delusion or error in perception, although the final version chose the second option.[42] Interestingly, Chéreau cast the same actor, Wladimir Yordanoff, in the roles of the Ghost, of the player king and of the second grave-digger, the former being a synthesis of the latter two, since the Ghost actualises the historical past (mediated by the grave-digger) in the here and now of the performance (mediated by the player). Whereas the Ghost in Besson's *Hamlet* failed to strike a balance between the opposite terms of the dialectic of motion and immobility, the armour that impeded his movements turning him into a comical figure, Chéreau overcame the technical problem by having the apparition ride a horse. An allegory of death with a gaunt face, prominent veins and sunken eyes, the Ghost set the Honour Court in motion while petrifying both characters and audience. Hamlet fell to his knees in a posture that, by contrast, magnified the supernatural creature. Besson's Hamlet, Horatio, Bernardo and Marcello similarly froze in dismay, like Vilar's Macbeth confronted with Banquo's spectre. But the Ghost in Chéreau's production also stunned the spectators as it made the venue unfamiliar, turning the audience into other guards watching from the battlements of Elsinore Castle. As a result of this contamination, the whole scene became spectral and still haunts the memory of those who attended the performances.[43]

Staging the supernatural in the Honour Court inspired other strategies of defamiliarisation, such as personifying the venue while dehumanising the characters who inhabit it. Constantly in movement, the stage platform designed by Peduzzi as a dynamic version of the monumental façade for Chéreau's *Hamlet* invited comparisons with 'a huge breathing womb',[44] the two walls figuring 'both the foundations and the gestation',[45] not only of the past and the present respectively, but also of the historical venue and the production it hosted. In *The Winter's Tale* directed by Lavelli, the wind ruffled under 'the immense crumpled dress'[46] of the Court that 'shivered'[47] as it came to life. For Vincent's *Macbeth*, scenographer Carlo Tommasi dressed the venue in deep mourning and covered its façade with black tulle sucked in by the window frames, suggesting 'dark, sunken eyes.'[48] Like a mask on the face of the Court, the veil signalled its theatricality. Visually echoing the three hags' long, black robes, it turned the Honour Court itself into a monstrous witch, emphasising its magic potential.

Performing the supernatural in this historic monument leads directors to engage with its unnatural proportions. Monstrosity thus contaminates the dramatic characters. In Vilar's *Macbeth*, Prassinos turned the witches into animals, gigantic night birds, halfway between owls and vultures. In his working notes, Vilar warned actress Mona Dol, who played the first witch, against making sharp movements with her wings, which would reveal her arms.[49] The dehumanising process also involved alienating their voices. Yet the use of microphones missed its point as it produced burlesque animalisation, the witches 'voices sounding exactly like that of an angry Donald Duck in Walt Disney cartoons'.[50] Not only did their voices sound strange, they seemed to speak a foreign language. A critic ironically underlined the coherence between the visual aspect of the ghostly night birds and their incomprehensible chatter.[51] Their bestiality contaminated Macbeth, a borderline character who is the only one to see Banquo's ghost. Prassinos dressed him in a long, woollen coat made using the technique of Mykonos rugs, meant to thicken Vilar's figure and give the impression that he was wearing a black and silver animal skin.[52] On the battlefield, the caparisoned warriors looked like green and gold beetles.[53] A similar zoomorphic process was also at work in Vincent's *Macbeth* whose costumes by famous *haute couture* designer Thierry Mugler were the most expensive in the history of the Comédie-Française. Highlighting their huge proportions, in keeping with those of the Honour Court, Vincent called these costumes 'monstrous'.[54] Lady Macbeth's 2.5 metre-wide dress turned her into a golden insect,[55] and male actors in black, quilted and studded costumes with big shoulder and leg pads, helmets and gloves, resembled 'insects caught in a giant cobweb'.[56] As for the witches, they blurred genders, as though the unsexing that Lady Macbeth called for at the end of Act 1 applied to them. Inspired by Frans Hals's *Regentesses of the Old Men's Almhouse* (1664) in particular, and Rembrandt's paintings in general, the witches wore long robes that hid their body forms, topped by enormous black millstone collars from which their bald pates emerged. In Arias's production of *The Tempest*, Ariel was also dressed in a long-sleeved, loose, black gown and a cloak of the same colour suggesting bat wings. The ghost rider in Chéreau's *Hamlet* also conjured up an animal image, that of a black centaur. Already visually united by the same colour, horse and rider were even more connected as the ghost's cloak was wrapped around the animal's rump. The sudden intrusion of a mythological creature into the Honour Court not only set the venue into motion but provoked the audience's emotions as they experienced an 'aesthetic shock'.[57]

Although the dual structure of illusion, both theatrical and metaphysical, tends to deepen the divide between the natural and supernatural worlds, some of the productions under study also develop a logic of continuity which tended to erase such dichotomy. Supernatural elements thus ensure the connection between past and present, the permanence of stone and the transience of performance. In *The Winter's Tale* directed by Lavelli, the allegory of Time was embodied by Maria Casarès, a famous actress who had marked the history of the Avignon Festival since her successful performance of Lady Macbeth in Vilar's 1954 production. She spun around, draped in an immense white veil decorated with discrete, linear grey motifs like lines of writing, suggesting a huge palimpsest of all the texts and scripts that had been performed in the Honour Court since 1947. The allegory took on double significance, as absolute Time, thus fulfilling its dramatic function, and as historical time, referring to the twofold memory of the heritage monument and of the Avignon Festival. Taking advantage of her ambivalent role as chorus, which allowed her to address the audience directly, Casarès asked them boldly '[d]o you recognise me?' Blurring the difference between person and *persona*, the actress and her role, she anchored the ephemeral performance in the history of the Avignon Festival which she instantly unfolded, along with the white veil, in front of the spectators. Continuity was enhanced as Casarès's gesture could also be read as an invitation to complete the palimpsest of stage writings. Aesthetically and symbolically powerful, this sequence has acquired legendary status, like the ghost scene in Chéreau's *Hamlet*. In the latter production, the spectre also performed circular movements to connect various temporal dimensions. At a dramatic level, the Ghost brought Danish history, to which he contributed as king, into the present of his successor's reign. At the level of performance, he linked the medieval wall from which he entered with the Palladian stage platform on which he rode his horse, thus connecting the time when the venue was erected and the time when the play was composed. Both a transgression and a transition, the apparition defined the Honour Court as an in-between, reversible space-time.

However, continuity in the representation of the natural and supernatural worlds sometimes results in the absorption of one by the other. In some productions, the supernatural prevailed. In Planchon's *Richard III*, continuity was ensured visually by the colour code of the costumes. Designer Claude Lemaire opted for a beige colour scheme which ranged from off-white to brown, thus providing variety within unity. Her choice evoked the white rose, emblematic of the York dynasty which has just acceded to the throne at the beginning of the play. Merging with the stone façade of the Petit Palais, the costumes emphasised the fact that the dramatic action and the venue both harked back to the Middle Ages. The embodied ghosts were not dressed differently from the other characters, nor were they dealt with in a spectacular way. For Lemaire, white already signalled immateriality, which meant that all the characters qualified as living dead.[58] The world of the dead did not appear as a world of shadows, a mere reflection of the world of the living, but as the reference. The supernatural became the norm, against which the real world qualified as an illusion. Lavaudant's *Richard III* also relied on transforming the characters into spectres. The immaterial apparitions manifested their presence through disembodied voices, while Richard (Ariel Garcia-Valdès), preparing for combat, wrapped himself in white bandages. Even as he dealt with inner ghosts, Richard became the shadow of himself.[59]

In other productions, the opposite approach resulted in the complete denial of the supernatural in favour of extreme realism. Besson thus cut out the *deus-ex-machina* Hymen from *As You Like It*. His 'caricatural realism' disappointed expectations: 'the realism of the stage arrangement, its materiality, proved his refusal to play with the magic inherent to the venue'.[60] Similarly, in Heiner Müller and Matthias Langhoff's adaptation of *Hamlet* directed by Besson, the Ghost was treated as a historical heritage rather than a supernatural creature. The show, which premiered in the Volksbühne, in East Berlin, three months before being re-created in French at the Avignon Festival, proposed an iconoclastic, ideological reading of Shakespeare's tragedy that stripped it of all metaphysical dimension to focus on the socio-political elements of the fable.[61] From the beginning, the Ghost symbolised the festivalgoers' frustration, which derived from the disconnection between the representation of the late king and the monumental, legendary venue. Embodied by a fat man hindered by his armour, helmet, shield, sword and flail, speaking in a paradoxically quavering, whining voice, the de-spectralised spectre seemed out of place in the haunted Honour Court.[62] *Richard III* by the Rustaveli Company, directed by Sturua, also kept the supernatural at a distance to advance a political allegory. The famed production that was played at Tbilisi in 1978, Edinburgh in 1979 and London in 1980, was met enthusiastically in Avignon the following year. Aiming to burlesque dictatorial regimes, Sturua resorted to Brechtian theatrical techniques, 'modified by the concepts of the carnival and the grotesque as set out by Mikhail Bakhtin'.[63] The critics of the play in Avignon – in Georgian without surtitles – unanimously celebrated the evocative power of the last scene, which here again merged the ghosts' apparitions and the duel opposing Richard and Richmond.[64] As they fought, their heads and swords sticking through a gigantic map of Britain, Richard and Richmond visually composed a single monstrous body, in keeping with the disproportionate venue, and symbolically merged into the same body politic, suggesting that the pattern of despotism is cyclical and that tyranny, far from being expunged by Richard's death, would continue in other forms. Dressed in white, the ghosts attending the duel were all too realistic witnesses of history, just like the real audience facing them. The spectacular staging of the medieval map, a metonymy of history, proposed a resolution of the dialectic opposing monument to movement, the permanent to the transient. In this highly theatrical ghost scene, poetry and history interacted to revive the memory of the Honour Court while stimulating its magnifying power.

The Shakespearean supernatural at the Avignon Festival celebrates the encounter of theatre, a hauntological art based on the disjunction between presence and absence, with a haunted heritage monument, the Popes' Palace. Characterised by a dual structure, the theatre is grounded on the dialectic of person and *persona* at the level of performance, and of illusion and denial at the level of reception. A shadow of the world which it duplicates onstage, theatrical performance is recurrently embodied by the figure of the ghost as 'spectracle' or 'spectre-as-spectacle' in Shakespeare's drama. Plays dramatising supernatural manifestations are doubly theatrical, since they are fables about shadows performed by shadows. The supernatural thus induces metatheatricality and reflects on the medieval Honour Court – a spectacular venue, with its monstrous architecture and rich history – to such an extent that staging the supernatural magnifies the theatrical medium and the Honour Court, while simultaneously deconstructing their nature and function.

The Shakespearean productions analysed in this chapter provide a wide range of supernatural manifestations, from ghosts to witches, fairies and spirits. They delineate a typology depending on how they deal with the apparitions, both dramatic and historical, and how they deal with the dialectics of monument and movement, the permanent and the transient, so as to reconcile two different modes of spectacularity. These productions hold a special place in the history of the Avignon Festival, a showcase of contemporary theatre and a laboratory for creation. Stimulating inventiveness, the performance of the supernatural has inspired national and international productions, many of which still haunt the memories of festivalgoers.

Notes

1 I wish to express my utmost gratitude for their unfailing help to the staff of the Performing Arts Department at the Bibliothèque nationale de France: its director Joël Huthwohl, Lenka Bokova, curator at the Maison Jean Vilar in Avignon, and her assistants Catherine Cazou, Muriel Delage and Estelle Richard, as well as to the staff of the Association Jean Vilar at the Maison Jean Vilar, particularly its former director Jacques Téphany and project manager Frédérique Debril, for their generous assistance and sound advice. My heartfelt thanks go to Jean-Michel Déprats, the translator of *Richard III* and *Macbeth* for Lavaudant's and Vincent's productions respectively; Ariel Garcia-Valdès, who played Richard III in 1984; Claude Lemaire, set and costume designer for Planchon's production of *Richard III* in 1966; Jacques Le Marquet, set designer for Wilson's *Hamlet* in 1965; and

Jean-Pierre Vincent, who directed *Macbeth* in 1985, as they all kindly agreed to answer my questions. I would like to extend my deepest gratitude to Janice Valls-Russell, the reviews and managing editor of *Cahiers Élisabéthains*, for her invaluable help and constant support.

2   Valérie Nativel, '"Such a questionable shape": pour une lecture de l'entrée en scène du Spectre dans l'*Hamlet* de Patrice Chéreau', *Revue d'histoire du théâtre*, 250 (2011), p. 167.

3   Respectively 'Banquo spectre – cagoule?' and 'Fantôme Banquo'. Fonds Jean Vilar, 4-JV-127, 5. The Jean Vilar archives are kept at the Performing Arts Department of the Bibliothèque nationale de France in Avignon (Maison Jean Vilar). All translations from the French are mine, unless otherwise specified.

4   'Perruque Deschamps', Fonds Jean Vilar, 4-JV-127, 14. Besson: 'perruque Deschamps à changer', Prassinos: 'perruque Deschamps spectre est mauvaise'. Fonds Jean Vilar, 4-JV-127, 15.

5   'Les sorcières seront-elles vivantes?' Fonds Jean Vilar, 4-JV-127, 13.

6   John Dover Wilson, *Vous avez dit Hamlet?* (*What Happens in Hamlet*, Cambridge: Cambridge University Press, [1935] 1990), trans. Dominique Goy-Blanquet, foreword by Patrice Chéreau and Claude Stratz (Paris: Aubier and Nanterre, Théâtre des Amandiers, 1988). Dominique Goy-Blanquet, whose translation was commissioned by Chéreau, recently issued a monograph on the stage and film director: *Shakespeare in the Theatre: Patrice Chéreau* (London: Bloomsbury, The Arden hakespeare, 2018). Chapter IV in particular is devoted to his production of *Hamlet* (pp. 87–112).

7   Clément Rosset, *The Real and its Double* (*Le Réel et son double: essai sur l'illusion*, Paris: Gallimard, 1976), trans. Chris Turner (Chicago: University of Chicago Press, 2012).

8   William Shakespeare, *The Tragedy of Macbeth*, ed. Henri Suhamy, a bilingual edition, trans. Jean-Michel Déprats, in *Œuvres completes*, vol. II, coll. Bibliothèque de La Pléiade (Paris: Gallimard, 2002), 4.1.110, 3.4.107 and 5.5.24. As Déprats translated *Macbeth* and *Richard III* for two of the productions under study, quotations from these texts and all plays by Shakespeare refer to his bilingual edition of the complete works.

9   William Shakespeare, *The Tragedy of Richard III*, ed. Gisèle Venet, a bilingual edition, trans. Jean-Michel Déprats, in *Œuvres completes*, vol. III, coll. Bibliothèque de La Pléiade (Paris: Gallimard, 2008), respectively: 5.3.216, 5.3.217, 1.1.26 and 1.2.267.

10 William Shakespeare, *A Midsummer Night's Dream*, ed. Gisèle Venet, a bilingual edition, trans. Jean-Michel Déprats, in *Œuvres completes*, vol. V, coll. Bibliothèque de La Pléiade (Paris: Gallimard, 2013), respectively: 3.2.347 and 5.1.406.

11 See for instance Jean-Pierre Thibaudat in *Libération*, 23 July 1984, and Guy Dumur in *Le Nouvel Observateur*, 3 August 1984.

12 See programme as well as press review: RPFA-1965, Bibliothèque nationale de France at Maison Jean Vilar, especially André Paris, 'Le *Hamlet* intelligent, mais appliqué, du TNP ne vaut pas celui de "notre" Théâtre national…', *Le Soir*, 31 July 1965.

13 'On dirait en somme que le mur d'Avignon s'est abattu d'un coup, qu'on a dessiné l'empreinte de sa ruine.' François Régnault, Chéreau's dramaturge, quoted by Valérie Nativel, 'Such a questionable shape', p. 163.
14 See the website of the Royal Shakespeare Company. Available at: www.rsc.org.uk/richard-iii/past-productions/1963–2003, accessed 26 April 2019.
15 'Les fantômes, venus tourmenter le souverain, sont multipliés en nombre gigantesque sur les pierres…'. Pierre Mazars, 'Michel Aumont dans *Richard III*', *Le Figaro*, 23 July 1972.
16 Interview with Richard Peduzzi by Georges Banu. Available at: http://fresques.ina.fr/en-scenes/fiche-media/Scenes05019/richard-peduzzi.html, chapter 17: 'Un cabinet de curiosités. Dévoilé et caché. L'esthétique allemande. Appia', accessed 21 July 2016.
17 Press review RPFA-1980 (13), Bibliothèque nationale de France at Maison Jean Vilar.
18 Gisèle and Jean Boissieu, *Nos Années Vilar*, preface by Paul Puaux (Gémenos: Éditions Autres Temps, 1994), p. 86.
19 In an interview in 1952, Maurice Jarre divided his musical compositions for the Théâtre National Populaire into two categories: 'background music' ('musique-décor'), meant to recreate a certain historical atmosphere, and 'dramatic music' that aims to enhance the text and the characters' psychological evolution. Vilar considered stage music as an essential element in a theatre production. *Cahiers Jean Vilar*, 112 (2012), 51.
20 Jean Vilar, *Notes de service, Lettres aux acteurs et autres textes, 1944–1967*, eds Frédérique Debril and Jacques Téphany (Arles: Actes Sud, 2014), p. 182.
21 'Il a fallu travailler dans un état troublant, une sorte d'hypnose, un état second auquel conduit naturellement l'étude en profondeur de la pièce.' Jean Vilar, 'Declaration of Mr Vilar in Genève on 9 June 1959', Fonds Jean Vilar, 4-JV-147, 3.
22 Vilar, *ibid*.
23 The phrases 'palpitations of nature' and 'palpitations of the night' ('palpitations de la nature', 'palpitations nocturnes') constantly recur in the French text of the play, annotated for the conducting of the music. Fonds Jean Vilar, 4-JV-147, 1.
24 'Le Palais… donne aux ombres, aux visages et aux mots un cadre magique.' Bertrand Poirot-Delpech, '*Les Troyennes* et *Hamlet*', *Le Monde*, 31 July 1965.
25 Yves Bonnefoy, 'Le lieu, l'heure, la mise en scène', in Sylvie de Nussac (ed.), *Nanterre-Amandiers, les années Chéreau, 1982–1990* (Paris: Éditions de l'Imprimerie nationale, 1990), p. 16.
26 An interview with Jean Vilar: 'Jean Vilar met en scène *Le Songe d'une nuit d'été*', 1min 27sec. Available at: www.ina.fr/video/I04328872, accessed 26 April 2019.
27 'Exciter l'imagination du public.' An interview with Terry Hands about *Richard III*, Fonds Paul Puaux, 4-FA-494/4-ACOL-1 (482, 4)/321.
28 See Pierre Sahel, 'Shakespeare au Festival d'Avignon. *Le Conte d'hiver*. Adaptation française de Claude-André Puget. Mise en scène de Jorge Lavelli. Le Théâtre de la Ville (Paris). Cour d'honneur du Palais des Papes, le 18 juillet 1980', *Cahiers Élisabéthains*, 18 (1980), 111–14, especially p. 112.

29 Quoted by Marvin Carlson in *The Haunted Stage: The Theatre as Memory Machine* (Ann Arbor: University of Michigan Press, 2001), p. 1. In his book, Marvin Carlson explores the close relationships between theatre and memory, and documents the ubiquity of 'ghosting' in word, body and performance site. This is also the subject of Monique Borie's *Le Fantôme ou le théâtre qui doute, essai* (Arles: Actes Sud/ Académie Expérimentale des Arts, 1997).

30 'Les fantômes de Jean-Pierre Vincent', an interview with Jean-Pierre Vincent by Jean-Bernard Pouy, in Jean Viard (ed.), *Avignon*, journal *Autrement*, series France 1 (1990), p. 186.

31 See Dominique Vingtain (ed.), *Le Palais des Papes, monument de l'histoire: construire, reconstruire, XIVe siècle–XXe siècle*, the catalogue of the exhibition 29 June–29 September 2002 (Avignon: Éditions RMG, 2002).

32 The concept of hauntology was theorised by Jacques Derrida in *Specters of Marx: The State of the Debt, the Work of Mourning and the New International* (*Spectres de Marx*, Paris: Galilée, 1993), trans. Peggy Kamuf (London and New York: Routledge, 1994). A portmanteau of haunting and ontology, hauntology replaces 'the priority of being and presence with the figure of the ghost as that which is neither present, nor absent, neither dead nor alive'. Colin Davis, '*État présent.* Hauntology, spectres and phantoms', *French Studies*, LIX:3 (2005), p. 373.

33 'Ce lieu est plein de fantômes, mais ce sont de bons fantômes.' 'Ariane Mnouchkine, entretien serein', an interview with Ariane Mnouchkine by Pouy, in Viard (ed.), *Avignon*, p. 176.

34 'Peut-être que pour *Macbeth*, les fantômes y sont pour quelque chose, définitivement défavorables, ceux de la pièce contre ceux de la Cour.' 'Les fantômes de Jean-Pierre Vincent,' an interview with Vincent by Pouy, in *ibid.*, p. 188.

35 Fernand Bertal, 'Le Festival d'Avignon, merveilleux spectacle d'art populaire', *Le Nouvelliste*, 5 August 1954, and Boissieu, *Nos Années Vilar*, pp. 72 and 75.

36 'Un lieu théâtral mais dans le plus mauvais sens du mot'; 'un mauvais lieu théâtral parce que l'Histoire y est trop présente'. Jean Vilar, 'Un lieu théâtral: Avignon', in Denis Bablet and Jean Jacquot (eds), *Le Lieu théâtral dans la société moderne* (Paris: Éditions du CNRS, [1963] 1969), p. 153.

37 'L'accord entre la pierre nue d'Avignon et Shakespeare… fut immédiat.' Jean Vilar, 'Mémorandum,' in *Le Théâtre, service public* (Paris: Gallimard, 1975), p. 242.

38 On this reference to Brueghel's painting, see François Laroque, '*Hamlet*, directed by Patrice Chéreau, Cour d'Honneur du palais des papes, festival d'Avignon, 18 July 1988, centre stalls', *Cahiers Élisabéthains*, 34 (1988), p. 95.

39 Fonds Jean Vilar, 4-JV-127, 19. An audio recording of the production in Avignon in 1954 can be found on the website of the French National Audiovisual Institute (INA). Available at: www.telerama.fr/radio/l-archive-ina-de-la-semaine-macbeth,100372.php, accessed 26 April 2019.

40 William Shakespeare, *The Winter's Tale*, ed. Line Cottegnies and Margaret Jones-Davies, a bilingual edition, trans. Jean-Michel Déprats, in *Œuvres completes*, vol. VII, coll. Bibliothèque de La Pléiade (Paris: Gallimard, 2016), 1.2.108. Play dated 1609–10.

41 Dating back to 1996, Daniel Mesguich's coinage is quoted by Catherine Treilhou-Balaudé in '*Hamlet* de la scène française à la scène européenne: omniprésence et diversité', in Treilhou-Balaudé (ed.), *Hamlet. Énigmes du texte, réponses de la scène* (Paris: CNDP, 2012), p. 29.
42 Jean-Louis Curtis first translated 'sights' and 'strange things' (3.4.117 and 146) by 'spectacles' and 'étrange illusion', before opting for 'aberration étrange' and 'hallucination'. Fonds Jean Vilar, 4-JV-127, 1: working texts annotated by Vilar, 1st version 1954, p. 43.
43 A *sociétaire* (member) of the Comédie-Française, Denis Podalydès, wrote about the horse in Chéreau's production as 'haunting memories' ('[c]e cheval... hante la mémoire') in *Album Shakespeare*, coll. Bibliothèque de La Pléiade (Paris: Gallimard, 2016), p. 211. A former *sociétaire* of the Comédie-Française, Philippe Torreton, evokes it as one of his best memories as a spectator, in *Thank you, Shakespeare!* (Paris: Flammarion, 2016), p. 69.
44 'Un grand ventre qui respire.' Marcel Freydefont, 'Les Scénographies *d'Hamlet* au Festival d'Avignon', *Perspectives Shakespeare, Cahiers Jean Vilar*, 117 (2014), p. 108.
45 Interview with Richard Peduzzi by Teilhou-Balaudé: '*Hamlet* de la scène française à la scène européenne: omniprésence et diversité', in *Hamlet. Énigmes du texte, réponses de la scène*, p. 44.
46 'La robe immense du plateau couverte de rides.' Jean-Jacques Lerrant, 'Festival d'Avignon 1980. *Le Conte d'hiver*: un Shakespeare "machiné" par Lavelli', *Le Progrès*, 15 July 1980.
47 'Frissonne'. Dominique Jamet, 'Avignon: *Le Conte d'hiver* de Shakespeare mis en scène par Jorge Lavelli. Le plaisir d'une nuit d'été', *Le Matin*, 28 July 1980.
48 'Des yeux noirs et creux'. A private interview with Jean-Pierre Vincent by Florence March, 13 March 2014. See also interview with Vincent by Carole Guidicelli: '*La Tragédie de Macbeth*: "Une extraordinaire histoire d'amour sous forme de messe noire", selon Jean-Pierre Vincent, entretien réalisé par Carole Guidicelli', in Estelle Rivier, *Shakespeare dans la Maison de Molière* (Rennes: Presses Universitaires de Rennes, 2012), pp. 251–9, in particular p. 253.
49 'Notes on the last rehearsal of *Macbeth*', Fonds Jean Vilar, 4-JV-127, 19. The costumes of the production are kept at the Maison Jean Vilar.
50 'Leur voix... est exactement celle de Donald Duck en colère dans les dessins animés de Disney.' Hubert Engelhard, '*Macbeth*', *Réforme*, 29 January 1955.
51 Marcelle Capron, '*Macbeth* au Théâtre National Populaire', *Combat*, 27 January 1955.
52 Boissieu, *Nos Années Vilar*, p. 75.
53 'Au Xe Festival d'Avignon, le TNP a vaincu la malédiction qui pèse sur Macbeth', *Le Provençal*, 23 July 1956.
54 Interview with Vincent, in Rivier, *Shakespeare dans la Maison de Molière*, p. 258.
55 *Ibid.*
56 'Insectes pris dans une toile géante'. Rivier, *Shakespeare dans la Maison de Molière*, p. 138.
57 'Choc esthétique'. Nativel, 'Such a questionable shape', p. 160.
58 Private interview with Claude Lemaire by the author, 23 July 2016.

59 Private interview with Ariel Garcia-Valdès by the author, 23 July 2016.
60 'Réalisme caricatural', 'le réalisme décoratif, sa matérialité, témoignent d'un refus d'utiliser la magie propre du lieu'. Claude Baignières, '*Comme il vous plaira*, un réalisme caricatural', *Le Figaro*, 15 July 1976.
61 See Teilhou-Balaudé, '*Hamlet* de la scène française à la scène européenne: omniprésence et diversité', in *Hamlet. Énigmes du texte, réponses de la scène*, p. 28–30.
62 See Pierre Marcabru, '*Hamlet* vu par Benno Besson. Une farce ricanante', *Le Figaro*, 12 July 1977; Dominique Jamet, '*Hamlet* aux fines herbes!', *L'Aurore*, 18 July 1977; Robert Kanters, 'Avignon: Claudel, bravo! *Hamlet*, hélas!', *L'Express*, 25 July 1977.
63 William Shakespeare, *The Tragedy of Richard III*, ed. John Jowett (Oxford: Oxford University Press, Oxford World's Classics, 2000), p. 103.
64 See 'Le triomphe du Théâtre Roustaveli', *Le Provençal*, 28 July 1981; Jean-Pierre Leonardini, 'Shakespeare venu de loin. Honneur aux Géorgiens…', *L'Humanité*, 29 July 1981; Gilles Sandier, '*Le Cercle de craie caucasien* de Brecht et *Richard III* de Shakespeare par le théâtre Roustavelli (*sic*)', *Le Matin*, 29 July 1981. A video extract from the last scene is available at www.youtube.com/watch?v=bKBcFg9ndsM, accessed 26 April 2019.

Bibliography

Boissieu, Gisèle and Jean, *Nos Années Vilar*, preface by Paul Puaux (Gémenos: Éditions Autres Temps, 1994).
Bonnefoy, Yves, 'Le lieu, l'heure, la mise en scène', in Sylvie de Nussac (ed.), *Nanterre-Amandiers, les années Chéreau, 1982–1990* (Paris: Éditions de l'Imprimerie nationale, 1990).
Borie, Monique, *Le Fantôme ou le théâtre qui doute, essai* (Arles: Actes Sud/Académie Expérimentale des Arts, 1997).
Carlson, Marvin, *The Haunted Stage: The Theatre as Memory Machine* (Ann Arbor: University of Michigan Press, 2001).
Davis, Colin, 'État présent. Hauntology, Spectres and Phantoms', *French Studies*, LIX:3 (2005), 373–9.
Derrida, Jacques, *Specters of Marx: The State of the Debt, the Work of Mourning and the New International* (*Spectres de Marx*, Paris: Galilée, 1993), trans. Peggy Kamuf (London and New York: Routledge, 1994).
Fonds Jean Vilar. Performing Arts Department of the Bibliothèque nationale de France in Avignon (Maison Jean Vilar).
Fonds Paul Puaux. Performing Arts Department of the Bibliothèque nationale de France in Avignon (Maison Jean Vilar).
Freydefont, Marcel, 'Les Scénographies d'*Hamlet* au Festival d'Avignon', *Perspectives Shakespeare, Cahiers Jean Vilar*, 117 (2014).
Goy-Blanquet, Dominique, *Shakespeare in the Theatre: Patrice Chéreau* (London: Bloomsbury, The Arden Shakespeare, 2018).
Laroque, François, '*Hamlet*, directed by Patrice Chéreau, Cour d'Honneur du palais des papes, festival d'Avignon, 18 July 1988, centre stalls', *Cahiers Élisabéthains*, 34 (1988), 95–7.
Mnouchkine, Ariane, 'Ariane Mnouchkine, entretien serein', interview with Ariane Mnouchkine by Jean-Bernard Pouy, in Jean Viard (ed.), *Avignon*, journal *Autrement*, series France 1 (1990), 176–9.
Nativel, Valérie, '"Such a questionable shape": pour une lecture de l'entrée en scène du Spectre dans l'*Hamlet* de Patrice Chéreau', *Revue d'histoire du théâtre*, 250 (2011), 159–67.
Podalydès, Denis, *Album Shakespeare*, coll. Bibliothèque de La Pléiade (Paris: Gallimard, 2016).
Rivier, Estelle, *Shakespeare dans la Maison de Molière* (Rennes: Presses Universitaires de Rennes, 2012).
Rosset, Clément, *The Real and its Double* (*Le Réel et son double: essai sur l'illusion*, Paris: Gallimard, 1976), trans. Chris Turner (Chicago: University of Chicago Press, 2012).
RPFA, Bibliothèque nationale de France at Maison Jean Vilar, Press reviews.
Sahel, Pierre, 'Shakespeare au Festival d'Avignon. *Le Conte d'hiver*. Adaptation française de Claude-André Puget. Mise en scène de Jorge Lavelli. Le Théâtre de la Ville (Paris). Cour d'honneur du Palais des Papes, le 18 juillet 1980', *Cahiers Élisabéthains*, 18 (1980), 111–14.

Shakespeare, William, *The Winter's Tale*, ed. Line Cottegnies and Margaret Jones-Davies, a bilingual edition, trans. Jean-Michel Déprats, in *Œuvres complètes*, vol. VII, coll. Bibliothèque de La Pléiade (Paris: Gallimard, 2016).
—— *A Midsummer Night's Dream*, ed. Gisèle Venet, a bilingual edition, trans. Jean-Michel Déprats, in *Œuvres complètes*, vol. V, coll. Bibliothèque de La Pléiade (Paris: Gallimard, 2013).
—— *The Tragedy of Richard III*, ed. Gisèle Venet, a bilingual edition, trans. Jean-Michel Déprats, in *Œuvres complètes*, vol. III, coll. Bibliothèque de La Pléiade (Paris: Gallimard, 2008).
—— *The Tragedy of Macbeth*, ed. Henri Suhamy, a bilingual edition, trans. Jean-Michel Déprats, in *Œuvres complètes*, vol. II, coll. Bibliothèque de La Pléiade (Paris: Gallimard, 2002).
—— *The Tragedy of Richard III*, ed. John Jowett (Oxford: Oxford University Press, Oxford World's Classics, 2000).
Torreton, Philippe, *Thank you, Shakespeare!* (Paris: Flammarion, 2016).
Treilhou-Balaudé, Catherine (ed.), *Hamlet. Énigmes du texte, réponses de la scène* (Paris: CNDP, 2012).
Viard, Jean (ed.), *Avignon*, journal *Autrement*, series France 1 (1990).
Vilar, Jean, *Notes de service, Lettres aux acteurs et autres textes, 1944–1967*, eds Frédérique Debril and Jacques Téphany (Arles: Actes Sud, 2014).
—— *Cahiers Jean Vilar*, 112 (2012).
—— *Le Théâtre, service public* (Paris: Gallimard, 1975).
—— 'Un lieu théâtral: Avignon', in Denis Bablet and Jean Jacquot (eds), *Le Lieu théâtral dans la société moderne* (Paris: Éditions du CNRS, [1963] 1969).
Vincent, Jean-Pierre, 'La Tragédie de Macbeth: "Une extraordinaire histoire d'amour sous forme de messe noire", selon Jean-Pierre Vincent, entretien réalisé par Carole Guidicelli', in Estelle Rivier, *Shakespeare dans la Maison de Molière* (Rennes: Presses Universitaires de Rennes, 2012), pp. 251–9.
—— 'Les fantômes de Jean-Pierre Vincent', interview with Jean-Pierre Vincent by Jean-Bernard Pouy, in Jean Viard (ed.), *Avignon*, journal *Autrement*, series France 1 (1990), 186–9.
Vingtain, Dominique (ed.), *Le Palais des Papes, monument de l'histoire: construire, reconstruire, XIVe siècle–XXe siècle*, catalogue of the 29 June–29 September 2002 exhibition (Avignon: Éditions RMG, 2002).
Wilson, John Dover, *Vous avez dit Hamlet?* (*What Happens in Hamlet*, Cambridge: Cambridge University Press, [1935] 1990), trans. Dominique Goy-Blanquet (Paris: Aubier and Nanterre: Théâtre des Amandiers, 1988).

Part III

Supernatural utterance and haunted texts

6

Prophecy and the supernatural: Shakespeare's challenges to performativity

Yan Brailowsky

> A lioness hath whelped in the streets,
> And graves have yawn'd and yielded up their dead;
> Fierce fiery warriors fight upon the clouds...
> And ghosts did shriek and squeal about the streets. (*Julius Caesar*, 2.2.17–19, 24)[1]

Supernatural phenomena in Shakespeare's plays are frequently embodied: they take a physical shape onstage with characters such as the Weird Sisters in *Macbeth* or Ariel in *The Tempest*, or with apparitions and ghosts as in *Richard III*, *Hamlet* or *Julius Caesar*, or they appear through portentous signs which work like props, either through staging effects (thunder and lightning), or by oral reports, with talk of 'horrid sights seen by the watch' (*Julius Caesar*, 2.2.16) such as those recounted by Calphurnia in my epigraph. Despite their uncertain origins, these supernatural elements seemingly take a material form onstage, and are given meaning by the characters and the audience alike, contributing to making the supernatural tangible.

The supernatural can also be embodied in a different manner, however, and this chapter will analyse how it can be produced through *language*, notably through prophetic utterances. Prophecies, particularly in plays with a well-known historical background, foreshadow events, helping audiences to orientate their interpretation of the characters' – often tragic – choices. In so doing, the prophecies add a teleological dimension to a play, giving it a pre-ordained purpose and meaning.[2] Whatever will be, will be... Omens, divinatory practices, amphibological warnings or predictions: all seem to partake in producing the dramatic tension which fuels a play. Prophetic warnings are justified by what ensues, suggesting that prophecies have a performative function, capable of *making* things *happen*. In the words of linguist J. L. Austin, prophecies seem to be 'performative' utterances; they have both an 'illocutionary' force (characters make prophecies through speech) and a 'perlocutionary' effect (these speeches have an effect on the audience, for instance persuading them of an impending doom).[3]

This chapter explores the language of prophecies to understand and question early modern conceptions of the supernatural from a linguistic perspective. Can language produce supernatural effects? How is the supernatural expressed through language? Does the language of prophecy work differently from ordinary language? In what follows, I first consider the context of early modern theatre in which the preternatural, or supernatural, power of prophecies was highly problematic, in a context in which Church and state endeavoured to counteract prophetic practices in Elizabethan and Jacobean England in the hope of avoiding the spread of seditious rumours. The evocative power of the language of prophecy resisted these regulatory efforts, however, and even monarchs such as James I could not help but recognise the close link between prophecies and poetry. This link dated back to the figure of the poet-prophet in antiquity, a relationship that may explain why Shakespeare's plays so frequently draw on prophecies to fuel a dramatic narrative. In the second part, I will discuss how the language of prophecy could trick audiences into *believing* in the supernatural power of prophecies, despite the fact that the language used to utter such prophecies turns out to be, paradoxically, *non*-performative. Instead, to borrow a concept from Gilles Deleuze, I will argue in the third part that prophecies make language 'stutter', rather than actually serving to advance the plot.[4] As we shall see, prophecies ultimately posit a number of hypothetical futures, perennially questioning our interpretation of historical narratives and supernatural phenomena. By producing the supernatural through language, rather than through characters or special effects, prophecies challenge our interpretations of the plays and all 'the things that we have heard and seen' (*Julius Caesar*, 2.1.15).

Kings and queens, prophets and poets

As religious reformists in England attempted to implement key Protestant ideas to purify the Church of England from Popish customs and to extirpate superstitious practices from the populace, Elizabethan and Jacobean authorities exercised a parallel effort to maintain the royal supremacy in matters of religion, prosecuting attempts at dabbling in witchcraft and unlicensed prognostications which could sow the seeds of heresy and sedition amongst parishioners. In England, Elizabeth I had talk of prophecies closely monitored, and laws against such practices were revived in 1563, early in her reign, with *An Act against Fond and Phantastical Prophesies*, first passed under Henry VIII and Edward VI, and *An Act against Conjurations, Enchantments and Witchcrafts*, which promised to punish with one year's imprisonment all who 'advance, publish and set forth by writing, printing, signing or any other open speech or deed, to any person or persons, any fond, fantastical or false prophecy' liable to concern the monarch and trouble peace in the realm.[5] In Scotland similar measures were taken, and James I/VI had another *Act against Conjuration* passed in 1604 shortly upon his accession to the English throne, suggesting the urgency of these matters for newly crowned monarchs.[6]

Of the two English monarchs, James was no doubt the most enthralled by talk of prophecies and witchcraft, having witnessed witch trials first-hand in the early 1590s, and having penned a treatise on *Daemonologie* in 1597.[7] Now on the throne of England, the king went one step further: not only was he the Supreme Governor of the Church of England, and thus responsible for the spiritual well-being and orthodoxy of his people, he was actually divinely inspired. According to the official historiography, it was James himself who discovered the Gunpowder Plot by deciphering the true import of a treasonous letter that had been intercepted by his secret police. In a sermon marking the first anniversary of the discovery of the Plot on 5 November 1606, bishop Lancelot Andrewes compared James to Joseph in Genesis:

> But then commeth *God* againe (God most certainly) and (as in the *Prov* 16.10) puts..., a very *divination*, a very *oracle, in the Kings lips*, and his mouth missed not the matter; made him, as *Joseph*, the revealer of secrets, to read the riddle: giving him wisdome to make both explication, what they would doe and application, where it was they would doe it. This was God certainly. This, *Pharaoh* would say, none could, unless he were *filled with the Spirit of the holy God*. It was *A domino factum*.[8]

That Andrewes should consider the king to be 'filled with the Spirit of the holy God' would have come as no surprise: in the monarch's own estimation, James was king by divine right.[9] More interestingly, he was also a professed poetry enthusiast, having authored several poetic works, including a small booklet on Scottish verse, several translations of French and Latin poems, and a number of palindrome poems and acrostics in his *Essays of a Prentise, in the Divine art of Poesie* published in Edinburgh in 1585.[10] The term 'Divine' used in the title was to be taken literally, conflating poetry and divination, echoing what Sir Philip Sidney argued when recalling the etymology of 'poets' in antiquity. Poets, Sidney noted, were the augurs and divines of yore:

> Among the Romans a poet was called *vates*, which is as much as a diviner, foreseer, or prophet, as by his conjoined words *vaticinium* and *vaticinari* is manifest: so heavenly a title did that excellent people bestow upon this heart-ravishing knowledge... And altogether not without ground, since both the oracles of Delphos and Sibylla's prophecies were wholly delivered in verses. For that same exquisite observing of number and measure in words, and that high flying liberty of conceit proper to the poet, did seem to have some divine force in it.
>
> And may not I presume a little further, to shew the reasonableness of this worde *vates*, and say that the holy David's Psalms are a divine poem? If I do, I shall not do it without the testimony of great learned men, both ancient and modern. But even the name psalms will speak for me, which being interpreted, is nothing but songs.[11]

The Scottish king's poetic production betrayed his interest in secret messages, buttressing claims that he was a modern-day *vates*, a poet-prophet, in the tradition of Apollo's sibyls to whom he regularly referred in his writings.[12]

Supernatural and ordinary language

The king claimed a divinely inspired, poetic, interpretative dexterity. In the fictional world of the stage, Shakespeare was also a poet-prophet as he portrayed characters who appeal to spirits to divine their future or that of their country. The playwright's inclusion of a great number of prophecies in his plays suggests that, contrary to other public venues, the stage afforded a greater degree of liberty concerning political prophecies, otherwise viewed with suspicion by the authorities. This suggests that theatrical prophecies could have a political use, underlining either their perniciousness, or their heuristic qualities, furthering the views and myths of the prevailing regime.

Take *Richard III*, for instance. The play famously begins with 'a prophecy which says that G/Of Edward's heirs the murtherer shall be' (1.1.39–40), a ruse which Richard himself calls 'subtle, false, and treacherous' (1.1.37). The series of synonyms imitated the redundant style of legal jargon, while recalling the epithet applied to the snake in the Garden of Eden ('the serpent was more subtil than any beast of the field', Genesis 3:1).[13] Richard's use of this 'false' prophecy, with its religious and political underpinnings, prepares the audience for the scene of his supposed coronation by popular acclaim, when he appears before the assembled populace in religious garb with a 'book of prayer' (3.7.98), stressing the intimate links between Church and Crown in the period.

Despite Richard's assertion that the prophecy is 'false', the audience quickly realises that the prophecy is true, as it is Richard of Gloucester who kills Edward's children, not Edward's brother George, Duke of Clarence. Richard's prophecy in G can be tuned to another key, revealing other 'secret' names in 'G' in the play, notably Richmond, later crowned as Henry VII, whose name is, 'rightly sounded', *Rougemont*.[14] The two names are distinguished by the only two affricates used in English: /tʃ/ and /dʒ/, thus making Richmond a 'G' name by paronomasia. The aural confusion was credible as they are hardly distinguishable when pronounced by an Irishman, as Richard says the name is.[15] For Howard Dobin, such 'misnomer prophecies rely for their polysemy on the random play of proper names'.[16] Shakespeare's *Richard III* thus suggests the double-edged nature of prophecies, which may be 'false' but prove true to those that utter them, as Richard is eventually defeated by a man whose name contains, in effect, the fateful letter 'G'.[17]

The ambiguous nature of prophecies is also illustrated by other characters in the play, notably Margaret of Anjou, whose 'curses' (Act 1, Scenes 3 and 4) rightly ought to be considered prophetic, although the others believe them to be the product of her incipient madness. As argued by Jessica L. Malay, in *Richard III* prophecies turn out to be true, but the playwright 'expresses grave doubts that prophecy can actually benefit those to whom it pertains... Shakespeare plainly sees prophecy as more likely to mislead and cause harm', a point shared by other early modern writers critical of prophetic practices.[18]

The ambivalent, yet prescient manner in which prophecies are used in *Richard III*, which portrays the last episode of the Wars of the Roses, is echoed by a host of other examples in the tetralogies, depicting earlier episodes of these wars. In *Richard II*, for example, written after *Richard III* but depicting the *beginning* of the feud between the houses of York and Lancaster, the Bishop of Carlisle promises fire and brimstone to all who participate in the downfall of the legitimate monarch. This betrayal, he warns, will ignite a civil war, depicted in the other plays of the tetralogies:

> And if you crown him [Henry Bolingbroke], let me prophesy,
> The blood of English shall manure the ground,
> And future ages groan for this foul act.
> Peace shall go sleep with Turks and infidels...
> Prevent it, resist it, let it not be so,
> Lest child, child's children, cry against you 'woe!' (4.1.136–9, 148–9)

Similar prophecies are uttered in the *Henry VI* plays performed in the early 1590s, and Margaret's curses partake in this eschatological vision of history, one that critics have often interpreted as contributing to the so-called 'Tudor myth', glorifying the Elizabethan regime by depicting events leading up to the victory of her illustrious grandfather over Richard III, putting an end to the Wars of the Roses.[19] According to this reading, the prophecies included in Shakespeare's historical plays are 'efficacious' in the religious sense (as when one speaks of 'efficacious grace', which grants the faithful eternal salvation). The characters' prophecies are true – or become so in due time – betraying a supposed divine plan that oversaw the crowning of Elizabeth and a Golden Age for England with half a century of peace and prosperity.

A closer analysis of the wording of some of these prophecies suggests that they are far more fragile than one might believe, however. Carlisle's speech quoted earlier, for instance, is not meant to predict the future, as the bishop speaks in hypotheticals: '*if* you crown him...' As he himself suggests, his 'prophecy' is not destined to divine the future but to '[p]revent it, [to] resist it'. The prophecy, in other words, is not meant to be efficacious. The term can be taken in its theological sense as well as its linguistic sense, in terms of performative utterance. From a pragmatist perspective, the bishop's statement sounds like a warning ('the blood *shall* manure the ground... Peace *shall* go sleep with Turks'), which endows his speech with a strong perlocutionary effect, as he threatens his listeners with civil war. From a different perspective, however, his speech may be considered as *non*-performative. As J. L. Austin argues, a performative utterance is 'felicitous' when certain 'conditions' are met.[20] If audiences did not recognise the bishop of Carlisle's religious stature, his apocalyptic prophecy would be seen as fraudulent and infelicitous. Given that audiences know how English history unfolded and can recognise the messianic nature of the bishop's speech (entitled as a man of God to speak in religiously charged terms), Carlisle's prophecy may well appear to be a performative utterance. However, its conditional formulation ('if you crown him') can mark the speech as *unperformative* in Austinian terms, in the same manner as a change of tense makes a warning necessarily infelicitous ('I prophesied' or 'I warned them' are not performative utterances; neither are they promises).[21] In this case, Carlisle's utterance is not meant to immediately 'do' something 'with words' (unlike when a minister declares 'I now proclaim you husband and wife' in a church wedding). Even examples of conjuration of spirits, such as those found in Marlowe's *Doctor Faustus* and analysed by Andrew Sofer, at least *seem* to provoke the appearance of devils, although the play 'probes the uncertain boundary between hollow performance and magical performativity'.[22] In *Richard II*, however, virtually *nothing* occurs immediately as a consequence of the bishop of Carlisle's speech; the other characters may not even feel threatened by his words, which can therefore be void of perlocutionary power. If anything, his warning will eventually prove true… in *other* plays from the tetralogies.[23]

The distinction between a prophecy and the moment of its accomplishment is of the essence, a point noted by Francis Bacon in *The Advancement of Learning*:

> History of Prophecy, consisteth of two relatives, the prophecy and the accomplishment;… being of the nature of their author [God], with whom a thousand years are but as one day; and therefore are not fulfilled punctually at once, but have springing and germinant accomplishment throughout many ages, though the height or fulness of them may refer to some one age.[24]

According to this reasoning, which distinguishes prophecies from their 'germinant accomplishments', one could argue that some Shakespearean prophecies survived the Elizabethan era in which they were written, becoming true *post facto*, as when one suggests that the late tragedies of the *sixteenth* century may have announced the tribulations of the Civil War in the *seventeenth* century – an argument made by Richard Wilson in an analysis of *Julius Caesar*.[25] The same reasoning also highlights the cultural and historical difficulties in analysing speech acts from previous eras, as argued by Dawn Archer and others, for whom defining context is key to 'captur[ing] participants' mental representations'.[26] Trying to understand how the language of prophecies works in early modern plays thus rests on a number of interpretative and linguistic assumptions, although we could also argue that an interpretation of Shakespeare's language from a contemporary perspective is also valid, as the plays are still being successfully performed today.

Unlike the example quoted earlier from *Richard II*, which uses a conditional form, other prophecies in the tetralogies can appear to have a more straightforward performative wording, but they too can be equally infelicitous – proof that so-called prophecies do not have, *ipso facto*, performative qualities, even where the playwright's resort to ambiguity and supernatural powers makes the prophecies *seem* to be effective. Unlike a king such as James, who claimed he was God's representative on earth, possessing God's prophetic gifts, and whose word was law – 'such is the breath of kings', marvelled Bolingbroke (*Richard II*, 1.3.215) – several characters in Shakespeare's plays, such as Eleanor, Suffolk, Somerset and Macbeth, have no such direct link to God, depending on the words of Satan to further their ambitions, generally to ill effect.

In *Henry VI, Part 2*, for instance, Eleanor is said to have ordered a witch, Margery Jordan, along with Roger Bolingbrook, a conjurer, to divine the future of the realm. A priest, Hume, begins the conjuration scene by implicating her and promising a performative utterance, one capable of actually raising a spirit through words: 'Come, my masters, the Duchess [Eleanor, Duchess of Gloucester], I tell you expects *performance* of your promises' (1.4.1–2, emphasis added). The conjuration scene is discovered moments later by the Duke of York, however, who proceeds to read aloud the prophecy uttered by the conjured spirit, allowing the audience a second chance to reflect on the meaning of the supposed prophecy, and affording York an opportunity to point out its ambiguous structure:

> YORK. Now pray, my lord, let's see the devil's writ.
> What have we here? (*Reads.*)
> 'The duke yet lives that Henry shall depose;
> But him out-live, and die a violent death.'
> Why, this is just
> 'Aio te, Aecida, Romanos vincere posse.' (1.4.57–62)

York's comment on the 'devil's writ' is a Latin quotation that refers to a famous prophecy quoted by Cicero, who recalled that the Oracle of Delphi promised Pyrrhus that he would vanquish Rome… or that Rome would vanquish him – an amphibological structure which spelled Pyrrhus' eventual demise after a few promising victories.

The ambiguous structure of the Pythia's Apollonian prophecy is an interpretative key that allows audiences to realise the ambivalent nature of prophecies as a whole, and the troubled minds of the characters who rely on them – Satan works through devious means.[27] By eschewing divine Providence and listening to the ambiguous words of the Devil in the hope of quickly reaching their goals, characters such as Eleanor unknowingly fall prey to doubt and despair which, in turn, ultimately precipitate their downfall.

To illustrate this point, it is instructive to compare speeches from two plays which contain several ominous prophecies: *Julius Caesar* and *Macbeth*. While the Soothsayer's prophecies in the Roman tragedy are fairly straightforward and repeated (notably with his warning '[b]eware the ides of March', 1.1.18, 23), other visions are not so clear-cut, such as the extraordinary natural phenomena observed by Casca in Act 1, Scene 3, or Calphurnia's dream, which is interpreted as either threatening or hopeful in Act 2, Scene 2. In the Scottish play, the prophecies are all uttered by decidedly strange characters, the Weird Sisters, who systematically speak in memorable riddles, a fact compounded by their use of trochaic tetrameters, which could be deemed a prosodic sign of the supernatural.[28]

Both plays highlight the problematic nature of interpretation, the difficulty in performing bloody deeds and, consequently, the difficulty in making prophecies come true. This is suggested by the manner in which Brutus and Macbeth share similar misgivings before deciding to commit cataclysmic murders. The speeches could almost be interchangeable:

> BRUTUS.   Between the acting of a dreadful thing,
> And the first motion, all the interim is
> Like a phantasma or a hideous dream.
> The Genius and the mortal instruments
> Are then in council, and the state of a man,
> Like to a little kingdom, suffers then
> The nature of an insurrection. (*Julius Caesar*, 2.1.63–9)

> MACBETH.   Present fears
> Are less than horrible imaginings:
> My thought, whose murther yet is but fantastical,
> Shakes so my single state of man that function
> Is smother'd in surmise, and nothing is
> But what is not. (*Macbeth*, 1.3.137–42)

In addition to expressing the same doubts about the route they are to embark on, the two characters have a common destiny: they murder their ruler by treacherous means; their victims come back to haunt them; and they both perish without reaching their avowed goal – preserving the republic for one, planting a new dynasty on the Scottish throne for the other.

What distinguishes the speeches is their rhetorical and theological underpinnings. Whereas Brutus develops a political metaphor, Macbeth concludes his existential disquisitions with an antithesis ('nothing is but what is not') that betrays the amphibological basis of his doubts – an antithesis which echoes the Weird Sisters' words moments earlier, '[f]air is foul, and foul is fair' (1.1.11), or his own reformulation '[s]o foul and fair a day I have not seen' (1.3.38). Although both Brutus and Macbeth speak of the 'state of [a] man', Macbeth speaks of 'my *single* state of man', inscribing his doubts in a more Christian perspective, as his expression can recall several passages from the Gospels in which duplicity and honesty are discussed, notably Matthew 6:22 and Luke

11:34.²⁹ While both characters apparently use the same lexical field of dreams ('phantasma... hideous dream', or 'horrible imaginings... [thought] fantastical'), it is only Macbeth's speech which contains the seeds of Satan, whose name in Hebrew means the Adversary, the Accuser, or the Enemy, symbolising the existential contradiction from which Macbeth suffers. Thus, when Macbeth reflects on '[his] single state of man' he betrays his willingness to serve Satan, rather than God, a choice between the 'two truths' (1.3.128) he spoke of moments earlier. In choosing Mammon, he reveals the demonic nature of his treachery. In contrast, Brutus' betrayal partakes in a political choice that excludes the individual's personal wishes.

Thus, although Brutus is as doubt-ridden as Macbeth, his objective is unwavering: defending the republic. What occurs *after* his death is of no concern to the Roman warrior, unlike Macbeth who becomes obsessed with his lack of progeny – an obsession that pushes him to commit monstrous acts, which will, in turn, precipitate his downfall. If, according to Young Siwain, Macbeth is the Devil incarnate, it is because Macbeth has become his own worst enemy, an instrument of his own end.

In this demonic context, Macbeth's obsession with an enemy 'none of woman born' (4.1.80), following the witches' prophecy describing his nemesis, unravels into a messianic parable or, rather, a story prefiguring the Antichrist, as Macbeth refuses to believe in the performative nature of divine language capable of breathing life through speech ('the Word was made flesh', John 1:14). According to the Gospels, the faithful or 'sons of God' are 'born, not of blood, nor of the will of the flesh, nor of the will of man, but of God' (John 1:13). In this context, Macduff, 'not born of woman' (5.7.3) because he 'was from his mother's womb/ Untimely ripp'd' (5.8.15–6), may be the prime example of the true believer, the saviour come to rid Scotland of tyrannous Macbeth, 'this fiend of Scotland' (4.3.233).³⁰ If Macduff is the saviour, Macbeth is akin to the Antichrist. The latter's refusal to believe that Macduff was 'not of woman born' turns the tyrant into a representative of the Devil, '[f]or many deceivers are entered into the world, who confess not that Jesus Christ is come in the flesh. This is a deceiver and an antichrist' (2 John 7). In other words, by refusing to believe in the possibility of a 'miraculous' birth, Macbeth refuses to believe in the miracle of Christ. Instead, Macbeth prefers to believe in the power of spirits, whose language has been shown to be ambiguous, as well as in ghostly apparitions, whose meaning is equally unclear. Knowing his soul to be devoted to 'the common enemy of man' (3.1.68), i.e. Satan, Macbeth takes fate to task, ultimately betraying his tragic hubris when he promises to embrace his fate: 'come, fate, into the list/And champion me to th' utterance!' (3.1.70–1). Alas, this battle to the bitter end, 'to th' utterance', which echoes the French origin of 'utterance' as '*à outrance*' (i.e. outrageously), is not only a duel, it is also a battle of words, of outrageous *utterance*.

Prophetic 'utterances' and the 'stuttering' of language

The term used by Macbeth recalls a line by Mark Antony in *Julius Caesar* as he bemoans the death of Caesar whose body lies at his feet. Mark Antony calls on the gods '[t]o beg the voice and utterance of my tongue' (3.1.261) in order to 'prophesy' to the bitter end, announcing his intent to seek 'revenge' against Caesar's murderers: 'Over thy wounds now do I prophesy… /A curse shall light upon the limbs of men… /And Caesar's spirit, ranging for revenge,… / [Shall] Cry "Havoc!" and let slip the dogs of war' (3.1.259, 262, 270, 273).

Macbeth does not address the gods. Instead, he lurches into a battle that he cannot win without divine assistance. The 'list' he 'champion[s] to th' utterance' is both an armed battle and a verbal joust. Unlike the Apostles, to whom 'the Spirit [gave] utterance' (Acts 2:4) on the day of the Pentecost, Macbeth cannot properly decipher the Weird Sisters' prophecies. Lacking divine inspiration from the Holy Ghost, which would have enabled him to speak another language, that of the spirits, Macbeth is bound to lose despite a promising start, not unlike Pyrrhus. After losing the verbal joust, he will succumb in the armed duel.

The antithesis of Macbeth, James I, performed the opposite: inspired by the Holy Ghost, the king successfully deciphered the letters of the Gunpowder Plotters, vanquishing the most diabolical plot of his enemies – without even needing to take up arms. The example of the spirits in Macbeth point to the theological issues posed by divine 'possession', such as when the Apostles spoke in tongues on the Pentecost. Unlike the language of divine inspiration, the language of demonic spirits rests on equivoque, where appearances and apparitions are deceitful, uttering words which are false or half-truths, contradicting one of Austin's conditions for a 'felicitious' utterance (i.e. to believe what one is saying). Supernatural beings such as demons act on language in a manner that voids univocal meaning, in the same manner as dramatic prophesies do in these plays.

One could thus reinterpret Mark Antony's promise '[t]o beg the voice and utterance of my tongue' as a promise to make language stutter, a notion first developed by Gilles Deleuze in *Critique et clinique* (1993). Deleuze also spoke of 'inclusive' or 'included disjunctions', i.e. moments when more than one meaning is possible, mapping out a range of possible, yet conflicting, interpretations in literature which makes language stutter. Arguably, such disjunctions are characteristic of prophecies and, more generally, divinatory practices: disjunctions can be temporal, as prophecies become true after a period of latency; they can also be spatial, as there are unstable, prophetic spaces; lastly, they can be verbal, as disjunctions affect language. For Deleuze,

> [a]s long as language is considered as a system in equilibrium, the disjunctions are necessarily exclusive (we do not say 'passion', 'ration', 'nation' at the same

time, but must choose between them), and the connections, progressive (we do not combine a word with its own elements, in a kind of stop-start or forward-backward jerk). But far from the equilibrium, *the disjunctions become included or inclusive, and the connections, reflexive*, following a rolling gait that concerns the process of language and no longer the flow of speech.[31]

The conjunction *if*, which serves as a linguistic marker of the type of 'inclusive disjunction' Deleuze is discussing, famously served as a motto decorating the temple of Apollo in Delphos. In Plutarch's 'On the E in Delphi' (*c*. 1 BCE), the Greek letter *E* could refer to Apollo (the deity is synonymous with permanence: 'you are'), or to the conditional, as well as to the dialectical or logical. In Plutarch's dialogue, Theon thus recalls that dialectics is the Apollonian art *par excellence*: 'when the god gives out ambiguous oracles, he is promoting and organizing logical reasoning as indispensable for those who are to apprehend his meaning aright'.[32] Thanks to logic promoted by Apollo, men can divine what links objects between them, deriving causal links where there used to be only incomprehensible correlations. The dialogue goes on to say that logical reasoning will allow men to prophesy: '[w]hat now is, and in future shall be, and has been of aforetime'.[33] This quotation, which Plutarch takes from Homer's *Iliad* (I.70), comes moments before Agamemnon rails against Calchas, the prophet. Calchas had divined what was needed to appease the ire of Apollo, much to the king's chagrin – kings rarely appreciate the recommendations of their prophets. The story is well known: forced to separate from his captive, Chryseis, Agamemnon takes Briseis, Achilles' captive, for himself, thus provoking his fellow warrior's anger.

One may well wonder what would have happened with the Greek army had Agamemnon refused to follow Calchas' advice. After all, the Homeric epic provides ample examples of the gods' anger subsiding, and patience often helps to triumph over 'ambiguous oracles' by the power of a 'revelation'. In Shakespeare's theatre, such 'revelations' are generally reserved for prophets, augurs and Apollo's priests, the divinely inspired sick and dying, or to certain exiled characters – in short, to a series of marginal (or marginalised) characters whose prophecies make language stutter 'to th' utterance'. The language stutters with prophecies because the sibylline dictums survive throughout the ages: they are rediscovered, given new currency; their meaning is revivified. They are, in the words of Bacon, 'germinant accomplishments'.

The underlying question is whether prophetic language in Shakespeare's plays is somehow *supra naturam*, 'above nature' or 'extra-ordinary', a uniqueness and difference that may even mimic the extra-mural location of Elizabethan theatre.[34] How else should one understand the link between the two roots of the word 'utterance'? One refers to a verbal statement, in the sense put forward by ordinary language philosophy; the other refers to quite the opposite, to that which is outrageous, excessive, what in French is (still) called *outrance*.

How, then, could one describe prophetic utterances, as opposed to a regular statement? In his introduction to *Speech Acts,* John R. Searle opposed meaningful and meaningless speeches:

> What is the difference between a meaningful string of words and a meaningless one? What is it for something to be true? or false? ... in some form or other some such questions must make sense; for we do know that people communicate,... that people's utterances do relate to the world in ways we can describe by characterizing the utterances as being true or false or meaningless, stupid, exaggerated or what-not. And if these things do happen it follows that it is possible for them to happen, and if it is possible for them to happen it ought to be possible to pose and answer the questions which examine that possibility.[35]

Searle took after J. L. Austin's work when he reflected on how 'things… happen'. In the context of prophetic utterances, Searle's remarks could be reformulated as follows: if events occur, must they *necessarily* occur? When does an 'ordinary' statement become 'prophetic'? What is a *real* prophecy? Or what does it mean for a prophecy to be *false*? In Deleuze's analysis, the French philosopher implicitly refers to Austin when he wonders what a writer can '*do*' or '*[say] without doing*', before offering 'a third possibility: *when saying is doing*.'[36] If making language stutter corresponds to this third option, which in Austinian terms recalls the notion of 'illocution', one could believe that prophetic utterances are performative only in so far as prophetic words *do* things by circuitous routes.

This is what seems to occur in *Julius Caesar*. The Soothsayer's warning to 'beware the ides of March' works through the stuttering of language with the use of paronomasia. As I argued elsewhere, the warning may be interpreted as alluding to sides, tides or tidings, as well as Mars (Caesar's tutelary god).[37] As suggested earlier, the same process occurs with the 'G' prophecy in *Richard III*, where the phoneme reappears in several guises, or in *Henry VI, Part 2* and *Macbeth*, in which the prophecies are repeated as if the characters were stammering, as when Macbeth meets every foe in his last scene by recalling that he cannot be vanquished 'by man that's of a woman born' (5.7.14; echoed 5.7.3–4, 5.8.12–3). The fact that these prophecies are structured amphibologically further contributes to this stuttering effect, interrupting the flow of meaning, if not of sound. This also explains why characters stop at the first interpretation of prophecies uttered by supernatural spirits, just as when a stutterer struggles to go beyond the first syllables of a word. In the words of Macbeth, the demonic language of prophecy is like haggling, a tug of war of promises and deception: '[a]nd be these juggling fiends no more believ'd,/That palter with us in a double sense,/That keep the word of promise to our ear,/And break it to our hope' (5.8.19–22).

In these plays, prophetic language may *appear* to be performative, as when the Soothsayer's and the Bishop of Carlisle's warnings in *Julius Caesar* or *Richard II* go unheeded, only to be proven right, like latter-day Cassandras. However, as I have tried to argue, a closer analysis shows that these prophecies are *not* models of performative utterance. Establishing a correlation between an utterance and its 'realisation' does not suffice to determine a *causal link*, particularly when cause is not *immediately* followed by effect. For performative utterances, as well as for prophecies, *temporality* is of the essence, but with opposing requirements – realisation must be proximate in the first instance, and remote in the second.

Rather than playing a performative role, I would argue that prophecies in these plays serve as lessons in interpretation.[38] Saying that one will prophesy invites the audience to reflect on what it means to write history and consequently to think about a different past, or a different future. The linguistic marker of such reflections falls on the conjunction *if*, one which is closely linked to the history of prophecy in the Apollonian tradition. In the comedies, to quote Touchstone, '[y]our If is the only peacemaker; much virtue in If' (*As You Like It*, 5.4.102–3). In the tragedies and the histories, the conjunction serves the opposite purpose, as the Bishop of Carlisle uses 'if' to prophesy the Wars of the Roses ('*[i]f* you crown him… let me prophesy…'). This conditional use is also an invitation for the *audience* to prophesy as well, that is, to think about what *could* have been, or what *could* be – what *if* Bolingbroke had relented, what *if* Henry VIII had not broken with Rome, what *if* Elizabeth were to be toppled, what *if* the Armada had managed to invade England or Jesuits succeeded in blowing up Parliament? The lack of definitive answer to these questions subtly produces the required anxiety among the audience to make prophecies *dramatically* efficacious onstage, if not actually *performative*. If anything, they become performative because they are afterwards rehearsed by the audience, who can recall the prophecy's message and connect the dots.[39] Hence, while Shakespeare's prophecies are paradoxically non-performative on stage because they are never properly presented, nor even perhaps acknowledged as such, they become efficacious *offstage* and assert the powers of the poet-*vates* to fashion history. In this sense, one can assert that Shakespeare succeeded, as a poet-prophet, in producing the supernatural through language.

Notes

1 All quotations from *The Riverside Shakespeare*, George Blakemore Evans (ed.) (Boston: Houghton Mifflin, 2nd edn, 1997). The author thanks Urszula Kizelbach for her helpful suggestions, along with those from anonymous reviewers.

2 Marjorie Garber, '"What's Past Is Prologue": Temporality and Prophecy in Shakespeare's History Plays', in Barbara Kiefer Lewalski (ed.), *Renaissance Genres: Essays on Theory, History, and Interpretation* (Cambridge, MA: Harvard University Press, 1986), pp. 301–31.

3 John L. Austin, *How to Do Things with Words* (Oxford: Clarendon Press, 1962).

4 Gilles Deleuze, *Critique et Clinique* (Paris: Minuit, 1993). In English: 'He Stuttered', Gilles Deleuze, *Essays Critical and Clinical*, trans. Daniel W. Smith and Michael A. Greco (London and New York: Verso, 1998), pp. 107–14. The French philosopher spoke of 'bégaiement de la langue' in his analysis of the style of three Russian writers: Biely, Mandelstam and Khlebnikov.

5 These acts posit the particular notion that words themselves, rather than acts, could constitute treason, which flew in the face of customary legal thought. That said, this new definition of treason was rarely, if ever, used by government authorities. See Jonathan K. van Patten, 'Magic, Prophecy, and the Law of Treason in Reformation England', *The American Journal of Legal History*, 27:1 (1983), 1–32. The history of the Elizabethan 1563 legislation is described in Michael Devine, 'Treasonous Catholic Magic and the 1563 Witchcraft Legislation: The English State's Response to Catholic Conjuring in the Early Years of Elizabeth I's Reign', in Marcus Harmes and Victoria Bladen (eds), *Supernatural and Secular Power in Early Modern England* (Farnham: Ashgate, 2015), pp. 67–91. Elizabeth's wary attitude regarding such practices did not prevent her from seeking the advice of people like John Dee. See Benjamin Woolley, *The Queen's Conjurer: The Science and Magic of Dr John Dee, Adviser to Queen Elizabeth I* (New York: Henry Holt, 2001).

6 Arguably, Elizabeth's and James' obsession was itself the direct by-product of Henry VII's own dynastic preoccupations at the beginning of his reign, positing a structural link between dynastic politics and interest in (political) prophecies. See Tim Thornton, *Prophecy, Politics and the People in Early Modern England* (Woodbridge: Boydell & Brewer, 2006).

7 James VI, *Daemonologie in Forme of a Dialogue, Diuided into Three Bookes* (Edinburgh: Printed by Robert Walde-graue printer to the Kings Majestie, 1597).

8 Lancelot Andrewes, *Ninety-Six Sermons*, J. P. Wilson and J. Bliss (eds) (Oxford: Library of Anglo-Catholic Theology, 1841), vol. IV, p. 217. See also Garry Wills, *Witches and Jesuits: Shakespeare's Macbeth* (Oxford, New York: Oxford University Press/NYPL, 1995).

9 See, for instance, James VI, *A Trew Law of Free Monarchs, or the Reciprock and Mutuall Duetie Betwixt A Free King and His Naturall Subiects* (Edinburgh: Printed by Robert Walde-graue printer to the Kings Majestie, 1598).

10 James VI, *The Essayes of a Prentise, in the Divine Art of Poesie* (Edinburgh: Thomas Vautrouillier, 1585).

11 Sir Philip Sidney, *An Apology for Poetry, Or the Defence of Poesy*, eds R. W. Maslen and Geoffrey Shepherd (Manchester: Manchester University Press, 3rd edn, 2002), pp. 83–4. On the link between poetry and prophecy, see the introductory chapter in James L. Kugel (ed.), *Poetry and Prophecy: The Beginnings of a Literary Tradition* (Ithaca, NY: Cornell University Press, 1990).

12 The opening lines of 'Ane metaphoricall invention of a tragedie called Phoenix' conclude thus: 'From Delphos syne Apollo cum with speid,/Whose shining light by cairs will dim in deid'. James VI, *The Essayes of a Prentise*, p. 41. In another section, entitled 'A Table of Some Obscvre Wordis With Their Significations, efter the ordour of the Alphabet', James VI speaks of 'Delphien Songs: Poemes, and

verses, drawn from the Oracle of Apollo at Delphos... Phœmonoe: A woman who pronounced the Oracles of Apollo', *ibid.*, pp. 76–7.
13 Biblical quotations are taken from the 1611 Authorised Version.
14 In *Henry VI, Part 2*, Suffolk says to his nemesis, Walter Whitmore, '[t]hy name is Gualtier, being rightly sounded' (4.1.37).
15 Henry's name may also have recalled the red (*rouge*) castle of Exeter from whence he came. For an analysis of the 'G' prophecy in the play, see my paper: '"What's in a name?" The "G" Prophecy and the Voice of God in Shakespeare's *Richard III*', in Line Cottegnies et al. (eds), *Les Voix de Dieu: Littérature et prophétie en Angleterre et en France à l'âge baroque* (Paris: Presses Sorbonne Nouvelle, 2008), pp. 35–46.
16 Howard Dobin, *Merlin's Disciples: Prophecy, Poetry, and Power in Renaissance England* (Stanford, CA: Stanford University Press, 1990), p. 166. Dobin approaches the issue of prophecies from a post-structuralist perspective, arguing that they reveal 'texts as products of human, conventional systems of meaning rather than of God's absolute truth'.
17 From a historical perspective, political prophecies related to the early Tudor reigns could actually exculpate Richard, as suggested by Lesley Coote and Tim Thornton, 'Richard, Son of Richard: Richard III and Political Prophecy', *Historical Research*, 73:182 (2000), 321–30. For a contextual analysis of early Tudor prophecy, see Sharon L. Jansen, *Political Protest and Prophecy under Henry VIII* (Woodbridge: The Boydell Press, 1991).
18 Jessica L. Malay, 'Shakespeare's Tudor Sibyl: Sibylline Discourse in the Portrayal of Queen Margaret in *Richard III*', in *Représentations et identités sexuelles dans le théâtre de Shakespeare: Mises en scène du genre, écritures de l'histoire*, ed. Delphine Lemonnier-Texier (Rennes: Presses Universitaires de Rennes, 2010), p. 73. On sibyls in early modern drama, and Shakespeare's disdain for what he believed were 'true' yet 'demonic' and dangerous prognostications, see Jessica L. Malay, *Prophecy and Sibylline Imagery in the Renaissance: Shakespeare's Sibyls* (London: Routledge, 2010).
19 E. M. W. Tillyard, *Shakespeare's History Plays* (London: Chatto & Windus, 1944). A different version of the myth was later proposed by Henry Ansgar Kelly, *Divine Providence in the England of Shakespeare's Histories* (Eugene, OR: Wipf and Stock Publishers, 1970). For a critique of these readings, see Phyllis Rackin, *Stages of History: Shakespeare's English Chronicles* (Ithaca, NY: Cornell University Press, 1990), in particular pp. 40–5.
20 Austin, *How to Do Things with Words*, pp. 14–15, for instance. I disagree with Austin's argument that theatre cannot provide 'real' performative utterances because they are 'in a peculiar way hollow or void if said by an actor on the stage, or if introduced in a poem, or spoken in soliloquy... Language in such circumstances is in special ways – intelligibly – used not seriously, but in ways parasitic upon its normal use – ways which fall under the doctrine of the etiolations of language. All this we are excluding from consideration.' *Ibid.*, p. 22. This argument has been cogently dismissed by critics who have pointed out that Austin's example of a marriage ceremony can well be termed theatrical. 'Marriage is "like a play" to the extent that it is like modern realistic theater, a theater whose conventional "relations

of visibility and spectatorship," as Brecht long ago recognized, mask the ideological labor behind its claims to verisimilar representation': W. B. Worthen, 'Drama, Performativity, and Performance', *PMLA*, 113:5 (1998), p. 1097. John Searle, in *Expression and Meaning* (Cambridge: Cambridge University Press, 1979), also challenged Austin's taxonomy and presented his own, more flexible, taxonomy of illocutionary acts which can be used to analyse dramatic dialogue, as has been done by Shakespearean scholars such as Manfred Pfister and Keir Elam.

21 Austin, *How To Do Things With Words*, pp. 63, 98.
22 Andrew Sofer, 'How to Do Things with Demons: Conjuring Performatives in *Doctor Faustus*', *Theatre Journal*, 61:1 (2009), p. 20. See also Eric Byville, 'How to Do Witchcraft Tragedy with Speech Acts', *Comparative Drama*, 45:2 (2011), 1–33.
23 The issue of temporality may also serve to highlight the cultural and historical difficulties in analysing speech acts from previous eras. See Dawn Archer, 'Speech Acts', in Andreas H. Jucker and Irma Taavitsainen (eds), *Historical Pragmatics* (Berlin: De Gruyter Mouton, 2010), pp. 379–417.
24 Francis Bacon, *The Major Works*, ed. Brian Vickers, Oxford World's Classics (Oxford: Oxford University Press, 2002), pp. 184–5.
25 Richard Wilson, 'A Savage Spectacle: *Julius Caesar* and the English Revolution', in François Laroque and Franck Lessay (eds), *Histoire et secret à la Renaissance: Études sur la représentation de la vie publique, la mémoire et l'intimité dans l'Angleterre et l'Europe des XVIe et XVIIe siècles* (Paris: Presses de la Sorbonne Nouvelle, 1997), pp. 41–55.
26 See Archer, 'Speech Acts', p. 405; Jonathan Culpeper and Dawn Archer, 'Requests and Directness in early modern English Trial Proceedings and Play Texts, 1640–1760', in Andreas H. Jucker and Irma Taavitsainen (eds), *Speech Acts in the History of English* (Amsterdam: John Benjamins, 2008), pp. 45–85.
27 On the notion that prophecies were intrinsically corrupt and proof of Satan's use of 'perverted syllogisms', see Armando Maggi, *Satan's Rhetoric: A Study of Renaissance Demonology* (Chicago: Chicago University Press, 2001). On prophecies and amphibology in Shakespeare, see my paper: 'Amphibologie et parole jésuitique à la Renaissance: entre poétique et politique', *Bulletin de la Société de Stylistique Anglaise*, 27 (2006), 11–26.
28 The prosodic sign of the supernatural could also be the seven-syllable lines. See Robert Stagg, 'Shakespeare's bewitching line', in Peter Holland (ed.), *Shakespeare Survey* (Cambridge: Cambridge University Press, 2018), vol. 71, pp. 232–41.
29 'The light of the body is the eye: if therefore thine eye be *single*, thy whole body shall be full of light./But if thine eye be evil, thy whole body shall be full of darkness. If therefore the light that is in thee be darkness, how great is that darkness!/No man can serve two masters: for either he will hate the one, and love the other; or else he will hold to the one, and despise the other. Ye cannot serve God and Mammon.' Matthew 6:22–4, emphasis mine. See also: 'The light of the body is the eye: therefore when thine eye is *single*, thy whole body also is full of light; but when thine eye is evil, thy body also is full of darkness.' Luke 11:34, emphasis mine.

30 Macbeth's order for the massacre of Macduff's wife and children is thus aptly turned into a Scottish equivalent of Herod's Massacre of the Innocents.
31 Deleuze, *Essays Critical and Clinical*, p. 110.
32 Plutarch, *Moralia*, trans. Frank Cole Babbitt (London: William Heinemann, 1936), vol. V, p. 212.
33 *Ibid.*, p. 213.
34 Steven Mullaney, *The Place of the Stage: License, Play, and Power in Renaissance England* (Ann Arbor/Chicago: University of Michigan Press/University of Chicago Press, 1995).
35 John R. Searle, *Speech Acts: An Essay in the Philosophy of Language* (Cambridge: Cambridge University Press, 1969), p. 3.
36 Deleuze, *Essays Critical and Clinical*, p. 107. Emphasis in the original.
37 'Ides' may evoke the bruised or bloodied sides of dogs in bear-baiting (to which Caesar's dead body is compared), or it may recall the ominous tides or tidings that abound throughout the play; whereas 'March' may evoke Caesar's tutelary god, Mars, which the general had both honoured and desecrated during Lupercalia a month earlier, when the feast meant to honor the god of war was interrupted by Mark Antony's attempt to crown Caesar thrice (that is, by repetition, as if it were a stuttering gesture); finally, 'beware' may announce the upcoming civil war by sundering in half the word to produce 'be war'. Yan Brailowsky, 'Du détournement au délire interprétatif: les figures de l'excès dans *Julius Caesar* de Shakespeare', *Actes des congrès de la Société française Shakespeare*, 25 (2007), 3–23.
38 Yan Brailowsky, '"Let me Prophesy": Apocalypse et inspiration prophétique dans *Richard II* de Shakespeare', in Michel Naumann and Dominique Daniel (eds), *L'Autre: Journée d'étude sur les Auteurs et Sujets des Concours 2006*, GRAAT (Tours: Presses universitaires François-Rabelais, 2017), pp. 81–99.
39 The participation of an audience is a key element to make an utterance performative in the Austinian sense, since something that is 'spoken in soliloquy' does not succeed in becoming performative: it requires an audience. Austin, *How To Do Things With Words*, p. 18.

Bibliography

Andrewes, Lancelot, *Ninety-Six Sermons*, eds J. P. Wilson and J. Bliss, vol. IV (Oxford: Library of Anglo-Catholic Theology, 1841).

Archer, Dawn, 'Speech Acts', in Andreas H. Jucker and Irma Taavitsainen (eds), *Historical Pragmatics* (Berlin: De Gruyter Mouton, 2010), pp. 379–417.

Austin, John L., *How to Do Things with Words* (Oxford: Clarendon Press, 1962).

Bacon, Francis, *The Major Works*, ed. Brian Vickers, Oxford World's Classics (Oxford: Oxford University Press, 2002).

Brailowsky, Yan, '"Let me Prophesy": Apocalypse et inspiration prophétique dans *Richard II* de Shakespeare', in Michel Naumann and Dominique Daniel (eds), *L'Autre: Journée d'étude Sur Les Auteurs et Sujets Des Concours 2006*, GRAAT (Tours: Presses universitaires François-Rabelais, 2017), pp. 81–99.

—— '"What's in a name?" The "G" Prophecy and the Voice of God in Shakespeare's *Richard III*', in Line Cottegnies, Claire Gheeraert-Grafeuille, Tony Gheeraert, Anne-Marie Miller-Blaise and Gisèle Venet (eds), *Les Voix de Dieu: Littérature et prophétie en Angleterre et en France à l'âge baroque* (Paris: Presses Sorbonne Nouvelle, 2008), pp. 35–46.

—— 'Du détournement au délire interprétatif : les figures de l'excès dans *Julius Caesar* de Shakespeare', *Actes des congrès de la Société française Shakespeare*, 25 (2007), 3–23.

—— 'Amphibologie et parole jésuitique à la Renaissance: Entre poétique et politique', *Bulletin de la Société de Stylistique Anglaise*, 27 (2006), 11–26.

Byville, Eric, 'How to Do Witchcraft Tragedy with Speech Acts', *Comparative Drama*, 45:2 (2011), 1–33.

Coote, Lesley, and Tim Thornton, 'Richard, Son of Richard: Richard III and Political Prophecy', *Historical Research*, 73:182 (2000), 321–30.

Culpeper, Jonathan, and Dawn Archer, 'Requests and Directness in early modern English Trial Proceedings and Play Texts, 1640–1760', in Andreas H. Jucker and Irma Taavitsainen (eds), *Speech Acts in the History of English*, (Amsterdam: John Benjamins, 2008), pp. 45–85.

Deleuze, Gilles, *Essays Critical and Clinical*, trans. Daniel W. Smith and Michael A. Greco (London and New York: Verso, 1998).

—— *Critique et Clinique* (Paris: Minuit, 1993).

Devine, Michael, 'Treasonous Catholic Magic and the 1563 Witchcraft Legislation: The English State's Response to Catholic Conjuring in the Early Years of Elizabeth I's Reign', in Marcus Harmes and Victoria Bladen (eds), *Supernatural and Secular Power in Early Modern England* (Farnham: Ashgate, 2015), pp. 67–91.

Dobin, Howard, *Merlin's Disciples: Prophecy, Poetry, and Power in Renaissance England* (Stanford, CA: Stanford University Press, 1990).

Garber, Marjorie, '"What's Past Is Prologue": Temporality and Prophecy in Shakespeare's History Plays', in Barbara Kiefer Lewalski (ed.), *Renaissance Genres: Essays on Theory, History, and Interpretation* (Cambridge, MA: Harvard University Press, 1986), pp. 301–31.

James VI, *A Trew Law of Free Monarchs, or the Reciprock and Mutuall Duetie Betwixt A Free King and His Naturall Subiects* (Edinburgh: Printed by Robert Walde-graue printer to the Kings Majestie, 1598).
—— *Daemonologie in Forme of a Dialogue, Diuided into Three Bookes* (Edinburgh: Printed by Robert Walde-graue printer to the Kings Majestie, 1597).
—— *The Essayes of a Prentise, in the Divine Art of Poesie* (Edinburgh: Thomas Vautrouillier, 1585).
Jansen, Sharon L., *Political Protest and Prophecy under Henry VIII* (Woodbridge: The Boydell Press, 1991).
Kelly, Henry Ansgar, *Divine Providence in the England of Shakespeare's Histories* (Eugene, OR: Wipf and Stock Publishers, 1970).
Kugel, James L. (ed.), *Poetry and Prophecy: The Beginnings of a Literary Tradition* (Ithaca, NY: Cornell University Press, 1990).
Maggi, Armando, *Satan's Rhetoric: A Study of Renaissance Demonology* (Chicago: Chicago University Press, 2001).
Malay, Jessica L., *Prophecy and Sibylline Imagery in the Renaissance: Shakespeare's Sibyls* (London: Routledge, 2010).
—— 'Shakespeare's Tudor Sibyl: Sibylline Discourse in the Portrayal of Queen Margaret in *Richard III*', in Delphine Lemonnier-Texier (ed.), *Représentations et identités sexuelles dans le théâtre de Shakespeare: Mises en scène du genre, écritures de l'histoire* (Rennes: Presses Universitaires de Rennes, 2010), pp. 61–78.
Mullaney, Steven, *The Place of the Stage: License, Play, and Power in Renaissance England* (Ann Arbor/Chicago: University of Michigan Press/University of Chicago Press, 1995).
Patten, Jonathan K. van, 'Magic, Prophecy, and the Law of Treason in Reformation England', *The American Journal of Legal History*, 27:1 (1983), 1–32.
Plutarch, *Moralia*, trans. Frank Cole Babbitt, vol. V (London: William Heinemann, 1936).
Rackin, Phyllis, *Stages of History: Shakespeare's English Chronicles* (Ithaca, NY: Cornell University Press, 1990).
Searle, John R., *Expression and Meaning* (Cambridge: Cambridge University Press, 1979).
—— *Speech Acts: An Essay in the Philosophy of Language* (Cambridge: Cambridge University Press, 1969).
Shakespeare, William, *The Riverside Shakespeare*, ed. George Blakemore Evans (Boston: Houghton Mifflin, 2nd edn, 1997).
Sidney, Sir Philip, *An Apology for Poetry, Or the Defence of Poesy*, eds R. W. Maslen and Geoffrey Shepherd (Manchester: Manchester University Press, 3rd edn, 2002).
Sofer, Andrew, 'How to Do Things with Demons: Conjuring Performatives in *Doctor Faustus*', *Theatre Journal*, 61:1 (2009), 1–21.
Stagg, Robert, 'Shakespeare's Bewitching Line', in Peter Holland (ed.), *Shakespeare Survey*, vol. 71 (Cambridge: Cambridge University Press, 2018), pp. 232–41.
Thornton, Tim, *Prophecy, Politics and the People in Early Modern England* (Woodbridge: Boydell & Brewer, 2006).
Tillyard, E. M. W., *Shakespeare's History Plays* (London: Chatto & Windus, 1944).
Wills, Garry, *Witches and Jesuits: Shakespeare's Macbeth* (Oxford and New York: Oxford University Press/NYPL, 1995).

Wilson, Richard, 'A Savage Spectacle: *Julius Caesar* and the English Revolution', in François Laroque and Franck Lessay (eds), *Histoire et secret à la Renaissance: Études sur la représentation de la vie publique, la mémoire et l'intimité dans l'Angleterre et l'Europe des XVIe et XVIIe Siècles* (Paris: Presses de la Sorbonne Nouvelle, 1997), pp. 41–55.

Woolley, Benjamin, *The Queen's Conjurer: The Science and Magic of Dr John Dee, Adviser to Queen Elizabeth I* (New York: Henry Holt, 2001).

Worthen, W. B., 'Drama, Performativity, and Performance', *PMLA*, 113:5 (1998), 1093–107.

7

Puck, Philostrate and the *locus* of *A Midsummer Night's Dream*'s topical allegory

Laurie Johnson

The supernatural world framing the action in *A Midsummer Night's Dream* is populated by figures derived from a range of pre-Shakespearean sources.[1] Yet the most elevated of these figures, Oberon and Titania, have long been thought by scholars to contain topical allusions to Elizabeth and her relationships with one or more courtiers. The play thus seems to be a *locus* for potentially competing fields of influence on the playwright: borrowing from the past while also writing directly to the present moment, most likely to excite the interest of his audiences and their yen for gossip or scandal. I argue here that the supernatural elements of *Midsummer*, rather than surrounding the drama with the unworldly or unfamiliar, provide an anchor for audiences to read locally by identifying supernatural figures on the basis of local knowledge. The semantic field within which the names of the supernatural figures circulate thus requires the audiences' local knowledge in order to signify coherently. Conversely, the world of the Athenians is populated by anachronisms drawn from multiple classical sources, thus remaining constantly at odds with itself and any attempt at local reading. By isolating the Athenians from their source worlds and putting them into contact with the supernatural world in a site that recognisably operates as the *locus amœnus* – the 'pleasant place' of classical literature, an idyllic setting removed from the routine of city life in which characters can give themselves over to natural desires and fears – Shakespeare enables these figures to signify as topical references, unmoored from the classical sources from which they have been drawn. The forest thus becomes the site for a clash between modes of signification – sources and topicality – enabled by allowing the audience to anchor supernatural elements to familiar figures derived from the audience's local experience, and responding to contemporary issues.

Northrop Frye famously argued that Shakespeare recalibrates this *topos* through a 'green world' in his most successful comedies, in which pastoral setting the characters are transformed by their exposure to forces both natural and supernatural – their metamorphosis both resolves the comedy and reshapes the characters' normal world upon their return.² Just as the Shakespearean version of the *locus amœnus* transfers the transformative effects of the non-place back onto the world from which the characters originated, my argument here will be that the play itself is not simply a fictional non-space of playing set apart from the world of the audience. Instead, in *Midsummer*, the forest and its supernatural inhabitants repeatedly call on the audience to make sense of the fictional world by applying local knowledge and, in so doing, transform the literary *topos* into a field of contemporary topical allegory. The initial audience for any play was the Master of the Revels, whose licence was required before it could be performed to any other audience. Accordingly, for the play to attempt to achieve a genuine transformation in its audience, it must first negotiate a change in relationship between the players and their chief censor. My argument will ultimately be that the supernatural subject matter of *Midsummer* frames a set of precise topical allusions that the man who held the Revels position would have easily recognised, and through which the play seeks to make amends for recent offences in which the company had been embroiled.

Sources

Scholars have established a range of sources for the various plots and characters intertwined in *Midsummer*, from Plutarch's *Life of Theseus* as a likely source for the Duke of Athens and Ovid's *Metamorphoses* as a source for Titania, to sources of rather more recent vintage such as John Lyly's *Endymion, the Man in the Moon* (1591), which foreshadows several aspects of Shakespeare's play. Perhaps what is most striking is just how many sources are likely to have been used by Shakespeare in the construction of this play. Geoffrey Bullough's eight volumes of *Narrative and Dramatic Sources of Shakespeare* bear out the unusual breadth of materials used: for the majority of Shakespeare's plays, Bullough excerpts only around three to four possible sources, alongside one or more analogues; for *Midsummer*, Bullough excerpts eight source texts and three analogues, in addition to which he discusses both Plutarch and Lyly at length in his introductory comments on the play. Bullough recognises ten sources in all,³ a figure exceeded only by the eleven sources he identifies for *King Lear*.⁴ To Bullough's ten sources for *Midsummer*, Kenneth Muir adds Thomas Mouffet's *Of the Silkewormes, and their Flies* (c. 1589), to which he traces much of the language used in the Pyramus and Thisbe story and, perhaps, Bottom's name.⁵ We might thus say of *Midsummer* that, even by the Bard's gregarious standards of appropriation, *Midsummer* stands rivalled only by *Lear* for breadth of coverage of source materials. The number of source materials is worth noting, in particular, when considering how this might have impacted on the sense of location that contemporary audience members were able to attach to the drama.

In 1596, the fairy realm represented in the play might have seemed rather loosely constituted. From the outset, the play signals its location as Athens and its sources as ancient, meaning that here the audience can expect to find the inhabitants of Olympus in close proximity. It is rather anachronistic to find the Athenians using the name of the Roman Diana instead of Artemis, Venus instead of Aphrodite, and Cupid instead of Eros, but this is attributable to Plutarch's use of the Roman equivalents, a convention to which Thomas North adhered in his 1579 English translation. The supernatural realm is thus aligned early in the play with Greco-Roman mythos. Yet this classical location seems to be upset soon after with the introduction to the fairy realm in Act 2, Scene 1. The scene begins with Robin Goodfellow, 'a puck' – although the defining phrase is missing from the relevant stage direction in the First Quarto of 1600 – and a fairy, whom Robin calls 'spirit' (2.1.1), in conversation.[6] This spirit tells Robin that she serves 'the Fairy Queen' (2.1.8), signalling a very contemporary analogue: the second instalment of Edmund Spenser's *Faerie Queene* was published in 1596 (the first in 1590). Spenser's Gloriana is of course the stuff of Arthurian romance, drawn from Malory's *Morte d'Arthur* (c. 1470) and other related *chansons de geste*,[7] which in itself might be cause for an early modern audience to have done a double-take at the shift from the Athenian setting to the Arthurian fairy realm.

Immediately afterward, though, Robin changes things still further by naming the King of this fairy realm as Oberon, who had been well known to Europeans as the Eastern dwarf king of the fairies since the thirteenth century *chanson Huon de Bordeux*, and was certainly also known as such in English after Lord Berners translated the tale around 1534.[8] Oberon's wife – that is, his 'fairy Queen' – is named in *Midsummer* as soon as she enters the stage: '[i]ll met by moonlight, proud Titania' (2.1.60). Oberon's words signal two potential points of disjuncture for the early modern audience: for those who knew Ovid's *Metamorphoses* well enough, the reference is to the daughter of Titan, shifting the sense of setting once more back to Greco-Roman mythology. However, for those who knew Spenser or his sources for *The Faerie Queene*, the 'fairy queen' in Shakespeare's *Midsummer* is not equated by name with Spenser's Gloriana, thus distancing the character from a text that might otherwise have been signalled as a 'source'.

In the midst of all this meandering through a variety of myths and romances, there appears 'that shrewd and knavish sprite/Called Robin Goodfellow' (2.1.33–34), who some call 'hobgoblin' and some 'sweet puck' (2.1.40). It is important to note that much of what we now understand to have been the early modern association of these terms was not, in fact, a commonly held view until *after* Shakespeare's *Midsummer* was first performed – indeed, as Albert Hamilton suggests, it may well be the case that it was 'under the influence of this play and Mercutio's Queen Mab speech in *Romeo and Juliet* that a coherent English tradition of fairies and fairy lore [was] generated in literature out of various traditions'.[9] In his *Discoverie of Witchcraft* (1584), Reginald Scot mentions Robin Goodfellow and the Hob-goblin several times as a related pair of 'bugs speciallie spied and feared of sick folke, children, women, and cowards, which through weaknesse of mind and bodie, are shaken with vaine dreams and continuall fear',[10] but he also makes clear their different traditions and locations. Importantly, we find no mention of 'Puck' by this name in Scot – there is but one passing mention to 'the puckle' in a list of no fewer than thirty-four different creatures and, he says, 'other such bugs' that remain sources of fear in the regional lore.[11] Robin Goodfellow and the Hob-goblin are also listed here, but this is not by way of conflation – Scot's list is intended to demonstrate how many different creatures still exist in the minds of Britain's people, which is precisely why the discovery of witchcraft remains a fraught exercise in the face of widespread collective fantasy persisting around the counties.

Puck comes from a range of traditions, all of which are perhaps so ancient that even by the time of Scot they seemed scarcely worth examining in any detail: in what is still one of the most comprehensive studies of Shakespeare's debt to local lore, Thiselton Dyer points out in his 1883 *Folk-lore of Shakespeare* that variations on the word 'puck' can be found scattered throughout Europe as generic terms for evil sprites – for example, 'puki' in Iceland, 'piskey' in Devon, the Cornish 'pixie', Worcestershire's 'poake', Ireland's 'pooka', and the Welsh 'pwcca', along with a possible connection to the Scottish 'pawkey', which by Dyer's time meant simply 'sly'.[12] Curiously, not one of these traditional terms is in fact the word 'puck' as it appears in Shakespeare's play. Yet Dyer may well have inadvertently created a convention among English folklorists when he concludes that 'it is evident, then, that the term Puck was in bygone years extensively applied to the fairy-race, an appellation still found in the west of England'.[13] In spite of the many words Dyer has listed as precedent alternatives, he suggests that the word 'Puck' existed in this form in 'bygone years', and it is a suggestion that seems to have worked its way into many accounts of the history of the term. For example, we find in the *Oxford Dictionary of Phrase and Fable* this definition: 'more generally (from the Old English period), puck meant a mischievous and evil sprite. The use of the name for one particular spirit seems to derive from the character in Shakespeare's *Midsummer Night's Dream* (1600).' The second part of this definition is correct, so far as the scholarship of Dyer and others such as Katharine Mary Briggs, Gillian Edwards and Winfried Schleiner attest.[14] Prior to Shakespeare, the varieties of what we might call puck-words referred generically to a class of spirit or sprite, so that there were 'pookas' (plural) or 'a poake' (singular) but no proper name for any single such creature. As Schleiner notes, then, perhaps Scot's 'the puckle' is the closest early analogue we have to Shakespeare's invention of the proper name 'Puck'.[15] As for the first part of the definition for 'puck' in the *Oxford Dictionary of Phrase and Fable*, its wording is misleading and carries with it the suggestion, as in Dyer's inflated claim, that 'puck' existed as a generic word before

Shakespeare. Yet no scholar has identified a single example of any previous use of the word in this form. So far as we currently know, 'Puck' is Shakespeare's invention, not only as a proper name but also in this particular form. The spelling of the name, as we shall see below, can serve as an interpretative key.

Names

In addition to the sources, I now wish to focus on the functions of the proper names within the drama. The place name 'Athens', as I have suggested already, signals more than just a geographical location; it cues a complete set of geo-mythological associations, replete with numerous additional proper names ('Olympus', 'Theseus', 'Hippolyta' and so forth). The name 'Oberon' signals the presence within the drama of a second geomythological tradition, but it need not be altogether incompatible with the Greco-Roman tradition established by the first set of proper names, especially when he is linked to Titania, whose name belongs to the tradition to which Athens, Theseus and others belong. It is a potentially complex manoeuvre to tie the Eastern fairy Oberon to figures from Greco-Roman *mythos*, but it ensures the audience do not mistakenly assume from the outset that the supernatural beings in the play are simply inhabitants of Olympus. The fairy realm in *Midsummer* exists alongside, not above, the urban setting of Athens, thereby signalling its potential to function as *topos* within the drama; that is, as a *locus amœnus*. The proper names are drawn from a range of sources, but perhaps this is the point: all of the names we have identified from 'Athens' to 'Titania' can be traced to a written source text – the geolocational cues for the audience occur within a written tradition of *historia*. In a manner befitting the character, the presence of Robin Goodfellow upsets this literary apple cart. Whereas Bullough lists Scot's *Discoverie* as a 'probable source' for *Midsummer*,[16] he is also keen to point out in the introductory comments that Shakespeare needed 'no books to define Robin Goodfellow's qualities, which were well-known in the countryside'.[17] This cursory observation removes from the artist any sense of insular self-sufficiency and resituates the playwright's life and practice in a community. Accordingly, Scot may well have been read by Shakespeare but not necessarily as a source 'text' for Robin Goodfellow or any of the other 'bugs' invoked in *Midsummer*. Both Scot *and* Shakespeare refer to those '*we* call' or '*some* call' – their names are thus tied directly to the community that *calls* each figure this or that name as a part of their own local, oral history.

Laura Aydelotte argues that the inhabitants of the fairy realm really only have just one thing in common: their shared lack of a 'local habitation' – 'the fairy world', she writes, 'is defined as one inhabited by moving creatures, unfixed, outpacing the moon in their global flight, and wandering "everywhere" while belonging nowhere'.[18] Against this idea, though, the names of the fairies who serve Titania are derived from rather familiar things: the fairy servant Peaseblossom and his parents 'Mistress Squash' and 'Master Peascod' (3.1.178–80) reference a widely used 'staple fodder', which as Vivian Thomas and Nicki Faircloth note was 'eaten more by ordinary people than served at feasts',[19] and Cobweb, Mustardseed, and Moth would be instantly recognisable to any audience. While the figures may seem to belong nowhere, their names enable 'ordinary people' to instantly locate them within a familiar field of knowledge. I suggest the same process is at work in the multiple names given to the puck figure in this play: just as the names potentially intersect with any number of oral traditions, this flexibility provides audiences with the scope to give the fairy realm their own, very local flavour, as it leaves the figures open to interpretation based on any of the local legends that an audience might bring to a theatre as part of their experience of belonging to a community. Each to their own, or make of puck what you will. This is thus a form of geolocation that relies on the local habitation of each audience to create a plausible or at least familiar fairy realm in the surroundings of Athens.

Shakespeare's Theseus, echoing Scot, dismisses the 'shaping fantasies' presented by the lovers, declaring that it is to the 'poet's pen' that 'airy nothing' owes its 'local habitation and a name' (5.1.5–17), yet Theseus contradicts himself; that is, he contradicts his self, his own *raison d'être* – as he earlier claims 'I never may believe/These antique fables, nor these fairy toys' (5.1.2–3), notwithstanding that Theseus owes his own existence to Shakespeare's use of classical sources or, as it were, 'antique fables'. The words with which the last act of the play gets under way should therefore be understood ironically, such that the antique fables that give to Theseus his existence are placed on a par with these fairy toys from which Robin Goodfellow and his aliases and compatriots are drawn. Their local habitation and their names are not the products of the poet's pen; instead, they derive from the audience's own local habitation and the names they give to the 'bugs', as Scot had dismissively called them all. Puck may admit to being 'that merry wanderer of the night' (2.1.42) and boast of being able to 'put a girdle round about the earth/In forty minutes' (2.1.175–76), but to any given member of the audience, his presence in the drama also provides a potentially localised anchor, based on their own knowledge of or belief in the existence of a puckle, a pouka, a Robin Goodfellow or what-have-you.

Topicality

We have noted, of course, that Shakespeare's version of this puckle figure is 'Puck', a proper name that does not predate *Midsummer* in any known source. I want to return now to the question of a possible source from which Shakespeare might have drawn this name, but this will bring us into the domain of topical reading. For more than a century there has been a well-established reading of the play focused on the identification of the fairy queen, Titania, with Elizabeth.[20]

Since David Bevington argued in 1968 that Elizabeth and her courtiers were well known to have engaged in 'political lock-picking', so any allegory likely to still be discernible several centuries later surely would not have gone unnoticed and therefore unpunished,[21] there have been a number of attempts to map the play's treatment of gendered authority while excluding any direct topical reference to the queen herself.[22] Maurice Hunt, on the other hand, suggests that *Midsummer* could more safely encrypt an allegory about Elizabeth that was not intended for her instruction but was aimed at 'the amusing reinforcement of the political opinions of one or more earls and their coteries with influence over the playwright'.[23] Taking Hunt's suggestion further, I would like to consider the extent to which topical material is encrypted into the play not solely for the amusement of earls and their coteries; it is my contention that the topical material also *includes* these coteries with influence over the playwright.

In the case of *Midsummer*, the topical analogues may function in the service of a commentary on questions of censorship and the professionalism of the players. Censorship was an issue Shakespeare's company had directly experienced in 1595 and 1596: as Janet Clare and others have argued, the deposition scene in *Richard II* and parts of *Henry VI, Part 3* were suppressed prior to publication, with the responsible censor on both occasions being the Master of the Revels, Edmund Tylney;[24] and the name of the fat knight in *Henry IV, Part 1* was changed from Oldcastle to Falstaff before the Christmas court performances of 1596 owing to rumblings regarding the use of the name Oldcastle made by William Brooke, Lord Cobham, around the time that he gained the role of Lord Chamberlain in August 1596.[25] Censorship and the limits of the censor's powers would have been likely targets for topical scrutiny after any of these occasions.[26] Indeed, Philostrate, who oversees the 'revels' in the play, would seem by this role alone to be an analogue for Tylney, but I suggest the allegory is further encrypted via a pun derived from Chaucer's *The Knight's Tale*. In Chaucer's text, Philostrate is the name taken by Arcite, squire to Theseus, the knight on whom the tale is based. Arcite adopts the name upon returning to Athens to become 'Page of the chambre' to Emelye.[27] As Arcite intends to woo and win Emelye – a portion of the tale is devoted to his rivalry with Palamon for her affections – it surprises me that the pun relating Arcite's chosen pseudonym to his job description has not yet been noted by scholars: 'philo' is of course 'lover' (from the Greek prefix) and 'strate' is, among other things, synonymous in early modern English with 'chamber'.[28] Such puns would of course seem to have nothing at all do with any attempt to lampoon Tylney, on face value. Yet Shakespeare could readily draw on Chaucer's pun to draw attention to Tylney's family: his father's name was Phillip, and his mother was Malyn Chambre – the resonances between these names and Philostrate ('lover of the *chambre*'), page to Emelye, must surely be no mere coincidence.

If Philostrate represents Tylney, then I suggest the play extends the allegory to include a well known contest for the reversion of the Revels position he held at that time. The man who was promised the reversion in 1596 or 1597 was George Buck,[29] who served with Robert Devereux, Earl of Essex, on the acclaimed Cadiz expedition of June 1596, and who was entrusted with reporting the expedition's success to the queen.[30] Buck did not receive the formal patent until 23 June 1603, when he assumed some of the Revels duties during Tylney's declining years, but there is some evidence that he had been made an informal promise much earlier than the issuing of the patent.[31] It is known that John Lyly believed himself to have also been made the same promise, and that he wrote to Elizabeth herself on two occasions to complain in quite vehement terms that she had not yet made good on her promise – in one he laments being left to 'onely lyve on dead hopes', and complain 'that I haue played the foole, soe longe, and yet lyve',[32] and in the second he goes so far as to bemoan 'yf I bee Borne to haue noethinge, I may haue a Protection to paye noethinge, wth Suite', and boldly requests '[t]enn yeares, ffor Recompence of his service'.[33] Just when this earlier promise might have been made is not certain – the editor of Lyly's *Complete Works*, R. Warwick Bond, claims that the promise must date to 1585, and the ten years and thirteen years named respectively in the two letters situates them in 1595 and 1598. However, this hinges ultimately on the much firmer date of 22 December 1597 attached to a letter written by Lyly to Robert Cecil, complaining about 'ye Reuells countenanced upon Buck' that dashes the promises made to him twelve years earlier.[34]

What is known is that Buck's stock at court peaked when he presented news of the success at Cadiz in July 1596, in a report that was reproduced in John Stow's *Annals of England to 1603*,[35] and yet he had been already passed over for preferment earlier in 1596 when the appointment of Secretary for the French Tongue had gone to Thomas Edmondes despite a direct plea from the Lord Admiral, Charles Howard, for Buck to be considered next in line for the post.[36] Arguably no time would have been more suited to a promise of royal favour than in the wake of Buck's report following the triumph at Cadiz. The competition between Buck and Lyly for the office occupied by Tylney would seem therefore to have been entirely topical in late 1596 or definitely by 1597. Of course, the name given to the 'poake' figure by Shakespeare is phonetically consonant with the name of one of these competitors: Puck is thus potentially a topical reference to Buck. Strengthening the association, in the epilogue to *Midsummer*, he identifies as Puck twice – 'as I am an honest puck' (Ep. 9) and '[e]lse the puck a liar call' (Ep. 13) – in a speech that uses a language strikingly familiar to the censor himself. Puck's first two lines address the question of offence and of how to make amends: '[i]f we shadows have offended,/Think but this, and all is mended' (Ep. 1–2). Tylney's surviving marginal comment on the manuscript copy of *Thomas More* from the early 1590s is remarkably echoed here: '[m]end this', he had written next to lines describing civil unrest in London.[37] It stands to reason he had used the same phrase in censoring Shakespeare's plays in 1595 and 1596. If the reference is missed, it is repeated:

'[g]entles, do not reprehend./If you pardon, we will mend' (Ep. 7–8), and then again, 'to 'scape the serpent's tongue,/We will make amends ere long' (Ep. 11–12). At the close, Puck becomes the voice agreeing to self-censorship, by explicitly echoing the language of the official censor.

If the Puck–Buck relation is clarified by this, what, then, of Lyly? In Bottom, who begins the play as hapless but who is then brought even further undone by Puck's magic, we might find a reference to the author of *Endymion*, on which so much of Shakespeare's play seems based: Bottom plays Pyramus, who is described by Flute as being 'most lily-white of hue' (2.2.87), and it is Bottom whose comic sub-plot seems most insistently to recall that of Sir Tophas, the gentleman who falls in love with the sorceress Dipsas in *Endymion*. The inversion from Sir Tophas to Bottom is also possibly a reference to another very public 'reversion'. It is after this time that Lyly's public fortunes noticeably began to wane. A play based heavily on his *Endymion* may thus contain a wry gesture toward the writer's own demise and the loss of his desired role to the high-flying, far-travelling Buck. The Puck figure is of course also called Robin Goodfellow. The name certainly existed before *Midsummer*, as we have noted, but it might be no coincidence that Shakespeare seeks to conflate his invented 'Puck' with this better known name in a play that gains some of its topical force from the Cadiz expedition. *Midsummer* would not have been the first play to promote this context: *The Merchant of Venice* was written in 1596, with Salarino's mention of the ship named *Andrew* an explicit reference to one of the ships captured by Essex, for example, among a raft of references to Essex's exploits of the time.[38] To an Elizabethan ear, *circa* 1596, the name of Robin would doubtless have been heard as a potential reference to the man who was considered by many to have had the highest political stock in the land: Essex was known widely as the favourite to the queen, her 'sweet Robin', as she called him on more than one occasion in public, after a habit she had developed for her previous favourite, Robert Dudley, Earl of Leicester.[39] By the end of the play – '[a]nd Robin shall restore amends' (Ep. 16) – the trickster figure has been turned into a restorative, healing Robin, who closes the play's account with the audience. The treatment of a comically translated 'lily-white' Bottom by the Puck–Buck figure carries with it the force of the conflation of the Puck–Robin figures into a single powerful entity, capable of wreaking havoc if unleashed but also of restoring amends, but perhaps only this last option 'if we be friends' (Ep. 15).

Censorship

I make this point about the epilogue because it is to be remembered that any reference understood by an Elizabethan audience *circa* 1596 also would not just have been understood by the monarch and her immediate, lock-picking court, but easily decrypted by the censor. If the censor was himself a target of the allegory, how could a playwright hope to quell the rage except, perhaps, to reference also the players' own powerful friends in high places, and by the offer to also 'be friends'? If Tylney saw himself in Philostrate – can we expect him to have failed to do so? – he might only have stayed any further request to 'mend *this*' if he could be helped to see that the players considered themselves to have an ally in the Earl of Essex and therefore, by association, with the man who had successfully outpaced Lyly for the reversion of the Master of the Revels position itself. Following a string of acts of censorship in 1595 and 1596 involving the company, this represented a particularly bold move – endgame, perhaps, or so it may have seemed. Having only been in existence in their current form for a little under two years come the end of 1596, the company was beset with two disasters: the Lord Chamberlain, Henry Carey, had died – Carey's son, George, became patron, but he did not replace his father as Lord Chamberlain, that honour being handed instead to Lord Cobham, who we have already seen at the centre of one of the company's censorship incidents – and the company's plans to purchase a large section of Blackfriars Estate for a playhouse were scuppered by a petition from the residents. Around this time, then, Shakespeare's company, or Hunsdon's Men as they became known, were vulnerable. Without a patron positioned close to the inner sanctum of the Queen's Privy Council, they could not count on protection should the censor's eye turn on them with intent to do more than merely remove any suspect sections of play text. In response to this situation, the players opted to use the tools at their disposal, both sources and topical materials, to construct an allegory with the censor himself in their sights.

The censor is not their only target – the players would seem to be part of the mischief in the text, since the presentation of the performers, these 'rude mechanicals' (3.2.11), is far from flattering. Yet I propose that the presentation of Bottom and his company participates in a response to the present moment, *c.* 1596 to 1597, in the very specific sense of fashioning theatrical value. I take my cue here from Paul Yachnin's study of the 'stage-wrights' like Shakespeare, who sought in their plays to distance themselves from the manual and material realities of their labour in order to improve their own standing within the wider 'knowledge marketplace' of their day.[40] On this basis, *Midsummer* represents a moment of writing back to the misfortunes of 1596. The mechanicals *are* inept, but much is made of their status as labourers, so they are prone to enduring the derision of their audience. The players who performed *Midsummer*, by contrast, could have revelled in their ability to portray ineptitude and derision with aplomb. Evidently absent from *Midsummer*, as Anita Gilman Sherman points out, is the *space* in which Philostrate would have seen Bottom audition sections of the play, so that he could advise Theseus of its poor quality.[41] Thus, the play consigns to the peripheral oblivion of an unseen space the site in which Tylney would have housed rehearsals and scrutinised scripts. For Sherman, the forgetting of the Priory at St John's contributes to a systematic forgetting of the labour of rehearsal and the mechanisms of state censorship, thus enabling the '*sprezzatura* of performance' by the professional actors to come to the fore.[42]

The exercise of geolocation which the play demands, as discussed earlier, puts the absence of the site of rehearsal and censorship into perspective. Constructed from an unusually large array of sources, *Midsummer* actively engages audience members in the formulation of a local habitation and a name, while at the same time positing two primary locations in which the action will take place: the Athens ruled by Theseus, and the fairy realm ruled by Oberon. The extent to which the fairy realm functions as the *locus amœnus*, set in opposition to urban Athens, demands in turn that the site be understood as a locale, prompting the audience to rely on their knowledge of the names offered to them: the Eastern fairy king Oberon, the fairy queen Titania, Puck, Robin Goodfellow and so on. These names resist being attached to a single historical source, leaving the audience to potentially situate the fairy realm of the play within their own local myths. In the same movement, the play also deals with the nature of allegory – Philostrate attempts to dissuade the King from allowing the play of *Pyramus and Thisbe* to be performed but only on the basis of it being 'tedious' (5.1.64), rather than because it obviously parallels the forbidden match of Hermia and Lysander.

Had the Master of the Revels to Theseus been sufficiently informed of current events, he might have dissuaded the King on the basis that the allegory struck a chord too close to home or at least thought in advance to order the players to mend this. Beyond Athens, within the *locus amœnus*, there are supernatural forces at work, playing with hapless figures like Bottom for their sport. The message encrypted within this presentation of a pastoral *topos* provides a cautionary tale for the Master of the Revels to Elizabeth – the *topos* concentrates a field of topical allusion that extends to the Master of the Revels himself, and to the power brokers who at that time seemed most effectively to be determining the future of the office, at the cost of those who, like Lyly, had proven themselves to be less capable of gaining preferment. As Lyly had once, like Bottom, found favour, his personality seemed incapable of carrying the weight of his literary gift, and his letters became more supererogatory with time and attendant failure. The puppet masters, like Buck and Essex, were also men of action, and on the heels of the triumph at Cadiz, seemed poised for yet bigger things. In the hurly burly of this field of topical allusion, Scot's 'bugs' are transformed via their familiarity to audiences into 'bug's-words' designed, I suggest, for the eye of the censor first and foremost.[43] The play's use and development of a supernatural location and names, the *locus amœnus* of the pastoral *topos*, thus responded to contemporary court politics, showing Shakespeare's appropriative use of fairies from local folklore for topical, even personal, purposes.

Notes

1 I wish to thank Victoria Bladen, Darryl Chalk, Mary Floyd Wilson, Brett Greatley-Hirsch, David McInnis and Paul Yachnin, as well as those who attended presentations of earlier versions of this material at the 'Shakespearean Reverie' symposium (University of Southern Queensland, 2011), the biennial conference of the Australian Universities' Languages and Literatures Association (University of Queensland, 2013), and 'The Afterlives of Pastoral' conference (University of Queensland, 2014), for their feedback and suggestions throughout the long life and various transformations undertaken by this essay.
2 Northrop Frye, *The Anatomy of Criticism* (New York: Atheneum, 1967), p. 182.
3 Geoffrey Bullough (ed), *Narrative and Dramatic Sources of Shakespeare*, 8 vols (London and Henley: Routledge and Kegan Paul, 1977), vol. 1, pp. 367–76.
4 *Ibid.*, vol. 7, pp. 269–414.
5 Kenneth Muir, *The Sources of Shakespeare's Plays* (London: Methuen, 1977), pp. 73–7. Bullough cites Muir's argument, but indicates that he is not convinced that Mouffet's work predates Shakespeare's (see Bullough, *Narrative and Dramatic Sources*, vol. 1, p. 375).
6 Unless otherwise indicated, all references to Shakespeare's plays are from *The Oxford Shakespeare: The Complete Works*, eds John Jowett, William Montgomery, Gary Taylor and Stanley Wells (Oxford: Clarendon Press, 2nd edn, 2005).
7 See Albert C. Hamilton's entry for 'fairies' in *The Spenser Encyclopedia* (Toronto: University of Toronto Press, 1997), pp. 295–6.
8 Bullough, *Narrative and Dramatic Sources*, vol. 1, pp. 370–71.
9 Hamilton, *Spenser Encyclopedia*, p. 295. For detailed discussion of the emergence of this English tradition during the early modern period, see Dianne Purkiss, *Troublesome Things: A History of Fairies and Fairy Stories* (London: Allen Lane, 2000), pp. 124–85; and Ronald Hutton, 'The Making of the early modern Fairy Tradition', *The Historical Journal*, 57:4 (2014).
10 Reginald Scot, *The Discoverie of Witchcraft* [1584], ed. Brinsley Nicholson (London: Elliott Stock, 1886), p. 122.
11 *Ibid.*
12 Reverend T. F. Thiselton Dyer, *Folk-lore of Shakespeare* (London: Griffith & Farran, 1883), p. 6.
13 *Ibid.*
14 See Katharine Mary Briggs, *The Anatomy of Puck: An Examination of Fairy Beliefs Among Shakespeare's Contemporaries and Successors* (London: Routledge and Kegan Paul, 1959); Gillian Edwards, *Hobgoblin and Sweet Puck: Fairy Names and Natures* (London: Bles, 1974); and Winfried Schleiner, 'Imaginative Sources for Shakespeare's Puck', *Shakespeare Quarterly*, 36:1 (1985).
15 Schleiner, 'Imaginative Sources', p. 66.

16 Bullough, *Narrative and Dramatic Sources*, vol. 1, pp. 394–7.
17 *Ibid.*, p. 371.
18 Laura Aydelotte, '"A local habitation and a name": The Origins of Shakespeare's Oberon', *Shakespeare Survey*, 65 (2012), p. 6.
19 Vivian Thomas and Nicki Faircloth, *Shakespeare's Plants and Gardens: A Dictionary* (London and New York: Bloomsbury, 2014), p. 260.
20 See, for example, Reverend N. J. Halpin, *Oberon's Vision in the Midsummer Night's Dream: Illustrated by a Comparison with Lylie's Endymion* (London: Shakespeare Society, 1843); William Aldis Wright, 'Preface', *Midsummer Night's Dream*, Clarendon Press Series (Oxford: Clarendon Press, 1877), pp. xii–xvi; Edith Rickert, 'Political Propaganda and Satire in *A Midsummer Night's Dream*', *Modern Philology*, 21:1 (1923); Marion Ansel Taylor, *Bottom, Thou Art Translated: Political Allegory in A Midsummer Night's Dream and Related Literature* (Amsterdam: Rodopi NV, 1973); and Mary Ellen Lamb, 'Taken by the Fairies: Fairy Practices and the Production of Popular Culture in *A Midsummer Night's Dream*', *Shakespeare Quarterly*, 51:3 (2000).
21 David Bevington, *Tudor Drama and Politics: A Critical Approach to Topical Meaning* (Cambridge, MA: Harvard University Press, 1968), p. 9.
22 See, for example, Louis Adrian Montrose, '"Shaping Fantasies": Figurations of Gender and Power in Elizabethan Culture', *Representations*, 2 (1983); and Lisa Hopkins, *Writing Renaissance Queens: Texts by and About Elizabeth I and Mary, Queen of Scots* (Danvers, MA: Rosemont Publishing, 2002), pp. 106–7.
23 Maurice Hunt, *Shakespeare's Speculative Art* (New York: Palgrave MacMillan, 2011), p. 155.
24 Janet Clare, *Art Made Tongue-tied by Authority: Elizabethan and Jacobean Dramatic Censorship* (Manchester: Manchester University Press, 1999), pp. 62–70.
25 *Ibid.*, pp. 97–100.
26 See also Richard Dutton, *Mastering the Revels: The Regulations and Censorship of English Renaissance Drama* (London: Macmillan, 1991).
27 Geoffrey Chaucer, *The Works of Geoffrey Chaucer*, ed. F. N. Robinson (Boston, MA: Houghton Mifflin, 2nd edn, 1957), p. 31.
28 See *Oxford English Dictionary*, 'strait', n. 2b and 'chamber'.
29 While Buck's name is more commonly presented in early modern scholarship as Buc, the spelling I adopt here was certainly used in his lifetime, not least when he was appointed to the Revels position on 21 June 1603: see Mary Anne Everett Green, ed., *Calendar of State Papers Domestic: James I, 1603–1610* (London: Her Majesty's Stationery Office, 1857), vol. 2, p. 16.
30 Mark Eccles, 'Sir George Buc, Master of the Revels', in Charles Jasper Sisson (ed.), *Thomas Lodge and Other Elizabethans* (Cambridge, MA: Harvard University Press, 1933), pp. 428–30.
31 W. R. Streitberger, 'On Edmond Tyllney's Biography', *The Review of English Studies*, 29:11 (February, 1978), pp. 28–9.
32 John Lyly, *The Complete Works of John Lyly*, ed. R. Warwick Bond (Oxford: The Clarendon Press, 1902), vol. 1, p. 65.
33 *Ibid.*, p. 71.

34 *Ibid.*, p. 68; Warwick Bond's assessment of the dates is made in his commentary, pp. 64–72.
35 Eccles, 'Sir George Buc', pp. 429–31.
36 Edmund Kerchever Chambers, *The Elizabethan Stage*, 4 vols (Oxford: Clarendon Press, 1923), vol. 1, pp. 98–9.
37 Clare, *Art Made Tongue-tied*, pp. 53–4.
38 William Shakespeare, *The Merchant of Venice*, Arden edn, ed. John Russell Brown (Cambridge, MA: Harvard University Press, 1959), p. xxvii. Other striking parallels to Essex are identified by Evelyn May Albright, 'Shakespeare's *Richard II* and the Essex Conspiracy', *PMLA*, 42:3 (1927); Chris Fitter, 'Historicising Shakespeare's *Richard II*: Current Events, Dating, and the Sabotage of Essex', *Early Modern Literary Studies*, 11:2 (2005), pp. 44–5; and Laurie Johnson, *The Tain of Hamlet* (Newcastle-upon-Tyne: Cambridge Scholars Publishing, 2010), pp. 128–32.
39 Taylor, *Bottom*, p. 203 n. 27.
40 Paul Yachnin, *Stage-Wrights: Shakespeare, Jonson, Middleton, and the Making of Theatrical Value* (Philadelphia: University of Pennsylvania Press, 1997), p. 45.
41 Anita Gilman Sherman, 'Forms of Oblivion: Losing the Revels Office at St John's', *Shakespeare Quarterly*, 62:1 (2011).
42 *Ibid.*, p. 101.
43 See *OED*, 'bug-word/bug's-word', and Richard Dutton, *Licensing, Censorship and Authority in Early Modern England* (Basingstoke: Palgrave Macmillan, 2000), p. ix, on the early modern use of 'buggesword' to refer to a word intended to cause dread in the reader or listener.

Bibliography

Albright, Evelyn May, 'Shakespeare's *Richard II* and the Essex Conspiracy', *PMLA*, 42:3 (1927), 686–720.

Aydelotte, Laura, '"A local habitation and a name": The Origins of Shakespeare's Oberon', *Shakespeare Survey*, 65 (2012), 1–11.

Bevington, David, *Tudor Drama and Politics: A Critical Approach to Topical Meaning* (Cambridge, MA: Harvard University Press, 1968).

Briggs, Katharine Mary, *The Anatomy of Puck: An Examination of Fairy Beliefs Among Shakespeare's Contemporaries and Successors* (London: Routledge and Kegan Paul, 1959).

Bullough, Geoffrey (ed.), *Narrative and Dramatic Sources of Shakespeare*, 8 vols (London and Henley: Routledge and Kegan Paul, 1977).

Chambers, Edmund Kerchever, *The Elizabethan Stage*, 4 vols (Oxford: Clarendon Press, 1923).

Chaucer, Geoffrey, *The Works of Geoffrey Chaucer*, ed. F. N. Robinson (Boston, MA: Houghton Mifflin, 2nd edn, 1957).

Clare, Janet, *Art Made Tongue-tied by Authority: Elizabethan and Jacobean Dramatic Censorship* (Manchester: Manchester University Press, 1999).

Dutton, Richard, *Licensing, Censorship and Authority in Early Modern England* (Basingstoke: Palgrave Macmillan, 2000).

—— *Mastering the Revels: The Regulations and Censorship of English Renaissance Drama* (London: Macmillan, 1991).

Eccles, Mark, 'Sir George Buc, Master of the Revels', in Charles Jasper Sisson (ed.), *Thomas Lodge and Other Elizabethans* (Cambridge, MA: Harvard University Press, 1933).

Edwards, Gillian, *Hobgoblin and Sweet Puck: Fairy Names and Natures* (London: Bles, 1974).

Everett Green, Mary Anne, ed., *Calendar of State Papers Domestic: James I, 1603–1610* (London: Her Majesty's Stationery Office, 1857).

Fitter, Chris, 'Historicising Shakespeare's *Richard II*: Current Events, Dating, and the Sabotage of Essex', *Early Modern Literary Studies*, 11:2 (2005), 1–47.

Frye, Northrop, *The Anatomy of Criticism* (New York: Atheneum, 1967).

Halpin, Rev. N. J., *Oberon's Vision in the Midsummer Night's Dream: Illustrated by a Comparison with Lylie's Endymion* (London: Shakespeare Society, 1843).

Hamilton, Albert C., *The Spenser Encyclopedia* (Toronto: University of Toronto Press, 1997).

Hopkins, Lisa, *Writing Renaissance Queens: Texts by and About Elizabeth I and Mary, Queen of Scots* (Danvers, MA: Rosemont Publishing, 2002).

Hunt, Maurice, *Shakespeare's Speculative Art* (New York: Palgrave MacMillan, 2011).

Hutton, Ronald, 'The Making of the early modern Fairy Tradition', *The Historical Journal*, 57:4 (2014), 1135–56.

Johnson, Laurie, *The Tain of Hamlet* (Newcastle-upon-Tyne: Cambridge Scholars Publishing, 2010).

Lamb, Mary Ellen, 'Taken by the Fairies: Fairy Practices and the Production of Popular Culture in *A Midsummer Night's Dream*', *Shakespeare Quarterly*, 51:3 (2000), 277–312.

Lyly, John, *The Complete Works of John Lyly*, 2 vols, ed. R. Warwick Bond (Oxford: Clarendon Press, 1902).
Montrose, Louis Adrian, '"Shaping Fantasies": Figurations of Gender and Power in Elizabethan Culture', *Representations*, 2 (1983), 61–94.
Muir, Kenneth, *The Sources of Shakespeare's Plays* (London: Methuen, 1977).
Purkiss, Dianne, *Troublesome Things: A History of Fairies and Fairy Stories* (London: Allen Lane, 2000).
Rickert, Edith, 'Political Propaganda and Satire in *A Midsummer Night's Dream*', *Modern Philology*, 21:1 (1923), 53–87.
Schleiner, Winfried, 'Imaginative Sources for Shakespeare's Puck', *Shakespeare Quarterly*, 36:1 (1985), 65–8.
Scot, Reginald, *The Discoverie of Witchcraft* [1584], ed. Brinsley Nicholson (London: Elliott Stock, 1886).
Shakespeare, William, *The Oxford Shakespeare: The Complete Works*, eds John Jowett, William Montgomery, Gary Taylor and Stanley Wells (Oxford: Clarendon Press, 2nd edn, 2005).
—— *The Merchant of Venice*, Arden edition, ed. John Russell Brown (Cambridge, MA: Harvard University Press, 1959).
Sherman, Anita Gilman, 'Forms of Oblivion: Losing the Revels Office at St John's', *Shakespeare Quarterly*, 62:1 (2011), 75–105.
Streitberger, W. R., 'On Edmond Tyllney's Biography', *The Review of English Studies*, 29:11 (1978), 11–35.
Taylor, Marion Ansel, *Bottom, Thou Art Translated: Political Allegory in A Midsummer Night's Dream and Related Literature* (Amsterdam: Rodopi NV, 1973).
Thiselton Dyer, Reverend T. F., *Folk-lore of Shakespeare* (London: Griffith & Farran, 1883).
Thomas, Vivian, and Nicki Faircloth, *Shakespeare's Plants and Gardens: A Dictionary* (London and New York: Bloomsbury, 2014).
Wright, William Aldis, 'Preface', *A Midsummer Night's Dream*, Clarendon Press Series (Oxford: Clarendon Press, 1877).
Yachnin, Paul, *Stage-Wrights: Shakespeare, Jonson, Middleton, and the Making of Theatrical Value* (Philadelphia: University of Pennsylvania Press, 1997).

8

'Strange intelligence': transformations of witchcraft in *Macbeth* discourse

William C. Carroll

The earliest Scottish chronicles of the reign of Macbeth do not mention witches, witchcraft, or the supernatural.[1] The first of these, the *Chronicle* of Marianus Scotus (written *c*. 1082, after the historical Macbeth's death in 1057), states the entire story in the briefest terms: 'Duncan, the king of Scotland, was killed in autumn (on the nineteenth day before the Kalends of September,) by his earl, Macbeth, Findlaech's son; who succeeded to the kingdom, [and reigned] for seventeen years'.[2] Other early accounts say even less: 'Macbeth, Findlaech's son, reigned for seventeen years. And he was killed in Lumphanan, by Malcolm, Duncan's son; and was buried in the island of Iona'.[3] Granted that these chronicles are primarily king-lists, still, the stories of Duncan's death and Macbeth's reign and death are terse. Later versions begin to fill in gaps and, increasingly, invent episodes, motivations and characters. This chapter will consider the historiography of the Macbeth narrative in its development of the supernatural witches.

John Fordun's fourteenth-century rendering – his *Chronica Gentis Scotorum* is apparently the first full-length narrative of Macbeth – describes Duncan's overthrow as in part his own fault: 'He was, it seems, too long-suffering, or rather easy-going, a king... [like the emperor Titus,] He was so gentle and mild that he punished no one at all', hence he was an easy mark for Macbeth, 'by whom he [Duncan] was privily wounded unto death at Bothgofnane' (vol. 4, p. 180).[4] Macbeth was 'hedged round with bands of the disaffected and at the head of a powerful force', and so 'seized the kingly dignity in AD 1040, and reigned seventeen years' (vol. 4, p. 180). No prophecy, no witchcraft, no Lady Macbeth, no supernatural elements to the story: just the same straightforward narrative of treachery and murder that – according to the English – had characterised the Scottish monarchy for centuries.

But then Andrew Wyntoun's *Original Chronicle of Scotland* (1406) says that Macbeth murdered Duncan – not simply slew him in battle – when

> he had... a dreme,
> That he sawe quhen he was ynyng,...

A nycht he thowcht, in hys dremyng,
That syttand he was besyd the King,...
He thowcht quhile he was swa syttand,
He sawe thre wemen than thowcht he,
Thre werd Systrys mast lyk to be;
The first he hard say gangand by,
'Lo, yhondyr the Thayne off Crwmbawchty!'
The tothir woman sayd agayne,
'Off Morave yhondyre I se the Thayne'.
All this he herd in his dremyng. (Wyntoun, vol. 2, ll. 1850–70)[5]

(he had... a dream,
That he saw when he was young,...
One night he thought in his dreaming
That sitting he was beside the King,...
He thought while he was so sitting,
He saw three women then, thought he,
Three weird Sisters most like to be;
The first he heard say going by,
'Lo, yonder the Thane of Cromarty!'
The other woman said again,
'Of Moray yonder I see thee Thane'.
All this he heard in his dreaming.)

The nature of the three women he thinks he sees remains ambiguous – they were most like to be 'thre werd Systrys,' but it was all a dream. Macbeth's motive for killing Duncan, then, originates (in Fordun) in 'the wickedness of a family... the head of which was Machabeus' (Fordun, vol. 4, p. 180), and in Wyntoun, in Macbeth's own mind, where he dreams the prophecies ('[t]he fantasy thus of his dreme/Movyd hym mast to sla hys eme [uncle]', [Wyntoun, vol. 2, ll. 1875–6]). Similarly, in his *Historia Majoris Britanniae Angliae quam Scotiae* (1521), John Major says that Duncan was 'secretly put to death by the faction which had been till then in opposition. He was mortally wounded by one Machabeda at Lochgowane... Now those kings showed a grave want of foresight, in that they found no way of union and friendship with the opposing faction... for to gain a kingdom many a wicked act is done.'[6] Wickedness, dreams of ambition, factional conflict: the secular nature of the crime, even though it is against royalty, could not be clearer.

It should be noted that Wyntoun (apparently) did first introduce a supernatural element into the Macbeth narrative, for Macbeth's mother, we are told in a later section, one day walking in the woods for the air, met a handsome man, 'proportyownd wele in all mesoure', slept with him, 'and on hyr that tyme to sowne gat/This Makbeth', and 'he the Dewïll wes that hym gat' (Wyntoun, vol. 2, ll. 1911–18, 1925), who then made the prophecy that 'na man suld be borne off wyff/Off powere to rewe hym hys lyff' (Wyntoun, vol. 2, ll. 1929–30). As several scholars have noted, Wyntoun's story has many elements of Norse and Celtic mythology, such as Macbeth's conception. According to Cowan, '[t]he story of MacBeth's father is basically a Celtic *compert* or conception tale and so is that relating to Malcolm's birth. MacBeth thus joins the ranks of other "fatherless" heroes – Taliesin in the *Mabinogion*, Ambrosius Aurelianus and St. Mungo.'[7] Dreams and visitations of course often derive from supernatural sources, but Wyntoun's 'thre wemen' are not further described, and are a 'fantasy' in Macbeth's head that moved him to commit the crime.

Hector Boece's 1527 narrative *Historia Gentis Scotorum* is a landmark (if not necessarily a positive one) in the evolution of the Macbeth narrative: it is full of new, invented scenes and events, ranging from the characters of Banquo and Fleance to the names and dates of the mythical first forty-five kings between Fergus I and Fergus II.[8] Boece also greatly developed Wyntoun's dream of the '[t]hre werd Systrys' into actual mysterious figures. Now, they are (in John Bellenden's Scots translation of *c.* 1536), 'clothit in elrage and uncouth weid', who 'suddanlie evanist out of sicht' (vol. 2, p. 259) after delivering the prophecies (not in a dream).[9] After killing Duncan, Macbeth recalls 'the prophecy of the foresaid wichis' and would have slain Macduff 'wer nocht ane wiche, in quhom he had gret confidence, said, to put him out of all feir, That he suld nevir be slane with man that wes borne of wife; no vincust, quhill the wod of Birnane wer cum to the castell of Dunsinnane' (vol. 2, p. 269). Boece also formalised the second set of prophecies, adding the one about Birnam Wood, all of them the product of 'fals illusionis of the devil' (vol. 2, p. 269; repeated 2.274). Boece also produced a Lady Macbeth, with dialogue, that greatly amplified the sparse (and in the earliest cases, non-existent) references to her in the preceding narratives:

> His wife, impacient of lang tary, as all wemen ar, specially quhare thay ar desirus of ony purpose, gaif him gret artation to persew the third weird, that scho micht be ane queen: calland him, oft timis, febil cowart, and nocht desirus of honouris; sen he durst not assailye the thing with manheid and curage, quhilk is offerit to him be benevolence of fortoun; howbeit sindry otheris hes assailyeit sic thingis afore, with maist terribil jeopardyis, quhen thay had not sic sickernes to succeed in the end of their labouris as he had (vol. 2, p. 260).

Macbeth, 'be [by] persuasion of his wife', gathered his allies (including Banquo), and 'slew King Duncan' forthwith.

Boece's account was largely taken over by Holinshed, Shakespeare's main source for his play. Holinshed describes 'three women in strange and wild apparel, resembling creatures of elder world' who give the first set of prophecies, then 'vanished immediatlie' (vol. 5, p. 268).[10] Holinshed then adds an interpretation of these figures: 'afterwards the common opinion was, that these women were either the weird sisters, that is (as ye would say) the goddesses of destinie, or

8.1 Raphael Holinshed, *The firste volume of the Chronicles of England, Scotlande, and Irelande* (London, 1577). Detail: Macbeth, Banquo, and the Witches.

else some nymphs or feiries, indued with knowledge of prophesie by their necromanticall science, because everie thing came to passe as they had spoken' (vol. 5, p. 269). Yet the famous illustration of the three witches in the 1577 edition of Holinshed (see figure 8.1) shows something less than 'strange and wild apparel', as the three women are more dowager-like than the typical period illustrations of witches.[11]

In his account of the attempt on Macduff, Holinshed has Macbeth hesitate: 'but that a certeine witch, whome hee had in great trust, had told that he should never be slaine with man borne of anie women, nor vanquished till the wood of Bernane came to the castell of Dunsinane' (vol. 5, p. 274). This (single) 'witch' seems, at least in Holinshed's phrasing, to be distinct from the three Weird Sisters, and distinct from yet another prophecy by 'certeine wizards, in whose words he put great confidence (for that the prophesie had happened so right, which the three faries or weird sisters had declared unto him) how that he ought to take heed of Makduffe, who in time to come should seeke to destroie him' (vol. 5, p. 274). Holinshed concludes Macbeth's reign by noting, as Boece had, that after Macbeth's years of good rule, 'by illusion of the divell, he defamed the same [deeds] with most terrible crueltie' (vol. 5, p. 277). Boece's elaborate portrait of Lady Macbeth, however, is boiled down to a single sentence in Holinshed: Macbeth is encouraged by the words of the 'three weird sisters… but speciallie his wife lay sore upon him to attempt the thing, as she that was verie ambitious, burning in unquenchable desire to beare the name of a queene' (vol. 5, p. 269).

John Leslie's 1578 history, *De origine, moribus et rebus gestis Scotorum*, also following Boece, initially relates (in Book 5, Chapter 84) that 'vainglory of spirit puffed up Macbeth, filling his mind with an insane lust for rule, insomuch that (his wife urging him on, when he was fearful, with hope of a happy outcome) he impiously murdered the saintly (*sanctissimum*) King Duncan'.[12] But later, in his chapter on David II (Book 7, Chapter 98), Leslie returns to the reign of Macbeth when he sets forth the origin of the Stewarts in Banquo's descendants: Macbeth 'understood, by the prophecy of some women – or rather Demons who assumed the likeness of women and were the sure causes of treason, hatred and strife – that after his line was extinct that of Banquo would flourish and reign for a long time etc.' (Bullough, vol. 7, p. 519). Leslie is so concerned to demonise Macbeth that in his main entry on Macbeth's reign (Book 5, Chapter 85; a passage not quoted by Bullough) he dismisses the entry in Marianus Scotus (otherwise considered an authority) that '[t]he king of Scotland, Macbeth, scattered money like seed to the poor, at Rome'[13] on the grounds that Macbeth's tyranny was too great for such a religious pilgrimage; instead, he says, '[I] am persuadet rather to believe the samyn to have beine of quhome how we sall make mentioune, to wit Malcolme', who during Macbeth's reign of terror, 'obteynet baith the ornament and glore of a Prince maist godlie and rychtuous, in visiting religious and haly places'.[14]

A few years after Holinshed's first edition of 1577, and a little more than two decades before Shakespeare wrote *Macbeth*, George Buchanan (1582) developed a parallel, secular reading of the narrative in depth, blaming both the victim and the murderer, while also reporting that the prophecies came through a dream:

> Mackbeth, who had always a Disgust at the un-active Slothfulness of his Cousin; and thereupon had conceived a secret Hope of the Kingdom in his Mind, was further encouraged in his Ambitious Thoughts, by a Dream which he had: For one Night, when he was far distant from the King, he seemed to see Three Women, whose Beauty was more August and Surprizing than bare Womens useth to be, of which, one Saluted him, *Thane* of *Angus* [etc.]... His Mind, which was before Sick, betwixt Hope and Desire, was mightily encouraged by this Dream, so that he contrived all possible ways, by which he might obtain the Kingdom.[15]

Given his 'Sick' mind, and 'spurred on, by the daily Importunities of his Wife (who was Privy to all his Counsels', Macbeth murdered Duncan 'at Innerness' (Buchanan, vol. 7, p. 210). Buchanan's 'Three Women' are of 'Surprizing' beauty, and the dream only 'further encouraged' the 'Ambitious Thoughts' that already possessed him. Indeed, Buchanan apparently dismissed the supernatural moments of the earlier chronicle histories sniffily: '[s]ome of our Writers do here Record many Fables, which are like Milesian Tales, and fitter for the Stage, than an History; and therefore I omit them' (Buchanan, vol. 7, p. 214). 'Milesian fables', he said in an earlier note, were 'so far from being true that they had not the least shadow of Truth in them' (Buchanan, vol. 2, p. 77).

In Buchanan's narrative, Duncan is an 'effeminate and slothful King' (vol. 7, p. 207), incapable of effective rule, as a result of which '*Mackbeth*… thereupon had conceived a secret Hope of the Kingdom in his Mind' (Buchanan, vol. 7, p. 210), prior to the dream. Moreover, Duncan made his son '*Malcolm*, scarce yet out of his Childhood, Governor of *Cumberland*. Mackbeth took this matter mighty Hainously; in regard, he look'd upon it as Obstacle of Delay to him, in his obtaining the Kingdom' since 'the Government of *Cumberland* was always look'd upon, as the first step to the Kingdom of *Scotland*' (vol. 7, p. 210). Duncan's naming of Malcolm, an attempt to reinstitute King Kenneth's change in the system of succession, is thus a prime but typical example of the perils of the new system, in which an incompetent could become king (Malcolm was 'scarce yet out of his Childhood', vol. 7, p. 210); moreover, the violation of the old system offends those who rest their belief in tradition. In Buchanan's version, Macbeth is certainly a violent warrior and an ambitious man, as he is in Shakespeare's, but he is also more clearly wronged, and in some ways had, as David Norbrook has noted in an important essay, 'half-buried associations with constitutionalist traditions', a figure in whom 'vestiges remain of a worldview in which regicide could be a noble rather than an evil act'.[16] Norbrook is referring here to the larger argument of Buchanan and others that the king derives his sovereign power from the consent of the people, in a contractual sense, and that it was not only possible but sometimes even necessary (as in the case of Mary Queen of Scots) for the monarch to be deposed or otherwise removed from power. The history of the Scottish monarchy, Buchanan showed through example after example, was that tyranny resulted from such impulses as Kenneth's, and tyrannicide was not only possible, but virtually an obligation for a free people. Such arguments resonated throughout the seventeenth century, particularly in times of constitutional crisis.[17]

To take one final example of the 'secular' narrative, almost exactly one century after Shakespeare's play, an anonymous author in 1708 published a novelisation of the Macbeth story entitled *The Secret History of Mack-Beth, King of Scotland. Taken from a very Ancient Original Manuscript*.[18] The printer, James Woodward, in the same year published another book entitled *Hypolitus Earl of Douglas. Containing some Memoirs of the Court of Scotland; with the Secret History of Mack-Beth King of Scotland*, in which the *Secret History* was simply reprinted.[19] Further reprintings, some under different titles, appeared in 1741, 1768, 1828 and 1841.

The Secret History follows Buchanan and the secular history, in which the ineffectual Duncan is '[a] Prince of too sweet, and easie a disposition to be at the Head of a Government so difficult to manage' (1708: A7ʳ). The 1768 revision and expansion of the *Secret History* is even more direct on the subject of the weak king: 'Duncan was of too soft and easy a disposition to be at the head of a government divided into a diversity of factions, every one of which making advantage of their monarch's inactivity, laboured to aggrandize their several families, without any sort of regard to the public-weal' (1768: B1^v).[20] Throughout all its versions, The *Secret History* resolutely banishes all traces of the supernatural. The prophecies Mack-Beth hears do not come from the Weird Sisters. Rather, he falls asleep one summer evening in his garden, as the Thane of Angus relates:

> He had not been long asleep, but a Vision appear'd to him most surprising, and pleasing; three Women appear'd to him, with Faces shining with celestial Glory, and Garments like the Beams of the Sun. The first salutes him by the Name of *Thane* of *Angus*; the second by that of *Murray*, and the third by the Title of King of *Scotland*. I know very well, that there is a Story spread abroad since his evil Administration, that he met three Witches in a Forest, who visibly, and by Day-Light gave him those Salutations, but I had it from his own Mouth long before, and take the Dream to be nothing else but the Effect of his perpetual Thoughts, how to bring that ambitious Design about, and to which his Lady, whose Soul was nothing but Ambition, push'd him on incessantly. (1708: C4^v)[21]

The 1768 revision is even more emphatic on this point, making even the dream a lie invented by Macbeth, and offering a completely secular explanation of the prophecies; the passage is worth quoting at length:

> *Macbeth* himself communicated to me the account of a vision he pretended to have been visited with the preceding evening. 'Ruminating (said he) last night in my garden, upon the party distractions which divide the Chiefs of this kingdom, without ever consulting about any measures that can tend to make the subjects either happier, or the nation itself less contemptible, I was, by the gentle murmurs of that purling brook which glides through it, and the softening even songs of drowsy birds, invited to repose: I had slumbered but a short while, when methought, after a voice like distant thunder, not noisy but awful, and a prospect of lightening, not glancing nor frightful, but permanent and shining, there appeared before me three most angelic female figures, whose loose garments resembled the waving beams of the sun, and whose heads seemed encircled with crowns of celestial glory. The first, in passing, saluted me with – All hail to *Macbeth*, Thane of *Murray*! The second, All hail to *Macbeth*, Thane of *Glamis*! And the third, All hail to *Macbeth*, King of *Scotland*!' Whether there was any such vision or no, no body can determine, but his ambitious wife, to whom, as to me, he had related it, quickly raised upon it the diabolic structure, which from that moment she pressed him to execute with so much vehemence. *It has been, I imagine, upon the foundation of that vision, that the ridiculous story was invented of his having been, in the same language, saluted by three witches, whom he visibly met in a forest in the middle of a day; and howsoever much the fiction of the witches may be better imagined, as better corresponding with the tyrannical conduct which followed it; yet I will vouch this dream, as now told by me, to be*

> as it was related by himself, long before the story of the witches was ever heard of; and I now consider it to have been nothing else than the effects of his perpetual thoughts, which incited him to form such a dream, to the end that he might observe the impressions which these epithets carried with them upon the minds of those who heard them. (1768: I6ʳ–K1ʳ; my emphasis)[22]

Two long-lived discourses of the Three Women thus parallel, overlap and at times contradict one another. The earliest accounts do not include women or prophecies at all, nor does the earliest full narrative by Fordun; in these versions, Duncan is a weak king, Macbeth's ambition is his own, arising partly from the power vacuum that seemed to invite him, and the witches are nothing more than a dream or even an outright invention. By the mid-eighteenth century, the 'fiction of the witches' is 'a ridiculous story', and it was Lady Macbeth who 'raised upon it the diabolic structure'. With Wyntoun and especially Boece, however, the process of demonisation begins, supernatural elements are added in and the various good deeds of the first ten years of Macbeth's seventeen-year reign begin to be erased. Holinshed provided a version of this narrative that Shakespeare, for the most part, followed.[23] But what I have termed the secular version of the witches also continued, in Buchanan's sceptical rendition, and in such texts as *The Secret History*.

Shakespeare's play seems to have both traditions in mind, for the 'three weïrd sisters' (2.1.20), to begin with, are physical entities outside of Macbeth's mind – Banquo testifies to having seen them, and it is he, not Macbeth, who offers the fullest description: 'What are these,/So withered and so wild in their attire,/That look not like th'inhabitants o'th'earth,/And yet are on it?' Each seems to understand him, he deduces, '[b]y each at once her choppy finger laying/Upon her skinny lips; you should be women,/And yet your beards forbid me to interpret/That you are so' (1.3.37–45).[24] When they disappear after uttering the first set of prophecies, it is Banquo who notes their absence: 'The earth hath bubbles, as the water has,/And these are of them. Whither are they vanished?' (1.3.77–8). Macbeth's response – 'Into the air, and what seemed corporal,/Melted, as breath into the wind' (1.3.79–80) – questions whether they were 'corporal' at all. The second set of prophecies is seen and heard by no one but Macbeth, however, and their corporeality definitely seems in question, as he asks Lennox '[s]aw you the weird sisters?... Came they not by you?', to which Lennox answers in the negative to both questions (4.1.134–6). The staging of the second set of prophecies allows the audience to believe that the witches are now somehow the product of Macbeth's fantasy, that the 'mind diseased' (5.3.41) that he asks the doctor about is his own.[25] The 'scorpions' (3.2.36) in his mind seem a more figurative and terrifying version of Buchanan's description of how '[h]is Mind, which was before Sick, betwixt Hope and Desire, was mightily encouraged by this Dream'. The first set of prophecies, we might say, tells Macbeth exactly what he wants to hear, an exact correspondence between inner desire and outer prophecy. When he asks the three witches 'what are you?', their answer is the three prophecies, as if their identity *is* the prophecies (not, say, their names), which culminate in '[a]ll hail Macbeth, that shalt be king hereafter' (1.3.48). To put it reductively, the play seems to offer both the supernatural and the secular interpretations as possibilities and never entirely settles on one or the other as true.

A few years after Shakespeare's play premiered, Simon Forman saw it at the Globe in 1611 (whether the Folio version or some earlier version is not clear), remarking 'howe Mackbeth and Bancko, 2 noble men of Scotland, Ridinge thorowe a wod, the[r] stode before them 3 women feiries or Nimphes, And saluted Macbeth, sayinge' the prophecies to him.[26] As Braunmuller and others have noted,[27] Forman seems to have read Holinshed's narrative, not only because of the episode with the horses, which are not in the play text, but also because of the echo of Holinshed's reference to 'some nymphs or feiries'. Forman, in any event, never mentions the witches again, and if they were shocking or unusual, they impressed him less than the other supernatural element in the play, the ghost of Banquo.

When Sir William Davenant revised the play for the Restoration stage (1663–4), he famously amplified the roles of Lady Macbeth and Lady Macduff (even having them meet and speak together) and introduced a new figure, the ghost of Duncan, but he also paid special attention to the witches, adding new scenes and, more importantly, new aspects of their representation. Now they both fly ('*Ex. Flying*' [1.1 s.d.; p. 1];[28] '*Enter three Witches flying*' [1.1 s. d.; p. 3]) and are highly musical, singing several songs (from Middleton's *The Witch*) and dancing ('*A dance of witches*' [2.1 s. d.; p. 28]; '*Musick. The witches Dance and Vanish*' [4.1 s. d.; p. 49]), and their number has multiplied, the traditional three in some scenes, four in others, plus Hecate, and possibly two others at the end of the second act. The witches appear to the Macduffs, moreover, with further ominous prophecies:

3 *Witch*.	Many more murders must this one ensue, As if in death were propagation too.
2 *Witch*.	He will.
1 *Witch*.	He shall.
3 *Witch*.	He must spill much more bloud, And become worse, to make his Title good. (2.1; p. 26)

The *Chorus* that follows expresses more directly the witches' anti-royalist nature: '[w]e shou'd rejoice when good Kings bleed./When cattel die, about we go,/ What then, when Monarchs perish, should we do?' (2.1; p. 27) and their second song follows suit: 'We gain more life by *Duncan*'s death' (2.1; p. 28). After Davenant, singing and dancing witches became the norm in productions throughout the eighteenth and nineteenth centuries, their numbers ever increasing. Kemble had a chorus of fifty or more singing witches in his 1794 production.[29] Davenant's singing and dancing witches had been parodied almost immediately by Thomas Duffett in the Epilogue to his burlesque *The Empress of Morocco. A Farce* in 1673, in which the witches were simply prostitutes working the city, and their entry was one of comic excess: '*Three witches fly over the pit, riding upon beesoms* [broomsticks], *Hecate descends over the stage in a glorious chariot, adorn'd with pictures of Hell and devils, and made of a large wicker basket*'.[30] Garrick commented in 1833 that '[i]t has been always customary, – heaven only knows why, – to make low comedians act the witches, and to dress them like old fishwomen… with as due a proportion of petticoats as any woman, letting alone witch, might desire, jocose red faces, peaked hats, and broomsticks'.[31] Samuel Phelps had attempted to break this tradition in a production at Sadlers Wells in 1847 – he would show 'Macbeth from the original text, dispensing with the Singing Witches'[32] – but such sobriety soon failed and some later productions, into the twentieth century, continued with comic witches, though more recent productions and films have featured sinister, uncanny and threatening witches.[33]

The Macbeth narrative, over a period of time, has thus been transformed from a typical Scottish account of secular ambition, rival factions and weak or strong kings, without any supernatural forces at work, to a narrative of supernatural intrusion and demonic prophecy. R. J. Adam has argued that as Macbeth was a man of Moray, the demonisation may have sprung from local politics: 'Moray remained the great danger to the Normanizing, Anglicizing house of Malcolm Ceann-mòr for almost a century after his death', and so the story of Duncan received a *post hoc* 'tragic colour which contemporaries had not seen' and 'projected on to the greatest *maormaer* of Moray something of the hatred and fear which the stubborn Celtic rearguard inspired'.[34]

No doubt many chroniclers indebted to the Scottish throne felt the pressure to demonise Macbeth and associate him with the supernatural, particularly through prophecy, which had been associated by many (but not all) writers with witchcraft, King James among them (in his *Daemonology*).[35] But there was a parallel sceptical (secular) discourse in which prophecy was the product of fabrication and illusion, with distinctly political implications, as Keith Thomas has shown.[36] Howard Dobin, Jr, has noted that '[i]n practical terms, all prophecies voiced outside the auspices of crown and church were treated as demonic or fraudulent', thus the demonic prophecies in *Macbeth* 'were intentionally duplicitous… Identifying such prophecies as multiple falsehoods preserved, by contrast, the ideology of univocal meaning; the devil's lies only validated God's truth'.[37] In an attack on the gullibility of the populace that listened to wild rumours and prophecies in the Armada year, John Harvey asked if anyone can imagine a more 'ludicrous, or ridiculous spectacle... than to see a wretched company of such woofull wights, and miserable creatures, scarcely woorth the ground they treade upon, and hardly deserving their daily bread: sodainly presented on a Theater, or comical stage, in their thredbare liveries, and stale gaberdines, of antique shape, and forlorne fashion? Is not their whole habite and gesture too notorious?'[38] He might have been describing the witches of *Macbeth*, but would have held his tongue had he been present on 29 August 1605, when King James and his court, who had journeyed to Oxford, witnessed an academic play by Matthew Gwinn, and were greeted after its performance with a brief, staged prophecy fawning over the relatively new king's power ('Hail, whom Scotland serves! Whom England, hail!' etc.) and his supposed lineage ('Thou dost restore the fourfold glory of Canute').[39] In terms of the present argument, the main item of interest is that the prophecies were spoken by '*three (as it were) Sibyls... as if from a wood*' ['*tres quasi Sibyllae, sic (Ut é sylva)*'] who identify themselves as '[w]e three same Fates'.

Any such prophetic figures associated with or emanating from sovereign power would be construed as sibyls, beautiful women, fairies, dream-like, while any such figures associated with opposition to sovereign power would be demonised, represented as the 'miserable creatures' Harvey mocked. As the anonymous author of the 1768 *Secret History* so aptly put it, 'the fiction of the witches may be better imagined, as better corresponding with the tyrannical conduct which followed it'. In Shakespeare's play, after all, the plot required a tricky rationalisation by which one king's murder – Duncan's – was condemned while another king's murder – Macbeth's – was rationalised; hence also the proliferation of the words 'tyrant' and 'tyranny', which appear eighteen times in Shakespeare's play, twice in Act 3, Scene 6 and the rest from Act 4, Scene 3 onwards, applied to Macbeth when the approaching murder of King Macbeth is being cast as a justifiable tyrannicide (though even tyrannicide could not be justified, James had argued in *The Trew Law of Free Monarchies* [1598]). Macduff urges Macbeth to surrender, promising (threatening) that he would 'live to be the show and gaze o'th'time./We'll have thee, as our rarer monsters are,/Painted upon a pole and underwrit,/"Here may you see the tyrant"' (5.8.24–7). Kings, it seems, may have sybils prophesy to them, but tyrants can have only witches. As a supreme example in the play, the saintly King Edward the Confessor, Malcolm reports to Macduff (who has come to the English court to appeal to Malcolm in Act 4, Scene 3), not only possesses the miraculous 'touch' that heals the 'Evil', but '[w]ith this strange virtue,/He hath a heavenly gift of prophecy' (4.3.148–59). You say demonic, I say heavenly.

The witches of Macbeth-discourse have been, first, invented and then, once established, radically transformed across the centuries, and their supernatural natures undermined and overdetermined in turn, as the political or religious winds suggest. A large cultural history would have to be mounted to provide a fuller explanation of how each era has constructed them, but one thing is certain: their form and nature seem as 'wayward' as any figures in the history of Shakespearean drama.

Notes

1 All quotations from *Macbeth* are cited in the text from A. R. Braunmuller (ed.), *Macbeth* (Cambridge: Cambridge University Press, 1997); hereafter cited as Braunmuller.
2 Alan O. Anderson (ed.), *Early Sources of Scottish History AD 500 to 1286*, 2 vols (Edinburgh: Oliver and Boyd, 1922), vol. 1, p. 579. Kenneth D. Farrow, 'The Historiographical Evolution of the Macbeth Narrative', *Scottish Literary Journal*, 21 (1994), points out that the Latin verb used – *occiditur* – does not necessarily mean 'murdered' (p. 8).
3 'Chronicle of the Kings of Scotland', *c.* 1187, in Anderson, *Early Sources*, vol. 1, p. 600.
4 W. F. Skene (ed.), *The Historians of Scotland* (Edinburgh: Edmonston and Douglas, 1872), vol. 4, *John of Fordun's Chronicle of the Scottish Nation*. Quotations are cited in the text. On Fordun (and the continuation by Walter Bower), see Sally Mapstone, 'Shakespeare and Scottish Kingship: A Case History', in Sally Mapstone and Juliette Wood (eds), *The Rose and the Thistle: Essays on the Culture of Late Medieval and Renaissance Scotland* (East Linton, East Lothian, Scotland: Tuckwell Press, 1998).
5 David Laing (ed.), *The Orygynale Cronykil of Scotland by Andrew of Wyntoun*, vol. 2 (Edinburgh: Edmonston and Douglas, 1872). Quotations are cited in the text. The third prophecy, that he 'suld be/A man off gret state and bownté', was made later in the narrative by the Devil.
6 John Major, *A History of Greater Britain*, trans. Archibald Constable (Edinburgh: Edinburgh University Press, 1892), pp. 120–1 (Book 3, Chapter 4).
7 E. J. Cowan, 'The Historical Macbeth', in W. D. H. Sellar (ed.), *Moray: Province and People* (Edinburgh: Scottish Society for Northern Studies, 1993), p. 132. See also Farrow, 'Historiographical Evolution', pp. 14–16.
8 See R. J. Adam, 'The Real Macbeth: King of Scots, 1040–1054', *History Today*, 7:6 (1957); Farrow, 'Historiographical Evolution'; and Nick Aitchinson, *Macbeth: Man and Myth* (Thrupp: Sutton, 1999). Prior to Boece's work, no such names as Banquo and Fleance had ever appeared in chronicles, court records or any other document. In 1605, Sir George Buc, in a work otherwise rhapsodic in its praises of James and his royal blood, discreetly said that this alleged descent, in which 'Fleanchus thane… begat unlawfully a sonne, whoe should be ancestor to all the Chiefe Stewards to his day… being not acknowledged by the best Scotish Historiographers, & the thing not honourable, I may well pretermit [i.e. omit] it', *Daphnis Polystephanos. An Eclog treating of Crowns, and of Garlands* (London, 1605), A4ᵛ.
9 Hector Boece, *The History and Chronicles of Scotland*, trans. John Bellenden, 2 vols (Edinburgh: Reprinted for W. and C. Tait, 1821); hereafter cited in the text.

10 Raphael Holinshed, *The Chronicles of England, Scotland, and Ireland* (London, 1587 [6 vols, London, 1808]).
11 They may represent three ages: old, middle, and young.
12 In Geoffrey Bullough (ed.), *Narrative and Dramatic Sources of Shakespeare*, 8 vols (New York: Columbia University Press, 1975), vol. 7, p. 518; hereafter cited in the text.
13 Anderson, *Early Sources of Scottish History*, vol. 1, p. 588.
14 Jhone [sic] Leslie, *The Historie of Scotland*, trans. Father James Dalrymple, 2 vols (Edinburgh: Scottish Text Society, 1888), vol. 1, p. 308.
15 George Buchanan, *The History of Scotland*, trans. T. Page (London, 1690), vol. 7, p. 210; hereafter cited in the text.
16 David Norbrook, '*Macbeth* and the Politics of Historiography', in Kevin Sharpe and Steven N. Zwicker (eds), *Politics of Discourse: The Literature and History of Seventeenth-Century England* (Berkeley: University of California Press, 1987), p. 116. Norbrook argues that Shakespeare seems to have been aware of Buchanan's account of Macbeth, perhaps through direct knowledge, perhaps through the 1587 edition of Holinshed's chronicles of Scotland, as the editor Francis Thynne had drawn 'on Buchanan to correct some points in earlier sections of the chronicle and to bring the narrative up to date beyond the point at which Boece [upon whose history Holinshed had drawn for the 1577 edition] had broken off' (p. 81), although, as Norbrook goes on to note, Thynne did so 'without enthusiasm' (p. 81), given Buchanan's controversial association with theories of deposition and regicide. Some of these 1587 additions were in any event ordered to be cut before publication.
17 Material in this paragraph, and some of the subsequent comments on *The Secret History*, first appeared in William C. Carroll, '"Two Truths Are Told": Afterlives and Histories of Macbeths', *Shakespeare Survey*, 57 (2004).
18 This edition of the *Secret History* is hereafter cited in the text as '1708'. The characters' names will be spelled 'Macbeth' and 'Lady Macbeth' in reference to Shakespeare's play, and 'Mack-Beth' and 'Lady Mack-Beth' in reference to the various editions of the *Secret History*.
19 The 1708 *Hypolitus* was reprinted yet again in 1711. Authorship of the *Secret History* has frequently been attributed by bibliographers and librarians to the French author, Marie-Catherine D'Aulnoy (c. 1650/51–1705), on the grounds that she is the author of the *Hypolitus* (published in France in 1690). The seventeenth-century editions of the *Histoire d'Hypolite*, however, do not include the *Secret History*, which seems purely an English invention. Best known today for her collections of fairy tales (*Les Contes des fées*, Paris, 1697 and *Contes nouveaux ou les Fées à la mode*, Paris, 1698), which were often reprinted and translated, Madame D'Aulnoy enjoyed a wave of popularity in England at this time. For her place in the genre of the memoir and travel-writing, and her influence on eighteenth-century English writers, see Melvin D. Palmer, 'Madame d'Aulnoy in England', *Comparative Literature*, 27 (1975).
20 *A Key to the Drama; or, Memoirs, Intrigues, and Atchievements, of Personages, who have been chosen by the most celebrated Poets, as the fittest Characters for Theatrical*

Representations... . Vol. I. Containing the Life, Character, and secret History of Macbeth. By a Gentleman, No professed Author, but a Lover of History, and of the Theatre (London: Printed for the author by J. Browne, 1768). Hereafter cited in the text as '1768'.

21 The Angus–Murray–King sequence marks this material as deriving from Buchanan.
22 Banquo, on the other hand, neither dreamed nor made up his prophecy, as Lady Mack-Beth learns from her spies 'that some *Gypsies* had assur'd *Bancho*, on enquiring his Fortune, that his Posterity shou'd be Kings of *Scotland*, and keep Possession of the Throne, as long as the Nation remain'd. This tho' an idle Story, was sufficient to alarm a Woman of her Temper' (1708: D1').
23 Among the many key differences in Shakespeare's play: the large expansion of Lady Macbeth's role; the erasure of any reference to Macbeth's ten years of enlightened rule; the introduction of Banquo's ghost; and the erasure of Banquo's role as co-conspirator with Macbeth against Duncan. Although he shows Duncan to be a fatally passive king, Shakespeare also suppresses the more openly contemptuous comments on Duncan in Holinshed – e.g. Macbeth spoke 'much against the kings softnes, and overmuch slacknesse in punishing offendors' (vol. 5, p. 265); Duncan was a 'dull coward and slouthfull person' (vol. 5, p. 267).
24 I pass over the implications of their apparent androgyny; many scholars have pursued this line of inquiry.
25 Neither Fordun, Wyntoun, Major, nor Buchanan, it should be pointed out, have anything equivalent to the play's Act 4, Scene 1 – much less a Hecate or a Show of Kings. The frontispiece illustration to Rowe's 1709 and 1714 editions featured the cauldron in this scene; see William C. Carroll, 'Spectacle, Representation, and Lineage in *Macbeth* 4.1', *Shakespeare Survey*, 67 (2014): 345–71. Deborah Willis argues, as many feminist critics have, that the cauldron becomes 'the *locus* of birth as well as death and dismemberment, suggestive of vagina and womb as well as cooking vessel', *Malevolent Nurture* (Ithaca, NY: Cornell University Press, 1995), p. 232.
26 Quoted from E. K. Chambers, *William Shakespeare: A Study of Facts and Problems* (Oxford: Clarendon, 1988), vol. 2, p. 337.
27 Braunmuller, p. 58.
28 Quotations are from *Macbeth, A Tragœdy. With all the Alterations, Amendments, Additions, and New Songs* (London, 1674); citations in the text are to the act/scene and page number.
29 Joseph W. Donohue, Jr, 'Kemble's production of *Macbeth* (1794)', *Theatre Notebook*, 21 (1967). For the stage history of the play, see among others Marvin Rosenberg, *The Masks of Macbeth* (Berkeley: University of California Press, 1978); Bernice W. Kliman, *Shakespeare in Performance: Macbeth* (Manchester: Manchester University Press, 1992); John Wilders (ed.), *Macbeth: Shakespeare in Production* (Cambridge: Cambridge University Press, 2004); and Dennis Bartholomeusz, *Macbeth and the Players* (Cambridge: Cambridge University Press, 1969).
30 Quoted in William C. Carroll (ed), *Macbeth: Texts and Contexts* (Boston, MA: Bedford, 1999), p. 179.
31 Quoted in Braunmuller, p. 68.

32 Quoted in William Shakespeare, *Macbeth*, eds Sandra Clark and Pamela Mason (London: Bloomsbury, 2015), p. 99.
33 See Victoria Bladen, 'Weird Space in *Macbeth* on Screen', in Sarah Hatchuel, Nathalie Vienne-Guerrin and Victoria Bladen (eds), *Shakespeare on Screen: Macbeth* (Rouen and Le Havre: Presses Universitaires de Rouen et du Havre, 2013), pp. 81–106. Some recent films and productions borrow from noir, horror and slasher film genres in attempting to outdo even the Shakespearean original in terms of demonism and the grotesque.
34 Adam, 'The Real Macbeth', p. 387.
35 King James VI, *Daemonology, In Form of a Dialogue* (Edinburgh, 1597).
36 Keith Thomas, *Religion and the Decline of Magic* (New York: Scribner's, 1971). Thomas argues that the publication of prophecies was prohibited by Tudor and Stuart authorities because political prophecies were usually deployed *after* some act of political radicalism, as a means of justification: 'at the heart of the belief in prophecies, there lay an urge to believe that even the most revolutionary doings of contemporaries had been foreseen by the sages of the past… Their function was to persuade men that some proposed change was not so radical that it had not been foreseen by their ancestors. This had the effect of disguising any essentially revolutionary step by concealing it under the sanction of past approval' (p. 423).
37 Howard Dobin, Jr, *Merlin's Disciples: Prophecy, Poetry, and Power in Renaissance England* (Stanford, CA: Stanford University Press, 1990).
38 *A Discursive Problem Concerning Prophecies* (London, 1588), p. 66.
39 The text is printed in Latin and translated into English in Bullough, vol. 7, p. 470–72. As Clark and Mason point out, in spite of some claims that it is a source for the play or that Shakespeare might even have been present, 'there is nothing to suggest that Shakespeare actually knew it or was even present in Oxford at the time; and the resemblances between it and the words of the Sisters [in *Macbeth*] may well be due to a common source in Holinshed', Shakespeare, *Macbeth*, eds Clark and Mason, p. 91.

Bibliography

A Key to the Drama; or, Memoirs, Intrigues, and Atchievements, of Personages, who have been chosen by the most celebrated Poets, as the fittest Characters for Theatrical Representations.... . Vol. I. Containing the Life, Character, and secret History of Macbeth. By a Gentleman, No professed Author, but a Lover of History, and of the Theatre (London: Printed for the author by J. Browne, 1768).

John of Fordun's Chronicle of the Scottish Nation, in W. F. Skene (ed.), *The Historians of Scotland*, vol. 4 (Edinburgh: Edmonston and Douglas, 1872).

The Secret History of Mack-Beth, King of Scotland. Taken from a very Ancient Original Manuscript (London: Printed for J. Woodward, 1708).

Adam, R. J., 'The Real Macbeth: King of Scots, 1040–1054', *History Today*, 7:6 (1957), 381–7.

Aitchinson, Nick, *Macbeth: Man and Myth* (Thrupp: Sutton, 1999).

Anderson, Alan O. (ed.), *Early Sources of Scottish History AD 500 to 1286*, 2 vols (Edinburgh: Oliver and Boyd, 1922).

Bartholomeusz, Dennis, *Macbeth and the Players* (Cambridge: Cambridge University Press, 1969).

Bladen, Victoria, 'Weird Space in *Macbeth* on Screen', in Sarah Hatchuel, Nathalie Vienne-Guerrin and Victoria Bladen (eds), *Shakespeare on Screen: Macbeth* (Rouen and Le Havre: Presses Universitaires de Rouen et du Havre, 2013), pp. 81–106.

Boece, Hector, *The History and Chronicles of Scotland*, trans. John Bellenden, 2 vols (Edinburgh: Reprinted for W. and C. Tait, 1821).

Buc, George, *Daphnis Polystephanos. An Eclog treating of Crowns, and of Garlands* (London, 1605).

Buchanan, George, *The History of Scotland*, trans. T. Page (London, 1690).

Bullough, Geoffrey (ed.), *Narrative and Dramatic Sources of Shakespeare*, 8 vols (New York: Columbia University Press, 1975).

Carroll, William C. (ed.), *Macbeth: Texts and Contexts* (Boston, MA: Bedford, 1999).

—— 'Spectacle, Representation, and Lineage in *Macbeth* 4.1', *Shakespeare Survey*, 67 (2014), 345–71.

—— '"Two Truths Are Told": Afterlives and Histories of Macbeths', *Shakespeare Survey*, 57 (2004), 69–80.

Chambers, E. K., *William Shakespeare: A Study of Facts and Problems* (Oxford: Clarendon, 1988).

Cowan, E. J., 'The Historical MacBeth', in W. D. H. Sellar (ed.), *Moray: Province and People* (Edinburgh: Scottish Society for Northern Studies, 1993).

Davenant, William, *Macbeth, A Tragœdy. With all the Alterations, Amendments, Additions, and New Songs* (London, 1674).

Dobin, Howard, Jr, *Merlin's Disciples: Prophecy, Poetry, and Power in Renaissance England* (Stanford, CA: Stanford University Press, 1990).

Donohue, Joseph W., Jr, 'Kemble's Production of *Macbeth* (1794)', *Theatre Notebook*, 21 (1967), 63–74.

Farrow, Kenneth D., 'The Historiographical Evolution of the Macbeth Narrative', *Scottish Literary Journal*, 21 (1994), 5–23.

Harvey, John, *A Discursive Problem Concerning Prophecies* (London, 1588).
Holinshed, Raphael, *The Chronicles of England, Scotland, and Ireland* (London, 1587 [6 vols, London, 1808]).
James VI, King, *Daemonology, In Form of a Dialogue* (Edinburgh: Printed by Robert Walde-graue printer to the Kings Majestie, 1597).
Kliman, Bernice W., *Shakespeare in Performance: Macbeth* (Manchester: Manchester University Press, 1992).
Leslie, Jhone [sic], *The Historie of Scotland*, trans. Father James Dalrymple, 2 vols (Edinburgh: Scottish Text Society, 1888).
Major, John, *A History of Greater Britain*, trans. Archibald Constable (Edinburgh: Edinburgh University Press, 1892).
Mapstone, Sally, 'Shakespeare and Scottish Kingship: A Case History', in Sally Mapstone and Juliette Wood (eds), *The Rose and the Thistle: Essays on the Culture of Late Medieval and Renaissance Scotland* (East Linton, East Lothian, Scotland: Tuckwell Press, 1998).
Norbrook, David, '*Macbeth* and the Politics of Historiography', in Kevin Sharpe and Steven N. Zwicker (eds), *Politics of Discourse: The Literature and History of Seventeenth-Century England* (Berkeley: University of California Press, 1987).
Palmer, Melvin D., 'Madame d'Aulnoy in England', *Comparative Literature* 27 (1975), 237–53.
Rosenberg, Marvin, *The Masks of Macbeth* (Berkeley: University of California Press, 1978).
Shakespeare, William, *Macbeth*, eds Sandra Clark and Pamela Mason (London: Bloomsbury, 2015).
—— *Macbeth*, ed. A. R. Braunmuller (Cambridge: Cambridge University Press, 1997).
Skene, W. F. (ed.), *The Historians of Scotland* (Edinburgh: Edmonston and Douglas, 1872).
Thomas, Keith, *Religion and the Decline of Magic* (New York: Scribner's, 1971).
Wilders, John (ed.), *Macbeth: Shakespeare in Production* (Cambridge: Cambridge University Press, 2004).
Willis, Deborah, *Malevolent Nurture* (Ithaca, NY: Cornell University Press, 1995).
Wyntoun, Andrew, *The Orygynale Cronykil of Scotland by Andrew of Wyntoun*, ed. David Laing, 3 vols (Edinburgh: Edmonston and Douglas, 1872).

Part IV

Magic, music and gender

9

Music and magic in *The Tempest*: Ariel's alchemical songs

Natalie Roulon

It has often been stressed that *The Tempest* is Shakespeare's most musical play:[1] the island's soundscape is uniquely rich and varied, its 'noises,/Sounds, and sweet airs' (3.2.127–8) enhance its supernatural atmosphere and Prospero's magic power is wielded largely through the music of Ariel and his fellow spirits. Unsurprisingly, music is one of the aspects of the play that has received the most critical attention, the perfect integration of this 'dangerously refractory material'[2] in the drama being regularly praised.[3]

Critics have long recognised that the play contains alchemical patterns and symbols. In the late eighteenth century, Thomas Warton recorded the affinity between Prospero and a 'chemical necromancer' from an Italian romance.[4] And yet it was only in the late twentieth century that the groundbreaking work of Michael Srigley[5] and Peggy N. Simonds[6] revealed the extent to which the play is steeped in alchemical lore.[7] To the best of my knowledge, however, the analysis of Ariel's songs from an alchemical perspective has never been undertaken. This is what I propose to develop in this chapter.

Ariel–Mercurius

As well as his mythological, folkloric, biblical and occult – and particularly cabalistic – associations, Ariel, the agent of Prospero's musical magic, has been correctly identified as the alchemical Mercurius.[8] Shakespeare's 'airy spirit' perfectly matches the description of Mercurius as 'an aerial spirit or soul… present everywhere and at all times during the alchemical *opus*'.[9] This 'protean, elusive' spirit is 'ambivalent, both destructive and creative'; he is 'the ultimate solvent', 'the grand master of the reiterated cycle of *solve et coagula* (dissolve and coagulate) which constitutes the alchemical work of purification'.[10] This is an apt delineation of Prospero's ethereal, dainty and at times mischievous attendant spirit, the swift shapeshifter he calls upon to control the actions of most of the characters on the island in order to enlighten them. Moreover, the representation of Mercurius as the *rebis* or hermaphrodite, 'the perfect integration of male and female energies',[11] parallels Ariel's androgynous role in the play.[12]

The alchemical quest for gold effected through the agency of Mercurius can be construed as a purely material one (*chrysopoeia*) and it is the alchemists so inclined, often nicknamed 'puffers', who are the butt of Ben Jonson's satire in the play *The Alchemist* (1610) and the masque *Mercury Vindicated from the Alchemists at Court* (1616).[13] However, for Renaissance practitioners of iatrochemistry such as Paracelsus, the philosopher's stone designated the panacea or all-healing elixir of life, and was another name for physical and spiritual purification.[14] As will become clearer in the course of this chapter, it is spiritual alchemy that Shakespeare is chiefly concerned with in *The Tempest*.

The alchemist's great work or *magnum opus*, the chemical wedding of sulphur and mercury, fixed and volatile, male and female, red king and white queen, sun and moon, Sol and Luna, creative will and wisdom,[15] could not take place without the intervention of Mercurius. He was present at the three main stages of the *opus*: the *nigredo* or black stage – putrefaction, the *albedo* or white stage – purification, connected with 'the dawning of consciousness',[16] and the *rubedo* or red stage – reunification, associated with Sol, the sun.[17] The *rubedo* marked the attainment of the philosopher's stone, a red powder or tincture that transmutes base metals into gold.

In the play, the black stage is exemplified among other episodes by 'the psychological death' of the Three Men of Sin[18] whom Ariel apostrophises in his role as harpy or 'minister of Fate' (3.3.53–82).[19] The white stage occurs when Prospero, having called for '[a] solemn air', describes the gradual effect of the musical cure he has devised for the sinners:

> The charm dissolves apace,
> And as the morning steals upon the night,
> Melting the darkness, so their rising senses
> Begin to chase the ignorant fumes that mantle
> Their clearer reason. (5.1.64–8)[20]

After having charmed or led the castaways astray to the sound of his voice and his instruments, Ariel contrives to assemble all the characters before Prospero's cell, a metaphor for the alchemical vessel: everything is ready for the red stage or final reconciliation to take place. Nevertheless, since Antonio and Sebastian remain unregenerate, the great work is only partly achieved at the end of the play. It is no accident that these two figures should prove immune to the allurements of music: '[t]he man that hath no music in himself,/Nor is not mov'd with concord of sweet sounds,/Is fit for treasons, stratagems and spoils'.[21]

That music accompanies each stage of Prospero's *magnum opus* is especially relevant considering the importance of this discipline in the alchemical tradition.

Alchemy was often called 'the musical art' because,[22] like music, it is governed by number.[23] Alchemists found in music the harmonious universe they sought to recreate by means of the philosopher's stone.[24]

Ariel–Mercurius as chemical mediator is 'the 'spirit' which joins 'soul' and 'body', 'form and matter'.[25] This aspect of his role calls to mind Marsilio Ficino's *spiritus*, the spirit or thin, clear vapour that mediates between *corpus* and *anima* and whose nature is akin to that of musical sound.[26] For Ficino, 'music has a stronger effect than anything transmitted through the other senses, because its medium, air, is of the same kind as the spirit'.[27] Ariel's name, which suggests both air, the element, and musical melody – specifically the ayre[28] – could not have been more apt from a Ficinian perspective.

Ficino used music to 'attract the spiritual influence of a particular planet' on the performers and listeners.[29] He was accustomed to singing Orphic hymns 'most often addressed to the sun' while accompanying himself on what was probably a *lira da braccio*.[30] Ariel–Orpheus and his cohort of spirits perform both instrumental and vocal music intended to control the castaways' behaviour. It can send them to sleep or wake them up, confuse them the better to edify or chastise them,[31] awe them by introducing and accompanying masque visions and dances, make them mad and cure their disturbed minds.

Ariel performs five songs:

- an invitation to a dance: 'Come unto these yellow sands' (1.2.375–86)
- a dirge: 'Full fathom five thy father lies' (1.2.396–403)
- a reveille or waking song: 'While you here do snoring lie' (2.1.297–302)
- a blessing song (the masque song): 'Earth's increase and foison plenty' (4.1.110–7)
- a freedom song: 'Where the bee sucks there suck I' (5.1.88–94)

As I shall argue, four of these pieces contain unmistakable alchemical allusions.

An invitation to a dance

Ariel's first song lures Ferdinand to the part of the island where Miranda and Prospero are stationed and simultaneously instructs his fellow spirits to join in song and dance:

> Come unto these yellow sands,
> And then take hands.
> Curtsied when you have, and kissed,
> The wild waves whist.
> Foot it featly here and there,
> And sweet sprites the burden bear.
> Hark, hark

> The watch-dogs bark
> Bow wow, bow wow.
>
> [*Spirits dispersedly echo the burden 'Bow wow'*]
>
> Hark, hark! I hear
> The strain of strutting Chanticleer,
> Cry cock-a-diddle-dow. (1.2.375–86)

The word 'sands', which stands out at the end of the first line, can be taken to refer to the sand-bath used during the cleansing process 'for the gentle, even heating of the matter of the Stone in the alchemical vessel'.[32] The invitation to take hands, kiss and dance looks forward to the chemical wedding that is to take place between Ferdinand and Miranda,[33] the play's sulphur and mercury.

'And sweet sprites the burden bear' is an implicit stage direction for the spirits who accompany Ariel to sing the burden of his song (the undersong), but also to bear the burden in the sense that they will contribute to the completion of the great work. Whether or not the 'sweet sprites' refer specifically to the seven alchemical spirits that are said to 'allow elevation and escape the fire',[34] it seems clear that there is a subjacent pun on the musical meaning of the word 'burden'.[35]

The imitation of farmyard animal cries at the end of the song has long puzzled critics. Erin Minear, for example, calls the piece 'a *nonsequitur*, both in mood and meaning'.[36] As David Lindley observes, 'the burden of the song, sung by "watch-dogs" and "Chanticleer", jars with the lyric's romantic opening', hence the 'uncertainty of response' elicited in the listener.[37] Richmond Noble is undoubtedly right to point out that 'the illusion is given of terra firma by the noise of dogs barking and cocks crowing';[38] the mention of the familiar literary braggart Chanticleer is also likely to reassure Ferdinand, disoriented by the music ('[w]here should this music be?', line 387). And yet this explanation does not seem sufficient. The reference to dogs and cocks becomes clearer, on the other hand, if one recalls that they are two of the most common symbols of sulphur – the male principle – mentioned in alchemical treatises.[39] I therefore regard the inclusion in the song of animal cries as Shakespeare's humorous suggestion that the male aspect of the matter (the dog,[40] as well as the cock) must be united to the female aspect (the bitch and the hen) for the chemical wedding to take place. The alchemical joke would not have been lost on the more learned members of a Jacobean audience, given 'the ubiquity of alchemy' at the time, attested to by the 'range of famous dabblers'.[41]

Furthermore, the cock was another name for the Bird of Hermes,[42] also known as Mercurius,[43] whose taming is 'a key task' for the alchemist who must turn it into 'a willing servant, a force controlled and directed rather than one which is overwhelming and out of control'.[44] Ariel's 'cock-a-diddle-dow' may thus be interpreted as a cheeky cry of defiance to the alchemist Prospero, who is challenged to catch him if he can. This is in keeping both with the spirit's reluctance to be ruled, and with the paradox that, although music is an instrument of Prospero's magic power, 'music and sound exceed his grasp, constitute a significant constraint upon, even a subversion of his considerable power', as Jacquelyn Fox-Good remarks.[45] Shakespeare seems to playfully suggest that whilst the dramatist-within-the-drama only exerts partial control over his musical spirit, he is in a position to show this limitation, which is evidence of his superior power. At the same time, since Prospero's art is a reflection of his own, the implication is that no artist is ever in full command of his medium.

Whatever the ironic undertones of Ariel's first song, the context makes it clear that it has fulfilled its task of calming the storm and assuaging Ferdinand: '[t]his music crept by me upon the waters,/Allaying both their fury and my passion/With its sweet air' (1.2.391–3). The contemporary setting of the song has not survived, which makes a musical analysis impossible.

The dirge

Fortunately, the same is not true for the dirge that follows almost immediately, and whose setting by 'Robert Johnson' has been preserved:[46]

> Full fathom five thy father lies,
> Of his bones are coral made;
> Those are pearls that were his eyes;
> Nothing of him that doth fade,
> But doth suffer a sea-change
> Into something rich and strange.
> Sea-nymphs hourly ring his knell.
> Hark, now I hear them, ding dong bell.
> [*Spirits dispersedly echo the burden 'ding dong bell'*] (1.2.396–403)

Ariel's second song may seem deceptive since Ferdinand's father Alonso has survived the shipwreck: he is not literally lying thirty feet deep in the sea. If read alchemically, on the other hand, the lyric foreshadows the moral transformation Alonso is about to experience and therefore suggests that Prospero's *magnum opus* is under way. Indeed, '[d]uring the process of becoming the Stone, the King [the raw matter for the Stone] has to undergo a death and resurrection.'[47] The *rex marinus*, who is 'almost drowned at sea' but ultimately 'saved' appears in many alchemical emblems of the period.[48] The dissolution of the king in the sea corresponds to the *nigredo* or black stage of the great work. 'After the black King's putrefied body is washed and cleansed of its impurities the white stage or *albedo* is attained.'[49] There is precisely an allusion to the white stage of the *opus* in the line '[t]hose are pearls that were his eyes', for pearls 'symbolize the *albedo* and the white stone'.[50] The connection between pearls and eyes is all the stronger as alchemists claim that when the matter becomes white at the *albedo*, 'there appear pearls or fishes' eyes in the vessel'.[51] The reference to 'coral' in the second line of the lyric is equally relevant since 'coral' is 'a synonym for the red stone… attained at the *rubedo*, the final stage of the *opus*'.[52] According to the *Turba Philosophorum* (twelfth century?), when the stone becomes red, 'it is called Flower of Gold, Ferment of Gold, Gold of Coral…'.[53]

The idea of transformation being central to alchemy, it is no coincidence that the metamorphosis facing the king, the 'sea-change' or marination, should be conjured up exactly in the middle of the poem and should therefore constitute its semantic core. 'Into something rich and strange' is a clear description of the transmutation of the base metal into gold or rather, in spiritual terms, of the purification of the King's soul which is the ultimate goal of the alchemist's quest.

The literal-minded reader or spectator is likely to interpret the mutation of eyes into pearls and bones into coral as no more than a denial of the body's irreversible decay through the poetic construction of beautiful artefacts. Indeed, from Rose A. Zimbardo's viewpoint, '[t]he process is not one of regeneration into something more nobly human… there is nothing here that suggests fertility, rather the human and impermanent is transfixed into a rich permanence, but a lifeless one. Potentially corruptible bones and eyes become incorruptible coral and pearls.'[54] An alchemical reading of the lyric, however, invites us to consider death or *nigredo* as only one stage in what is in effect a process of regeneration. This was perfectly captured by 'Robert Johnson', who did not set Ariel's song of mourning in a minor key but in G major, and who devised a melodic line the overall movement of which is rising rather than falling, with the exception of the last phrase – the knell – itself sung in major scales. The most important change in the harmony coincides with the 'sea change/Into something rich and strange': the F naturals in bars 11–12 indicate a modulation in D minor, a melancholic strain reminding the listener of the pain involved in the transmutation.[55]

John P. Cutts suggests that the music fits the lyrics perfectly and its general cheerfulness is only slightly tinged with sadness.[56] Fox-Good, on the other hand, contends that the music 'pulls against' the words: '[t]he song's words emphasize death, intensify and beautify its finality; its music enacts transformation, change, possibility'.[57] When the song is interpreted alchemically, the dichotomy between words and music is dissolved: it is a symbiosis of both, a fusion of sound and meaning which emerges.[58] It is not the music that 'pulls against' the words, but the conjunction of music and words that defeats our generic expectations: playwright and composer have produced a funeral song which is most unusual in that it is closer to a lullaby than to a sullen dirge.[59] Whether or not they collaborated on the song,[60] 'Johnson's' music supports the alchemical message of the text.

The song is strange (from Latin *extraneus*, foreign, from without) rather than sad, as evidenced by Ferdinand's response: '[t]his is no mortal business, nor no sound/That the earth owes. I hear it now above me' (1.2.405–6). He is convinced that he is hearing the harmony of the spheres, but the audience knows that the sounds are produced 'above' him in a literal sense, i.e. in 'the music-room above the stage'.[61] Consequently, Shakespeare allows practical music to enchant us whilst inviting us to distance ourselves from speculative music by reducing cosmic harmony to a metaphor.[62]

Ariel's role as water-nymph, harpy, and as Ceres in the masque song

When Ariel puts on a guise to sing a song, it is to perform a feminine role. Although he is invisible to Ferdinand, whom the first songs are intended to lull, he dons the attire of a 'water-nymph' (1.2.318 s. d.) for the benefit of the audience. He later probably enacts the part of Ceres in the betrothal masque,[63] in which he sings a duet with Juno. This is congruent with the fact that, in Shakespeare's works, the characters whose role it is to tune someone's *musica humana* or effect musical cures are women more often than not – witness Helena, Marina and Paulina.[64]

That said, Ariel's feminine guises also lend themselves to alchemical interpretations. 'Water' is 'the name for philosophical mercury... when it is dissolved,'[65] and the nymph, maid or virgin is a symbol of 'the receptive, feminine aspect of the dual-natured Mercurius'.[66] Even though Ariel's role as a harpy is not, strictly speaking, musical, his appearance in the banquet scene is framed by music and thunder: '[s]trange and solemn music' (3.3.17 s. d.), '[t]hunder and lightning' (3.3.52 s. d.) and 'soft music' (3.3.82 s. d.). His presence in this scene is far from benign, and yet, as a punisher of human sin,[67] he can be categorised as a harmonising figure.[68] In one of the *Ripley Scrolls*, a female Bird of Hermes is pictured as 'a proper harpy, with long blond hair and exposed breasts,'[69] which recalls both Ariel's mercurial function and his ambivalent gender identity. As for Ceres, she is present in alchemical emblem books,[70] which is hardly surprising since the alchemical process was often described 'in terms of an agricultural cycle: sowing, growth and harvesting'.[71]

Here is an excerpt from her masque speech, followed by the stanza she sings after Juno in the masque song:

> Ceres: Hail, many-coloured messenger, that ne'er
> Dost disobey the wife of Jupiter;
> Who, with saffron wings, upon my flowers
> Diffusest honey drops, refreshing showers,
> And with each end of thy blue bow dost crown
> My bosky acres, and my unshrubbed down,
> Rich scarf to my proud earth. Why hath thy queen
> Summoned me hither, to this short-grazed green? (4.1.76–83)

(*sung*) Earth's increase, and foison plenty,
       Barns and garners never empty,
       Vines, with clust'ring bunches growing,
       Plants with goodly burthen bowing;
       Spring come to you at the farthest,
       In the very end of harvest.
       Scarcity and want shall shun you,
       Ceres' blessing so is on you. (4.1.110–7)

Prospero's betrothal masque can be associated with the many-coloured stage in the alchemical process known as *cauda pavonis* or the peacock's tail,[72] which indicates that 'the dawning of the *albedo* is at hand'.[73] Ceres' speech and song are interspersed with alchemical allusions. Both are proleptic and form a kind of diptych, the eight spoken lines suggesting that the *albedo* or white stage is about to take place, the eight sung lines inviting the audience to imagine that the *magnum opus* has been accomplished.[74]

Iris, the 'many-coloured messenger' whose 'blue bow' is a sign that the '*albedo* is in sight'[75] sheds 'honey drops' on Ceres' 'flowers'. In the alchemical tradition, the flower is 'that which is an essential part of the matter, that which has attained the fullest perfection'. For Paracelsus, 'the matter of the stone doth discover most fair colours in the production of its Flower'.[76] Honey could refer to the philosophical solvent Mercurius or to the all-healing elixir or panacea,[77] the discovery of which was the aim of iatrochemistry. Iris's 'honey drops' and 'refreshing showers' are reminiscent of the 'dew' Prospero once ordered Ariel to fetch '[f]rom the still-vexed Bermudes' (1.2.288–9). Dew or rain is a central symbol in alchemy: it refers to 'the beneficial, healing aspect of the mercurial water which magically transforms the black *nigredo*... into the white *albedo*'.[78] 'In agreement with ecclesiastical symbolism, the alchemists' cleansing water is a "dew of grace"'. John Dee quoted the passage from Genesis (27:28), 'God give thee of the dew of heaven, and of the fatness of the earth' on the title page of his *Monas Hieroglyphica*. What is more, '[t]he ablution of rain or dew always precedes a new *coniunctio* or chemical wedding',[79] which perfectly fits the purpose of the masque.

In her song, the goddess of earth and harvest uses the imperative form 'come to you', the modal 'shall' and the performative utterance 'Ceres' blessing so is on you', thereby picturing the alchemist's goal as being achieved. Indeed, the harvest was synonymous with 'the attainment of the philosopher's Stone'.[80] The alchemical meaning is here reinforced by the mention of 'vines': George Ripley, amongst others, 'compares the cultivation of the red grapes on the vine to the production of the red stone of the alchemists'.[81]

The song's rhyming couplets have sometimes been dismissed as doggerel. It is true that the rhythm of the regular trochaic tetrameters may seem monotonous when the text is spoken, and that the combination of emphatic rhyme and alliteration has a clumsiness to it. But this is to forget that the lyric was meant to be sung:[82] when set to music, what sounds like a jingle may acquire a solemn or incantatory character, which would befit the masque song. Whether the composer succeeded in transmuting the text into a trance-like ceremonial song remains a matter of speculation, for the original music apparently has not survived. That this was the effect intended for the piece is borne out by Ferdinand's enthralled response: '[t]his is a most majestic vision, and/Harmonious charmingly' (4.1.118–9).

Even though the masque is soon interrupted by the discordant note of the conspiracy, I concur with Robin Headlam Wells in thinking that it is 'not the escapist fantasy it is often accused of being, but a qualified expression of human potentialities'.[83] As ever, Shakespeare disrupts the better to instruct. That he dissolves visual and musical illusions as soon as he creates them points to the transience of all things human at the same time as it attests to the power of his theatrical magic.

The freedom song

The masque of Ceres shares its pastoral imagery with Ariel's song of freedom, what with the 'love of flowers' typical of fairies,[84] the notion of bounty and fertility and the prospect of an eternal summer characteristic of the Golden Age:

> Where the bee sucks, there suck I;
> In a cowslip's bell I lie;
> There I couch when owls do cry;
> On the bat's back I do fly
> After summer merrily.
> Merrily, merrily, shall I live now,
> Under the blossom that hangs on the bough. (5.1.88–94)

Ariel's song mentions several creatures that belong to the alchemical bestiary. The bee refers metaphorically to 'the blessed spirits in Elysium' in Virgil's *Aeneid*;[85] it is also associated with the Golden Age in Cesare Ripa's *Iconologia*.[86] This is perfectly compatible with its alchemical meaning since 'bee' is another name for the 'mercurial solvent which destroys the old metal or outmoded state of being'.[87] The reference therefore suggests that the spirit owes his freedom to the role he has played in forwarding the transmutation, which was part of Prospero's plan. The identification of Ariel with the bee, rendered in the text by a chiasmus ('bee – sucks/suck – I') is emphasised in 'Robert Johnson's' setting by the fact that each pair is sung on the same note – 'bee' and 'I' are sung on the dominant (D) while 'sucks' and 'suck' are sung on an A.

Ariel pictures himself flying on a bat's back. In Christian iconography, the 'leathery black bat's wings' characterise 'the monstrous representatives of evil'.[88]

In alchemical lore, the bat was sometimes equated with the winged dragon, i.e. with 'Mercurius in his first dark chthonic phase'.[89] Its association with Mercurius is corroborated by an illustration from *Aurora Consurgens* (early fifteenth century) which shows an hermaphrodite whose female, mercurial side is holding a bat.[90] That Ariel flies on the bat's back implies that he has tamed his former, corrupt self.

As for the owl, it is usually a sign of 'gloom and doom', and the image cluster 'owl-night-death' is recurrent in Shakespeare, as Wilson observes.[91] This is congruent with the owl's connection with the *nigredo* or black stage of the *opus*.[92] A possible interpretation of this image in the context of the song is that Ariel having carried out his task as Prospero's chemical agent, he can now rest or hide 'in a cowslip's bell' since his assistance is no longer required: his confrontation with the owl is behind him.

In Act 1, Prospero reminds Ariel that he was confined by Sycorax in 'a cloven pine' (1.2.274–7) and threatens to 'rend an oak/And peg thee in his knotty entrails' (1.2.294–5) if he keeps moaning. As post-colonial readings of the play stress, Prospero's attitude can legitimately be called tyrannical.[93] And yet, it can also be envisaged differently since '[t]he truncated tree is one of a number of images expressing the torture motives that occur in alchemical texts'.[94] The torture of Mercurius is a *topos* in such treatises for he is regarded as an 'inconstant, teasing spirit which, when captured and tamed by the alchemist, is magically transformed into a willing, faithful, helpful ally or ministering servant'.[95] Significantly, Sycorax's pine tree becomes an oak in Prospero's threat:[96] the hollow oak being a common image for 'the alchemical vessel or the oven in which the vessel is placed',[97] I read this substitution as a sign that the *opus chymicum* is about to commence.

Since at the end of the play Ariel sings about his future life '[u]nder the blossom that hangs on the bough', his trajectory can be defined as a progress from the cleft tree to the philosophical tree, the latter being a symbol of 'growth and fruition, in both a physical and spiritual sense'.[98] This is in keeping with the Christian interpretation of Ariel's last line, which Grace Hall connects 'with the mystery plays' recurrent image of Christ, blossom of the Virgin Mary'. The Marian subtext in the song is borne out by the presence of the bee, a symbol of the Blessed Virgin,[99] and by the choice of the flower in which Ariel takes refuge, the cowslip being dedicated to the Virgin.[100] Drawing on Hall's study, Robert L. Reid sees the last image of the song as one of the crucifixion.[101] Here again, Christian imagery and alchemical imagery intersect: the Christian's joy at being redeemed by the Saviour parallels that of the alchemist's servant who has contributed to the quest for the philosopher's stone. This conflation need not surprise us: alchemical discourse is 'suffused with the language of Christianity',[102] and in many treatises the philosopher's stone is equated with Christ.[103]

The final song is the only one which has not been summoned by Prospero. That music is no longer an instrument of his magic is a sign that he is about to abjure his power. The lyric is emphatically about Ariel's now free self: the personal pronoun 'I', in a prominent position at the end of the first line, is 'the word the most rhymed upon'[104] in the lyric ('I'/'lie'/'cry'/'fly'/'merrily'). Unlike the previous songs, all aimed at others, this piece could aptly be described as Ariel's self-charming melody.[105] As Patricia Buccellato comments, 'from an articulatory point of view, the succession of plosives (/k/,/p/,/b/,/d/) in the first four lines necessitate closure, consecutive mounting tension followed by liberation of accumulated air. This corresponds to a feeling of relief and release consonant with Ariel's mood.'[106] The flowing liquid (/l/) heard throughout the verse and the pleasure-filled nasals (/m/ and /n/) prevalent in the last three lines convey a sense of perfect bliss.

'Robert Johnson' placed a musical emphasis on the key words in the text by setting them to high-pitched notes or prolonged notes or both: 'I', 'lie', 'fly', 'merrily', 'now' and 'bough' stand out, thus providing a perfect sound image of Ariel's state of mind. The melisma on 'blossom' is also worth mentioning in this respect. 'Johnson' was praised for the 'melodic mimesis of the sense' noticeable in many of his songs;[107] 'Where the bee sucks', like 'Full fathom five', is a case in point.

Sadly, his other settings for *The Tempest* are unknown. It is intriguing, nonetheless, that the composer should have set the two songs that have come down to us in (notated) G major. The aim of the *magnum opus*, as I mentioned previously, is to attain gold or the sun, often called Sol, which in solmisation can denote G.[108] Accordingly, we are left with the tantalising possibility that Sol is the key chosen by 'Johnson' for Ariel's alchemical music.[109]

The Tempest's four alchemical songs share several traits. They are effective in that they succeed in enchanting or perplexing onstage and offstage listeners alike. They are proleptic: the invitation to a dance and the dirge foreshadow the chemical wedding of Ferdinand and Miranda as well as Alonso's regeneration; the blessing song and the freedom song both conjure up an idyllic future for the young couple and Ariel. The four songs therefore partake of the idealising current of the play.[110] That musical magic is ironised or undercut in several ways does not prevent the songs from imprinting themselves lastingly on our minds, as befits a play that constantly reminds us of the importance of memory. The ideal, euphoric state they project remains an ongoing quest for an object which is possibly unattainable. The songs play a key role in constructing what Kiernan Ryan has suitably termed a 'precursive fiction' – his definition of the Shakespearean romance.[111]

Prospero may well have failed to find the philosopher's stone that would have transmuted into gold the base metal of Antonio's and Sebastian's souls. On the other hand, the chemical wedding that was part of the magus's design has been achieved, largely through Ariel's musical magic, i.e. through the conjunction of Shakespeare's sulphur and 'Johnson's' mercury.

With *The Tempest*, Shakespeare produced theatrical gold powerful enough to out-Jonson Jonson by showing that there is more to alchemy than quackery,[112] and perhaps to do away with some of King James's misgivings about magic by inciting him to identify with the magician-king.[113] If this elusive play will never yield all its secrets, an awareness of its status as an alchemical palimpsest can no doubt allow us to probe ever deeper Shakespeare's polyphonic imagination.

Notes

1 I am much indebted to Victoria Bladen for inviting me to lecture on *The Tempest* ('Shakespeare for All' in Oxford, July 2016), to Patricia Neville Buccellato, Ross W. Duffin, Joscelyn Godwin, Christopher R. Wilson, Penelope Gouk and Peter J. Forshaw for commenting on an early draft of this article and/or for providing me with valuable information on music and alchemy. All quotations from the play are from David Lindley's edition of *The Tempest* [2002] (Cambridge: Cambridge University Press, 2004).

2 R. W. Ingram, 'Musical Pauses and the Vision Scenes in Shakespeare's Last Plays', in Waldo F. McNeir and Thelma N. Greenfield (eds), *Pacific Coast Studies in Shakespeare* (Eugene: University of Oregon, 1966), p. 245.

3 In Catherine Dunn's words, '[i]n *The Tempest* music is woven into the very fabric of the play': 'The Function of Music in Shakespeare's Romances', *Shakespeare Quarterly*, 20 (1969), p. 400.

4 Warton describes the main character of the romance, possibly entitled *Aurelio and Isabella*, as 'a chemical necromancer, who had bound a spirit like Ariel to obey his call and perform his services. It was a common pretence of the dealers in the occult sciences to have a demon at command. At least *Aurelio*, or *Orelio*, was probably one of the names of this romance, the production and multiplication of gold being the grand object of alchemy. Taken at large, the magical part of *The Tempest* is founded in that sort of philosophy which was practised by John Dee and his associates, and has been called the Rosicrusian': Anon., *The History of English Poetry* [1778–81] (London: Reeves and Turner, 1871), p. 936.

5 Michael Srigley, 'A Furnace of Tribulation: *The Tempest* and Alchemy', in *Images of Regeneration* (Uppsala: Acta Universitatis Upsaliensis, 1985), pp. 21–46.

6 Peggy N. Simonds, '"My charms crack not": The Alchemical Structure of The Tempest', *Comparative Drama*, 31:4 (Winter 1997–8), 538–70. Although Simonds mistakenly conflates Ariel's first two songs, she has identified an alchemical motif in them (p. 546), as has Srigley (p. 32). That said, neither critic offers a detailed analysis of the songs.

7 The play's very title has an alchemical meaning: 'it is a boiling process which removes impurities from base metal and facilitates its transmutation into gold': John S. Mebane, *Renaissance Magic and the Return of the Golden Age. The Occult Tradition and Marlowe, Jonson, and Shakespeare* (Lincoln and London: University of Nebraska Press, 1989), p. 181.

8 See Katherine Briggs, *The Anatomy of Puck* [1959] (London and New York: Routledge, 2003), pp. 52–5; W. Stacy Johnson, 'The Genesis of Ariel', *Shakespeare Quarterly*, 2:3 (1951), pp. 206–9; Frank Kermode's edition of *The Tempest* [1954] (London: Methuen, 1979), pp. 142–5; Dympna Callaghan, 'Irish Memories in *The Tempest*', in *Shakespeare without Women* (New York: Routledge, 1999), pp. 97–138; Virginia Mason Vaughan's edition of *The Tempest* [1999] (London: Thomson Learning, 2001), pp. 27–8; Srigley, 'A Furnace of Tribulation', pp. 43, 46; Robert R. Reed, 'The Probable Origin of Ariel', *Shakespeare Quarterly*, 11:1 (1960), 61–5.

9 Lyndy Abraham, *A Dictionary of Alchemical Imagery* (Cambridge: Cambridge University Press, 1998), p. 125.

10 *Ibid.*, pp. 125–6.

11 *Ibid.*, p. 98.

12 As Stephen Orgel notes, 'all the roles he plays at Prospero's command are female: sea nymph, harpy, Ceres': *The Tempest* [1987] (Oxford: Oxford University Press, 1998), p. 27. Christopher R. Wilson points out that '[i]n F[irst Folio], Ariel is clearly male, played by a musician boy actor. From the Restoration to the 1930s, however, he was invariably played by a female': *Shakespeare's Musical Imagery* (New York and London: Continuum, 2011), p. 221. See also Roger Covell, 'Seventeenth Century Music for *The Tempest*', *Studies in Music*, 11 (1968), p. 46; Irena Cholij, '"A Thousand Twangling Instruments": Music and *The Tempest* on the Eighteenth-Century London Stage', *Shakespeare Survey*, 51 (1998), pp. 84, 88–92; Mason Vaughan (ed), *The Tempest*, pp. 30, 78, 82, 93, 109, 150, 157. Even today, the role is often performed by a female actor or singer, whether in the theatre or the opera house.

13 In *Mercury Vindicated from the Alchemists at Court*, Jonson puns on the phrase *aurum potabile* (a cordial made from gold), which becomes '*aurum palpabile*' or touchable gold, i.e. money. Stephen Orgel (ed.), *Ben Jonson: Selected Masques* (New Haven, CT and London: Yale University Press, 1970), p. 136.

14 As Penelope Gouk explains, Paracelsian alchemy was 'about discovering compounds that might prove beneficial to the health of mankind'. She further notes 'its emphasis on improving the spiritual health of mankind': 'Transforming Matter, Refining the Spirit: Alchemy, Music and Experimental Philosophy around 1600', *European Review*, 21:2 (2013), p. 147.

15 Abraham, *A Dictionary*, pp. 35, 189, 146.

16 *Ibid.*, p. 5.

17 As M. E. Warlick points out, 'polarized masculine and feminine terms' serve to describe matter, and he concludes that '[w]hile alchemy offers a model of equality between the sexes, culminating in the perfection of both feminine and masculine qualities, there is a degree of sexism embedded within alchemical texts, for feminine silver tarnishes beneath the perfection of masculine gold': 'Fluctuating Identities. Gender Reversals in Alchemical Imagery', in Jacob Wamberg (ed.), *Art and Alchemy* (Copenhagen: Museum Tusculanum Press, 2006), pp. 103, 106.

18 Srigley, 'A Furnace of Tribulation', p. 31.

19 On the harpy in the play, see Yves Peyré, 'Les "Masques" d'Ariel. Essai d'interprétation de leur symbolisme', *Cahiers Elisabéthains*, 19 (1981), pp. 63–4.

20 Quoted by Srigley, 'A Furnace of Tribulation', p. 36, and Simonds, 'My charms crack not', 560.
21 *The Merchant of Venice*, 5.1.83–5.
22 See Jacques Rebotier, '"Art de Musique" et "Art d'Hermès". Recherches sur le symbolisme alchimique de la post-Renaissance' (Diplôme de l'Ecole Pratique des Hautes Etudes, 1972); Serge Hutin, *Les Alchimistes au Moyen Age* [1977] (Paris: Hachette, 1995), pp. 73–4; Jacques Van Lennep, *Alchimie. Contribution à l'histoire de l'art alchimique* (Brussels: Crédit Communal de Belgique, 1984), p. 57; Joscelyn Godwin, 'Musical Alchemy', in *Harmonies of Heaven and Earth* (London: Thames and Hudson, 1987); Godwin, 'Music and the Hermetic Tradition', in Roelof van den Broek and Wouter J. Hanegraaff (eds), *Gnosis and Hermeticism from Antiquity to Modern Times* (New York: State University of New York Press, 1998), pp. 183–96; Peter J. Forshaw, '*Oratorium—Auditorium—Laboratorium*: Early Modern Improvisations on Cabala, Music, and Alchemy', *Aries*, 10:2 (2010), 169–95.
23 See Van Lennep, *Alchimie*, p. 172. Thomas Norton advised his reader to join 'erth, watyr, fyre, and ayer… to-gedir also Arismetically,/Bi subtile nombres proporcionally… Ioyne your elementis Musicallye, [because musical intervals]/ with theire proporcions cawsen Armonye,/Moch like proporcions be in Alchymye…': *The Ordinal of Alchemy* [1477], ed. John Reidy (London, New York, Toronto: Oxford University Press, 1975), p. 53.
24 Van Lennep, *Alchimie*, p. 172.
25 Abraham, quoting Petrus Bonus, *A Dictionary*, p. 127.
26 Gouk, 'Transforming Matter', p. 149. Neoplatonic and alchemical thought come together at this point. As Gouk observes, music 'is linked to alchemy at a number of different levels by virtue of *spiritus*, an extremely active substance that, according to Paracelsus, also figured in the alchemical transformation of matter' (*ibid.*). Gary Tomlinson notes that 'man's spirit linked him to the cosmos through its resemblance to the *spiritus mundi*… [It] could be enhanced and refreshed by contact with the *spiritus mundi*, and it was this contact that Ficino aimed to achieve through his musical magic': *Music in Renaissance Magic. Toward a Historiography of Others* (Chicago and London: University of Chicago Press, 1993), p. 88. Peter J. Forshaw points out 'the identification of the *spiritus mundi*, the spirit of the world… with the alchemical *coelum* or fifth essence' in Ficino's *De vita libri tres*: 'Marsilio Ficino and the Chemical Art', in Stephen Clucas, Peter J. Forshaw and Valery Rees (eds), *Laus Platonici Philosophi. Marsilio Ficino and his Influence* (Leiden and London: Brill, 2011), p. 260. Since the fifth essence, otherwise known as the fifth element or quintessence, is one of the names of Mercurius (Abraham, *A Dictionary*, p. 128), the connection is obvious.
27 D. P. Walker, *Spiritual and Demonic Magic from Ficino to Campanella* (London: The Warburg Institute, 1958), p. 7.
28 See Christopher R. Wilson and Michela Calore, *Music in Shakespeare. A Dictionary* (London and New York: Thoemmes, 2005), pp. 26–30, and Francis Guinle, '"Noises,/Sounds and sweet airs" – Les chansons de *La Tempête*: texte et contexte', in Claude Peltrault (ed.), *La Tempête. Etudes critiques* (Besançon: Université de

Franche-Comté, 1993), pp. 220–1. In *Hymenaei* (1606), a masque which influenced *The Tempest*, Ben Jonson describes 'musicians seated, figuring airy spirits, their habits various, and resembling the several colors caused in that part of the air by reflection': *Ben Jonson: Selected Masques*, p. 69.

29 Walker, *Spiritual and Demonic Magic*, pp. 13–14.
30 *Ibid.*, p. 19.
31 Commentators sometimes resent the fact that Ariel should resort to music to lure the sinners into a muddy pool, from which they emerge smelling of 'horse-piss' (4.1.198): '[e]ven if we read this as an appropriate – or even improving – punishment, the music plays a morally doubtful role', writes Erin Minear, *Reverberating Song in Shakespeare and Milton. Language, Memory, and Musical Representation* (Farnham and Burlington, VT: Ashgate, 2011), pp. 144–5. I would object that the joke involving Ariel as a mock-Orpheus in this scene becomes less distasteful if one remembers that in alchemical recipes 'urine' is 'an ingredient in making a powerful solvent' to cleanse and unite sulphur and mercury (Abraham, *A Dictionary*, p. 206).
32 Abraham, *A Dictionary*, p. 177.
33 This chemical wedding foreshadows that of Frederick V, Elector Palatine, and Princess Elizabeth, the alchemical *sponsus* and *sponsa*. See Frances Yates, *The Rosicrucian Enlightenment* [1972] (Oxford and New York: Routledge, 2002), p. 194. My thanks to Ross Duffin for reminding me of this reference.
34 Martin Rulandus, *Lexicon alchemiae* (1612), quoted in Gareth Roberts, *The Mirror of Alchemy* (London: The British Library, 1994), p. 112.
35 For other aspects of its polysemy, see Michael Neill, '"Noises,/Sounds and Sweet Airs": The Burden of Shakespeare's *Tempest*', *Shakespeare Quarterly*, 59:1 (Spring 2008), 36–59.
36 Minear, *Reverberating Song*, p. 147.
37 David Lindley, 'Music, Masque, and Meaning in *The Tempest*', in The *Court Masque* (Manchester: Manchester University Press, 1984), p. 49.
38 Richmond Noble, *Shakespeare's Use of Song* (London: Oxford University Press, 1923), p. 100.
39 Abraham, *A Dictionary*, pp. 58, 43. In an alchemical engraving, a cock and a hen are pictured at the feet of a man and a woman embodying the sun and the moon. The motto reads '[t]he Sun needs the Moon, as the cock needs the hen'. Michael Maier's *Atalanta Fugiens* (1617), trans. and ed. Joscelyn Godwin (Grand Rapids, MI: Phanes Press, 1989), emblem 30, p. 165.
40 As Albert Poisson explains, the dog is used most often: *Théories et symboles des alchimistes. Le grand œuvre* [1891] (Angoulême: Editions maçonniques de France, 2013), p. 72.
41 Charles Nicholl, *The Chemical Theatre* (London: Routledge and Kegan Paul, 1980), pp. 15–17.
42 The cock was Hermes–Mercury's favourite bird because his crow heralded the coming of daylight every morning: Pierre Gordon, *Le Mythe d'Hermès*, quoted in Robert Marteau, *La Récolte de la rosée. La tradition alchimique dans la littérature* (Paris: Belin, 1995), p. 144.

43 It is essential to make a distinction between quicksilver, the common metal mercury or *argent vive*, the female aspect of the *prima materia*, and Mercurius or philosophical mercury. What makes this terminology very complex is the fact that the word 'mercury' can be used in all three senses. On this conceptual nexus, see Abraham, *A Dictionary*, p. 124, Poisson, *Théories et symboles*, p. 84, and Rebotier, '"Art de Musique" et "Art d'Hermès"', p. 6.
44 Abraham, *A Dictionary*, pp. 25–6. In *Mercury Vindicated*, Vulcan orders the alchemists to 'bind' Mercury 'if he will not obey'. The latter replies: 'I know what your aims are, sir, to tear the wings from my head and heels, and lute me up in a glass with my own seals…'. *Ben Jonson: Selected Masques*, p. 134.
45 Jacquelyn Fox-Good, 'Other Voices: The Sweet, Dangerous Air(s) of Shakespeare's *Tempest*', *Shakespeare Studies*, 24 (1996), p. 257.
46 See John P. Cutts, *La Musique de la troupe de Shakespeare: The King's Men sous le règne de Jacques Ier* (Paris: C. N. R. S., 1959), pp. 131–2. For an extended musicological commentary on the two songs, see Howell Chickering, 'Hearing Ariel's Songs', *Journal of Medieval and Renaissance Studies*, 24:1 (Winter 1994), 131–72, and Fox-Good, 'Other Voices'. In his *Shakespeare's Songbook* (London: Norton, 2004), pp. 157–9, 454–6, Ross W. Duffin presented the two settings with a caveat that they were late. He has since challenged the assumption that they were written for the original production of *The Tempest*. In an article which he has kindly allowed me to see prior to publication, he writes '[i]t is much more likely that Robert Johnson – if it was Johnson and not some later composer – created these settings as art songs based on extracted play lyrics': 'Thomas Morley, Robert Johnson, and Songs for the Shakespearean Stage', in Christopher R. Wilson (ed), *Research Companion to Shakespeare Music* (Oxford: Oxford University Press, forthcoming). I have put Johnson's name in inverted commas to alert the reader to the fact that the attribution and dating of the settings are now disputed.
47 Abraham, *A Dictionary*, p. 110.
48 *Ibid.*, p. 111. Simonds, '"My charms crack not"', p. 546. See, for example, Maier, *Atalanta Fugiens*, emblem 31, p. 167.
49 Abraham, *A Dictionary*, p. 112.
50 *Ibid.*, p. 143.
51 *Ibid.*, p. 77.
52 *Ibid.*, p. 47. See also Maier, *Atalanta Fugiens*, emblem 32, p. 169.
53 The Alchemy Website, n. p. Similarly, Penotus describes the stone as 'a Red Powder, which the Philosophers call… their Red Coral': *Alchymist's Enchiridion* (1692), 3.3, The Alchemy Website.
54 Rose A. Zimbardo, 'Form and Disorder in *The Tempest*', *Shakespeare Quarterly*, 14:1 (1963), p. 51. The same goes for R. S. White: 'Ariel reminds us of the crucial limitation of finished art. However æsthetically fascinating, it is essentially static and dead, a transmutation of one person's feelings and fluctuating experience into a jewellike object': *Let Wonder Seem Familiar* (New Jersey: Humanities Press; London: Athlone Press, 1985), p. 171.
55 Alternatively, 'a lutenist realizing the bass might add F# [at the end of the sixth phrase] to make it D major… This would give a fine harmonic flourish,

something more "rich" than "strange"': Chickering, 'Hearing Ariel's Songs', pp. 159, 60n.
56 'La musique s'harmonise parfaitement avec les vers, et elle est pleine d'une gaîté spontanée, à peine teintée de tristesse': Cutts, *La Musique de la troupe de Shakespeare*, p. 132. I would object to the notion of spontaneity in this context, for the song is artfully self-referential: Ariel disguised as a sea nymph sings about sea nymphs ringing a watery knell. Yet I agree with Cutts's general appreciation of the song's mood.
57 Fox-Good, 'Other Voices', p. 253.
58 This is in keeping with musical humanists' tenet that there should be 'complete subordination of music to text': D. P. Walker, *Music, Spirit and Language in the Renaissance*, P. Gouk (ed.) (London: Variorum Reprints, 1985), p. 9.
59 Chickering speaks of 'the mood of a lullaby' with reference to the song: 'Hearing Ariel's Songs', p. 161.
60 If Cutts is correct, such a collaboration is highly likely since 'Johnson' wrote dramatic songs and incidental music for the Blackfriars productions of the King's Men on a regular basis during the first two decades of the seventeenth century. See 'Robert Johnson: King's Musician in His Majesty's Public Entertainment', *Music and Letters*, 36:2 (April 1955), 110–25.
61 Lindley, *The Tempest*, p. 123. Wilson, commenting on a similar effect in Act 3, Scene 3, notes its irony, the audience being aware of the characters 'deceptive perception since they can see Prospero on the stage gallery performing his magic power': Wilson and Calore (eds), *Music in Shakespeare*, p. 198.
62 I am using 'metaphor' in the modern sense of the term. On the changing perception of speculative music, see John Hollander, *The Untuning of the Sky: Ideas of Music in English Poetry, 1500–1700* [1961] (New York: W. W. Norton, 1970).
63 See Irwin Smith, 'Ariel as Ceres', *Shakespeare Quarterly*, 9 (1958), 430–2, and 'Ariel and the Masque in *The Tempest*', *Shakespeare Quarterly*, 21 (1970), 213–22. It is sometimes argued that Ariel plays the part of Iris – this is Karol Berger's contention on the grounds that '[t]he role of Iris, the mediatrix between heaven and earth, was most appropriate for Ariel, who is the mediator himself': 'Prospero's Art', *Shakespeare Studies*, 10 (1977), p. 239. Kermode suggests this as a possibility (*The Tempest*, p. 105) but, as Orgel points out, 'sheer theatrical economy would argue in favour of Shakespeare using his singer Ariel in a major role in the masque of Prospero's spirits, and Iris is not required to sing' (*The Tempest*, p. 182). Lindley adds that 'there is no Shakespearean precedent for having three boy singers in a single play' (*The Tempest*, p. 192).
64 See Natalie Roulon, *Les Femmes et la musique dans l'œuvre de Shakespeare* (Paris: Honoré Champion, 2011), pp. 243–79.
65 Abraham, *A Dictionary*, p. 213.
66 *Ibid.*, p. 210.
67 Lindley, *The Tempest*, p. 174.
68 In Berger's words, '[l]ike the harpies, Ariel functions to convince sinners of the value of reconciliation and peace': 'Prospero's Art', p. 226.
69 Warlick, 'Fluctuating Identities', pp. 117, 121.

70 Ceres appears twice in *Atalanta Fugiens:* she is shown breast-feeding her son in emblem 35 (p. 175), and as Nature guiding the alchemist in emblem 42 (p. 189). In emblem 27 of Mylius's *Philosophia Reformata* (1622), she is depicted sitting in front of a cornfield with a baby at her breast: The Alchemy Website.

71 Roberts, *The Mirror of Alchemy*, p. 82.

72 Noted by Peggy Simonds, '"My charms crack not"', p. 552.

73 Abraham, *A Dictionary*, p. 142. There is a famous illustration showing a peacock encased in a glass vessel in Salomon Trismosin, *Splendor Solis*, ed. Stephan Hoebeeck (Bruxelles: Editions SPRL, 2013), p. 49. See also Van Lennep, *Alchimie*, p. 62, and Poisson, *Théories et symboles*, p. 124.

74 On numerical proportion in the masque, see John Orrell, 'The Musical Canon of Proportion in Jonson's *Hymenaei*', *English Language Notes*, 15:3 (1978), p. 178, n. 14.

75 Abraham, *A Dictionary*, p. 163.

76 *Ibid.*, p. 80.

77 *Ibid.*, p. 103.

78 *Ibid.*, p. 52. See also Marteau, *La Récolte de la rosée*, pp. 150–61.

79 Abraham, *A Dictionary*, p. 54.

80 *Ibid.*, p. 95.

81 *Ibid.*, p. 90.

82 It is easy to show that when set to music, the poem's jingle-like characteristics disappear. See Duffin's adaptation of the text to fit the tune of 'In Crete' (*Shakespeare's Songbook*, pp. 203–4) – with a recording of the piece on the companion CD – or that of Andrew Charlton to the tune of 'Tread Juno's Steps Who List': *Music in the Plays of Shakespeare: A Practicum* (New York and London: Garland Publishers, 1991), pp. 225–9.

83 Robin Headlam Wells, *Elizabethan Mythologies: Studies in Poetry, Drama, and Music* (Cambridge: Cambridge University Press, 1994), p. 63.

84 Briggs, *The Anatomy of Puck*, p. 54.

85 Kermode, *The Tempest*, p. 118.

86 Pierre Iselin, '"My Music for Nothing": Musical Negotiations in The Tempest', *Shakespeare Survey*, 48 (1995), 143–4.

87 Abraham, *A Dictionary*, p. 20.

88 Clare Gibson, *How to Read Symbols* (London: Herbert Press, 2009), p. 200.

89 Abraham, *A Dictionary*, p. 59.

90 See Van Lennep, *Alchimie*, pp. 56–7.

91 *Shakespeare's Musical Imagery*, pp. 104–6.

92 See Van Lennep's comment on an illustration from *Splendor Solis* in *Art et alchimie* (Brussels: Meddens, 1971), p. 59. I have encountered a more favourable image of the owl in an engraving from *Aurora Consurgens*, on which Van Lennep comments thus: Athena's bird being a symbol of wisdom because of its ability to see in the dark, its role was to help the alchemist to discover the secrets of the art: *Alchimie*, p. 58. This reading is less likely in the present context since Ariel is not associated with the owl in its function as a guide: it is clearly an antipathetic creature from which he is eager to hide.

93 Paul Brown, for example, characterises Prospero's constant reminders to 'Ariel of his indebtedness to the master' as 'a mode of "symbolic violence"': '"This thing of darkness I acknowledge mine": The Discourse of Colonialism in *The Tempest*', in Jonathan Dollimore and Alan Sinfield (eds), *Political Shakespeare: New Essays in Cultural Materialism* (Manchester: Manchester University Press, 1985), p. 60.
94 Abraham, *A Dictionary*, p. 205.
95 Ibid., p. 126. In *Mercury Vindicated*, the titular character calls his life 'an exercise of torture': *Ben Jonson: Selected Masques*, p. 131.
96 The substitution usually passes unnoticed. Mason Vaughan, for instance, writes of Ariel's 'being imprisoned in Sycorax's mighty oak' (*The Tempest*, p. 87). White makes the same mistake (*Let Wonder Seem Familiar*, p. 169).
97 Abraham, *A Dictionary*, p. 137.
98 Ibid., p. 150. Even though he shows that Prospero and Sycorax have much in common, Anthony Harris rightly opposes the witch's pine and the magician's oak: '[s]ince primaeval times the oak has been associated with ceremonies conducted by priest-like figures – such sacred groves existed in both ancient Greece and Celtic Europe, for example. In contrast, pine forests were regarded as the haunts of trolls and other demonic figures of North European mythology': *Night's Black Agents* (Manchester: Manchester University Press, 1980), p. 145.
99 See Fiona J. Griffiths, *The Garden of Delights. Reform and Renaissance for Women in the Twelfth Century* (Philadelphia: University of Pennsylvania Press, 2007), pp. 101–2.
100 'In Norse mythology, the flower was dedicated to Freya, the Key Virgin, and in northern Europe the idea of dedication to the goddess was transferred to the Virgin Mary': Ann Ball, *Catholic Traditions in the Garden* (Huntington, IN: Our Sunday Visitor Publishing Division, 1998), p. 66. My thanks to Maurice Bower for confirming that the association can be traced back to the Middle Ages.
101 Robert Reid, 'Sacerdotal Vestiges in *The Tempest*', *Comparative Drama*, 41:4 (Winter 2007–8), pp. 500, 508.
102 Roberts, *The Mirror of Alchemy*, p. 78. In Ben Jonson's *The Alchemist*, Mammon asks Face if he has 'descry'd the flower, the *sanguis agnis*' (2.2.28). Here the lamb's blood is a Christian metaphor for the *rubedo*.
103 The philosopher's stone is 'often identified with Christ as creative *Logos*': Abraham, *A Dictionary*, p. 145. Aksel Haaning dates the equation from the first half of the fourteenth century: 'The Philosophical Nature of Early Western Alchemy', in Wamberg (ed), *Art and Alchemy*, p. 34.
104 Chickering, 'Hearing Ariel's Songs', p. 168.
105 Wilson records the polysemy of the word 'charm' (from Latin *carmen*, song) in the Renaissance: '[i]n his Latin-English *Thesaurus* (1565), Thomas Cooper equates "charme" with "songe". Other usages suggest charm is a melody, particularly associated with birds… There is also evidence to suppose charm, as a song, could have magical connotations relating to the practice of chanting or reciting verse with magic power, going back to the fourteenth century': *Music in Shakespeare*, p. 93.
106 Personal communication.

107 Chickering, 'Hearing Ariel's Songs', p. 140. On the notion of mimetic music, see Walker, *Music, Spirit and Language*, pp. 12–14, 289.
108 My thanks to Christopher Wilson for his assistance with this technical point.
109 'Johnson' does not seem to have had a predilection for G major, hence the significance of this choice for the songs of *The Tempest*.
110 On the darker, Dionysian aspect of music in the play, see Simonds, 'Sweet Power of Music'.
111 'The last plays employ a host of techniques and devices designated to convert their plotlines into precursive rather than recursive fictions, into prefigurative parables that couch desirable futures in the forms and languages of the past': Kiernan Ryan, 'Introduction', in *Shakespeare. The Last Plays* (London: Longman, 1999), p. 16.
112 Mason Vaughan recalls that Ben Jonson was 'no fan of the play, judging from his (perhaps tongue-in-cheek) Introduction to *Bartholomew Fair* [1614]' (*The Tempest*, p. 7).
113 See Mebane, *Renaissance Magic*, pp. 107–8. As Harris notes, 'James's main objection to theurgy was its reliance on spirits to effect its unnatural powers and there is no doubt that, however benevolent might be the ends to which Prospero employs his "Art", he performs his magical deeds with the aid of spirits': *Night's Black Agents*, p. 134.

Bibliography

The Alchemy Website. www.alchemywebsite.com. Accessed 15 August 2019.
The History of English Poetry [1778–81] (London: Reeves and Turner, 1871).
Abraham, Lyndy, *A Dictionary of Alchemical Imagery* (Cambridge: Cambridge University Press, 1998).
Ball, Anne, *Catholic Traditions in the Garden* (Huntington, IN: Our Sunday Visitor Publishing Division, 1998).
Bate, Jonathan, *Shakespeare and Ovid* (Oxford: Clarendon Press, 1993).
Berger, Karol, 'Prospero's Art', *Shakespeare Studies*, 10 (1977), 211–39.
Briggs, Katherine, *The Anatomy of Puck* [1959] (London and New York: Routledge, 2003).
Brumble, H. David, *Classical Myths and Legends in the Middles Ages and Renaissance* (London and Chicago: Fitzroy Dearborn, 1998).
Callaghan, Dympna, *Shakespeare without Women* (New York: Routledge, 1999).
Chan, Mary, *Music in the Theatre of Ben Jonson* (Oxford: Oxford University Press, 1980).
Charlton, Andrew, *Music in the Plays of Shakespeare: A Practicum* (New York and London: Garland Publishers, 1991).
Chickering, Howell, 'Hearing Ariel's Songs', *Journal of Medieval and Renaissance Studies*, 24:1 (Winter 1994), 131–72.
Cholij, Irena, '"A Thousand Twangling Instruments": Music and *The Tempest* on the Eighteenth-Century London Stage', *Shakespeare Survey*, 51 (1998), 79–94.
Coletti, Theresa, 'Music and *The Tempest*', in R. C. Tobias and Paul G. Zolbrod (eds), *Shakespeare's Late Plays* (Athens: Ohio University Press, 1974).
Councell, R. W., *Apollogia Alchymiae* (London: John M. Watkins, 1925). www.levity.com/alchemy/counsell.html.
Covell, Roger, 'Seventeenth Century Music for *The Tempest*', *Studies in Music*, 11 (1968), 43–63.
Cutts, John P., *La Musique de la troupe de Shakespeare: The King's Men sous le règne de Jacques Ier* (Paris: C. N. R. S., 1959).
—— 'Robert Johnson: King's Musician in His Majesty's Public Entertainment', *Music and Letters*, 36:2 (1955), 110–25.
Dollimore, Jonathan, and Alan Sinfield (eds), *Political Shakespeare: New Essays in Cultural Materialism* (Manchester: Manchester University Press, 1985).
Duffin, Ross W., *Shakespeare's Songbook* (London: Norton, 2004).
Dunn, Catherine, 'The Function of Music in Shakespeare's Romances', *Shakespeare Quarterly*, 20 (1969), 391–405.
Faivre, Antoine, *Toison d'or et alchimie* (Milan: Arché, 1990).
Forshaw, Peter J., 'Marsilio Ficino and the Chemical Art', in Stephen Clucas, Peter J. Forshaw and Valery Rees (eds), *Laus Platonici Philosophi. Marsilio Ficino and his Influence* (Leiden and London: Brill, 2011), pp. 249–71.
—— '*Oratorium—Auditorium—Laboratorium*: Early Modern Improvisations on Cabala, Music, and Alchemy', *Aries*, 10:2 (2010), 169–95.
Fox-Good, Jacquelyn, 'Other Voices: The Sweet, Dangerous Air(s) of Shakespeare's *Tempest*', *Shakespeare Studies*, 24 (1996), 241–74.
Gibson, Clare, *How to Read Symbols* (London: Herbert Press, 2009).

Godwin, Joscelyn, *Harmonies of Heaven and Earth* (London: Thames and Hudson, 1987).
—— 'Music and the Hermetic Tradition', in Roelof van den Broek and Wouter J. Hanegraff (eds), *Gnosis and Hermeticism from Antiquity to Modern Times* (New York: State University of New York Press, 1998), pp. 183–96.
Gouk, Penelope, 'Transforming Matter, Refining the Spirit: Alchemy, Music and Experimental Philosophy around 1600', *European Review*, 21:2 (2013), 146–57.
Griffiths, Fiona J., *The Garden of Delights. Reform and Renaissance for Women in the Twelfth Century* (Philadelphia: University of Pennsylvania Press, 2007).
Guinle, Francis, '"Noises, / Sounds and sweet airs" – Les chansons de *La Tempête*: texte et contexte', in Claude Peltrault (ed.), *La Tempête. Etudes critiques* (Besançon: Université de Franche-Comté, 1993), pp. 219–38.
Haaning, Aksel, 'The Philosophical Nature of Early Western Alchemy', in Jacob Wamberg (ed.), *Art and Alchemy* (Copenhagen: Museum Tuscularum Press, 2006), pp. 23–39.
Halleux, Robert, *Les Textes alchimiques* (Turnhout: Brepols, 1979).
Harris, Anthony, *Night's Black Agents* (Manchester: Manchester University Press, 1980).
Hollander, John, *The Untuning of the Sky: Ideas of Music in English Poetry, 1500–1700* [1961] (New York: W. W. Norton, 1970).
Hutin, Serge, *Les Alchimistes au Moyen Age* [1977] (Paris: Hachette, 1995).
Ingram, R. W., 'Musical Pauses and the Vision Scenes in Shakespeare's Last Plays', in Waldo F. McNeir and Thelma N. Greenfield (eds), *Pacific Coast Studies in Shakespeare* (Eugene: University of Oregon, 1966), pp. 234–47.
Iselin, Pierre, '"My Music for Nothing": Musical Negotiations in *The Tempest*', *Shakespeare Survey*, 48 (1995), 135–45.
—— '"My Music for Nothing": *The Tempest* comme comédie de l'air', in Claude Peltrault (ed.), *La Tempête. Etudes critiques* (Besançon: Université de Franche-Comté, 1993), pp. 239–52.
Johnson, W. Stacy, 'The Genesis of Ariel', *Shakespeare Quarterly*, 2:3 (July 1951), 205–10.
Kahn, Coppélia, 'The Providential Tempest and the Shakespearean Family', in Murray M. Schwartz and Coppélia Kahn (eds), *Representing Shakespeare: New Psychoanalytic Essays* (Baltimore, MD, and London: The Johns Hopkins University Press, 1982), pp. 217–43.
Knight, G. Wilson, *The Shakespearian Tempest* (London: Oxford University Press, 1932).
Lindley, David, 'Music, Masque, and Meaning in *The Tempest*' in *The Court Masque* (Manchester: Manchester University Press, 1984), pp. 47–59.
Long, John H., *Shakespeare's Use of Music: The Final Comedies* (Gainesville: University of Florida Press, 1961).
Lyne, Raphael, 'Ovid, Golding, and the "Rough Magic" of *The Tempest*', in A. B. Taylor (ed.), *Shakespeare's Ovid* (Cambridge: Cambridge University Press, 2000), pp. 150–64.
Maier, Michael, *Atalanta Fugiens* (1617), trans. and ed. Joscelyn Godwin (Grand Rapids, MI: Phanes Press, 1989).
Marteau, Robert, *La Récolte de la rosée. La tradition alchimique dans la littérature* (Paris: Belin, 1995).
Masson, Hervé, *Dictionnaire initiatique* (Paris: Jean-Cyrille Godefroy, 1995).

Maynard, Winifred, *Elizabethan Lyric Poetry and Its Music* (Oxford: Clarendon Press, 1986).
Mebane, John S., *Renaissance Magic and the Return of the Golden Age. The Occult Tradition and Marlowe, Jonson, and Shakespeare* (Lincoln and London: University of Nebraska Press, 1989).
Mellers, Wilfrid, *Harmonious Meeting: A Study of the Relationships between English Music, Poetry and Theatre c. 1600–1900* (London: Dennis Dobson, 1965).
Minear, Erin, *Reverberating Song in Shakespeare and Milton. Language, Memory, and Musical Representation* (Farnham and Burlington, VT: Ashgate, 2011).
Mowatt, Barbara, 'Prospero's Book', *Shakespeare Quarterly*, 52:1 (Spring 2001), 1–33.
Neill, Michael, '"Noises, / Sounds and Sweet Airs": The Burden of Shakespeare's *Tempest*', *Shakespeare Quarterly*, 59:1 (Spring 2008), 36–59.
Nicholl, Charles, *The Chemical Theatre* (London: Routledge and Kegan Paul, 1980).
Noble, Richmond, *Shakespeare's Use of Song* (London: Oxford University Press, 1923).
Norton, Thomas, *The Ordinal of Alchemy* [1477], ed. John Reidy (London, New York, Toronto: Oxford University Press, 1975).
Orgel, Stephen (ed.), *Ben Jonson: Selected Masques* (New Haven, CT and London: Yale University Press, 1970).
Orrell, John, 'The Musical Canon of Proportion in Jonson's *Hymenaei*', *English Language Notes*, 15:3 (1978), 171–8.
Paracelsus, *Paracelsus (Theophrastus Bombastus von Hohenheim, 1493–1541). Essential Theoretical Writings*, trans. and ed. Andrew Weeks (Leiden and Boston: Brill, 2008).
Peyré, Yves, 'Les "Masques" d'Ariel. Essai d'interprétation de leur symbolisme', *Cahiers Elisabéthains*, 19 (1981), 53–71.
Poisson, Albert, *Théories et symboles des alchimistes. Le grand œuvre* [1891] (Angoulême: Editions maçonniques de France, 2013).
Poole, William, 'False Play: Shakespeare and Chess', *Shakespeare Quarterly*, 55:1 (2004), 50–70.
Rebotier, Jacques, '"Art de Musique" et "Art d'Hermès". Recherches sur le symbolisme alchimique de la post-Renaissance' (Diplôme de l'Ecole Pratique des Hautes Etudes, 1972).
Reed, Robert R., 'The Probable Origin of Ariel', *Shakespeare Quarterly*, 11:1 (1960), 61–5.
Reid, Robert L., 'Sacerdotal Vestiges in *The Tempest*', *Comparative Drama*, 41:4 (2007–8), 493–513.
Ripley, George, *The Mistery of Alchymists*, in Elias Ashmole (ed.), *Theatrum Chemicum Britannicum: containing severall poeticall pieces of our famous English philosophers, who have written the hermetique mysteries in their owne ancient language* (London, 1652), pp. 380–8.
Roberts, Gareth, *The Mirror of Alchemy* (London: The British Library, 1994).
Roulon, Natalie, *Les Femmes et la musique dans l'œuvre de Shakespeare* (Paris: Honoré Champion, 2011).
Ryan, Kiernan, *Shakespeare. The Last Plays* (London: Longman, 1999).

Schwartz, Murray M., and Coppélia Kahn (eds), *Representing Shakespeare: New Psychoanalytic Essays* (Baltimore, MD, and London: The Johns Hopkins University Press, 1982).

Srigley, Michael, *Images of Regeneration* (Uppsala: Acta Universitatis Upsaliensis, 1985).

Seng, Peter J., *The Vocal Songs in the Plays of Shakespeare: A Critical History* (Cambridge, MA: Harvard University Press, 1967).

Shakespeare, William, *The Tempest* [2002], ed. David Lindley (Cambridge: Cambridge University Press, 2004).

—— *The Tempest* [1999], ed. Virginia Mason Vaughan (London: Thomson Learning, 2001).

—— *The Tempest*, ed. Stephen Orgel [1987] (Oxford: Oxford University Press, 1998).

—— *The Tempest*, ed. Frank Kermode [1954] (London: Methuen, 1979).

Simonds, Peggy N., '"My charms crack not": The Alchemical Structure of *The Tempest*', *Comparative Drama*, 31:4 (Winter 1997–8), 538–70.

—— '"Sweet Power of Music": The Political Magic of "The Miraculous Harp" in Shakespeare's *The Tempest*', *Comparative Drama*, 29:1 (Spring 1995), 61–90.

Simonis, Annette, 'Geräusch—Klang—Melodie. "Strange music" in *The Tempest*', in U. Jung-Kaiser and A. Simonis (eds), *'Dis süße Macht des Töne', Zur Bedeutung der Musik in Shakespeares Werken und ihrer Rezeption* (Hildesheim, Zürich, New York: Georg Olms Verlag, 2014).

Sisson, C. J., 'The Magic of Prospero', *Shakespeare Survey*, 11 (1958), 70–7.

Smith, Hallett, 'Introduction to *The Tempest*', in G. Blakemore Evans (ed.), *The Riverside Shakespeare* (Boston: Houghton Mifflin, 1974).

Smith, Irwin, 'Ariel and the Masque in *The Tempest*', *Shakespeare Quarterly*, 21 (1970), 213–22.

——'Ariel as Ceres', *Shakespeare Quarterly*, 9 (1958), 430–2.

Srigley, Michael, *Images of Regeneration* (Uppsala: Acta Universitatis Upsaliensis, 1985).

Tomlinson, Gary, *Music in Renaissance Magic. Toward a Historiography of Others* (Chicago and London: University of Chicago Press, 1993).

Trismosin, Salomon, *Splendor Solis*, ed. Stephan Hoebeeck (Brussels: Editions SPRL, 2013).

Van Lennep, Jacques, *Alchimie. Contribution à l'histoire de l'art alchimique* (Brussels: Crédit Communal de Belgique, 1984).

—— *Art et alchimie* (Brussels: Meddens, 1971).

Walker, D. P., *Spiritual and Demonic Magic from Ficino to Campanella* (London: The Warburg Institute, 1958).

—— *Music, Spirit and Language in the Renaissance*, P. Gouk (ed.) (London: Variorum Reprints, 1985).

Wamberg Jacob (ed.), *Art and Alchemy* (Copenhagen: Museum Tuscularum Press, 2006).

Warlick, M. E. 'Fluctuating Identities. Gender Reversals in Alchemical Imagery', in Jacob Wamberg (ed.), *Art and Alchemy* (Copenhagen: Museum Tuscularum Press, 2006), pp. 103–28.

Wells, Robin Headlam, *Elizabethan Mythologies: Studies in Poetry, Drama, and Music* (Cambridge: Cambridge University Press, 1994).

White, R. S., *Let Wonder Seem Familiar* (New Jersey: Humanities Press; London: Athlone Press, 1985).
Wilson, Christopher R. (ed), *Research Companion to Shakespeare Music* (Oxford University Press) (forthcoming).
—— *Shakespeare's Musical Imagery* (New York and London: Continuum, 2011).
—— and Michela Calore, *Music in Shakespeare. A Dictionary* (London and New York: Thoemmes, 2005).
Yates, Frances, *The Rosicrucian Enlightenment* [1972] (Oxford and New York: Routledge, 2002).
Zimbardo, Rose A., 'Form and Disorder in *The Tempest*', *Shakespeare Quarterly*, 14:1 (1963), 49–56.

10

From Prospero to Prospera: transforming gender and magic on stage and screen

Katharine Goodland

Over the past two decades, an increasing number of female actors have stepped into the role of Shakespeare's protagonist in *The Tempest*, transforming Prospero, a character long viewed as the quintessential patriarch, into Prospera, an icon of womanly power.[1] The apparent seamlessness of this change suggests that its time has come. As Virginia Mason Vaughan writes: '[e]ach production represents a moment in time, when the cultural forces outside the theatre – political, social, economic and aesthetic – come together in a theatrical performance, which by its nature is a collaborative activity, between and among the actors, and between and among the actors and audience'.[2] To this collaborative activity I would add the dynamic between the text and the actors' bodies. For, as Robert Weimann observes, a 'performed play thrives on the mutual engagement of text and bodies'.[3] The meaning produced in a theatrical performance is the alchemical product, if you will, of what happens when a particular body, with all its ideological and cultural associations at a particular moment in time, inhabits the script. With respect to *The Tempest*, a number of directors and actors have noted that, as Andrew Hartley puts it, '[i]n a character like Prospero there is relatively little that asserts the character's essential maleness... Remove that male body, replace it with a female body, and much that seems "male" about Prospero changes.'[4] And yet, Shakespeare's text sets up an opposition between male and female forms of magic in the figures of Prospero and Sycorax. What happens, then, to the magic in the play when Prospero becomes Prospera?

I address this question by examining how magic is wielded in performance by three of the most prominent Prosperas to date, two on stage and one on screen: Blair Brown (2003, McCarter Theatre, directed by Emily Mann), Helen Mirren (2010 film directed by Julie Taymor) and Olympia Dukakis (2012, Shakespeare & Company, directed by Tony Simotes).[5] As an exploration of the nature of art and more specifically of the theatre, *The Tempest* is the play most closely associated with Shakespeare himself, who, like Prospero, created and controls the magic of theatrical illusion in the play. It is therefore appropriate that in all three of these productions featuring women in the central role, women were also significant creative forces behind the scenes. Two of the productions were directed by women, Emily Mann and Julie Taymor, while the third was influenced by a feminist adaptation of the play penned by leading actor Olympia Dukakis herself. These Prosperas differ in many respects, not least of which is the age of the actors at the time they played the role (Brown was 53, Mirren 62 and Dukakis 81). Because the magic in the play endows the protagonist with authority and control, these productions help us to understand how, at this moment in time, our culture envisions powerful, creative women.

In the course of its 400-year performance history, *The Tempest* has been interpreted on stage in a remarkably wide-ranging number of ways. The Victorian era focused on Prospero as Victorian 'paterfamilias' in James Macready's actor-manager interpretation. This was followed at the end of the nineteenth century by a shift in the spotlight to Caliban as an exemplar of Darwinian evolutionary theory. Next came John Gielgud's and Derek Jacobi's Freudian interpretations, which, as one reviewer wrote, energised the play by 'switching our interest from the power of Prospero to his psychology'.[6] The Darwinian and Freudian interpretations gave way after the Second World War to post-colonial *Tempests*, which have left an indelible mark on our understanding of the play and made it central to an understanding of post-colonial theory. The play was among the first in mainstream professional theatre productions to include actors of colour, not only in the roles of Caliban and Ariel, but also of Prospero. Ariel has long been routinely cast with both male and female actors, with the gender of the sprite either following that of the actor or being performed as androgynous (most often when a male actor is cast in the role). Until recently, however, Prospero's gender has been sacrosanct, remaining resolutely male, even when played by a female actor, as in Vanessa Redgrave's polarising performance at the Globe in 2000.[7] As approaches to gender, casting and the play itself have changed, so have the interpretations and portrayals of Prospero's magic.[8]

The three productions I discuss in this chapter represent a new moment in the history of *The Tempest* in performance, one that both imagines and reminds us of the ways in which women are and have always been creative, intellectual and political forces to be reckoned with. Blair Brown's 2003 stage portrayal conjured the dream of a Renaissance queen; Olympia Dukakis's 2012 theatre performance evoked the goddesses of matriarchal prehistory; while Helen Mirren's 2010 Prospera materialises on screen as a scientist with the ingenuity of Galileo and the keenness of Madame Curie. These three Prosperas invite us to consider them in the context of feminism and rethink the text's opposition between male and female forms of magic.

'Native and endued unto that element?': Prospera as earth goddess

Blair Brown (2003) and Olympia Dukakis (2012)

The Prosperas of Blair Brown and Olympia Dukakis were goddess-like in that the magic they wielded was depicted as a natural extension of their feminine natures rather than as a skill derived from the knowledge-based pursuit of science and alchemy. In Emily Mann's 2003 McCarter Theatre production, Blair Brown's Prospera (figure 10.1) was at the centre of a relatively diverse cast that seemed intended to prevent it from eliciting the play's customary post-colonial motifs.[9] The actors of colour, Ezra Knight and Caroline Stefanie Clay, were cast as nobility, Sebastian and Alonsa respectively. Despite this attempt to avoid conjuring post-colonial images, the production's setting established a contrast between east and west, portraying Prospera as a red-haired

10.1 Blair Brown as Prospera (2003).

European noblewoman reminiscent of Elizabeth I.[10] Her lavish Renaissance-style gown contrasted sharply with the spare Asian ambiance of the stage, which was bare except for Prospera's elaborately carved, throne-like chair, which substituted for Prospero's traditional book-lined cell. A narrow bar of sand ran the length of the front, suggesting the shoreline. An upper level was framed by panels of rice-paper and bamboo screens. Looming over the stage from its high perch at the centre of the deck was an enormous window in the shape of a full moon through which Ariel entered and exited. A smaller image of the full moon moved slowly across the sky over the course of the production, indicating the passage of time. The moon, Renaissance symbol of the goddess Diana, was an ever-present reminder that Prospera's magic partook of this feminine cosmic force.

The opposition between East and West was further developed in the casting of Ariel, played by Julyana Soelistyo, an American actor born in Indonesia. While Brown's Prospera was statuesque and strong, Ariel was slight and waifish. Throughout the production Brown's Prospera physically intimidated Soelistyo's spritely and graceful Ariel. This Prospera needed no magic cape, books or spells, and her Ariel seemed to derive whatever magic she could conjure from her queen rather than her own essence. The setting also suggested that this was Ariel's island rather than Caliban's.

Caliban was played by a white actor, Ian Kahn, who was no deformed monster, but instead looked so much like Lorenzo Pisoni's Ferdinand that it was easy to confuse the two, especially in the scene when Ferdinand hauled logs for Prospera. Ferdinand was dressed like Caliban in burlap sackcloth that barely covered his body. Both actors were tall, muscular and handsome. There was a discernible hint of erotic tension in the relationship between Prospera and Caliban throughout the production that recalled Elizabeth I's dalliances with members of her court. Caliban's passionate gaze upon his duchess suggested either a former intimacy or hope for a future one that Prospera finally seemed to acknowledge when she aborted his plot to kill her and, turning to him with an edge of desire in her voice, gave new meaning to the line, 'this thing of darkness I acknowledge mine'.[11]

The storm sequence emerged from Prospera's imagination as a dream, suggesting that the entirety of the unfolding action was Prospera's queenly dream of power. The show opened as the lights came up on Prospera asleep in her throne, her heavy blue and red brocade Renaissance-style gown flowing onto the floor, and her red, wavy hair draped about her shoulders. She thrashed in her throne. Rising, she moved to centre stage where, with her feet planted firmly, she slowly jerked her head from left to right with sharp muscular turns. Lightning flashed and, to the rumbling of thunder, we heard the voices of her victims being tossed in the storm as they cried out from the aisles of the theatre. Prospera punched the air with her powerful arms in a stately and controlled, if violent, dance, and the elements responded again with lighting and thunder. Blair Brown's Prospera possessed and was possessed by her magic in the manner of an earth goddess, for it appeared to be innate, rather than the result of learning.

This production's portrayal of magic embodied several feminist cross-currents. On one hand, it presented an inherently powerful woman. Brown's physique, voice and manner were authoritative and regal. On the other hand, the suggestion that the events transpired as a dream distanced her from responsibility for her magic.[12] Further, as a queen her power was an entitlement that took precedence over her gender. At the same time, the allusion to Elizabeth I is a reminder that, throughout history, as Igor Kopytoff observes, women like Indira Ghandi in India, Benazir Bhutto in Pakistan, Sirimavo Bandaranaike in Sri Lanka, to name only a few who inherited power in caste societies like that of Elizabeth I, also ruled supremely well.[13]

The production was greeted with interest on the part of critics, though none of them commented on the significance of the allusions to Elizabeth I, an interpretation that aligns Prospera's magic with political authority and power. Instead, they implicitly viewed this Prospera in traditional constructions of femininity, focusing on how a female Prospera shed new light on the relationships in the play. Robert L. Daniels, for example, domesticated the magic wielded by Blair Brown's Prospera into that of a mother: 'she glows with comforting maternal wisdom'.[14] Another reviewer made a similar move, noting that the regendering of both Prospero and Alonso as women (Prospera and Alonsa) 'brought a female spark to traditionally male roles of power, and as they [gave] feminine life to masculine dialogue their commanding performances encompass[ed] both motherly warmth and harrowing strength'.[15] Peter Filchia wrote that casting a woman was 'Mann's most daring move', and that it worked, 'for it suggests that jealous brother Antonio usurped power and banished his sister because he felt a man should be on the throne. As a result, there's a strong subtext of women's rights.' He also felt that 'the right woman is playing Prospera', noting that she 'cuts a bold figure', that can fill her throne. But what he found 'most endearing' is the scene when Prospera, unseen, watches Miranda and Ferdinand: '[a]s she stands unnoticed by the two lovers, she has her arms crossed, head cocked and a steely glint in her eye. In other words, she's all mother.'[16] Here Filchia engages in a common tendency to praise Prospera's motherhood. In each instance cited here, Prospera's characteristics as a mother eclipse her power as a magician, thereby indicating how much the general population, for whom reviewers write, associates the idea of womanhood with motherhood, and how important being a good mother is to contemporary society's idea of what it means to be a good woman. Filchia's comment also implies that if a powerful woman is also a good mother, her magic is less disturbing and more palatable.

In contrast to Blair Brown's Prospera who, at 53, was entering middle age, Shakespeare & Company's *Tempest*, directed by Tony Simotes, starred the

10.2 Olympia Dukakis as Prospera (2012).

dauntingly vigorous 81-year-old Academy Award-winner Olympia Dukakis (figure 10.2).[17] This production was set in a deliberately neutral landscape – at once familiar and strange – both inside and outside time and place. While Brown's Prospera was intended to conjure a Renaissance queen, Dukakis's evoked a Greek matriarch. Thus her Prospera engaged with an icon of motherhood writ large. Her Prospera drew upon her Greek heritage as well as a previous theatre piece funded by the Dodge Foundation, called 'The Goddess Project'.[18] As Jeffrey Borak explains, Dukakis 'saw… Prospera as emblematic of the matriarchal forces and spirit of pre-history'.[19]

Tony Simotes, who was at the time Shakespeare & Company's artistic director as well as the director of this production, insisted they perform Shakespeare's play rather than Dukakis's adaptation.[20] The 'Goddess Project' nevertheless shaped the production's Prospera. Dukakis was personally invested in this project because, as she explained in an in-depth interview with Virginia Mason Vaughan, she felt a profound sense of betrayal and anger when, 'in the wake of first wave feminism... she [learned] that before the Greeks conquered Asia Minor, worship of the Great Mother, a female goddess of sexuality and power, flourished in the ancient world'.[21] In the interview related by Vaughan, Dukakis sees her own betrayal mirrored in this historical shift. Dukakis created Prospera's backstory out of this mythic past: 'Prospera's life in Milan was pre-patriarchal... but when her brother steals her crown, a fragmentation of the spirit tears her apart'.[22]

Dukakis conceived her Prospera as finding a new kind of power on the island that draws from nature and connects with '"the old consciousness," one in which she felt the ancient mothers guiding and empowering her'.[23] The opening scene manifested this idea, as Dukakis's Prospera stirred the storm using a branch in a churning motion as though she were stirring up these ancient mothers through their native medium, the elements of earth and water. As Dukakis explained to Jeffery Borak, '[t]he knowledge and wisdom that Prospera... brings is from prehistory... Spirituality is within plants, within nature. It is not transcendent and if it is not transcendent who carries it? Woman.'[24] Dukakis's statement is problematic from the standpoint of current feminist and gender theory, yet she is an actor, not a scholar, and her passionate belief certainly contributed to a powerful and moving performance.

According to Vaughan, the production set up a contrast between feminine and masculine drives for power, with Dukakis's Prospera at the center of and central to the struggle. Dukakis saw her Prospera primarily as wrathful, as possessing rage that was necessary and empowering: '[s]he wants vengeance... She wants to get back at all of them. She's been disempowered. She is acting out of deep humiliation. She wants her power back.'[25] Most reviewers responded well to this interpretation and felt that it came through in performance, and yet her anger, like that of Brown, was not received by most reviewers as frightening or disturbing. Joan Mento observed, 'Dukakis's delivery in *The Tempest* was powerful. As Prospera, she embodied both vengeance and forgiveness, recognizing the need to enact all aspects of self. Instead of a colonialist interpretation, this *Tempest* envisioned a feminist goddess approach, representing the matriarchal reign of pre-history.'[26] Many reviewers saw Dukakis's Prospera as tough and hard, but they perceived this toughness as an aspect of motherhood, rather than of her magic power. Jeffrey Borak felt that 'the stakes become just a bit higher as a parent–child relationship takes on a different texture; gains in layers of complexity, rivalry, coming together... Prospera is not just any mother – this is a tough, hard, vengeful woman.' Yet he also commented on her softer moments: '[a]s she leans over to forgive Caliban, she grazes his cheek with her hand; the act of a loving mother acknowledging her own responsibility for the misshapen emotional state of this, in effect, orphan son'.[27] Frank Rizzo observed that the perspective gained in a female Prospero is that 'of a strong, maternal monarch… and Dukakis is magnificent in the role'.[28] Chris Rohmann agreed, 'it's the female star in the traditionally male lead who brings special impact to *The Tempest*… The sex change poignantly shifts the parent–child relationship, even as it sharpens Prospera's bitterness toward the male usurpers.'[29] With regard to Prospera's magic, like Dukakis herself who understood her Prospera as having a special connection with the forces of nature and with the consciousness of the ancient goddesses immanent there, several critics remarked on the magic of her stern maternalism, which Ben Brantley turned into a joke about all moms:

> As your own mom probably told you many times, mothers have magic powers, like reading their children's thoughts and making them feel guilty like nobody else. So just imagine what might be accomplished by a mother with full command of the mystic arts: I mean the sort that can rule the elements and call up armies of sprites and goblins with the wave of a rod. Kind of a scary thought, huh? Well brace yourself and allow me to introduce the mighty, moody, Prospera, the stay-at-home-sorcerer played by Olympia Dukakis… Fail to call this mother on her birthday at your mortal peril.[30]

Further, he quips '[w]hen the monster Caliban… dares to complain about his treatment, she pierces him with a leveling glare that requires no additional witchcraft'.[31] Brantley mockingly implies that of course this woman is just a mom. He eschews taking Dukakis's goddess research seriously. Brantley's is an extreme version of the tendency for critics to endeavour to contain Prospera's power by domesticating it under a stereotypical idea of motherhood, and the patriarchal control over her body that this implies.

Bob Goepfert similarly domesticates Dukakis's Prospera, writing that

> [t]he change [to a woman] is more significant than altering the name. Rather than portray the character as a powerful individual who has learned magic to control the environment, Dukakis brings a more maternal attitude to the character… Her interaction with her exceedingly innocent daughter… is patient and protective. Too, her interaction with the ephemeral spirit Ariel… is also motherly. Even her dominance over Caliban… is more gentle and teacher-like in this production.'[32]

Goepfert's remarks about Merritt Janson's Miranda, whose rebelliousness and sexual desire for Ferdinand were barely contained, are especially curious here. The confrontation between Janson's Miranda and Dukakis's Prospera throbbed with tension and conflict. It is entirely possible that the evening Goepfert saw the production this exchange was more conciliatory than on the several evenings I saw the production. At the same time, it also suggests that the critical response is implicitly biased. As Frank Rizzo put in a more positive way: '[n]o one can give a wary look better than this actress, her eyebrows forming two great diagonals of doubt as her eyes bore into another character's falseness'.[33] Yet, as these remarks demonstrate, many reviewers view a woman in power through the framework of our culture's construction of motherhood by which a woman's strength and power are domesticated and contained: the word 'mother' in our culture is associated with compassion and selflessness while also implying dependency.

In contrast to the reviewers, Vaughan sees the concept of motherhood in the production as a feminist statement. She argues that Dukakis's interpretation of Prospera as re-embodying the consciousness of the ancient goddesses aligned itself with that of Medea: '[l]ike the Great Mother, Medea had extraordinary powers... Flooded with primordial wrath, Medea took a horrible revenge, killing her own children in the process. As a female Prospero, Dukakis could tap into the darkest passions, making her decision to forgive more difficult, yet more convincing.'[34] Vaughan's point raises questions, about gender dynamics not only in the play, but also our own. For Vaughan's statement suggests that, as a woman, Dukakis had greater access than a man would to the forces of passion and magic – that she could more readily tap into the darkest passions, thereby making her decision to forgive more moving and realistic than a male actor could in the same role. In contrast, the reviewers of both Dukakis's portrayal and Brown's felt that Prospera's forgiveness was more realistic for the opposite reason: because women are naturally more compassionate. The arguments on both sides imply essentialist differences between the biological sexes that are difficult to substantiate, particularly now when notions of gender identity are in kaleidoscopic flux.

Perhaps even more to the point is the difference in constructions of motherhood represented in Euripides's Medea and Shakespeare's Sycorax and those of our own time. Medea and Sycorax are mothers but, like the ancient goddesses that inform their portrayals, their motherhood is construed as terrifying and wild, and their magic is viewed with awe and fear.[35] In contrast, as these stage productions show, there is a tendency in our contemporary culture to neutralise the potency of these powerful portrayals by viewing their magic as an extension of a domesticated construction of motherhood that is premised upon patriarchal control. Shakespeare's powerful magus becomes akin to Elizabeth Montgomery's character Samantha in the popular 1960s television show *Bewitched*, where the beautiful woman uses her magic to perform domestic tricks to please and bemuse her husband.

'I have bedimmed the noontide sun'

Helen Mirren, 2010

While the Prosperas of Blair Brown and Olympia Dukakis wielded magic that seemed to extend from their feminine natures in the manner of earth goddesses,

From Prospero to Prospera 227

10.3 Helen Mirren as Prospera (2010).

Helen Mirren's Prospera in the Julie Taymor film is depicted as a scientist/magus whose magic derives from the knowledge she has acquired from her studies and experiments (figure 10.3). She uses her knowledge to devise a complex lens apparatus through which she can see the inhabitants on the island while remaining unseen by them. She watches them from the secrecy of her underground cave-cell, creating illusions on the screen of the sky to manipulate them with the help of Ariel, who is himself a filmic projection within the intradiegetic world of the film. His androgynous, nude body is entirely encapsulated in a separate film that is superimposed upon the main film. Taymor's Prospera thus uses film in a way that is analogous to that by which Shakespeare's original protagonist deployed theatrical illusion.[36]

Samuel Crowl sees the film as evoking a Darwinian struggle for survival on the island setting with its 'hard black volcanic rock', which he finds reminiscent of 'Darwin's Galapagos'. He argues that 'Prospera's island is as much a laboratory for her experiments as is her cell'.[37] I would suggest that the Darwinian elements in the film are rather Taymor's directorial wink of acknowledgment to the earlier, Darwinian phase of *Tempest* productions. For while the story of this film certainly involves survival on the island, as Crowl emphasises, it seems to me that, as Sebastian Lefait shows, the film is more concerned with investigating the 'scopic regimes' of theatre and film that illuminate the parallels between the use of surveillance during Shakespeare's era and our own.[38] A scopic regime is one in which dominance rests in the hands of those with the greatest power to see others unseen and to control the structuring relationships between observer, image and subject. This is the magic that Prospero possesses in Shakespeare's original play, and it is what endows Mirren's Prospera with her dominance in the film.

Further, this reading shows that Julie Taymor construes her art of filmmaking as a contemporary analogue of Shakespeare's playmaking, which the film encourages us to ascertain through her allusions to earlier films. Samuel Crowl relates, 'Taymor has said that the triangular design of the entrance to [the] underground cell, with its two symmetrical flights of steps angling down from a high doorway, is meant to evoke an open book'.[39] Here Taymor pays homage to Greenaway's *Prospero's Books* while also marking her point of departure for the feminist vision of her film. For, as Crowl points out, '[w]hen Taymor's camera enters Prospera's underground cave-cell it lingers lovingly not on her books but rather on the scientific and alchemical apparatus through which she exercises her powers'.[40] As a filmmaker rather than a playmaker, Taymor implies, her magic emanates from this prototype of a film camera through which she presciently explores the powers and dangers of the screen-fixated lives we live today. Taymor's Prospera has thus adapted one of the most significant discoveries of the Renaissance – Galileo's telescope – to devise what Sebastian Lefait aptly describes as a 'proto-cinematic' contraption of lenses.[41] Further, he explains:

> Prospera's protocinematic instruments adumbrate the era of ubiquitous CCTV units and display devices, and create a bridge between two eras. As a result, Taymor's adaptation relates *The Tempest* to the scopic culture of Shakespeare's time on the one hand, and to surveillance and screen societies on the other. It shows that *The Tempest* reflexively focuses on theatrical practices, but also on an early modern scopic culture based on surveillance practices and displays of authority that have a lot in common with drama… [The film] reminds that Shakespeare used the scopic regime of his art to study the scopic culture of his time.[42]

Thus, as in the original play, Prospera's power 'comes from showing as well as watching'.[43] The film de-mystifies Prospera's magic while at the same time commenting on the politics of power in both Shakespeare's time and our own: 'Prospera's arrangement of lenses is not only a part of the Renaissance collective imagination regarding the connection between vision and knowledge. It is also a way of acknowledging the play's analysis of synoptic power by condensing, into a single apparatus, the power to capture reality and the power to display it'.[44] In wielding this magic, Mirren's Prospera relies upon Ariel for carrying out her illusions. Their relationship in the film parallels that between Prospero and the spirit in the text, where the dynamics of magic are symbiotic and it is difficult to know where the power begins and ends. Prospera relies on Ariel for information and for carrying out her filmic displays, but Ariel is also the magus's captive whose filmic existence, like that of a character on the stage, only exists in the medium of performance. Further, '[a]s a picture that can see, Ariel roots the play's surveillance into contemporary scopic culture, where the telescreens of Orwell's *Nineteen Eighty-Four* have become concrete.'[45]

Taymor's film engages with the play's post-colonial implications in the relationship between Prospera and Caliban, who is played by West African actor Djimon Hounsou. Samuel Crowl notes that the score 'acknowledges Caliban as a universal figure of colonial dispossession' in its use of 'African drum and the Australian didgeridoo'.[46] Francesca Royster describes the film's handling of colonialism as 'muddled'.[47] I would suggest that colonialism, particularly as it is portrayed in Shakespeare's text, is itself a complex affair, and that the film's handling of it is bracingly honest and alert to the playtext's complexity. Royster notes that Mirren's Prospera is palpably afraid of Caliban: '[t]here is frustration in Prospera's eyes and her throaty voice, compounded by barely contained fear, especially in the lines that allude to Caliban's attempted rape of Miranda… She stands between Caliban and her daughter and brandishes her large black staff at him, her own black phallus countering his, shaken but determined'.[48] Mirren uses her black staff frequently throughout the film to hold Caliban at bay, and the effort appears to take all of her strength and will, leaving her shaken and depleted each time. For his part, Hounsou's Caliban looks at her with knowledgable, perceptive eyes that reveal the depth of his intelligence and ability to resist. As Crowl points out, Caliban retains his dignity. Instead of kneeling, he adopts poses from Butoh dance in graceful, meditative protest.[49] Butoh is 'an expressionist contemporary dance form which originated in Japan in the late 1950s'.[50] In Butoh the intent of the dance is to preserve and repossess the traumatised body: 'the body is regarded as a repository of repressed cultural memory; the grimaces and tortured gestures reflect the dancer's attempt to overcome physical and social inhibitions and to reconnect with primal energy'.[51] Caliban's silent poses eloquently bespeak his resistance, as well as, perhaps, his deeper bodily connection to the primal energies of the universe from which Prospera's technologically based power has distanced her. Further, as Courtney Lehmann points out, 'Caliban's skewed surfaces resemble the white-chalked and visibly scarred bodies of the dancers in Benin's annual voodoo festival, who engage in ritual self-mutilation as language for communicating the horrors of slavery'.[52] Caliban's dance measures the trauma of technological progress on the human body, for even as he enacts resistance to colonial dispossession, that dispossession is written on his body. In another reference to an earlier film, Taymor, as Lehmann notes, 'underscores the ultimate futility of Caliban's attempted revolt' as the silhouette of Caliban, Trinculo and Stephano is 'an unmistakable allusion to Ingmar Bergman's *The Seventh Seal* (1957)'.[53]

Francesca Royster sees the relationship between Prospera and Caliban as opaque: when Mirren acknowledges Caliban as her own 'thing of Darkness', she writes, 'the two lock eyes in silence, a mystery language of unsaid tenderness exchanged'.[54] Unlike Royster, I see a mutual sense of loss in their eyes, not affection. Or if it is affection, I would not call it tenderness, but rather the respect that emerges between two equally worthy and differently oppressed adversaries.[55] Caliban's elevation, symbolised in his slow ascent up the stairs and out of the underground cell, depends upon Prospera's sacrifice of her freedom in leaving the island. Lehmann sees in their silent exchange an 'acknowledge[ment of] the prisons they share'.[56] In contrast to Shakespeare's Prospero, who is set free by the audience's applause in the epilogue, Taymor's Prospera is 'disturbingly silent after this point'.[57] Crowl, Garcia and Royster all read Prospera's decision to leave her magic behind and return to Milan as an excruciating sacrifice of her freedom in order to ensure her daughter's future. Lehmann also sees the decision as a sacrifice, but without any payoff in terms of her motherhood: '[m]ore than anything else, in Taymor's film, Prospera is a scientist in search of an inhabitable – though clearly not hospitable epistemology'.[58] The corseted gown in which she willingly, if painfully, imprisons herself, embodies this sacrifice, which 'is not merely sartorial – it is ontological'.[59]

As with stage productions I discussed, some reviewers could not see past Mirren's gender and the fact of Prospera's motherhood to attend to the complexity and originality of Taymor's vision. There were well-known film reviewers who succumbed to the tendency to see any woman playing Prospera as an earth goddess or as a mom. Andrew O'Hehir, writing for *Salon*, described Mirren's Prospera as a 'sadly elegant mom-magician'.[60] It is unlikely that a male Prospero would be described in a similar way, say as a 'sadly elegant dad-magician'. O'Hehir makes it sound as though Mirren spends her time in the film doing fun magic crafts in the kitchen with her daughter. *New Yorker* film reviewer David Denby similarly is unable to recognise the protagonist of the film as a scientist, leaving him struggling with contradictory terminology: 'Prospera is a magician/earth goddess, with conceptual rather than generative fecundity'.[61] By definition an earth goddess has generative fecundity, so, according to Denby's own choice of words, Mirren is not primarily an earth goddess. 'Conceptual fecundity' is the creative output of the human scientist of the film. Marcia Garcia, writing for *Cineaste*, also construes Mirren's Prospera as an earth goddess, though in a more positive way: '[t]his Prospera is Demeter, a Great Mother with sufficient power to engineer a new world order, Miranda's brave new world'.[62] Her evidence for this claim, however, is primarily derived from the credentials Mirren brings to the role, rather than from the characterisation of Prospera in the film: 'Mirren – a Dame in real life and *The Queen* in the imaginations of many movie-goers – is the closest any female actor comes to royalty or to Demeter's divinity'.[63] True, perhaps, but as with O'Hehir's and Denby's critiques, Garcia does not discern the film's emphasis upon Mirren's Prospera as a woman of learning.

Rather, I would suggest that the Demeter/Persephone allusions which Garcia finds in the costumes and setting work instead as motifs that lend mythic import to Taymor's enterprise in creating the film, offering a feminine deity to offset Western civilisation's preoccupation with a male god as emblematic of the artistic drive. Garcia details how Prospera's costumes, especially her magician's cloak, 'seemingly constructed of obsidian, connect her to the island and the earth, to Demeter who, along with her daughter Persephone, represent the eternal cycle of birth, death, and rebirth that we are witness to' in the film.[64]

Where Crowl found the setting Darwinian, Garcia construes 'the volcanic Hawaiian isles… [as] a manifestation of eternity' and the eternal feminine.[65] She sees 'symbols of the Eternal Feminine' in 'the moon-shaped cistern, the rounded flasks of Prospera's laboratory, and their transformation into the circles of eclipsing moon and sun'.[66] This last image of the sun and moon, of course, points to the indelible Renaissance symbols of the feminine and masculine forces of the cosmos.[67] In their celestial dance, as they each, in turn, eclipse one another, we find another example of Taymor's wit and her nuanced adaptation of Shakespeare's script.

Francesca Royster, like Garcia, points out that Mirren's fame as an actor in previous roles contributes to how we view this Prospera. But Royster sees her primarily, and more accurately to my mind, as a remarkable woman rather than a goddess: 'Mirren, 62 and fresh from her machine gun-toting role as a trained assassin in the graphic remake, *Red* (2010), as well as her signature tough woman work in *Prime Suspect* (1991–2006) and toughness of another kind in *The Queen* (2006) brings to the role a combination of warmth, vulnerability, and haughtiness… Mirren's Prospera is most definitely female and human.'[68] Similarly, Crowl describes Mirren's Prospera as 'a deeply ambivalent figure', who is 'a scientist as well as a magician'.[69] I emphasise these contrasts among the reviewers, critics and scholars because they demonstrate how difficult it can be to see a woman's identity as distinct from her role as a mother.

What, then, is at stake in these different views of Helen Mirren's Prospera, and of the similarly conflicting responses to the Prosperas of Blair Brown and Olympia Dukakis? What difference does it make whether we see Prospera as a mom-magician, Demeter or a scientist, who also happens to be a woman and a mother? This query returns us to the question at the beginning of this chapter: what happens to the magic in the play when Prospero becomes Prospera? What changes, as I have shown, is not the magic itself, but rather the illusion of the magic, how it appears when it emanates from a differently gendered body. When a woman plays the role, many reviewers see the magic as an aspect of a domesticated form of motherhood, one that implies that the 'mom-magician' is under patriarchal control. Yet it is the reviewers themselves who exert this patriarchal control in reverting to implicitly biased ideas about women.[70]

When a man plays Prospero, his role as a parent is incidental rather than central to his magic; but when a female actor plays the role, many, though not all, see it as the reverse: the fact of motherhood is seen as the wellspring of the magic. Further, when a male actor plays Prospero, the implicit bias works in a different direction. He is viewed as less caring, more authoritative and principally concerned about controlling the value of his daughter's body as an object of patriarchal exchange. And yet the text indicates that he conceives of himself as a mother as well as a father to his daughter. In particular is his tender recollection that he lived for Miranda who gave him strength to survive their treacherous sea journey. To Miranda's exclamation that she must have been 'trouble' for him, he responds:

> O, a cherubin
> Thou wast that did preserve me...
> When I have decked the sea with drops full salt,
> Under my burden groaned, which raised in me
> An undergoing stomach, to bear up
> Against what should ensue. (1.2.153–8)

This passage portrays an inconsolable, grieving Prospero who sees himself blessed by his 3-year-old daughter Miranda, who saves him by giving him courage: the 'undergoing stomach'. Yet these words also feminise Prospero, showing his vulnerability, as he groans and weeps under the burden of a raised stomach like a woman giving birth. This poetic play on words aligns him with Sycorax, who was similarly exiled to the island pregnant and vulnerable.

This moment, early in the play, establishes Prospero's complex parallel with Sycorax and invites the audience to attend carefully to the play's tangled exploration of gender and magic. For much of the play, Prospero repeatedly pits his male, white magic against Sycorax's female, black witchcraft. This is the first of two key moments of dramatic irony when the playwright indicates, through the poetic allusions made by his unwitting protagonist, that Prospero and Sycorax might be more alike than different.

Julie Taymor suggests as much in the scene that opens her film, where we find Mirren's blue-eyed Prospera perched raven-like in her black obsidian cloak high above the sea commanding the storm. Further, she gives her Prospera a new backstory. Set in a period evocative of the Renaissance, we learn that Prospera's husband was the ruler of Milan who supported his wife's experiments. We see flashbacks of Mirren in her laboratory in Milan with baby Miranda in the cradle. Prospera's husband dies and bequeaths the duchy to her, but his brother Antonio accuses her of witchcraft and seizes power.[71] Taymor carries the alignment between Prospero and Sycorax a step further in her film's scene in which they part. The camera closes in first on the blue eyes of Mirren's Prospera and then on Hounsou's Caliban, who has one brown eye and one that is the same shade of blue as Mirren's. In suggesting not merely a parallel, but a kinship between Prospera and Sycorax, Taymor prompts us to rethink the text's contrast between the two exiles. Apart from their gender, what is the difference in the nature of the magic wielded by Prospero and Sycorax, between the learned male magus and the blue-eyed female witch?

Shakespeare's dramaturgy suggests that there may be no difference at all. In the second moment of dramatic irony in the play, as Prospero abjures his 'rough magic', Shakespeare has him ventriloquise history's most famous sorceress, Medea, thereby collapsing the opposition between gendered modes of magic.[72]

At this moment, the playwright invites us to see yet another illusion vanish into thin air.[73]

Yet illusions are powerful. They form the foundation of magic in the play, in which theatrical illusion elicits the characters' fears and desires. The play's dramaturgical structure similarly tests the audience's imaginative acuity in noticing that Prospero opposes his magic to Sycorax's for most of the play only to collapse that opposition in his abjuration of it. Further, it is likely that only the literate and educated in the original audience would have recognized the allusion to Ovid's Medea in Prospero's abjuration speech. In this way, the play embodies and interrogates the contradictory constructions of magic, alchemy and witchcraft circulating at the time the play was first performed, a time when women who participated in scientific experiments, herbal remedies or religious practices that were viewed as outside the norm were much more likely to be construed and prosecuted as witches than men similarly engaged.[74]

This analysis shows that, upon closer inspection, the replacement of a male body with a female body is not so seamless after all. Bodies matter. In Taymor's film the trauma of slavery and post-colonialism is written on Caliban's body, and the patriarchal society that will imprison Prospera once again encloses her body in a corseted gown in the film's final moments. The biases of our twenty-first-century culture are written in the laws that endeavour to control women's bodies and in the reviews that construe their value to society under the category of motherhood rather than as individuals who are leaders and scientists. Scholars and reviewers in general perceive Prospera's magic in different terms. Reviewers write on short deadlines for a readership that often needs to recognise pre-existing concepts rather than be challenged by new research. Reviews therefore are more inclined to be based in opinions and quick judgements that repeat and reinforce existing biases rather than challenge them. The purpose of scholarship is quite different in purpose and scope. The result is that where scholars might find strong feminist statements, reviewers' comments incline toward revealing implicit biases about women on the margins of an implicit social norm. In all three instances of the Prosperas I have discussed, the artistic teams and the actors themselves understood their Prosperas as angry, intimidating, creative, strong and complex, regardless of whether they were portrayed as earth goddesses or scientists. All three actors playing the role were past child-bearing age. Yet, in all three cases, reviewers tended to view them primarily as mothers rather than magi. This proclivity is not a matter of life or death as it was in Shakespeare's time when women on the margins of society, particularly those who were older, poor and single, were prosecuted for witchcraft.[75] Yet it is worth considering that, now as then, our culture manifests anxiety over independent women in its inclination to contain exceptional women within a stereotyped idea of motherhood.

In our current moment, the emergence of Prospera in *The Tempest* has expanded roles in Shakespeare's canon for seasoned female actors, giving them a significant opportunity to portray older women as sexually complex, intellectually vibrant and creative. In turn, the role of Prospera opens up an exploration of how our contemporary society views women in positions of power and authority. These portrayals elicit responses by reviewers that expose our culture's implicit biases.[76] Perhaps with time, as more Prosperas tread the boards, these biases will give way and more audiences and reviewers will meet portrayals of strong women on their own terms. For the experience of seeing these female actors in a major Shakespearean role, one that is most closely associated with the playwright himself, produces its own alchemy. As if by magic, they show how performance transforms an oppressive patriarch into a complex woman of singular strength and empathy.

Notes

1 Here I extend Francesca T. Royster's point that Helen Mirren's Prospera becomes a new female Shakespearean icon, to include the character of Prospera in general. See Royster, 'Introduction to "Shakespeare's Female Icons": Sorcerers, Celebrities, Aliens, and Upstarts', *Upstart Crow: Special Edition*, 31 (2012).
2 Virginia Mason Vaughan, *Shakespeare in Performance: The Tempest* (Manchester: Manchester University Press. 2011), p. 1; hereafter cited as *The Tempest*.
3 Robert Weimann, 'Playing with a Difference: Revisiting "Pen" and "Voice" in Shakespeare's Theatre', *Shakespeare Quarterly*, 50:4 (1999), p. 420.
4 Andrew James Hartley, 'Prospera's Brave New World: Cross-Cast Oppression and the Four-Fold Player in the Georgia Shakespeare Festival's *Tempest*', in *Shakespeare Re-Dressed: Cross-Gender Casting in Contemporary Performance* (Madison, NJ: Fairleigh-Dickinson Press, 2008), p. 140.
5 I have selected these productions for two reasons: first, they represent the trends in textual adaptation, critical response and the portrayal of Prospera's magic since the first woman, Marie Peckinpah, assumed the magic mantle at the Synthaxis Theatre in Southern California in 1977. By my count, there have been approximately thirty productions to date in the United States, Canada and Britain combined in which women have played the role as 'Prospera', including three female actors of colour. Second, I have seen these three productions, and so am able to write about them from first-hand experience in conjunction with drawing on reviews and scholarship.
6 Anonymous, *The Sunday Times* (18 August 1957); cited in Vaughan, *The Tempest*, p. 78.
7 My research shows that to date three female actors have played Prospero as a man. Performance artist Rose English played the magus in a 1999 experimental, avant-garde production directed by Nick Philippou for Actors Touring Company that used only three actors, video screens, techno-sound effects and Beckett-like images. Most recently, Harriet Walters took on the role as part of a Shakespearean trilogy (*Julius Caesar*, 2012; *Henry IV*, 2014; *The Tempest*, 2016) directed by Phyllida Lloyd with an all-female cast and set in a women's prison. Vanessa Redgrave's

performance was more challenging sociologically and semiotically since she cross-dressed in a production in which the other actors' genders were aligned with their characters. In contrast, Rose English and Harriet Walter were in productions the frameworks of which re-contextualised the play in ways that distanced the actors from the character they were playing. On Redgrave's Prospera, see Elizabeth Klett, 'Gender in Exile: Vanessa Redgrave's Prospero in *The Tempest* (2000)', in *Cross-Gender Shakespeare and English National Identity: Wearing the Codpiece* (Basingstoke: Palgrave, 2009), Chapter 4, pp. 87–114.

8 In the history of performances of *The Tempest*, some of the main ways in which magic has been interpreted are: magic as dream, gunpowder as magic in post-colonial productions, and 'magic as love, magic as theatre, and magic as illusion' (Vaughan, *The Tempest*), p. 211.

9 This evasion of the colonial reading of the play is common in productions of *The Tempest* when a woman plays the role of the protagonist. For a sensitive and provocative analysis of how this evasion can go awry, see Hartley, 'Prospera's Brave New World'.

10 Parts of my discussion here are taken from my published review: Katharine Goodland, '*The Tempest*', *Shakespeare Bulletin*, 21:2 (2003), p. 26.

11 This is the one point upon which Bruce Weber and I approached agreement, as he also commented upon the actors playing Caliban and Ferdinand, writing that they were 'strikingly brawny enough… to be emblems of sexuality', and that 'their bodies are being exploited here, which in a gender-bending production… is certainly part of Ms Mann's intention': see 'Full Fathom Five Thy Mother Lies', *New York Times* (24 February 2003), E3. In a feature article about the production, Mann and Brown confirmed their intent to 'emphasize the chemistry between Brown and her Caliban': see Eric Grode, 'Prospera's "Rough Magic"', *American Theatre* (July/August 2003), 51.

12 The use of the dream to account for the magic occurs with male Prosperos as well, especially those that focus on the play as an exploration of the relationship between the artist and his art.

13 See Igor Kopytoff, 'Women's Roles and Existential Identities', in Peggy Reeves Sanday and Ruth Gallagher Goodenough (eds), *Beyond the Second Sex: New Directions in the Anthropology of Gender* (Philadelphia: University of Pennsylvania Press, 1990), p. 77.

14 Robert L. Daniels, 'Review of *The Tempest*', *Daily Variety* (6 March 2003), 10.

15 *Daily Princetonian*, 'Review of *The Tempest*', 26 February 2003.

16 Peter Filchia, '*Tempest* tossed – McCarter's Mann bends genders to update Shakespeare for today', *The Newark Star-Ledger* (17 February 2003), 27.

17 I served as dramaturge on this production, which in this instance involved little more than writing the programme note. I was present in the room during many of the rehearsals, and so have a sense of how Dukakis and Simotes approached the role, but I was not included in the artistic choices. My discussion of this production draws exclusively on the critical reviews and scholarly articles I found in researching it, as well as my experience as an audience member for several performances.

18 Jeffrey Borak, 'Prospero becomes goddess', *The Berkshire Eagle* (27 July 2012), D1.
19 *Ibid.*
20 *Ibid.*
21 Virginia Mason Vaughan, '"Miranda, Where's Your Mother?": Female Prosperos and What They Tell Us', in Gordon McMullan, Lena Cowen Orlin and Virginia Mason Vaughan (eds), *Women Making Shakespeare, Text Reception and Performance* (London: Bloomsbury, 2014), p. 225.
22 *Ibid.*
23 *Ibid.*, p. 226.
24 Jeffrey Borak, '*The Tempest*: Change a vowel, the earth tips', *The Berkshire Eagle* (4 August 2012), D4.
25 *Ibid.*
26 Joan Mento, 'Shakespeare & Company, Lenox, Massachusetts, 2012–2013', *New England Theatre Journal*, 24 (2013), p. 162.
27 Jeffrey Borak, '*The Tempest*', D4.
28 Frank Rizzo, 'Dukakis memorable in *Tempest*', *The Hartford Courant* (31 July 2012), D1.
29 Chris Rohmann, 'King and Goddess: Shakespeare & Company reinterprets two pillars of the canon', *The Valley Advocate* (2 August 2012), Arts and Entertainment.
30 Ben Brantley, 'A Family and Mom's in charge', *The New York Times* (31 July 2012), C1.
31 *Ibid.*
32 Bob Goepfert, '*The Tempest* at Shakespeare & Company', *The Record* (30 July 2012), Entertainment.
33 Rizzo, 'Dukakis memorable in *Tempest*'.
34 Vaughan, 'Miranda, Where's Your Mother?', p. 227.
35 See Nicole Loraux, *Mothers in Mourning*, trans. Corrine Pache (Ithaca, NY and London: Cornell University Press, 1998), and Jeanne Addison Roberts, *The Shakespearean Wild: Geography, Genus, and Gender* (Lincoln: University of Nebraska Press 1992).
36 For an analysis of how the medium of film itself is magic, see Victoria Bladen, 'Screen Magic in Greenaway's *Prospero's Books* and Taymor's *The Tempest*', in Sarah Hatchuel and Nathalie Vienne-Guerrin (eds), *Shakespeare on Screen: The Tempest and Late Romances* (Cambridge: Cambridge University Press, 2017).
37 Samuel Crowl, 'Film review: Julie Taymor's *Tempest*', *Shakespeare Bulletin*, 29:2 (2011), p. 177.
38 Sebastian Lefait, 'Prospera's Looks: Adapting Shakespearean Reflexivity in *The Tempest* (Julie Taymor 2010)', *Literature Film Quarterly*, 43:2 (2015), p. 137.
39 Crowl, 'Film review', p. 177.
40 *Ibid.*, p. 178.
41 Lefait, 'Prospera's Looks', p. 137.
42 *Ibid.*, p. 142.
43 *Ibid.*, p. 133.
44 *Ibid.*, p. 138.
45 *Ibid.*, p. 137.

46　Crowl, 'Film Review', p. 181.
47　Royster, 'Introduction', p. 8.
48　*Ibid.*
49　Crowl, 'Film Review', pp. 178–9.
50　'Butoh' in Debra Krane and Judith Mackrell (eds), *The Oxford Dictionary of Dance* (Oxford: Oxford University Press, 2010).
51　M. Cody Poulton, 'Butoh', in Dennis Kennedy (ed.), *The Oxford Companion to Theatre and Performance* (Oxford: Oxford University Press, 2010).
52　Courtney Lehmann, '"Turn off the dark": A Tale of Two Shakespeares in Julie Taymor's *Tempest*', *Shakespeare Bulletin*, 32:1 (2014), p. 55.
53　*Ibid.*, p. 56.
54　Royster, 'Introduction', p. 8.
55　For provocative explorations of the ways in which white women and black men have been differently oppressed, see Hartley, 'Prospera's Brave New World'. See also Hilton Als, *White Girls* (San Francisco: McSweeney's, 2013).
56　Lehmann, 'Turn off the dark', p. 60.
57　*Ibid.*
58　*Ibid.*, p. 62.
59　*Ibid.*, p. 59.
60　Andrew O'Hehir, 'Helen Mirren's sadly elegant mom-magician', Salon.com, 10 December 2010.
61　David Denby, 'Roundup', *The New Yorker* (20 December 2010), 144.
62　Maria Garcia, '*The Tempest*', *Cineaste* (Winter 2010), p. 50.
63　*Ibid.*, p. 51.
64　*Ibid.*
65　*Ibid.*
66　*Ibid.*
67　See Bladen, 'Screen Magic', pp. 218–9, for an analysis of the film's Renaissance iconography in relation to Mirren's Prospera.
68　Royster, 'Introduction', p. 6.
69　Crowl, 'Film review', p. 181.
70　On implicit bias, see Mahzarin R. Banaji and Anthony Greenwald, *Blindspot: Hidden Biases of Good People* (New York: Delacorte Press, 2013).
71　Crowl notices the parallel but does not analyse it: 'Film review', p. 178.
72　See Judith Buchanan, 'Not Sycorax', in Gordon McMullan, Lena Cowen Orlin and Virginia Mason Vaughan (eds), *Women Making Shakespeare, Text Reception and Performance* (London: Bloomsbury, 2014), for an argument that the conflation of Prospera and Sycorax, as in Julie Taymor's film, 'cannot but forfeit some of the darkly stimulating, and specifically gender-dynamic animus of the play's inner life' (p. 222).
73　Courtney Lehmann reads this moment differently. She sees it as Prospero's 'attempt to differentiate "white magic" from "black magic" or, for that matter, male from female sorcery', in 'Turn off the dark', p. 59. I find this reading difficult to support since Prospero speaks Medea's words as if they are his own. See Buchanan, 'Not Sycorax'.

74 Willem de Blécourt, 'The Making of a Female Witch', *Gender and History*, 12:2 (2000); Elspeth Whitney, 'The Witch "She"/The Historian "He": Gender and the Historiography of the European Witch-Hunts', *Journal of Women's History*, 7:3 (1995).
75 See Brian P. Levack, *The Witch-Hunt in Early Modern Europe* (Harlow: Pearson, 3rd edn, 2006); James Sharpe, *Witchcraft in Early Modern England* (Harlow: Longman, 2001); Victoria Bladen, 'Shaping Supernatural Identity in *The Witch of Edmonton* (1621)', in Marcus Harmes and Victoria Bladen (eds), *Supernatural and Secular Power in Early Modern England* (Farnham: Ashgate, 2015).
76 For an in-depth examination of this issue with reference to Julie Taymor's career, see Ralph Turner, 'Taymor's tempests: sea change, or seeing little change in responses to gender and leadership?', *Journal of Gender Studies*, 24:6 (2015).

Bibliography

Als, Hilton, *White Girls* (San Francisco: McSweeney's, 2013).
Banaji, Mahzarin R., and Anthony Greenwald, *Blindspot: Hidden Biases of Good People* (New York: Delacorte Press, 2013).
Bladen, Victoria, 'Screen Magic in Greenaway's *Prospero's Books* and Taymor's *The Tempest*', in Sarah Hatchuel and Nathalie Vienne-Guerrin (eds), *Shakespeare on Screen: The Tempest and Late Romances* (Cambridge: Cambridge University Press, 2017).
—— 'Shaping Supernatural Identity in *The Witch of Edmonton* (1621)', in Marcus Harmes and Victoria Bladen (eds), *Supernatural and Secular Power in Early Modern England* (Farnham: Ashgate, 2015).
de Blécourt, Willem, 'The Making of a Female Witch', *Gender and History*, 12:2 (2000), 287–309.
Borak, Jeffrey, '*The Tempest*: Change a vowel, the earth tips', *The Berkshire Eagle* (4 August 2012), D4.
—— 'Prospero becomes Goddess', *The Berkshire Eagle* (27 July 2012), D1.
Brantley, Ben, 'A Family and Mom's in charge', *The New York Times* (31 July 2012), C1.
Buchanan, Judith, 'Not Sycorax', in Gordon McMullan, Lena Cowen Orlin and Virginia Mason Vaughan (eds), *Women Making Shakespeare, Text Reception and Performance* (London: Bloomsbury, 2014).
Butler, Judith, *Bodies That Matter* (London and New York: Routledge, 1993, 2011).
Cartelli, Thomas, *Repositioning Shakespeare: National formations, postcolonial appropriations* (London and New York: Routledge, 1999).
Crowl, Samuel, 'Film review: Julie Taymor's *Tempest*', *Shakespeare Bulletin*, 29:2 (2011), 177–81.
Daily Princetonian, The, Review of *The Tempest*, 26 February 2003.
Daniels, Robert L., 'Review of *The Tempest*', *Daily Variety* (6 March 2003), 10.
Denby, David, 'Roundup', *The New Yorker* (20 December 2010), 144.
Filchia, Peter, '*Tempest* tossed – McCarter's Mann bends genders to update Shakespeare for today', *The Newark Star-Ledger* (17 February 2003), 27.
Garcia, Maria, '*The Tempest*', *Cineaste* (Winter 2010), 50–2.
Gilbert, Helen, and Joanne Tompkins (eds), *Post-colonial Drama: theory, practice, politics* (London and New York: Routledge, 1996).
Goepfert, Bob, '*The Tempest* at Shakespeare & Company', *The Record* (30 July 2012).
Goodland, Katharine, '*The Tempest*', *Shakespeare Bulletin*, 21:2 (2003), 26.
Graff, Gerald, and James Phelan (eds), *William Shakespeare, The Tempest: a case study in critical controversy* (Boston, MA, and New York: Bedford/St Martins, 2nd edn, 2009).
Grode, Eric, 'Prospera's "Rough Magic"', *American Theatre* (July/August 2003), 51.
Hartley, Andrew James, 'Prospera's Brave New World: Cross-Cast Oppression and the Four-Fold Player in the Georgia Shakespeare Festival's *Tempest*', in *Shakespeare Re-Dressed: Cross-Gender Casting in Contemporary Performance* (Madison, NJ: Fairleigh Dickinson Press, 2008).

Klett, Elizabeth, 'Gender in Exile: Vanessa Redgrave's Prospero in The Tempest (2000)', in *Cross-Gender Shakespeare and English National Identity: Wearing the Codpiece* (Basingstoke: Palgrave, 2009), pp. 87–114.

Kopytoff, Igor, 'Women's Roles and Existential Identities', in Peggy Reeves Sanday and Ruth Gallagher Goodenough (eds), *Beyond the Second Sex: New Directions in the Anthropology of Gender* (Philadelphia: University of Pennsylvania Press, 1990).

Krane, Debra, and Judith Mackrell (eds), *The Oxford Dictionary of Dance* (Oxford: Oxford University Press, 2010).

Lefait, Sebastian, 'Prospera's Looks: Adapting Shakespearean Reflexivity in *The Tempest* (Julie Taymor 2010)', *Literature Film Quarterly*, 43:2 (2015), 131–45.

Lehmann, Courtney, '"Turn off the dark": A Tale of Two Shakespeares in Julie Taymor's *Tempest*', *Shakespeare Bulletin*, 32:1 (2014), 45–64.

Levack, Brian P., *The Witch-Hunt in Early Modern Europe* (Harlow: Pearson, 3rd edn, 2006).

Loraux, Nicole, *Mothers in Mourning*, trans. Corrine Pache (Ithaca, NY and London: Cornell University Press, 1998).

Mento, Joan, 'Shakespeare & Company, Lenox, Massachusetts, 2012–2013', *New England Theatre Journal*, 24 (2013), 161–4.

Nash, Margo, 'When a Man Becomes a Woman', *The New York Times* (16 February 2003).

O'Hehir, Andrew, 'Helen Mirren's sadly elegant Mom-magician', Salon.com, 10 December 2010.

Orgel, Stephen, 'Review of Shakespeare Santa Cruz's *The Tempest*', *Theatre Journal*, 48:1 (1996), 91–3.

Pao, Angela, *No Safe Spaces: Recasting race, ethnicity, and nationality in American Theater* (Ann Arbor: University of Michigan Press, 2010).

Poulton, M. Cody, 'butoh', in Dennis Kennedy (ed.), *The Oxford Companion to Theatre and Performance* (Oxford: Oxford University Press, 2010).

Quart, Leonard, 'Letter from New York', *The Berkshire Eagle* (14 September 2012), A7.

Rizzo, Frank, 'Dukakis memorable in *Tempest*', *The Hartford Courant* (31 July 2012), D1.

Roberts, Jeanne Addison, *The Shakespearean Wild: Geography, Genus, and Gender* (Lincoln: University of Nebraska Press 1992).

Rohmann, Chris, 'King and Goddess: Shakespeare & Company reinterprets two pillars of the canon', *The Valley Advocate* (2 August 2012), Arts and Entertainment.

Royster, Francesca T., 'Introduction to "Shakespeare's Female Icons": Sorcerers, Celebrities, Aliens, and Upstarts', *Upstart Crow: Special Edition*, 31 (2012), 5–13.

Sharpe, James, *Witchcraft in Early Modern England* (Harlow: Longman, 2001).

Solomon, Alisa, *Re-dressing the Canon: Essays on theater and gender* (London and New York: Routledge, 1997).

Turner, Ralph, 'Taymor's tempests: sea change, or seeing little change in responses to gender and leadership?', *Journal of Gender Studies*, 24:6 (2015), 689–704.

Vaughan, Virginia Mason, *Shakespeare in Performance: The Tempest* (Manchester: Manchester University Press, 2011).

—— '"Miranda, Where's Your Mother?": Female Prosperos and What They Tell Us', in Gordon McMullan, Lena Cowen Orlin and Virginia Mason Vaughan (eds), *Women Making Shakespeare, Text Reception and Performance* (London: Bloomsbury, 2014).

Weber, Bruce, 'Full Fathom Five Thy Mother Lies', *New York Times* (24 February 2003), E3.

Weimann, Robert, 'Playing with a Difference: Revisiting "Pen" and "Voice" in Shakespeare's Theatre', *Shakespeare Quarterly*, 50:4 (1999), 415–32.

Whitney, Elspeth, 'The Witch "She"/The Historian "He": Gender and the Historiography of the European Witch-Hunts', *Journal of Women's History*, 7.3 (1995), 77–102.

Part V

Contemporary transformations

11

'I'll put a girdle round the earth in forty minutes': representing the supernatural in film adaptations of *A Midsummer Night's Dream*

Gayle Allan

A Midsummer Night's Dream is one of the most often-performed Shakespeare plays, and one of his most popular comedies.[1] It is also a favourite of film directors, with a number of adaptations made since its first known appearance on the silver screen in 1909.[2] The play's popularity is due in no small part to the supernatural elements in the play, and more particularly the supernatural beings that populate it – the fairies.

In any adaptation of a play that features the supernatural, there are decisions to be made about the performance of these elements. All performances, whether on stage or on screen, rely on costuming, set design, lighting, music, sound and special effects to contribute to the realisation of the supernatural. While it is true that some stage productions of the play remain abstract or symbolic in their representation of the supernatural, generally the impulse to literally realise some aspects of the supernatural has been consistently strong in the stage and performance history of the *Dream*.

While fairy flight appears in a number of stage productions, and numerous film adaptations, the play text does not require it. As Martin White observes, the play itself (with its original stage directions) '[m]akes few technical demands'.[3] In the play, the word 'fly' or 'flying' is used seven times, mostly in reference to the lovers or Bottom, to describe the leaving of a place or person. The word 'flight' is only mentioned four times, also mostly referring to the lovers or Bottom.[4]

What is more pertinent is the requirement and expectation of great speed from the fairies. The word 'swift' is used often in terms of the fairies' comings and goings. Early in Act 2, the fairy tells Puck they have wandered 'swifter than the moon's sphere' (2.1.7). Oberon asks Puck to go 'swifter than the wind' (3.2.94) to find Helena, and Puck responds he will go '[s]wifter than arrow from the Tartar's bow' (3.2.101). However, the key moment in the play, which sets the expectation for fairy flight, comes when Oberon instructs Puck to return quickly from his journey to retrieve the flower. In response to this, Puck promises to 'put a girdle round about the earth/In forty minutes' (2.1.175–76). Flying, or some other kind of supernatural propulsion, would be required in order to achieve this feat in such a short amount of time, unless Puck is using hyperbole, as he is wont to do.

Added to this are questions around the fairies' corporeality. Even though the fairies are performed by human actors (and the play is very clear about the fairies' sexual relationships with mortals, suggesting that they are human in size and function),[5] the fairies are not always seen by the lovers, the mechanicals or members of the Athenian court.[6] Their speed, invisibility and ability to be both human-like and supernatural presents numerous challenges (and possibilities) in realising the fairies' materiality in performance.

From the beginning, performances often used the latest technology available at the time to show some of the supernatural aspects of the play – whether it was hidden trapdoors, wires, fireworks, ropes or harnesses.[7] Jay Halio describes how, in the earliest performances of the *Dream* in the late sixteenth or early seventeenth centuries, Puck would most likely have made his entrances spectacularly through a trapdoor in the stage.[8] Performances following the Restoration saw the introduction of dancing and music; a semi-opera was composed, and by the early nineteenth century, pageant and spectacle were the order of the day. These performances cut a lot of the text out of the play as it was felt too difficult or cumbersome to perform.[9] Towards the end of the nineteenth century, the play was being performed once again in its entirety but now had acquired Mendelssohn's and Purcell's music, and the inherited custom of dancing and singing fairies in gauzy tutus.[10]

Nineteenth-century reviewer Henry Morley touched on the perceived difficulty of the play's performance in his 1853 review of *A Midsummer Night's Dream*, which he described as:

> ... the most essentially *unactable* [my emphasis] of all his plays. It is a dramatic poem of the utmost grace and delicacy; its characters are creatures of the poet's fancy, that no flesh and blood can properly present.[11]

Film adaptation seems to offer something Morley could barely imagine – a means of representing 'creatures of the poet's fancy' with the requisite 'grace and delicacy'. From the outset, cinema promised to be the perfect medium for this rendering of the supernatural. Murray Leeder argues that, in the late 1890s, 'trick' filmmakers, such as George Méliès and George Albert Smith were keen to 'show off the capacity of the medium for wonderful appearances and disappearances, animations and transformations'.[12] As Peter Mollen argues, '[t]he cinema, after all, is an art of ghosts, projections of light and shadow, which seem while we watch them to have the substance of real beings'.[13]

Any adaptation of the play invokes the referent Shakespeare text and all the intertextuality around its history of performance.[14] A film adaptation adds numerous layers to this, as cinema is inherently intertextual.[15] Along with the original source text, there is the potential for references and homage to previous adaptations and films through editing, shooting styles, shot construction, special effects, backgrounds and *mise-en-scène*. Even the actors bring an intertextuality to the work.[16] Film is constantly self-referential; as Cook and Bernink claim, 'no film is a self-contained organic whole, but many films'.[17] Not surprisingly, the intertextuality of film adaptations of the *Dream* not only refers to previous adaptations of the play itself, but also to other notable films of the era or genre. While screen adaptation in one sense 'frees' the fairies from the fixed materiality of the stage, they are in another sense charged and weighed down with layers of meaning from various other intertexts.

In this respect, cinema plays a defining role, changing the audience's experience of time and motion. While stage's ephemeral nature is often seen as a limitation for those who enjoy 'playback', its transience is actually more in keeping with the material instability of the fairies and the supernatural. Yet stage performances are limited by the bodies on the stage who perform in real time and can only do so within the confines of what is humanly possible. Even though cinema appears to represent reality, time is not contiguous when making the film. This gives film the ability to create special effects with editing, which in turn offers exciting potential for representing the supernatural in Shakespeare's plays. André Bazin originally thought that, because photography was a vestige of a past spectacle, one would expect 'animated photography', or film, to also be a remnant of past motion.[18] However, Christian Metz argues that motion or movement is always perceived as being in the present.[19] Rick Altman takes this further by arguing that the cinema event (not only the film itself, but all the texts, institutions, agents, business, etc. which relate to a film) is not just always in the present, but is 'a continuing interchange, neither beginning or ending at any specific point'.[20] Does cinema, as Morley demands, offer a means of translating Shakespeare's creatures of fancy in ways the stage cannot? In this chapter I consider this question through a survey of some notable film adaptations of *A Midsummer Night's Dream* from the early twentieth to the early twenty-first century. The list of films is not exhaustive but it illustrates a number of approaches to representing fairy flight and Puck's girdling of the earth as the supreme expression of the fairies as supernatural beings.

Early days: 1909–35

The first known film of the *Dream* was directed by Stuart Blackton and Charles Kent and released in 1909 by American film producer Vitagraph (followed by two other film adaptations in 1913).[21] The film was mostly shot outdoors on location in a wood, where things unfold gently and playfully. One of the most interesting interventions in the play has nothing to do with film effects, but a change in the gender of the characters. Oberon is replaced by Penelope, and she and Titania are reunited at the end of the film. While it has been argued that this was for the practical reason of the studio having two female stars, changing Oberon from a man to a woman impacts the story and Judith Buchanan argues that the producers would have been aware of this.[22]

Blackton and Kent's *Dream* enthusiastically embraced the new technology of cinema and, as Buchanan comments, 'the film proudly vaunts its capacity to create illusions of a sort beyond theatre'.[23] The film made significant innovations in the way the play could be presented, and clearly establishes film adaptation as different from theatre.[24] Double exposure and stop action were used to achieve Puck's girdling of the earth, although the wires of the older stage adaptations are still visible. The dangling figure of Puck (with arms outstretched) is superimposed over a rapidly moving, revolving landscape which appears to be a globe of the world. Stop action enables Puck to suddenly disappear then reappear from her flight (Puck was played by female actor, Gladys Hulette).

In principle, Puck's and Penelope's ability to appear from and disappear into thin air should have had the effect of showing them to be the 'airy spirits' of the play text, but in practice, the effects were not yet developed enough to be in any way smooth or appear 'natural'. A quarter of a century later, the film industry had developed exponentially – not only in technical advances (with the advent of synchronised sound on film), but also as an art form, with new camera techniques, special effects and devices made specifically for film.

In 1935, German director Max Reinhardt released *A Midsummer Night's Dream*. While sometimes employing an expressionist aesthetic to his film, Reinhardt unexpectedly revisited gauzy tutus and dancing fairies from the nineteenth-century spectacle tradition, even including Mendelssohn's music in his film. Titania gracefully and delicately sings most of her lines, Oberon is menacing and Puck is frenzied. This approach differs greatly from Blackton and Kent's adaptation and the technical differences between the films are also marked. Reinhardt makes much more judicious use of stop motion in his film, and rarely includes fairies simply appearing or disappearing. Titania's entrances and exits are always made gracefully, rather than abruptly, while Puck's girdling of the earth is shown as a fast 'motion spiral' up into the heavens, with Puck on board a tree branch (which looks like a broomstick). It is the older traditions of acting style and sets/props, rather than the special effects employed in Reinhardt's film, which create the most interesting mediations with the fairies. The frenzied and hysterical actions and dialogue of Mickey Rooney's Puck vacillate between playful and delinquent, although the fast motion used in the film mirrors and amplifies this. He is unsettling and uncomfortable to watch. Rooney was only 14 years old at the time the film was shot and his performance shows that 'child' fairies were not necessarily benign nor sentimentally sweet. Oberon is also unlikeable and lacks any sense of grace and delicacy. Rather than flying, tripping or dancing, Oberon's main means of transport did not require stop motion, fast motion or double exposure but something far more prosaic. For most of Reinhardt's film, Oberon sits menacingly on a large, black horse – a very masculine, militaristic form of speed and strength.[25]

In these early film adaptations of the *Dream*, the exciting possibilities of film editing and effects to overcome the limits of the stage and regain some of the poetry of text in performance appear to fall short. While the film editing techniques of Blackton and Kent's film were quite clunky and jarring, fairy fight and their sudden appearances and disappearances nonetheless managed to add a playfulness to the film. Better, smoother editing techniques in Reinhardt's film added to the spectacle of the film in the tradition of nineteenth-century performances. Despite the superior technical qualities of Reinhardt's film, it is the director's *mise-en-scène* that accounts for the greater impact on the reading of the fairies in the play. The German director emphasised Oberon's masculine and authoritarian power, exemplified by the horse he sits on, and added strangeness with Puck's crazed and frightening unpredictability, achieved by Rooney's acting style and young age. The film effects, such as fast motion and stop action, only mirrored and amplified, rather than creating, Puck's frenzy. These effects are more the support act than the main feature.

Various adaptations of the *Dream* have drawn on Blackton and Kent's and Reinhardt's films as originators of the film language and tropes used to represent fairy flight and other aspects of the supernatural, especially stop action, fast motion and double exposure. While the aspirations of film to solve the 'problem' of fairy flight in *A Midsummer Night's Dream* were not fully realised in these early films, their contributions provided a base which further adaptations worked with and against.

The 1960s to the 1980s

It was a long time after Reinhardt's 1935 *Dream* before another notable film adaptation of *A Midsummer Night's Dream* made its way to the cinema.[26] In his *A History of Shakespeare on Screen*, Kenneth Rothwell only lists one *Dream* film adaptation between 1935 and 1964 – a puppet animation directed by Czechoslovakian Jiří Trnka in 1959, with voicing by Richard Burton amongst others.[27] In 1964, a television adaption was made by Joan Kemp-Welch, notable for its inclusion of comedian Benny Hill as Bottom; it featured Mendelssohn's music (as in Reinhardt's film) and also showed expressionist tendencies just below the surface.[28]

The next *Dream* film adaptation of note was Peter Hall's *A Midsummer Night's Dream* (1968), in which we see stop action, fast motion and 'double exposure' to represent fairy flight (by the 1960s the original technique of double exposure had evolved into blue screen/Chroma-key editing). Hall's *Dream* was produced two years before Peter Brook's famous 'White Box' production on the RSC stage,[29] and both Brook's and Hall's adaptations were responses to the controversial theories published by Polish theorist Jan Kott, which focused on the rampant sexuality and danger of the anarchic fairy world.[30]

Hall's film avoids elements of fantasy and grounds the supernatural firmly in the more earthly and earthy. Puck remains earth-bound, even when girdling the globe in forty minutes. The viewer gets the distinct impression that Puck is going to run, rather than fly. Like Reinhardt, Hall uses fast motion to indicate the fairy's speed. Added to this, Puck's quick departure is accompanied by a cartoonish 'whooshing' noise.[31] With alarming speed, Puck is back by Oberon's side (with another whooshing sound) using both fast motion and stop action. Like Rooney in Reinhardt's film, Puck (Ian Holm) delivers his lines at breath-taking speed, increasing the sense of chaos that he is so keen on creating and enjoying. In Puck's final soliloquy, where he jerkily appears at various points around the grounds, Hall exploits the jump cut (made popular a few years before by directors of the French New Wave), which makes his sudden appearance more obviously artificial and jarring.

Unlike Reinhardt, Hall made no attempt to smooth or normalise the stop-action editing techniques. Instead, he uses metacinematic techniques to draw attention to the film 'tricks' he used. Sarah Hatchuel argues that Hall used a 'strategy of alienation' in his film that is integrated into its amateurish filmmaking, drawing attention to the technological devices being used and the artificiality of the point of view.[32] By doing this, Hall subverts the notion that the fairies are different from the mortals. These efforts to show fairy flight as deliberately artificial clearly articulate the unsentimental way in which his film regards the fairies. Rather than trying to respond to Henry Morley's call to realise the creatures of Shakespeare's fantasy, and fulfil the promise film held for such a possibility, Hall used the cinema to dismantle the notion of this as being a desirable or legitimate goal.

Jonathan Miller's 1981 TV series for the BBC brought a new adaptation of *A Midsummer Night's Dream* to the screen, directed by Elijah Moshinsky. The series was made for television and, although they were presented as films, the plays generally followed stage conventions and used few or no special effects, focusing rather on the actors' performance. In places, Moshinsky's *Dream* is beautifully acted (Helen Mirren as Titania in particular), but the director did not use film editing effects to represent fairy flight or any other supernatural qualities of the fairies.

As in his production of *All's Well that End's Well* for the same series, Moshinsky introduced intertextuality into his *Dream* through montages of Dutch masters in his *mise-en-scène*.[33] Moshinsky also paid homage to Reinhardt's film, with Oberon seated on a large horse in order to travel through the woods. Moshinsky's film does not have the expressionist angst of Reinhardt's, however, and as a result his Oberon does not appear as menacing. Nevertheless, the horse gives a similar, hyper-masculine and authoritarian air to Oberon, and directly contrasts him with the ethereal, gentle and motherly Titania. Moshinsky's approach (in line with Miller's) retrieves the poetry of the play for the audience, focusing more on the language than exploiting film editing techniques.

The 1990s

Advances in computer-generated imagery (CGI) technology in the early 1990s meant that the filmmakers' repertoire could be further extended, freeing them from just film editing techniques such as stop action, fast motion, dissolves and double exposure/blue screen to more sophisticated and seamless integration of digitally produced images into the 'live action' of films. During this decade there were two stand-out film adaptations of *A Midsummer Night's Dream* that utilised CGI and other film editing techniques in different ways, and with very different effects.

Adrian Noble's *A Midsummer Night's Dream* (1996) used the everyday object of an umbrella to assist fairy flight. The umbrellas belong initially to the mechanicals but are swept into the air by the wind – one floats down again and, changed from black to green, falls into Puck's hand. Titania's pink umbrella is large and sumptuous (Mark Sinker describes it as 'vulva-pink')[34] and also operates as her bower when it is upturned. Noble used blue screen and careful shot constructions to create the effect of flight with ascending and descending umbrellas.

New CGI technology creates the most stunning effect in the film when the fairies and others arrive in the woods in bubbles.[35] This mode of transport is not fast, nor is it direct; rather, the fairies 'fly' by floating gently to earth in cradling bubbles. While Puck creates the first bubble from a raindrop on his umbrella, the boy narrator blows bubbles with his toy bubble pipe. Each one contains a fairy whose bubbles burst as they land on the stage/in the woods. In doing so, Noble's fairies appear indeed as the creations of the poet. The boy narrator, whom Mark Burnett describes as both 'narrative framer and dramaturge' of the film, functions as a framing device that Noble added for his film adaptation – it was not in the stage production the film is based on.[36] According to Burnett, the boy is often shown as literally 'pulling the ropes of the stage machinery'.[37]

Initially, the effect of this is that fairy flight in Noble's film is notable by its lack of speed, unlike in the earlier examples mentioned above. There is no rush and the film has a gentle and lyrical quality about it. This contrasts strongly with Puck's girdling the globe later in the film, however. Despite Noble's access to CGI, notably with the bubbles, Puck's journey to collect the flower uses traditional techniques similar to those found in Blackton and Kent. The film cuts to a shot of Puck with only his head and shoulders visible. He then raises his arms in flight, the camera pans up into the lightbulbs which feature in the *mise-en-scène* (the viewer does not see him leave the ground). This is followed by a cross-fade-out, then we are immediately given an extreme close-up of Puck's head with the wind blowing in his hair. Subtle wind sounds complete the effect.

This seemingly old-fashioned, rather unsophisticated approach to depicting fairy flight is quite surprising, especially coming so soon after the spectacular use of CGI bubbles. Noble's film is an adaptation which clearly signals its intertextuality and self-referential nature. As outlined above, the film is framed by a young boy and the film is his dream, both literally and literarily. Additionally, Noble references a number of motifs from children's literature and film. His use of the humble umbrella as a means of supernatural transport reminds us of Mary Poppins, who floated in and out of the Banks' family home in P. L. Travers story of 1934, as well as the 1964 film directed by Robert Stevenson.[38] Noble also includes allusions to Beatrix Potter's children stories, and to Lewis Carroll's Alice stories, to Steven Spielberg's *ET* (1982) and *Home Alone* (1990), directed by Chris Columbus. Bottom and Titania ride across the moon in silhouette, in much the same way as ET and Elliot do in Spielberg's film.

Noble's adaptation of the *Dream* is thus not only self-consciously referential to itself as a modern film of its time; it also links to a nostalgia for nineteenth-century children's literature. He draws on childhood memories and fondness of the 'everyday', of umbrellas and toy bubble pipes, to create the fairies and portray their insubstantial airiness.[39] While the fairies appear solidly adult and mortal in some parts of the film, in the parts where the child is the dramaturge, their materiality is much less certain.

The use of CGI for the fairy bubbles and blue screen techniques to effect the umbrella flight and motorcycle ride across the moon utilises twentieth-century tales and technologies to add to Noble's film what Samuel Crowl calls 'film dazzle'.[40] While Puck's 'girdle' is at odds with the dazzle in the film, it does fit in with the nostalgia and self-referential practice, reaching back to older techniques used by Blackton and Kent early in the twentieth-century. Fairy flight is presented inconsistently in the film, in keeping with the unstable narration of the film, which is sometimes controlled by the boy and sometimes not.[41] This inconsistency forces the audience to consider the subjectivity of the fairies' power, tying it very much to point of view, and destabilising the idea of the fairies' identity as fixed or definable. By combining new film techniques and older film effects, along with a great deal of deliberately self-referential intertextuality, Noble's representation of fairy flight complicates the film's 'reading' of the fairies and adds unresolved layers of meaning onto them. Mark Sinker argues that the addition of the boy was an attempt to please both an adult and a child audience, and Halio considers whether this lack of focus was the cause of the film's commercial failure.[42]

Spielberg's *ET* and the famous image of the bicycle as supernatural flight became a motif in further adaptations of the *Dream*. In Michael Hoffman's *A*

Midsummer Night's Dream (1998), Puck rides off on a bicycle so he can travel 'swifter than an arrow's bow'. In Ed Fraiman's *A Midsummer Night's Dream* (2005), the lovers chase each other around the woods on bikes. The Puck character (Timothy) in Tom Gustafson's *Were the World Mine* (2008) rides through the town on his bicycle (wearing costume wings) distributing his 'love juice' to unsuspecting townspeople.

Despite the play text's requirement for fairy speed, Michael Hoffman's *Dream* seems to be at pains to show Puck's slowness. Puck is not at all interested in the speed his boast of 'girdling the earth' implies. When Oberon tells him to fetch the flower, Hoffman's Puck seems to be quite content to remain lying on the ground with Oberon, observing the lovers, rather than take off on his strenuous journey. When gently encouraged by a few hand gestures from Oberon, who verbalises the 'whooshing' noise we hear in Hall's film, Puck rises to his feet and trots off with no great speed or urgency. Puck's general lack of speed, or desire for it, is further emphasised by his arrival in one scene on the back of a giant turtle, making painfully slow progress. The discovery of the bicycle in the same scene gives him the means by which the rest of his 'flying' is achieved in the film. Puck's flight is powered by mechanical, human technology, not by supernatural powers, nor by those of film editing and other special effects.

Hoffman sometimes does employ the trick of having the fairies appear when we do not expect them by using stop motion, but he does not embrace this technique with the excitement and enthusiasm of the early filmmakers, nor with the cynicism and self-consciousness of Hall. Any flying by fairies other than Puck is achieved when they become CGI pinpricks of light that swarm and fly away. Stop action is used in the critical moment when the fairies change shape, creating a sense of the fluid nature of their materiality.

The 2000s

As mentioned above, two *Dream*-inspired productions from the early 2000s, Ed Fraiman's *A Midsummer Night's Dream* (2005), from the BBC *Shakespeare Retold* series, and Tom Gustafson's musical *Were the World Mine* (2008), feature the bicycle motif in their stories. In Fraiman's film, the bicycles are solely used by the lovers (Hoffman's lovers also ride bicycles) but, as in Hoffman's film, Gustafson's Puck character (Timothy) uses a bicycle to deliver the love juice. Unlike *ET* and Noble's *Dream*, Timothy's bicycle does not leave the ground – so he does not 'fly'. Timothy is both Puck and lover, hoping to win the love of the football captain Jonathon, as well as challenge the heteronormative citizens of his town. In preparing to play Puck in the school play, Timothy becomes a disruptor, a bringer of chaos, and this all achieved on his bicycle, wearing fake wings his mother made for him. As improbable as this sounds, the musical film genre allows space for the fantastical elements of Gustafson's film to sit comfortably alongside the realistic setting of high school in an insular rural town. The film's musical genre expects non-naturalistic sequences and halted narrative in order to view the spectacle (usually of a song and dance sequence).[43] The musical genre is thus able to incorporate the fantastical nature of Puck's/ Timothy's powers, and it never needs to define whether Timothy's powers are supernatural or not.[44] While the *Dream*'s potential as a musical production was recognised early with Henry Purcell's masque (1692), and later in Benjamin Britten's opera (1960), these are very formal genres. Gustfason's use of the modern musical film genre to incorporate the fantastical nature of his story offers a thought-provoking meditation on how some genres, rather than film techniques or special effects, can better cope with the demands and challenges of the *Dream* that Morley was so concerned about.

In a recent adaptation of *A Midsummer Night's Dream* (2016), David Kerr utilises the science fantasy/fiction genre, to inform his representations of the fairies and their supernatural powers. While the film is not a science fiction/ fantasy, it harnesses some of the genre's tropes and pays homage to notable films.[45] Kerr's Athenian court is a totalitarian regime with a brutal and tyrannical Theseus, complete with stormtroopers and sets adorned with iconography that combines 1940's fascism and George Lucas's original *Star Wars* (1977) (also known as *Star Wars, Episode IV – A New Hope*).

In his film, Kerr pays homage to Hoffman, also expressing flying fairies as small points of light. However, Kerr's use of CGI incorporates newly developed techniques, bringing the idea of the fairies' materiality into even sharper focus. Kerr gives his fairies enormous speed and frightening energy in their flight. They fly around the woods as small sparks, at times appearing like fireflies. Puck, Titania and Oberon at different times all 'fly' by becoming small balls of flames, which shoot off at immense speed. But it is the means by which they take flight which differs from Hoffman's and other films' fairy flight discussed previously. Hoffman uses stop action to go from full-size fairy 'bodies' to pinpricks of light, but Kerr explicitly shows the dissolution of the fairy body into expressions of energy, fire and light. When Titania retreats from Oberon's wrath, she disintegrates from the feet upwards into a large pile of swirling leaves. When Puck takes off to girdle the earth, he leaps into the air, his body bursts into a ball of flame, which then zips off in a fizzing spark, with a voice-over of his sped-up, high-pitched voice. When Oberon and Titania fly back to Athens, their bodies turn into flames before whizzing off like meteors towards the city.

In each case, the fairies shed their mortal 'disguises' in order to realise their supernatural selves (the ones that can fly). Occasionally, some of these powers 'leak' out when they are in mortal form – Oberon exerts powerful 'death rays' from his hands, clearly referencing science-fiction film tropes (especially those of the light-sabre battles in the *Star Wars* films). Kerr's adaptation makes full use of CGI's capabilities to express the transience, perhaps duplicity, of the fairies' materiality, and also complicates their powers by representing them as perhaps not supernatural, but actually alien.

Throughout my discussion of some notable film adaptations of *A Midsummers Night's Dream*, I have measured some of the films against the views of nineteenth-century reviewer Henry Morley, who argued that the play was 'unactable' because it was impossible to capture the creatures of the poet's imagination. In 2014, acclaimed film director, Julie Taymor made a similar claim – she held that the *Dream* was 'unfilmable'.[46] So, rather than make a film adaptation, despite being known for her film direction, Taymor mounted a lavish and ambitious stage production of the *Dream* to great acclaim.[47]

Although not produced as a film adaptation (but rather a filmed record of her stage production), Taymor's *A Midsummer Night's Dream* mixes the conventions of both film and stage. Taymor's adaptation takes us full-circle from the early films of Blackton and Kent and Reinhardt, which combined existing and historical stage conventions with emerging film techniques, and the self-referential films of the 1990s and early 2000s, which celebrated and reproduced the film history of the *Dream*. Rather than stage and film, or film and film intertextuality, Taymor used film and CGI on stage to represent the fairies' supernatural natures and fairy flight, allowing film, a century later, to 'talk back' to a stage production of *A Midsummer Night's Dream*. The hybridity of Taymor's adaptation, a film of a stage production that uses film and film effects, offers a new dimension of possibility for the representation of fairy flight and supernatural powers.

Taymor used standard stage conventions for some fairy flight in her production – the fairies of Titania and Oberon's retinues are lifted by figures clothed in black (who also represent the forest.) However, as Puck addresses the fairies, their flight is shown as a series of filmed images of butterflies being projected onto moving sheets. Puck descends from a white cloth canopy onto which images of spreading ink or blood are projected. When Oberon describes the flower to Puck, a large purple flower is projected onto the background and when Puck promises to girdle the earth, he makes a 'whooshing' noise, does a high kick and the lights go down; a large circle (describing the girdle) is drawn on the backdrop using CGI and Puck runs towards it.

Taymor also references previous stage productions. Puck's trousers seem to be stretching as he/she heads toward the ground, but then a trapeze is revealed, an homage to Peter Brook's famous RSC 'White Box' stage production in 1970. Oberon's and Titania's flight towards Athens is achieved by mechanical technology as an open elevator lifts them off the ground towards the roof of the stage. The lift harks back to the mechanical lifts and pulleys often used on stage to lift and lower Titania's bower in earlier periods. Though much slicker and smoother than previous stage productions, Taymor also references the ropes and pulleys previously used for fairy flight.

Her production also created some of its own tricks. The billowing sheets, on which images were projected, also allowed Titania to 'disappear' (hide in the folds) and provided a canopy from which Oberon suddenly 'appeared' and descended. This created a sense of mysterious appearance and disappearance that stop action usually achieves in film adaptations, but with low-tech (and highly artistic) effects. Strategic use of low, often blue, lighting, and rippling cloud-like white sheets on the ground where the king and queen of the fairies walk (again, often with images projected on them), all conveyed an ethereal aura around Oberon and Titania, without the bodies being subjected to shimmering dissolves, stop motion jumps, or CGI disintegration and provides the 'grace and delicacy' and poetry that Henry Morley so longed for.

Conclusion

Has film lived up to its potential in resolving some of the issues that prompted Morley to declare the play 'unactable'? Techniques of double exposure, stop action and fast motion editing used by Blackton and Kent and Max Reinhardt in the early days of film, became *de rigueur* in later film adaptations of the *Dream* when depicting fairy flight. Blackton and Kent, as well as Reinhardt, demonstrated that editing techniques could imbue the fairies with a quickness and lightness in comparison to the mortal characters. Stop action editing demonstrated the different nature of the fairies' materiality, emphasising their 'airiness' and possibly even their impermanence. But although these techniques became smoother and more sophisticated as the years passed, Peter Hall's metacinema techniques in the 1960s undercut the notion that film could contain and express the supernatural nature of the fairies in a commodifiable way.

The *Dream* film canon grew, as did cinema history. By the 1990s, Adrian Noble's adaptation was weighed down and limited by the intertextual and self-reflexive tendency of his film, while Michael Hoffman's film reverted to a slow, non-flying Puck who harnessed human technology rather than the supernatural to propel himself. In the 2000s, both Tom Gustafson and David Kerr showed in their films that introducing conventions and styles from other genres could open spaces for meaningful interventions into well-known texts and provide a fresh way of approaching the *Dream*'s challenges. The musical film genre's allowance for spectacle enabled Gustafson to integrate the fantastical elements of his story, while the science fiction/fantasy genre enabled Kerr to interrogate the materiality of the fairies and their supernatural/alien powers.

In 2014, Julie Taymor's film of her stage production imagined a hybridity which took the best of what stage and film could offer. Taymor's lyrical depiction of fairy flight and materiality retains the poetry of the play that was mourned by Morley, but she also allowed film to write back to the stage. Or was stage writing back to film? In Taymor's film/stage production of the 'unactable' and 'unfilmable' play, *A Midsummer Night's Dream* found an expression that drew on the magic of both film and stage.

Notes

1. According to the Royal Shakespeare Company's website, www.rsc.org.uk/a-midsummer-nights-dream/past-productions, accessed 14 April 2019.
2. J. Stuart Blackton and Charles Kent produced a 12-minute version of *A Midsummer Night's Dream* for Vitagraph in 1909.
3. Martin White, *Shakespeare Handbooks: A Midsummer Night's Dream* (London: Palgrave Macmillan, 2009), p. 7.
4. All quotations from the play will be taken from the Norton 3rd edition.
5. White, *Shakespeare Handbooks*, p. 7.
6. White lists the props of Phillip Henslowe's Rose Theatre in 1598, which included 'a robe "for to go invisible"'. *Ibid.*, p. 7.
7. See Neil Forsyth, 'Shakespeare the Illusionist: Filming the Supernatural', in Russell Jackson (ed.), *The Cambridge Companion to Shakespeare Film* (Cambridge: Cambridge University Press, 2000), p. 274. According to Forsyth, Ben Jonson considered such tricks vulgar while other contemporaries condemned them as witchcraft.
8. See Jay Halio, 'The First Three Centuries', in Jay Halio, *Shakespeare in Performance: A Midsummer Night's Dream* (Manchester and New York: Manchester University Press, 2nd edn, 2003), Chapter 1, pp. 4–30, esp. p. 12.
9. See Halio, *Shakespeare in Performance*, pp. 15–26.
10. *Ibid.*, pp. 22–30.
11. Henry Morley quoted in Halio, *Shakespeare in Performance*, p. 26.
12. Murray Leeder, *The Modern Supernatural and the Beginnings of Cinema* (Calgary, Alberta: Palgrave Macmillan, 2017), p. 3.
13. Peter Mollen quoted in Leeder, *The Modern Supernatural*, p. 25.
14. Graham Allen, *Intertextuality* (Abingdon, New York: Routledge, 2nd edn, 2011), p. 104.
15. Susan Hayward, *Cinema Studies: Key Concepts* (London and New York: Routledge, 2nd edn, 2000) p. 201; Pam Cook and Mieke Bernink, *The Cinema Book* (London: BFI Publishing, 2nd edn, 1999) p. 289.
16. Hayward, *Cinema Studies*, p. 201; Robert Stam, 'Beyond Fidelity: The Dialogics of Adaptation', in James Narremore (ed.), *Film Adaptation* (New Brunswick, NJ: Rutgers University Press, 2000), p. 60. Stam refers to this as 'thespian intertext'.
17. Cook and Bernink, *The Cinema Book*, p. 289.
18. Christian Metz, *Film Language: A Semiotics of the Cinema* [1974], Michael Taylor (trans.) (Chicago: University of Chicago Press, 1991), p. 8.
19. *Ibid.*, p. 8.
20. Rick Altman in David Bordwell and Noël Caroll (eds), *Post Theory: Reconstructing Film Theory* (Madison: University of Wisconsin, 1996), p. 12.
21. Judith Buchanan, *Shakespeare on Silent Film: An Excellent Dumb Discourse* (Cambridge: Cambridge University Press, 2009), p. 131; Kenneth Rothwell, *A*

History of Shakespeare on Screen (Cambridge: Cambridge University Press, 2nd edn, 2004), p. 349.

22 For a more thorough discussion of this, see Judith Buchanan, 'Historically Juxtaposed Beans (I): *A Midsummer Night's Dream* on film' in *Shakespeare on Film* (London and New York: Routledge, 2005 reprint 2014), pp. 124–6. David Kerr's 2016 adaptation also features a same-sex relationship for Titania.
23 Buchanan, *Shakespeare on Film*, p. 124.
24 *Ibid.*, p. 14.
25 Elijah Moshinsky's 1981 adaptation of the *Dream* also used the motif of Oberon on a horse, effectively portraying his Oberon as authoritative and stern like Reinhardt's Oberon.
26 The BBC made a TV movie of *A Midsummer Night's Dream* in 1946, directed by I. Orr-Ewing: Daniel Rosenthal, *Shakespeare on Screen* (London: Hamlyn, 2000), p. 87.
27 Rothwell, *A History*, p. 349.
28 *Ibid.*, p. 104.
29 Peter Brook's 'White Box' production was performed in the Royal Shakespeare Theatre in Stratford-upon-Avon during the 1970 season, then moved to the Aldwych Theatre in London on 1971. It went on a world tour during 1972–3.
30 See Jan Kott, 'Titania and the Ass's Head', in *Shakespeare Our Contemporary* (New York: W. W. Norton 1974), pp. 213–36.
31 The cartoon trope of whooshing, as a recognisable sound to indicate when something is moving at great speed, is also used by Hoffman in his 1998 adaptation, albeit in a more self-conscious way.
32 Sarah Hatchuel, 'From Meta-fiction to Meta-cinema in Screen Versions of *A Midsummer Night's Dream*', in Sarah Hatchuel and Nathalie Vienne-Guerrin (eds), *Shakespeare on Screen: A Midsummer Night's Dream* (Rouen: Publications de l'Université de Rouen, 2004), p. 158.
33 See Rothwell, *A History*, p. 114–5.
34 Mark Sinker in Halio, *Shakespeare in Performance*, p. 149.
35 Glinda the good witch arrives in a bubble in *The Wizard of Oz* (1934), directed by Victor Fleming.
36 Mark Burnett, 'Impressions of Fantasy: Adrian Noble's *A Midsummer Night's Dream*' in M. T. Burnett and R. Wray (eds), *Shakespeare, Film, Fin de Siècle* (London: Palgrave Macmillan, 2000), pp. 89–101, p. 91.
37 *Ibid.*, p. 98.
38 Rob Marshall's *Mary Poppins Returns* (2019) retains the umbrella.
39 Burnett, 'Impressions of Fantasy', p. 91.
40 Samuel Crowl in Halio, *Shakespeare in Performance*, p. 150.
41 See Burnett, 'Impressions of Fantasy', pp. 90–92 for a fuller discussion of the boy's role as director and narrator in Noble's film.
42 Sinker in Halio, *Shakespeare in Performance*, p. 149.
43 See David Bordwell and Kristen Thompson, *Film Art: An Introduction* (New York: McGraw Hill, 6th edn, 2001), pp. 105–8.

44 See Matt Kozusko, 'Shakesqueer, the Movie: *Were the World Mine* and *A Midsummer Night's Dream*', *Shakespeare Survey*, 65 (2012), 168–80. Kozusko argues that the comfortable nature of the musical genre effectively defuses the queer reading of the text, and of Timothy/Puck, and makes the film safer for a general cinema audience.
45 This is not surprising as the adaptation was co-written with Russell T. Davies, writer of the *Dr Who* TV series (from 2005–10).
46 See Geoffrey O'Brien, 'Shakespeare's Unfilmable Dream', *The New York Review of Books*, 25 June 2015, www.nybooks.com/daily/2015/06/25/shakespeare-taymor-unfilmable-dream/, accessed 14 April 2019.
47 Taymor's *A Midsummer Night's Dream* played in The Polonsky Shakespeare Centre, Fort Greene, Brooklyn in 2013.

Bibliography

Allen, Graham, *Intertextuality* (Abingdon and New York: Routledge, 2nd edn, 2011).

Altman, Rick in David Bordwell and Noël Caroll (eds), *Post Theory: Reconstructing Film Theory* (Madison: University of Wisconsin, 1996).

Berthomieu, Pierre, 'Shakespeare Should have Emigrated to Hollywood', in Sarah Hatchuel and Nathalie Vienne-Guerrin (eds), *Shakespeare on Screen: A Midsummer Night's Dream* (Rouen: Publications de l'Université de Rouen, 2004).

Bordwell, David and Kristen Thompson, *Film Art: An Introduction* (New York: McGraw Hill, 6th edn, 2001).

Buchanan, Judith, *Shakespeare on Film* (Oxford: Routledge, 2005 reprint 2014).

—— *Shakespeare on Silent Film: An Excellent Dumb Discourse* (Cambridge: Cambridge University Press, 2009).

Burnett, Mark, 'Impressions of Fantasy: Adrian Noble's *A Midsummer Night's Dream*' in M. T. Burnett and R. Wray (eds), *Shakespeare, Film, Fin de Siècle* (London: Palgrave Macmillan, 2000), pp. 89–101.

Cook, Pam, and Mieke Bernink, *The Cinema Book* (London: BFI Publishing, 2nd edn, 1999).

Crowl, Samuel, *Shakespeare at The Cineplex: The Kenneth Branagh Era* (Athens: Ohio University Press, 2003).

Forsyth, Neil, 'Shakespeare the Illusionist: Filming the Supernatural', in Russell Jackson (ed.), *The Cambridge Companion to Shakespeare Film* (Cambridge: Cambridge University Press, 2000).

Halio, Jay L., *Shakespeare in Performance: A Midsummer Night's Dream* (Manchester: Manchester University Press, 2nd edn, 2003).

Hatchuel, Sarah, 'From Meta-fiction to Meta-cinema in Screen Versions of *A Midsummer Night's Dream*', in Sarah Hatchuel and Nathalie Vienne-Guerrin (eds), *Shakespeare on Screen: A Midsummer Night's Dream* (Rouen: Publications de l'Université de Rouen, 2004).

—— and Nathalie Vienne-Guerrin (eds), *Shakespeare on Screen: A Midsummer Night's Dream* (Rouen: Publications de l'Université de Rouen, 2004).

Hayward, Susan, *Cinema Studies: Key Concepts* (London and New York: Routledge, 2nd edn, 2000).

Jackson, Russell, 'Introduction', in Russell Jackson (ed.), *The Cambridge Companion to Shakespeare Film* (Cambridge: Cambridge University Press, 2000).

Kliman, Bernice W., 'Video Clips as Clues to a Whole Film and Companion to the Playtext', in Sarah Hatchuel and Nathalie Vienne-Guerrin (eds), *Shakespeare on Screen: A Midsummer Night's Dream* (Rouen: Publications de l'Université de Rouen, 2004).

Kott, Jan, 'Titania and the Ass's Head', in *Shakespeare Our Contemporary* (New York: W. W. Norton 1974).

Kozusko, Matt, 'Shakesqueer, the Movie: *Were the World Mine* and *A Midsummer Night's Dream*' *Shakespeare Survey*, 65 (2012), 168–80.

Leeder, Murray, *The Modern Supernatural and the Beginnings of Cinema* (Calgary, Alberta: Palgrave Macmillan, 2017).

Metz, Christian, *Film Language: A Semiotics of the Cinema* [1971, English edn 1974], trans. Michael Taylor (Chicago: University of Chicago Press, 1991).

O'Brien, Geoffrey, 'Shakespeare's Unfilmable Dream', *The New York Review of Books*, www.nybooks.com/daily/2015/06/25/shakespeare-taymor-unfilmable-dream/, accessed 14 April 2019.

Rosenthal, Daniel, *Shakespeare on Screen* (London: Hamlyn, 2000).

Rothwell, Kenneth, *A History of Shakespeare on Screen* (Cambridge: Cambridge University Press, 2nd edn, 2004).

Shakespeare, William, *The Norton Shakespeare*, eds Stephen Greenblatt, Walter Cohen, Suzanne Gossett, Jean E. Howard, Katherine Eisaman Maus and Gordon McMullan (New York: Norton, 3rd edn, 2016).

Stam, Robert, 'Beyond Fidelity: The Dialogics of Adaptation' in James Narremore (ed.), *Film Adaptation* (New Brunswick, NJ: Rutgers University Press, 2000).

White, Martin, *Shakespeare Handbooks: A Midsummer Night's Dream* (London: Palgrave Macmillan, 2009).

12

Ophelia and her magical daughters: the afterlives of Ophelia in Japanese pop culture

Yukari Yoshihara

In *Hamlet*, Ophelia has nothing to do with the supernatural. She is not a witch, fairy or deity; nor does she return to life as a zombie or a ghost for revenge, in spite of the mistreatment and injustice she suffered in life. But in her afterlives in Japanese popular culture Ophelia has metamorphosed into a supernatural woman in various forms, such as a powerful sea goddess, a guardian of the tree of life and a grim reaper. This chapter explores these various afterlives, and contextualises Ophelia's metamorphosis from an innocent victim, gendered as a passive woman, into a vehemently powerful, active, supernatural presence.

In the play, Polonius calls Ophelia 'a green girl/Unsifted in such perilous circumstance' (1.3.101–2). In her afterlives, as Stephen O'Neill observes, Ophelia has been variously represented as 'an ideal of femininity and beauty, the teenage girl-in-crisis, regulated female sexuality, and the spectacularization of female death'.[1] As Elaine Showalter outlines, in her groundbreaking essay 'Representing Ophelia', Ophelia and her afterlives 'bring to the foreground the issues in an ongoing theoretical debate about the cultural links between femininity, female sexuality, insanity, and representation'.[2] More recently, Kaara L. Peterson and Deanne Williams convincingly argue that representations of Ophelia reflect 'each era or culture's characteristic constructions of women's roles, madness, and essentialized notions of femininity'.[3] Supernaturally powerful Ophelias in Japan constitute a part of 'the dynamic, ongoing process of regeneration and reinvention' found in 'Ophelia's ever-flourishing afterlife'.[4]

In this chapter, I will first focus on Soseki Natsume's reworking of Ophelia in *Kusamakura* (1906), in which the protagonist, a painter, encounters O-Nami, a mysterious, strong-willed, rebellious woman rumoured to be subject to a supernatural curse.[5] She is curiously compared to Ophelia. Natsume's construction of this Ophelia figure is partially complicit with, yet also a challenge to, fetishised female victimhood. I then outline various Ophelia characters in twenty-first-century Japanese popular culture in which she appears in various roles that are all quite different from what one usually associates with Ophelia. I also consider certain Japanese legends and horror tales that link Ophelia with revengeful female ghosts and monsters, an image incongruous with Shakespeare's original character. I argue that these post-modern supernatural Ophelias are critical interventions in the conceptualisation of the character as an embodiment of 'natural' femininity.

Hamlet as a ghost story

Hamlet was adapted as a ghost story in late nineteenth-century and early twentieth-century Japan. The earliest kabuki-style adaptation of *Hamlet* by Robun Kanagaki (1886) is set in a feudal Japanese castle haunted by the ghost of King Hamlet in samurai armour;[6] an adaptation of *Hamlet* by Tsutomu Inoue (1888) is entitled *Dialogues with a Ghost*, and the novel *Tempest in Tohima clan* (1891), by Ouchi Sakurachi, has a female ghost, combining Gertrude and Ophelia, who urges the Hamlet figure for revenge. These fictional adaptations resonated with the critical reception of the play by Japanese academics, particularly by Soseki Natsume.

After studying British literature in London in 1900–2, Soseki Natsume (1867–1916) became the first Japanese professor of British literature at Tokyo Imperial University in 1903 and subsequently a famed novelist. In the eyes of Natsume, *Hamlet* is a gothic ghost story. He devotes a large section of his *Theory of Literature* (1907) – one of the earliest Japanese books on British literature – to the supernatural.[7] He analyses the ghosts in *Hamlet*, *Macbeth* and *Richard III*, as well as Alice's ghost in Walter Scott's *The Bride of Lammermoor* (1819), the phantoms in Horace Walpole's *The Castle of Otranto* (1764) and the ghosts in Ann Radcliffe's *The Mysteries of Udolpho* (1794) as exemplary tales of the supernatural. Strikingly, Natsume placed Shakespeare's works in the same category as gothic novels at a time when, as Anna-Marie Farrier notes, comparatively little critical attention was paid to gothic fiction.[8] Natsume's early work, pointing to the links between aspects of the supernatural in Shakespeare's work and in gothic novels, accords with the work of later critics such as Christy Desmet and Anne Williams, who have recognised Shakespeare's work as proto-Gothic.[9] In his *Theory of Literature*, Natsume argued that supernatural, mystic and occult elements in literature should be approached from 'the perspective of the discipline of psychology and sociology'.[10]

As Alexa Huang argues in analysing Natsume's *Kusamakura*, 'Ophelia is... central to the anxiety of modernity' in Japan.[11] More broadly, Huang places Asian attitudes to Ophelia in the context of Asia's 'deeply conflicted love–hate relationships with Western modernity'. In his theoretical and fictional works,

Natsume engaged with the dichotomies between the West and Japan – to his mind, the West represented science, modernity and rationality while Japan represented superstition, feudalism and a lack of enlightenment, at a time when the Japanese state's official policy was to 'enlighten' Japan by westernising it. Natsume and his contemporaries were thus divided between their desire for 'civilising' themselves through Western scientific knowledge and maintaining the legacy of their domestic culture, which drew heavily from supernatural concerns. He therefore took a keen interest in narratives involving the supernatural in Western literature.

Natsume was cognisant of the Victorian fascination with Ophelia, who is described by Bram Dijkstra as 'the later nineteenth-century's all-time favourite example of love-crazed self-sacrificial madness'.[12] In his novel, *Kusamakura*, Natsume combined the Victorian image of Ophelia with Japanese legends of female ghosts who drowned themselves for love. The unnamed protagonist, an artist, retreats to a spa resort in the mountains, looking for subjects for his paintings. He attempts to draw the mysterious hostess of his hotel, O-Nami, as an Ophelia in the style of John Everett Millais's painting *Ophelia* (1851–52). The artist learns about O-Nami's tempestuous life, including the forced separation from her lover, an unhappy marriage for money and divorce. In spite of her sad life, O-Nami is a highly intellectual, independent-minded and rebellious woman – a character that contrasts sharply with Shakespeare's Ophelia or Victorian Ophelias, generally portrayed as fragile and powerless female victims. Nevertheless, Natsume's protagonist seeks to contain O-Nami in Ophelia's image – an elegant, refined and beautiful corpse.

In the novel, it is rumoured that O-Nami Shinoda suffers from multiple curses. She inherits a family curse that makes the Shinoda women 'peculiar', 'crazies';[13] she is depicted as if she is a reincarnation of, or spiritually possessed by, a mythical princess who is likened to Ophelia. Even before meeting her in person, the narrator, when listening to the local people talk about her wedding ceremony and unhappy marriage, imagines her as Millais's 'Ophelia, floating, hands folded, down the stream'.[14] An old woman tells the narrator that O-Nami and the maid of Nagara (from an ancient legend) are much alike. When younger, O-Nami had a lover whom she was forced to leave to marry another man for money. Similarly, the maid of Nagara was loved by two men and was 'sorely torn between them'. Eventually she 'threw herself into a pool and drowned'. In the narrator's dream, the two men try to drag the maid of Nagara from a horse she is riding: '[t]he girl suddenly becomes Ophelia, lying upon a drifting willow branch in the water's flow, singing beautifully'.[15] O-Nami is thus represented as a version of the maid of Nagara, who is a version of Ophelia.

The narrator's desire to make O-Nami fit into a more manageable type of the maid of Nagara, whom he imagines like Ophelia, is transparent. The narrator immediately learns, however, that O-Nami is actually quite different from the maid of Nagara. O-Nami declares that if she had been the maid of Nagara, she would not have drowned herself; instead, she would have taken both suitors as her lovers,[16] rebelling against the idea that a woman must be faithful only to one man.

O-Nami even ridicules the narrator's fascination with Ophelia when she suggests to him that she might commit suicide soon. She asks the narrator, 'Please paint a beautiful picture of me floating there – not lying there suffering, but drifting peacefully off to the other world' in the fashion of Millais's Ophelia.[17] At first, the narrator takes her words literally, believing she desires suicide, but he realises he is being mocked when she grins and says, 'Aha, that surprised you, didn't it!' She is savvy and intelligent enough to mock the narrator's infatuation with the idea that there is 'something inherently aesthetic about a figure drifting or sunk'.[18] O-Nami is thus quite unlike Ophelia: she is independent, intelligent – and she does not die. In fact, she is the first of a number of Japanese Ophelias who fight against what Romanska calls 'Necr-Ophelia', a morbid fascination with dead wet beauties.[19]

Ophelias in mid-twentieth-century Japan

It is adaptations of *Hamlet* that have reinterpreted Japanese Ophelias as powerfully supernatural, not literary, translations of Shakespeare's original play. The first phase of free adaptations of Shakespeare's works occurred from the 1880s to the 1910s. The first staged performance of *Hamlet* in Japan was produced by Otojiro Kawakami (1864–1911), the founder of modern, westernized theatre in Japan, with himself playing both the title role and the ghost of King Hamlet, and Sada Yacco (1871–1946), his wife and the first professional actress, playing Ophelia. Kawakami produced three Shakespearean plays (*Othello*, *The Merchant of Venice* and *Hamlet*) consecutively in 1903 after his troupe's third tour to the United States and Europe (1901–02). All three productions were adaptations – *Othello* was set in Taiwan under Japanese colonisation, *The Merchant of Venice* with the Shylock figure as an indigenous man in Hokkaido and *Hamlet* was set in contemporary Japan. In contrast with the earlier adaptations of *Hamlet* as a ghost story in feudal Japan mentioned earlier, in Kawakami's *Hamlet* the ghost of King Hamlet is not a feudal samurai warlord, but a modern, westernized military commander with some references to Japan's military expansion in Asia at that time (for example, the Hamlet figure is exiled to Siberia). The combination of the supernatural (the ghost) and the contemporaneous issues (Japan as a westernized, military nation) shows Japan's anxiety over its tension between tradition and modernity.

In the 1910s, stage performance became dominated by literary, word-for-word translations, particularly by Shoyo Tsubouchi (1859–1934). Tsubouchi, who was to publish the first Japanese translation of Shakespeare's complete works in 1928, produced the 1911 performance of *Hamlet*, the first full performance of the play in literary translation. Stage performances based on literary translations, the dominant form in Japan from the 1920s onward, generally kept Ophelia faithful to Shakespeare's original character.

Some novels that adapt *Hamlet* have taken greater liberties with the original, however, endowing Ophelia with supernatural powers. Hideo Kobayashi's *Ophelia's Literary Remains* (1931) centres on the letter Ophelia writes to Hamlet just before her suicide. The novel gives the reader the impression that Ophelia might be a phantom or ghost. Intertextual references suggest that, when he created his novel, Kobayashi had Arthur Rimbaud's 'Ophélie' (1870) in mind, in which Rimbaud calls Ophelia a 'fantôme blanc' or 'white ghost'.[20] Kobayashi's phantom Ophelia, though gentle in manners, is actually self-assertive. She condemns Hamlet for his ill treatment of her, saying: 'You said to me, "Get thee to a nunnery", but it's you that should die… You said "To be, or not to be, that is the question". How wonderful, how splendid! What are you waiting for? Just go ahead and solve the problem.' Shohei Ooka created his *Hamlet's Diary* (first edition 1955; final edition 1989), in which Denmark is under Norway's military occupation, as an allegory of Japan under occupation by the Allied Powers (1945–52) after its defeat in the Second World War.[21] In the final edition, Hamlet dreams of Ophelia after her suicide, and wonders if she might be a ghost. In the eyes of Ophelia, who criticises him for his extravagant behaviour, Hamlet acts in a plainly misogynistic way, treating her as a simple-minded nuisance. He tries to dismiss her by saying 'You annoy me. You even contradict me? I, who have great ambition, have no time to listen to foolish words from a drowned girl. Dream or ghost, vanish!'[22] But she does not vanish: instead, she looks steadfastly at him, sadly, but accusingly. Kobayashi and Ooka's Ophelias are the predecessors of a series of post-modern, angry, supernatural Ophelias.

Post-modern, supernatural Ophelias

Nearly a century after Natsume's character, Japanese pop culture gave rise to many varieties of Ophelias who are quite different from what we would usually associate with the Shakespearean character.[23] The post-modern, supernatural Ophelias include a female fighter who turns into a water dragon, a guardian of the tree of life, a sea goddess, a grim reaper, high school girls under the curse of watery death and a survivor of domestic violence with the supernatural power to communicate with animals. They appropriate some elements from the original Ophelia, most notably their associations with water, flowers and plants. However, whereas the original Ophelia has no supernatural power, these post-modern incarnations are endowed with supernatural power to fight, renew the world and survive. They also constitute critical interventions in the conceptualisation of Ophelia as an embodiment of 'natural' femininity.

Post-modern, supernaturally powerful Ophelias in Japan combine the original Ophelia, Millais's Ophelia, Natsume's reconstruction of Ophelia as O-Nami, and vengeful female ghosts from Japanese feudal horror stories, who, having been killed in water, come back to take revenge. David Kalat coined the term 'dead wet girls' to describe these Japanese female ghosts.[24] One prominent example is O-Iwa, in *The Horror Tale of Yotsuya* (from the sixteenth and seventeenth centuries), who is poisoned, killed and dumped in a river by her husband. She returns as a vengeful ghost. Powerless and victimised in her life, O-Iwa achieves empowerment after her tragic death.

Among post-modern 'dead wet girls' in Japanese horror films based on feudal vengeful ghosts, Sadako in *Ringu* (1998), directed by Hideo Nakata, stands out.[25] She is represented as a combination of Ophelia and feudal revengeful female ghosts, not only in Nakata's original *Ringu* but also in its Hollywood adaptations. Like O-Iwa, Sadako is thrown into a well and returns as a vengeful ghost, crawling with her face covered with her iconic long, straight, black hair, reminiscent of Ophelia's long hair. Hollywood adaptations of *Ringu* – *The Ring* (2002), directed by Gore Verbinski,[26] and *The Ring 2* (2005), directed by Nakata[27] – have marked references to Ophelia. In *The Ring*, the protagonist, Rachael, finds the corpse of Samara (an equivalent to Sadako) at the bottom of a well. When her corpse emerges from below the water, it retains a lifelike quality reminiscent of Millais's *Ophelia* – a girl in a white smock with long hair in water. In *The Ring 2*, when Rachael explores the basement of the house where Samara and her birth mother lived, she finds a scrapbook that contains a clip of Millais's *Ophelia* with the handwritten caption, 'Vessels of Death'. Samara's spirit possesses Rachael's son, Aidan. Trying to exorcise Aidan of Samara, Rachael soaks her son in a bathtub. When Aidan, now a male version of Ophelia, disappears, Samara appears in a white dress and with long black hair, invoking images of Ophelia and Sadako. Post-modern, supernatural Ophelias are vehement and strong; whereas the original Ophelia remains simply, beautifully dead, these Ophelias as revengeful ghosts or 'dead wet girls' in globalised horror films are powerful avengers.

Likewise, while the original Ophelia does not fight, some of her post-modern variations are fighters. Norihiro Yagi's manga *Claymore* (manga 2001–14; anime 2007) has a character called 'Ophelia, the blood-soaked warrior', who transforms into a water dragon.[28] She had been a powerless young girl unable to defend herself from a monster's attack, resulting in the death of her brother, who sacrificed himself in order to save her. She hardened herself into 'the blood-soaked warrior' because of her anger and guilt over her earlier vulnerability. At first, the reason why the character is named Ophelia is a total mystery.

12.1 Ophelia of *Claymore* at her death.

When Clare, the female protagonist of the story, tries to help Raki, a young boy, escape from Ophelia's attack, Ophelia mocks Clare by saying that thinking you can be strong when you 'have something to protect' is 'the foolish illusion of the weak'.[29] At first Ophelia cannot recall where and when she got this idea, but subsequently recalls the suppressed memory of the death of her brother, for whom she was 'something to protect'. The name Ophelia is thus tied to this earlier state of vulnerability.

In the world of this fantasy manga, the dividing line between the human and the monstrous – or the natural and the supernatural – is precariously thin; a human fighter who is hunting monsters can turn, against her will (all the principal fighters in the manga are female), into a monster at crucially emotional moments. *Claymore*'s Ophelia changes into a gigantic water dragon when she remembers her despair at her brother's death and her intense rage at the monster that killed him. When she fights with Clare in a lake, Ophelia sees a reflection of herself as a water dragon in the water.[30]

Once Ophelia recognises the similarities between her history and Clare's – Clare is trying to protect Raki at the cost of her life, just as Ophelia's brother tried to protect her – she accepts her transformation. Ophelia lets Clare win, making Clare promise that she will destroy the monster who killed Ophelia's brother and save the world from monsters. Ophelia dies contentedly, remembering that her brother had a gentle smile on his face as he passed away because he knew his sister was safe. The final sequence shows Ophelia returning to her human form, floating in the water. With her long hair flowing over the water, she is strongly reminiscent of Millais's *Ophelia* (figure 12.1).[31] She shows calm satisfaction at the hope that she will be able to meet her brother after death.

Ophelia and her magical daughters

12.2 Ophelia in *Romeo × Juliet*.

The Ophelia of *Claymore* in her monstrous state – fierce, vile and venomous – is a direct opposite of the conventional image of Ophelia – overprotected, delicate and obedient. In flashbacks to her brother's death, however, Ophelia appears as a stereotypically powerless and vulnerable girl in need of protection, while her brother is overprotective of her, just like Laertes is of his sister. Fundamentally, the driving force that makes Ophelia a powerful fighter and then a water monster is the rage she feels at herself for being a damsel in distress in need of her brother's protection.

This Ophelia does not fall into powerless madness as Shakespeare's character does. On the contrary, the tragic loss of her brother empowers her to become a fighting woman. She thus questions and challenges the sexism ingrained in other typical images of the character involving female romantic madness, melancholic passivity and the beauty of victimhood. Even though it is also true that she sacrifices herself in the end to save the world, this Ophelia deliberately chooses to make herself a sacrifice out of rational determination, not out of frenzied madness.

In the animation series *Romeo × Juliet* (2007) directed by Fumitoshi Oizaki,[32] we have another mutated Ophelia – this time, she is a protectress of the tree of life (figure 12.2). The all-too-human story of the political power struggle between the Capulets and the Montagues turns out to be staged in the magical city of Neo Verona that floats in the air, supported by the tree of life named Escalus. Ophelia, a protectress of the tree of life, tells Juliet that 'when Escalus's life runs out… This world will be destroyed.'[33] The tree of life needs human sacrifice for its renewal. If this is not offered, Escalus will die, and Neo Verona would fall and be destroyed. Ophelia urges Juliet to sacrifice herself to revive Escalus, which Juliet eventually accepts. Romeo chooses to die with Juliet, and he becomes an integral part of the rebirth of Escalus. *Romeo × Juliet* endows Ophelia with the power of plants and trees because of the original Ophelia's association with flowers. When the ritual is accomplished, Ophelia dies like an old, sapless tree.[34]

When creating *Ponyo* (2008),[35] Hayao Miyazaki, creator of *My Neighbour Totoro* (1988), *Princess Mononoke* (1988), *Spirited Away* (2001), and *Howl's Moving Castle* (2004), was inspired by Millais's *Ophelia* and O-Nami in Natsume's *Kusamakura*. On the Studio Ghibli official website, it is reported that Miyazaki visited Tate Britain to see Millais' *Ophelia* before creating Ponyo.[36] Instead of repeating the stereotypical image of Ophelia as an exquisite but powerless maiden, however, Miyazaki transforms Ophelia into the powerful, gigantic sea goddess Granmamare, mother of Ponyo. Her husband (Fujimoto) has some aspects of Hamlet's character, evident in his emo-style indecision, and some elements of Prospero in his obsession to rule not only the natural world with science (as a counterpart to Prospero's magic), but also his daughter. In contrast to Fujimoto, who tries to dissuade Ponyo (a mermaid) from becoming a human, Granmamare encourages her. Granmamare is an Ophelia who supports her daughter, who is partially modelled on the little mermaid in Andersen's fairy tale and who, being a mermaid, reminds us of the original Ophelia who floated on water 'mermaid-like' (4.7.202).

Yana Toboso's *Black Butler* (2007–), a manga/animation set in Victorian England, parodies Ophelia's fetishised image as a dedicated lover and beautiful corpse, by presenting its Ophelia as a grim reaper who looks like a drag queen. The series is about a boy (Ciel) who has a contract with a devil (Sebastian), who agrees to serve Ciel as a butler dressed in black. Ciel is seeking the murderer of his parents, which makes him a Hamlet figure. In the process, he encounters a variety of supernatural incidents, including fights with grim reapers, zombies and werewolves.

One particularly vivid supernatural character in *Black Butler* is Grell Sutcliff, a grim reaper. The androgynous Grell is physically male but emphatically feminine in his/her looks and manner of speaking. In the scene where she/he fights with Sebastian, the devil, she/he cites *Romeo and Juliet*, to describe their inevitable confrontation: 'Aah, Sebastian Darling! Wherefore art thou, Sebastian Darling!'[37] Grell performs the part of Ophelia in a spin-off episode of the animated version of *Black Butler* (2011).[38] This episode shows a charity performance of *Hamlet* in which Ciel plays Hamlet and Sebastian plays Laertes. Grell's Ophelia departs wildly from the original character. This Ophelia falls in love with every handsome man around her, including her father. When Polonius punches her stomach and kicks her into the river, the floating corpse looks slightly like Millais's Ophelia. This Ophelia,

12.3 Ophelia from *Fatal Frame* (*Gekijô-ban: Zero*).

however, does not remain dead. When Laertes and Hamlet fight, she comes back to life, riding on a fancy gondola and singing 'Do not fight over me' in karaoke.

Admittedly, the scene is outrageously tacky, yet it accomplishes one of the important functions of parody, i.e. questioning that which is taken for granted as natural in the original Shakespeare. While, in *Hamlet*, Ophelia remains 'naturally' dead, the Ophelia played by Grell comes back to life. Grell/Ophelia effectively deconstructs assumptions underlying Ophelia's fetishised image as a dedicated lover and beautiful corpse.

Another Ophelia figure who decides to live on is in Eiji Otsuka's novel *Zero* (2014),[39] based on a series of computer games,[40] and its film version *Fatal Frame* (*Gekijô-ban: Zero*) (2014), directed by Mari Asato,[41] set in a Catholic girls' school in the Japanese countryside. The school is haunted by the beautiful ghosts of drowned girls. Allusions to Millais's *Ophelia* are deliberate: a large replica of Millais's painting is displayed on the wall of the school principal's room, the girls sing a version of Ophelia's song ('By his cockle hat and staff', 4.5.25) and they are repeatedly compared with Millais's Ophelia for their innocence, beauty and troubled adolescence. In one fantasy sequence, a girl dying in water is shown exactly in the manner of Millais's painting, floating down a stream in a white smock surrounded with flowers (figure 12.3). The novel and the film are suffused with an eerie atmosphere, including a gothic-style

Catholic girls' school with hidden rooms, mazes, dungeons, nuns, a girl who can see ghosts and a beautiful dead body in a glass coffin.

The 'dead wet girls' return as ghosts to haunt the school and lure living girls to their deaths in order to become exquisite corpses who retain eternal youth. Valerie Traub suggests that, in Shakespeare's original, 'Ophelia reclaims sexual desirability only as a dead, but perpetual, virgin',[42] when she is 'devoid of that which makes women so problematic: change, movement, inconstancy, unpredictability' and 'transformed into a fully possessable object'.[43] The living girls in *Zero*, tormented with fear for losing their youth and with anxiety over their unknown future, at some points wish to die young and beautifully like Ophelia. However, they decide to grow out of their Ophelia phase of disturbed adolescence. One of the surviving girls, who is able to see ghosts, loses her supernatural power when she chooses to grow up and graduate from the school to become an ordinary adult, rather than remaining in the perceived purity of adolescence. The girls say a melancholic goodbye to Ophelia, a symbol of their vulnerable, innocent and pure youth, refusing to fall victim to 'Necr-Ophelia'.

The most recent instance of a supernatural Ophelia in contemporary Japanese pop culture is a backstroke champion. She appears in a short animation film entitled 'Ophelia, Not Yet' (2015).[44] This Ophelia survives because of her sane mind, physical strength and sports training, using some of her supernatural powers to communicate with animals. The animation visually cites Millais's *Ophelia* with a twist. This Ophelia is sane enough to know that her abusive boyfriend, Hamlet, does not deserve her, and she determines to live on:

> My garments were pulling me down deep under the water. Suddenly I remembered, I am a national backstroke champion, am I not?… Not yet, not yet, it is not time for a watery death… My abusive boyfriend told me 'Get thee to a nunnery'… Dolphins and swordfishes are your friends. Almost native to that element, you can go anywhere in backstroke. Ophelia, Ophelia, don't give up, not yet.

This sporty Ophelia playfully, yet radically, challenges the objectification and sexualisation of the original Ophelia's death, just as various post-modern Ophelias examined in this chapter question and criticise the fetishised image of the innocent, fragile and powerless Ophelia.

In her afterlives in the twenty-first century, Ophelia in Japanese pop culture commonly becomes a woman with supernatural power. Her various transformations challenge the notion that women are 'naturally' fragile, beautiful and self-sacrificing, and deconstruct the romanticisation of female adolescence, melancholic passivity and the beauty of victimhood. They create a critical intervention in Ophelia's fetishised image as a dedicated lover, beautiful corpse, innocent adolescent and passive victim.

These Ophelias are very different from Shakespeare's original character, and sometimes it is not easy to understand the reasons why they are named after her. Shakespeare purists might argue that these Ophelias misappropriate the Bard's authority. I would like to suggest that these Ophelias actually revive Ophelia in meaningful ways in contemporary culture. The original character and her magical daughters stand, to borrow Douglas Lanier's term, in the relationship of 'reciprocal legitimation';[45] the original Ophelia places her supernatural daughters in the context of an aesthetics of fragile, beautiful and self-sacrificing female beauty, while Ophelia's magical daughters give the original character the chance to come back to raise an enraged, dissident voice against those who turned her into little more than a beautiful corpse.

Notes

1 Stephen O'Neill, 'Ophelian Negotiations: Remediating the Girl on YouTube', *Borrowers and Lenders*, 10:1 (2014).
2 Elaine Showalter, 'Representing Ophelia: Women, Madness, and the Responsibilities of Feminist Criticism', in Patricia Parker and Geoffrey Hartman (eds), *Shakespeare and the Question of Theory* (London: Methuen, 1984), p. 78.
3 Kaara L. Peterson and Deanne Williams, 'Introduction: The Afterlives of Ophelia', in Kaara L. Peterson and Deanne Williams (eds), *The Afterlife of Ophelia* (New York: Palgrave Macmillan, 2012), p. 2.
4 *Ibid.*, p. 8.
5 Soseki Natsume, *Kusamakura*, trans. and ed. Meredith McKinney (New York: Penguin Books, 2008).
6 For an insightful analysis of *Hamlet* in Japan, see Yoshiko Kawachi, '*Hamlet* and Japanese Men of Letters', *Multicultural Shakespeare*, 14:1 (2016).
7 Soseki Natsume, *Theory of Literature and Other Critical Writings*, eds Michael Bourdaghs, Atsuko Ueda, and Joseph A. Murphy (New York: Columbia University Press, 2010), p. 127.
8 Anna-Marie Farrier, Circulating Fictions: The Novels of Natsume Soseki and the Gothic (PhD dissertation, Princeton University, 2007), p. 166.
9 Christy Desmet and Anne Williams (eds), *Shakespearean Gothic* (Cardiff: University of Wales Press, 2009), p. 3.
10 Natsume, *Theory*, p. 46.
11 Alexa Huang, 'The Paradox of Female Agency: Ophelia and East Asian Sensibilities', in Kaara L. Peterson and Deanne Williams (eds), *The Afterlife of Ophelia* (New York: Palgrave Macmillan, 2012), p. 80.
12 Bram Dijkstra, *Idols of Perversity: Fantasies of Feminine Evil in Fin-de-Siècle Culture* (New York: Oxford University Press, 1986), p. 42.
13 Natsume, *Kusamakura*, p. 110.
14 *Ibid.*, p. 21.
15 *Ibid.*, p. 28
16 *Ibid.*, p. 51.
17 *Ibid.*, p. 103.
18 *Ibid.*, p. 78.

19 Magda Romanska, 'Necr-Ophelia: Death, Femininity and the Making of Modern Aesthetics', *Performance Research*, 10:3 (2005), p. 34.
20 At the beginning of the novel, Kobayashi cites Rimbaud's 'Fêtes de la Faim' (1872). Chuya Nakahara, a close friend of Kobayashi, translated Rimbaud's 'Ophélie' (1937).
21 Shohei Ooka, 'Hamlet's Diary', in *Nobi/Hamlet's Diary* (Tokyo: Iwanami, 1988), p. 356.
22 *Ibid.*, p. 341. All English translations in the chapter are mine.
23 For an analysis of Shakespeare in Japanese pop culture, see Ryuta Minami, 'Japanese Comics', in Richard Burt (ed.), *Shakespeares After Shakespeare* (Santa Barbara, CA: Greenwood Press, 2007), vol. 2; Ryuta Minami, 'Shakespeare for Japanese Popular Culture; Shojo Manga, Takarazuka and *Twelfth Night*', in Dennis Kennedy and Yong Li Lan (eds), *Shakespeare in Asia* (Cambridge: Cambridge University Press, 2010); Yukari Yoshihara, 'Tacky Shakespeare in Japan', *Multicultural Shakespeare*, 10:25 (2013); Yukari Yoshihara, 'Toward "Reciprocal Legitimation" between Shakespeare's Works and Manga', *Multicultural Shakespeare*, 14:1 (2016); Yukari Yoshihara, 'Manga and Shakespeare', in Fusami Ogi, Rebecca Suter, Kazumi Nagaike and John A. Lent (eds), *Women's Manga in Asia and Beyond* (London: Palgrave Macmillan, 2019).
24 David Kalat, *J-Horror: The Definitive Guide to The Ring, The Grudge and Beyond* (New York: Vertical, 2007), p. 13.
25 Hideo Nakata, *The Ringu* (Tokyo: Kadokawa, 1999).
26 Gore Verbinski, *The Ring* (Universal City: DreamWorks, 2002).
27 Hideo Nakata, *The Ring 2* (Universal City:DreamWorks, 2005).
28 Norihiro Yagi, *Claymore* (San Francisco: VIZ Media, 2007), vol. 6, p. 136.
29 *Ibid.*, vol. 7, p. 77.
30 *Ibid.*, p. 170.
31 *Ibid.*, vol. 8, p. 35.
32 *Romeo × Juliet*, dir. Oizaki Fumitoshi (Tokyo: GONZO K.K., 2007).
33 COM (artist) and William Shakespeare (original story), *Romeo × Juliet*, GONZO × SPWT, trans. Kate Beckwitt (New York: Yen Press, 2010), n. p.
34 In a detailed analysis of the anime, Jim Casey writes that it perpetuates 'the rhizome through a seed of Shakespeare… gives new life to' Shakespeare's *Romeo and Juliet*: 'HypeRomeo & Juliet: Postmodern Adaptation and Shakespeare', in Christy Desmet, Natalie Loper and Jim Casey (eds), *Shakespeare/Not Shakespeare* (New York: Palgrave Macmillan, 2017), p. 72.
35 Hayao Miyazaki, *Ponyo* (London: StudioCanal, 2010).
36 Studio Ghibli, 'Gakeno ueno Ponyo', www.ghibli.jp/ponyo/press/keyword/005001.html, accessed 3 August 2018. See also Lynley Stance and Daniel Hare, 'Film Study: *Ponyo* by Hayao Miyazaki', www.slaphappylarry.com/film-study-ponyo-by-hayao-miyazaki/, accessed 3 August 2018.
37 Yana Toboso, *Black Butler* (English edition) (New York: Yen Press World, 2014), vol. 3, pp. 66–7.
38 Toshiya Shinohara, *Black Butler: Complete First Season* (Flower Mound: Funanimation, 2012).

39 Eiji Otsuka, *Zero* (Tokyo: Kadokawa, 2014).
40 Makoto Shibata, *Fatal Frame* (Tokyo: Tecmo, 2001).
41 Mari Asato, *Zero* (Tokyo: Happinet, 2015).
42 Valerie Traub, 'Jewels, Statues and Corpses: Containment of Female Erotic Power in Shakespeare's Plays', in *Desire and Anxiety: Circulations of Sexuality in Shakespearean Drama* (New York: Routledge, 2014), p. 30.
43 *Ibid.*, p. 32.
44 Ryo Inoue, 'Ophelia, madamada', *Bijutune*, www.youtube.com/watch?v=v5xuP_FBMfI, accessed 20 August 2019.
45 Douglas Lanier, 'Recent Shakespeare Adaptation and the Mutations of Cultural Capital', *Shakespeare Studies,* 38 (2010), p. 112.

Bibliography

Black Butler: Complete First Season, dir. Toshiya Shinohara (Flower Mound: Funanimation, 2012).
Ponyo, dir. Hayao Miyazaki (London: StudioCanal, 2010).
Romeo × Juliet, dir. Oizaki Fumitoshi (Tokyo: GONZO K.K., 2007).
The Ringu, dir. Hideo Nakata (Tokyo: Kadokawa, 1999).
The Ring, dir. Gore Verbinski (Universal City: DreamWorks, 2002).
The Ring 2, dir. Hideo Nakata (Universal City: DreamWorks, 2005).
Zero, dir. Eiji Otsuka (Tokyo: Kadokawa, 2014).
Zero, dir. Mari Asato (Tokyo: Happinet, 2015).
Casey, Jim, 'HypeRomeo & Juliet: Postmodern Adaptation and Shakespeare', in Christy Desmet, Natalie Loper and Jim Casey (eds), *Shakespeare/Not Shakespeare* (New York: Palgrave Macmillan, 2017), pp. 175–218.
COM (artist), William Shakespeare (original story), GONZO × SPWT, *Romeo × Juliet*, trans. Kate Beckwitt (New York: Yen Press, 2010).
Desmet, Christy, and Anne Williams (eds), *Shakespearean Gothic* (Cardiff: University of Wales Press, 2009).
—— Nathalie Loper and Jim Casey (eds), *Shakespeare/Not Shakespeare* (New York: Palgrave Macmillan, 2017).
Dijkstra, Bram, *Idols of Perversity: Fantasies of Feminine Evil in Fin-de-Siècle Culture* (New York: Oxford University Press, 1986).
Farrier, Anna-Marie, 'Circulating Fictions: The Novels of Natsume Soseki and the Gothic' (PhD dissertation, Princeton University, 2007).
Huang, Alexa, 'The Paradox of Female Agency: Ophelia and East Asian Sensibilities', in Kaara L. Peterson and Deanne Williams (eds), *The Afterlife of Ophelia* (New York: Palgrave Macmillan, 2012), pp. 77–99.
Inoue, Ryo, 'Ophelia, madamada', Bijutune, www.youtube.com/watch?v=v5xuP_FBMfI, accessed 20 August 2019.
Inoue, Tsutomu, *Dialogues with a Ghost* (Tokyo: Kunogi Nobuyoshi, 1888).
Kalat, David, *J-Horror: The Definitive Guide to The Ring, The Grudge and Beyond* (New York: Vertical, 2007).
Kanagaki, Robun, *Hamuretto yamato nishiki-e* (Tokyo: Tokyo Eiri Shimbun, 1886).
Kawachi, Yoshiko, '*Hamlet* and Japanese Men of Letters', *Multicultural Shakespeare*, 14:1 (2016), 123–35.
Kobayashi, Hideo, Oferia Ibun *[1931]*, in Kobayashi Hideo Zenshu [*The Complete Works of Hideo Kobayashi*], vol. 2 (Tokyo: Shincho-sha, 1968).
Lanier, Douglas, 'Shakespearean Rhizomatics: Adaptation, Ethics, Value', in Alexa Huang and Elizabeth Rivlin (eds), *Shakespeare and the Ethics of Appropriation* (London: Palgrave Macmillan, 2014), 21–40.
—— 'Recent Shakespeare Adaptation and the Mutations of Cultural Capital', *Shakespeare Studies*, 38 (2010), 104–13.
Minami, Ryuta, '*Shakespeare for Japanese Popular Culture; Shojo Manga, Takarazuka and* Twelfth Night', in Dennis Kennedy and Yong Li Lan (eds), *Shakespeare in Asia* (Cambridge: Cambridge University Press, 2010), pp. 109–31.

—— 'Japanese Comics', in Richard Burt (ed.), *Shakespeares After Shakespeare* (Santa Barbara, CA: Greenwood Press, 2007), vol. 2, pp. 111–20.

Natsume, Soseki, *Kusamakura* [1906], trans. and ed. Meredith McKinney (New York: Penguin Books, 2008).

—— *Theory of Literature and Other Critical Writings* [1907], eds Michael K. Bourdaghs, Atsuko Ueda and Joseph A. Murphy (New York: Columbia University Press, 2010).

Ooka, Shohei, 'Hamlet's Diary' in *Nobi/Hamlet's Diary* (Tokyo: Iwanami, 1955, final edn 1988).

O'Neill, Stephen, 'Ophelian Negotiations: Remediating the Girl on YouTube', *Borrowers and Lenders*, 10:1 (2014).

Peterson, Kaara L. and Deanne Williams (eds), *The Afterlife of Ophelia* (New York: Palgrave Macmillan, 2012).

Romanska, Magda, 'Necr-Ophelia: Death, Femininity and the Making of Modern Aesthetics', *Performance Research*, 10:3 (2005), 34–53.

Sakurachi, Ouchi, *Toshima arashi* (Tokyo: Shunyo-do, 1895).

Shakespeare, William, *The Oxford Shakespeare: The Complete Works*, eds Stanley Wells and Gary Taylor (Oxford: Oxford University Press, 2nd edn, 2005).

Schilling, Mark, 'Fatal Frame: Mari Asato's Uncanny, Ghostly Doppelgangers', *The Japan Times*, 24 September 2014.

Shibata, Makoto, *Fatal Frame* (Tokyo: Tecmo, 2001).

Showalter, Elaine, 'Representing Ophelia: Women, Madness, and the Responsibilities of Feminist Criticism', in Patricia Parker and Geoffrey Hartman (eds), *Shakespeare and the Question of Theory* (London: Methuen,1984), pp. 77–94.

Stance, Lynley, and Daniel Hare, 'Film Study: *Ponyo* by Hayao Miyazaki', www.slaphappylarry.com/film-study-ponyo-by-hayao-miyazaki/, accessed 3 August 2018.

Studio Ghibli, 'Gakeno ueno Ponyo', www.ghibli.jp/ponyo/press/keyword/005001.html, accessed 3 August 2018.

Toboso, Yana, *Black Butler*, vol. 3 (New York: Yen Press, English edn, 2014).

Traub, Valerie, 'Jewels, Statues and Corpses: Containment of Female Erotic Power in Shakespeare's Plays', in *Desire and Anxiety: Circulations of Sexuality in Shakespearean Drama* (New York: Routledge, 2014), pp. 25–49.

Yagi, Norihiro, *Claymore*, vols 5–7 (San Francisco: VIZ Media, 2007).

Yamagishi, Kayo, *Hamlet* (Tokyo: Fuzanbo, 1903).

Yoshihara, Yukari. 'Manga and Shakespeare', in Fusami Ogi, Rebecca Suter, Kazumi Nagaike and John A. Lent (eds), *Women's Manga in Asia and Beyond* (London: Palgrave Macmillan, 2019), pp. 161–80.

—— 'Toward "Reciprocal Legitimation" between Shakespeare's Works and Manga', *Multicultural Shakespeare*, 14:1 (2016), 107–22.

—— 'Tacky Shakespeare in Japan', *Multicultural Shakespeare*, 10:25 (2013), 83–97.

Index

adaptation 17–18, 262–73
   see also anime; film; *manga*; popular culture
Aeneid 74
Agrippa, Cornelius 6
alchemy 4, 6, 16, 183–204, 220, 233–4
   philosopher's stone 194
   see also Agrippa, Cornelius; Dee, John; magic
Andrewes, Lancelot 139
anime 269–72
Antichrist *see* religion
Arias, Alfredo 115, 118–19, 122, 124
Augustine 4, 8

Bacon, Francis 8, 142
Balaack and Balaam 88–90
Besson, Benno 115, 117, 120, 123, 126, 132
Bible *see* religion
birth 50–65
   see also motherhood
Blackton, Stuart 247–9, 251–2, 255–6
Boece, Hector 175–6, 180
Bondy, Luc 115, 118–19, 122
Bonnefoy, Yves 120, 129
Brewer, Anthony 97
Brook, Peter 249–50, 255
Brown, Blair 218, 219, 220–6, 231, 235

Brueghel, Pieter 122, 130
Buchanan, George 177–8, 180
Buck, George 164–5, 167
Bullough, Geoffrey 177

cabalistic 193
Calvin, John 5
Carey, George, 2nd Baron Hunsdon 166
Carey, Henry, Lord Chamberlain 166
Casarès, Maria 121, 125
Catholicism *see* religion
Ceres 199–201
Certain relation of the hog-faced gentlewoman called Mistris Tannakin Skinker, A 52, 68
CGI *see* film, film effects
changelings 51, 56, 58–9
Chaucer, Geoffrey 163
Chéreau, Patrice 115–16, 119–20, 122–5, 128–31
Christ (Jesus) *see* religion
Chronicle of the Kings of England 173
Church *see* religion
Comédie-Française 115, 119, 121, 124, 131
Curtis, Jean-Louis 123, 131

dance 76, 119, 181, 195–6, 203, 221, 229, 231, 254

Davenant, William 99–100, 181–2
Dee, John 6–7, 200
Dekker, Thomas 94–5
Deleuze, Gilles 146–8
Demeter 230, 231
demons *see* Devil; religion
Deschamps, Jean 116–17, 128
Devereux, Robert, Earl of Essex 44, 164–5
Devil 4, 6, 32, 35, 39–40, 87, 90–5, 97–8, 100–2
 see also religion
digital technology *see* theatre, stage effects / staging
dreams 1–2, 8, 16, 33, 40, 43, 102, 121, 144–5, 175, 177–80, 183, 219, 221–2, 264
 see also Shakespeare's works, *Midsummer Night's Dream, A*
Dudley, Robert, Earl of Leicester 165
Duffett, Thomas 182
Dukakis, Olympia 218–26, 231, 235–6, 240

Edward VI 7, 138
effects *see* theatre, stage effects / staging; film, film effects
Eidinger, Lars 118
Elizabeth I 6–7, 44, 138, 149, 157, 162–4, 167, 221–2
emblems 197, 199
embodiment 11–13, 17, 33
Enough is as Good as a Feast 93–6
expressionism 248–50

fairies 4, 15, 17, 201, 245–6
feminism 219, 222, 224, 226, 228
 see also gender
Ficino, Marsilio 6, 16, 195
film 17–18, 37, 118, 182, 218, 226–33, 247–57, 267, 271–2
 film effects 247–56
 horror 267
Fordun, John 173–4, 180
Forman, Simon 181

Fraiman, Ed 253
France 114–27
Fulwell, Ulpian 91–2, 93, 95

Garcia-Valdès, Ariel 126, 127, 132
Garrick, David 182
Garter, Thomas 91
gender 5–6, 11, 16–17, 124, 163, 199, 218–34, 248, 262
 feminine 57, 199, 205, 220–2, 230–3, 262–3, 267, 270
 matriarchal 219, 223–4
 see also feminism; motherhood
generation *see* birth; motherhood
genre 1, 18, 57, 70, 187, 247, 253–4, 256
ghost 3–5, 10, 12–15, 31–45, 64, 87–104, 114–27, 130, 133, 137, 145, 181, 246, 262–7, 271–2
 see also Devil; Shakespeare's works, *Hamlet*
Golden Age 201
Greene, Robert 95
Gustafson, Tom 253–4, 256
Gwinn, Matthew 183

Hal, Frans 124
Hall, Peter 249–50, 253, 256
Hands, Terry 115, 119–20, 122
harpy 199
Harsnett, Samuel 91
Harvey, John 182–3
Haughton, William 92–3, 97
hauntology 121, 127, 130, 133
 see also ghost
Henry VIII 7, 138, 149
hermaphrodite 194, 202
Hermes 196, 199
Hoffman, Michael 252–3, 254, 256
Holinshed, Raphael 16, 57, 59, 99, 175–7, 180–1

illusion 116–19, 120, 123, 125–8, 131, 133
 see also theatre

intertextuality 246–7, 250, 252, 253–6
Iris 200

Jack Juggler 98
James VI/I 4, 7, 43, 138–40, 143, 146, 182–3, 204
Japan 262–73
Jarre, Maurice 120–1, 129
Johnson, Robert 197–8, 203
Johnson, Samuel 91
Jonson, Ben 97, 194, 204
Juno 199

Kemble, John Philip 182
Kemp-Welch, Joan 249
Kent, Charles 247–9, 251–2, 255–6
Kerr, David 254–5, 256
king's two bodies 31, 36–8, 41, 43
    see also power

Langhoff, Matthias 126
language 11–12, 14–15, 39, 57, 59, 64, 93, 124, 137–8, 140, 142, 145–9, 158, 164–5, 202, 229, 249, 251
Lavater, Ludwig 32, 100
Lavaudant, Georges 115, 118, 120, 126–7
Lavelli, Jorge 115, 120, 122, 124–5, 129, 131
law 2–3, 7, 35–6, 53, 57, 64–5, 103, 138, 140, 233
Leslie, John 177
Lupton, Thomas 91
Lyly, John 95, 158, 164–6

magic 2–7, 9–10, 13–18, 40, 22, 38, 49–54, 70, 74–5, 79, 115, 119–20, 122, 124, 126, 183–204, 218–22, 224–8, 230–2, 257, 269–70
    magician / magus 222, 226–8, 230, 232, 234, 237, 240
Major, John 174
manga 267–9
Mann, Emily 218–20, 222, 235
Marlowe, Christopher 7–8, 13, 142

Marprelate, Martin 95–6, 102
Marston, John 95
masque 13, 72–4, 79, 194–5, 199–201, 254
materiality 246, 252–6
maternity *see* birth; motherhood
matriarchal *see* gender
Medea 226, 232–3, 237
mercury, mercurial 193–5, 202
Mercury Vindicated from the Alchemists at Court 194
Mesguich, Daniel 123
metatheatricality *see* theatre
Millais, John Everett 264, 267–8, 270–2
miracles *see* religion
Mirren, Helen 218–19, 226–34
Miyazaki, Hayao 18, 270
Mnouchkine, Ariane 121, 130
monstrous 3, 12, 50–65, 119, 122, 124, 126, 127
Montgomery, Elizabeth 226
morality plays 87, 90, 92, 95–9
    see also Vice
More, Sir Thomas 57, 60, 68
Moshinsky, Elijah 250–1
motherhood 222–6, 230, 231, 233
    see also birth; gender
motion capture *see* theatre, stage effects / staging
Mugler, Thierry 124
Müller, Heiner 126
music 16, 120, 123, 181, 193–204, 245–6, 248–9, 253–6, 259
mystery plays 88–90, 103

Nashe, Thomas 95
Natsume, Soseki 262–5
nature 1–5, 17, 50, 53, 65, 147, 184, 220, 225–6
necromancy *see* magic
nigromancy *see* magic
Noble, Adrian 251–2, 253, 256

omens *see* portents
Orpheus 195

Ostermeier, Thomas 115, 117–18, 122
Ovid 61, 67n.31, 68–9

painting 122, 124
Paracelsus 194
Parnassus plays 96, 99
patriarch 218, 225–6, 231, 233–4
Pedlar's Prophecy, The 98–9
Peduzzi, Richard 119–20, 123, 129, 131
performativity 137, 141–3, 146, 149
Phelps, Samuel 182
Philipe, Gérard 121
philosopher's stone *see* alchemy
Pico della Mirandola, Giovanni 6
Planchon, Roger 115, 119, 125, 127
Plautus 98
Plutarch 147
popular culture 266–73
  see also adaptation
portents 1, 12, 50, 52, 54–5, 60–3
  omens 3, 8, 15, 137
  see also prophecy
post-colonialism 233
power 1, 6, 9, 12–13, 15, 17–18, 31–45, 50, 57, 61, 74, 97–8, 138, 145, 149, 166–7, 178, 180, 183, 193, 197, 203, 218, 221–2, 224–30, 232, 234, 249, 253, 262, 267, 272
preternatural 1–3, 11, 138
prophecy 8, 12, 14–15, 34, 38, 40, 43, 54–5, 60–1, 66, 98–9, 137–49, 174–7, 179–80, 182–3
  see also portents
Protestantism *see* religion
puppetry 70–80
Purgatory *see* religion, Catholicism

Reformation *see* religion, Protestantism
Reinhardt, Max 248–9, 250, 255, 256
religion
  Antichrist 145
  Bible 139–40, 144–6, 200
  Catholicism 3, 9, 31–2, 97, 102–3, 271–2
    Purgatory 3, 32

Christ (Jesus) 8, 145, 202
Church 3–6, 9, 138–9, 140–2, 182
  miracles 3, 8–9, 50, 145, 183
  Protestantism 3, 5, 8, 10, 31–2, 35, 87, 102, 138
  Virgin Mary 202
Rembrandt 124
Ripa, Cesare 201
Royal Shakespeare Company 13, 70, 73, 115, 119, 129

Sadler, John 52
scepticism 8–10, 34
scientist 219, 227, 230–1, 233
Scot, Reginald 8–9, 100, 160–1
Scotus, Marianus 173, 177
scripture *see* religion, Bible
Serreau, Dominique 117
shadow 117–20, 122, 126–7
Shakespeare & Company 218, 222–3, 236, 239
Shakespeare's works
  All's Well That Ends Well 9
  As You Like It 115, 126, 132, 149
  Cymbeline 1
  Hamlet 1, 12–14, 18, 31–3, 35–6, 38, 56, 87–104, 115–20, 122–9, 131–2, 137, 262–3, 265–5, 270–2
    Ophelia 262–73
    see also ghost
  Henry IV Part I 10, 54–5, 99, 163
  Henry VI Part II 1, 5, 14, 103, 141, 143, 148
  Henry VI Part III 51, 57, 59, 60–1, 141, 163
  Julius Caesar 1, 12, 14, 31, 33–5, 37–9, 54–5, 137, 142–4, 146, 148
    see also portents; prophecy
  King Lear 8, 10, 158
  Macbeth 1, 12, 15–16, 31, 33–5, 41–3, 55–6, 115–18, 120–4, 127–8, 130–1, 137, 143–6, 148, 180–4
    Lady Macbeth 175–6
    sources 173–80, 183

Merchant of Venice, The 165, 265
Midsummer Night's Dream, A 1, 15, 18, 56–7, 115, 117, 120, 128–9, 157–68
  censorship 163, 165–7
  film productions 247–56
  proper names 160–3
  Puck 159–62, 164–5, 167
  sources 158–61
  stage productions 249–50, 255–7
  topicality 157, 163, 166–8
  see also dreams
Othello 265
Rape of Lucrece, The 9
Richard II 44, 114, 141–3, 148–9, 163
Richard III 1, 12, 15, 31, 33, 35, 39–40, 51, 57–65, 115, 117, 119–20, 122, 125–9, 132, 137, 140–1, 148
  see also birth; monstrous; prophecy
Tempest, The 1, 6, 13, 16, 53–4, 70–80, 115, 118, 122, 124, 137, 183–204, 218–34
  Ariel 6, 13, 16, 70–80, 122, 124, 126, 137, 193–203, 219, 221, 225, 227–8
  Prospero 5–6, 10, 16–17, 54, 74–6, 193–7, 200–3, 218–34, 270
Twelfth Night 98, 100
Winter's Tale, The 1, 51, 115, 118–20, 122, 124–5, 130–1
Sidney, Sir Philip 139
slavery 229, 233
spectacle *see* theatre
spectre *see* ghost
stage directions *see* theatre
stage effects *see* theatre
staging *see* theatre
Sturua, Robert 115, 126
superstition 4, 8–9, 59, 72, 102, 138, 264
  see also religion

Tarlton, Richard 95
Taymor, Julie 218–19, 227–33, 236–8, 255–7

technodramaturgy *see* theatre
theatre 7, 9–11, 13–15, 31, 33–4, 44, 70–2, 78, 114, 116–21, 123, 127, 138, 147, 151, 162, 219–21, 227, 265
  metatheatricality 114, 116, 118, 127
    see also theatre, theatricality
  spectacle 70, 72–3, 77
  spectacular 114–16, 119, 120, 122–3, 126–7
  'spectracle' 123, 127
  stage directions 73, 159, 196
  stage effects / staging 11, 14, 72–3, 89, 103, 122–7, 137, 180, 246–8, 255–6
    digital technology 70–8
    motion capture 70–80
    stage machinery 73–4
  technodramaturgy 72, 74–5, 79
  theatricality 114–17
    see also theatre, metatheatricality
  see also dance; music
Théâtre National Populaire (TNP) 115–16
theurgy *see* magic
trauma 34, 37, 229, 233
Trinka, Jirí 249
True relation of the birth of three monsters in the city of Namen in Flanders, A 66n.13, 68
True report of the forme and shape of a monstrous childe, A 66n.17, 68
Tylney, Edmund 163–4, 167

Udall, Nicholas 96
uncanny valley 71

Vergil, Polydore 60, 62, 67n.30
Vice 87, 91, 93–8, 102
  see also morality plays
Vilar, Jean 114–18, 120–4, 128–31
Vincent, Jean-Pierre 115, 120–1, 124, 127, 130–1
Virgin Mary *see* religion

Wager, William 95
Wilson, Georges 115, 118, 120, 127
witchcraft 1–10, 12, 17, 51–7, 63, 65, 74, 100, 116–18, 120, 124, 127, 138–9, 143, 145, 160, 173–84, 225–6, 232–3, 262
    see also magic

witches *see* magic; witchcraft
wizards *see* magic; witchcraft
Wyntoun, Andrew 173–5, 180

Yordanoff, Wladimir 123

EU authorised representative for GPSR:
Easy Access System Europe, Mustamäe tee 50,
10621 Tallinn, Estonia
gpsr.requests@easproject.com